Our Nation's Heritage
Volume 1

Fifth Edition

F. Todd Smith
Guy Chet

THOMSON

Australia · Canada · Mexico · Singapore · Spain · United Kingdom · United States

Our Nation's Heritage, Vol. 1 Fifth Edition
F. Todd Smith and Guy Chet

Custom Editor:
Staci Powers

Project Development Editor:
Terry Isgro

Marketing Coordinators:
Lindsay Annett and Sara Mercurio

Production/Manufacturing Supervisor:
Donna M. Brown

Project Coordinator:
Jennifer Atwood

Pre-Media Services Supervisor:
Dan Plofchan

Rights and Permissions Specialist:
Bahman Naraghi

Senior Prepress Specialist:
Deanna Dixon

Acknowledgements

The content of this text has been adapted from the following products:

The Scotch-Irish
James G. Leyburn: American Heritage, December 1970, Copyright © December 1970 Forbes, Inc. All rights reserved. Reproduced by permission.

The Case of John Peter Zenger
Lincoln Barnett: American Heritage, December 1971, Copyright © 1971 Forbes, Inc. All rights reserved. Reproduced by permission.

Why Benedict Arnold Did it
Willard Sterne Randall: American Heritage, Sept. 1990, Copyright © Sept. 1990 Forbes, Inc. All rights reserved. Reproduced by permission.

The Horrid and Unnatural Rebellion of Daniel Shays
Alden T. Vaughan: American Heritage, June 1966, pp.50-53, 77-81, Copyright © 1966 Forbes, Inc. All rights reserved. Reproduced by permission.

Immense Mountains to the West
Stephen E. Ambrose: Undaunted Courage: Meriwether Lewis, Thomas Jefferson, and the opening of the American West. Simon & Schuster, 1996. Copyright © Simon & Schuster. All rights reserved. Reproduced by permission.

Marrats, Dantons, and Robespierres
July 1977: American History Illustrated, Copyright © American History Illustrated. All rights reserved. Reproduced by permission.

Eli Whitney: Nemesis of the South
Arnold Whitridge: American Heritage, April 1995, Copyright © 1995 Forbes, Inc. All rights reserved. Reproduced by permission.

Engineering the Erie Canal
John Tarkov: American Heritage of Invention & Technology, Vol. 2-1, Summer 1986, Copyright © 1986 Forbes, Inc. All rights reserved. Reproduced by permission.

The Trail of Tears
June 1972: American History Illustrated, Copyright © American History Illustrated. All rights reserved. Reproduced by permission.

All Men and Women are Created Equal
August 1998: American History Illustrated, Copyright © American History Illustrated. All rights reserved. Reproduced by permission.

Children of Darkness
Stephen B. Oates: American Heritage, Oct. 1973, Copyright © 1973 Forbes, Inc. All rights reserved. Reproduced by permission.

Gold!
Ralph K. Andrist: American Heritage, Dec. 1962, Copyright © 1962 Forbes, Inc. All rights reserved. Reproduced by permission.

The Unexpected Mrs. Stowe
David McCullough: American Heritage, August 1973, Copyright © 1973 Forbes, Inc. All rights reserved. Reproduced by permission.

The Father of American Terrorism
Ken Chowder: American Heritage, Vol. 51, I. 1, Feb. 2000, p.81. Copyright © 2000 Forbes, Inc. All rights reserved. Reproduced by permission.

Combat Trauma in the American Civil War
John E. Talbott: History Today, vol. 46, no.3, March 1996, pp. 41-47. Copyright © 1996 by History Today. All rights reserved. Reproduced by permission.

Alexander Hamilton's Alternative: Technology Piracy and the Report on Manufactures
Doron Ben-Atar: The William and Mary Quarterly, 3rd Ser., Vol. 52, No. 3 (Jul., 1995), 389-414, Copyright © The William and Mary Quarterly. All rights reserved. Reproduced by permission.

How Self-Sufficient Was Early America?
Carole Shammas: Journal of Interdisciplinary History, Vol. 13, No.2 (Autumn, 1982), 247-272, Copyright © Journal of Interdisciplinary History. All rights reserved. Reproduced by permission.

The Spirit of '54
Richard M. Ketchum: American Heritage, Aug/Sept 2002, Copyright © 2002 Forbes, Inc. All rights reserved. Reproduced by permission.

The Renegade
Steven Rinella: American Heritage, Sept 2001, Copyright © 2001 Forbes, Inc. All rights reserved. Reproduced by permission.

Mound Country
Michael S. Durham: American Heritage, April 1995, Copyright © 1995 Forbes, Inc. All rights reserved. Reproduced by permission.

Introduction

Our Nation's Heritage is a collection of essays intended to serve as supplementary reading in survey courses on the history of the United States from the colonial beginnings to 1865. Most of these essays appeared originally in *American Heritage,* a popular magazine that began publication during the 1950s. Many of the great historians of modern times have presented their views in *American Heritage,* and these readings offer soundly based interpretations of specific events and important individuals in American history. Moreover, because *American Heritage* was designed to interest the general reader as well as professional historians, the articles are presented in a lively and readable fashion.

This reader is produced in cooperation with American Heritage Custom Publishing in an effort to provide a volume that is inexpensive when compared to the choices available from other publishing companies.

Guy Chet
F. Todd Smith
University of North Texas
Denton, Texas

1

Mound Country

Michael S. Durham

Long before Europeans arrived in America, various Native American civilizations had already spread throughout the Western Hemisphere. About three millennia ago, a culture called Adena emerged in the Ohio River Valley. The Adena people lived in small villages of thatch-roofed houses, planted gardens of vegetables such as squash, and participated in long-distance trade. They also interred their dead in burial mounds, causing other Indians to follow their lead. By 1500 A.D., mounds—almost all of them abandoned by their builders—dotted the landscape of the Ohio and Mississippi valleys. This article discusses the mound builders themselves, as well as investigating the wonder they caused the Europeans, and the efforts Americans made in the nineteenth century to solve the mystery of who had produced such monuments.

Robert Maslowski and I made our way carefully across the tobacco field, trying not to disturb the neat rows of freshly plowed furrows. On the other side of the flat valley, a tractor moved slowly across the horizon "settin' tobacco," as they call planting seedlings in this part of West Virginia. Our destination was also far away: an oasis of greenery in the distance that was a prehistoric Indian mound.

Maslowski suddenly picked up something from a furrow and handed it to me. I could see it was a flint arrowpoint, less than two inches long, flatter on one side than the other, and unevenly shaped, but it wasn't until Bob said "Early Adena" that I realized I was holding a true prehistoric artifact in my hand, one that had been crafted by the Adena Indians hundreds of years before Christ and at least twenty centuries before Europeans set foot in this part of America.

Maslowski, an archeologist with the Army Corps of Engineers, explained that recently plowed fields were fertile grounds for finding prehistoric Indian artifacts. From time to time he would stop to pick up a fire-cracked rock, evidence of an ancient campsite, or to point out a grayish patch in the soil caused by the high ash content of prehistoric debris, probably mussel shells.

Our walk across the tobacco field came on the first day of a trip I took to the Indian mounds and other prehistoric earthworks of the upper Ohio River Valley, an area that includes sites on tributaries many miles away from the river itself. This part of the Ohio River has both heavy industry and great stretches of unspoiled scenery; it defines eastern and southern Ohio on one side and forms borders for western West Virginian and northern Kentucky on the other. An atlas published in 1814 shows how archeologically rich this region once was; dots on a map indicate large clusters of prehistoric sites, especially along rivers flowing into the Ohio, like the Muskingum, the Scioto, the Hocking, and the Great Miami. Most of these sites are gone, "plowed down," as they say, for agriculture or otherwise destroyed in the name of progress. But more survive here than in any other part of the country.

In the eighteenth and nineteenth centuries, the mounds were a source of wonder—and pride, in that they were thought to be much older than any man-made monument in Europe. Most Americans believed that they had been built by some prehistoric master race, the "ancient white aborigines of America," a people of skill and culture who came to be known as the Mound Builders. At the heart of the Mound Builder theory was the assumption that contemporary Indians lacked the intelligence, technical know-how, or energy to be Mound Builders—a theory bolstered by the fact that more modern Indians had no knowledge or collective memory of the mounds.

Ideas about where the ancient builders came from varied, ranging from Europe—Wales, Norway, Greece—to the Bible: the Lost Tribes of Israel or the sons of Shem. Ephraim Squier and Edwin Davis, authors of the important mid-nineteenth-century survey *Ancient Monuments of the Mississippi Valley*, thought the Mound Builders originally came from Mexico or Peru. Others claimed they were a superior indigenous race that had been driven south to Mexico by savage invaders.

There were dissenters from Mound Builder orthodoxy all along, enlightened souls who had no trouble believing that the mounds had been built by ancestors of modern Indians, and they grew in number as the nineteenth century wore on. Among them were Thomas Jefferson, who described excavating a mound in *Notes on the State of Virginia,* and the famous explorer John Wesley Powell, who dismissed the Mound Builder theory as a "romantic fallacy." In 1881, as the first head of the Bureau of Ethnology, Powell assigned the eminent archeologist Cyrus Thomas to survey prehistoric earthworks. Thomas and his crews excavated many mounds in the Ohio Valley, including the one toward which Maslowski and I were now heading. Thomas concluded in a 730-page report published in 1894 that there was "an unbroken chain connecting the moundbuilders and the historical Indians." Thomas's well-researched conclusions were supposed to put an end to the Mound Builder theory once and for all.

On my trip I would see more impressive mounds; even close up, this one looked more like a natural feature that farmers had plowed around rather than over. And I would see more accessible ones, with parking lots and visitors' centers, paved paths, and steps to the summit. Here access was difficult, and the top could be reached only by bushwhacking up through locust trees and brambles. The view from the top was blocked by vegetation, but on the ground we could make out a rock-filled indentation in the earth that, Bob informed me, had been dug by the Cyrus Thomas expedition in 1890.

I was disappointed. I had enjoyed the walk across the field, but compared with the thrill of finding the arrowpoint, this hole in the ground that amounted to no more than a shallow pit was an anticlimax. Only later, in retrospect, did its significance come into focus. Cyrus Thomas's 1894 report was a milestone, "the birth of American archaeology," Maslowski has written. By demolishing the myth of an ancient race of Mound Builders and determining that the mounds were constructed by American Indians, it put archeology on a scientific footing. This unimpressive hole in the ground was part of that process and therefore had a historical importance all its own. I understand that now, but at the time it was just a hole; I missed the point entirely.

"How much do you know about Woodland people?" Susan Yoho asked me. It was a question I was hoping to avoid. I knew that Woodland was a term that covered roughly three thousand years of human development before white men arrived in eastern America, but otherwise I had to admit that I knew very little prehistory (a curious term covering the centuries before man began writing down his story). And this despite some fancy schooling and a long association with publications in the American history field.

Yoho, who is curator of the Grave Creek Mound State Park in Moundsville, West Virginia, assured me I wasn't alone. "There is widespread ignorance about prehistoric sites," she said. "People still come here who think that the Grave Creek Mound is historic. When you tell them that it was built before the birth of Christ, they are astounded."

In historic times, after Moundsville was founded by white settlers, the local citizenry put the huge mound to a variety of uses, including building a racetrack around its base and a saloon on its pinnacle. ("After a long night of drinking, that first step must have been a doozy," Yoho says.)

When Yoho took over as curator in 1981, she ended the practice of draping the mound with lights at Christmas on the ground that "an Adena mound built several hundred years before the birth of Christ really had very little to do with Christmas." Yoho is not an archeologist, but, she warns, "like all amateurs, I have my own opinions."

Sixty-two feet high and two hundred and forty feet through at the base, Grave Creek Mound, built between 250 and 100 B.C., is one of the largest man-made earthworks in the world. It took people who had neither the horse nor the wheel the equivalent of three million basketloads of earth to build it. The Adena lived in this part of the country from roughly 1000 B.C. to A.D. 200; they came after the Late Archaic people and before the Hopewell (about 150 B.C. to A.D. 500), although as the dates show, there is considerable overlap between the Adena and the Hopewell cultures. The Adena lived throughout the southern half of Ohio and in adjacent parts of Indiana, Kentucky, West Virginia, and Pennsylvania. The Hopewell were concentrated in southwestern Ohio, at the hub of a trading network that extended from the Great Lakes to the Gulf of Mexico. The impact of their culture was felt throughout that vast territory.

The Adena were the region's first serious mound builders. They built them in stages, starting with a burial, sometimes in a log tomb like the one found at Grave Creek, which they then covered with earth. Then another burial and more earth, and so, depending on the number of burials, the mounds grew, sometimes to immense size.

The Hopewell had a different approach: their mounds were one-stage affairs. They first disposed of their dead in a charnel house, which, when filled with bodies, they covered with earth to construct a mound. Then they started all over again in another location. This is why Hopewell mounds are smaller than Adena mounds, the highest being barely half the size of the mound at Grave Creek.

What they lacked in size, the Hopewell mounds made up for in treasure. The burial goods found in them were far more abundant and finely crafted than the items buried with the Adena. Where an Adena mound might contain tools or simple neck ornaments called gorgets, Hopewell burials have yielded quantities of items crafted from mica or copper or gold or large numbers of precious freshwater pearls. Because they were in pristine condition when excavated, it appears that the Hopewell goods were produced solely for burials and went into the grave unused.

Both the Adena and the Hopewell mounds were for the elite only; archeology does not yet know, although it would dearly like to, where and how the common folk were laid to rest. There are many other unanswered questions. It isn't known if the Hopewell drove out the Adena or whether one culture simply melded into the other.

Archeologists don't even know the bare outlines of the story: where the prehistoric people of the region came from, where they went, or what happened to them. (There were no Indians living in their region when white settlers arrived. With the Adena and Hopewell, burial of the dead appears to have been an obsession amounting to a cult. But we don't know why they built mounds, or even what the people of these cultures called themselves. And because the Adena and Hopewell, like all of America's prehistoric peoples, had no written language, the answers to these questions may never be known.

The Grave Creek Mound was first excavated in 1838 by local amateurs, who dug two shafts, one vertical and one horizontal, into the earthwork and discovered two burial vaults, one above the other. The first excavation also produced the notorious Grave Creek Tablet, a "curious relic" that the early anthropologist Henry Rowe Schoolcraft saw "lying unprotected among broken implements of stone, pieces of antique pottery, and other like articles." The oval stone, which immediately became more famous than the mound itself, is less than two inches long and inscribed with more than twenty hieroglyphiclike characters.

The Grave Creek Tablet intrigued the experts and provided support for the argument that the mounds were built by a civilized race that had a written language. Schoolcraft speculated that four of the twenty-five characters were from an ancient Celtic alphabet; others saw evidence of Greek, Phoenician, and Canaanite letters.

Faith in the authenticity of the stone diminished as the century progressed, but there are still believers, Yoho told me. "Just the other day a man was in here telling me that he could prove the tablet was written in Welsh." The actual tablet is privately owned; only a replica is on display at the park's Delf Norona Museum and Cultural Centre. Yoho recognizes its worth—"historically it's one valuable little item"—and would like to obtain the original for the museum. But she is sorry that it deflects attention from the mound itself.

"You don't have to sensationalize the mound to make it interesting," she says. "The Adena and Hopewell led wonderful, peaceful, and complicated lives. To me that alone is sensational. There's no need here to look for the Loch Ness monster."

In my travels through the Ohio Valley, I must have seen fifty mounds. I discovered early on that there is something about a mound that makes me want to climb it. This isn't always possible, of course; some mounds are fenced or chained off, but others have steps spiraling around them like a corkscrew or going straight up the side. Often children and I were the only climbers.

Mounds are the stars of the prehistoric sites of the Ohio Valley. There are other ancient attractions—forts, quarries, a reconstructed village—but nothing with the visual impact of a mound. Some of them were in state or federal parks with trails and museums and other facilities, but they could be found almost anywhere, often in bizarre juxtaposition with the manmade environment. "They liked the same land we like," says N'omi Greber, a Hopewell expert at the Cleveland Museum of Natural History. "Land gets reused."

Most mounds that have been excavated have revealed burials—both skeletons and cremated remains—as well as tombs made of wood, graves lined with sheets of mica, and immense quantities of burial goods. These days it is also believed that mounds were used as astronomical observatories. "There is rarely just one reason for doing anything," says Robert Petersen, an archeologist at a large Hopewell complex in Chillicothe, Ohio. At Sunwatch, a prehistoric village reconstructed on its original site near Dayton, archeologists, guided by evidence found in the ground, have rebuilt a solar observatory.

Mounds located in old cemeteries—where the recently old and the really old come together—were particularly to my liking. In Marietta, Ohio, the Revolutionary War general Rufus Putnam is buried at the foot of Conus Mound, which is separated from the historic burial ground by a prehistoric moat. Putnam led the Ohio Company party that settled Marietta in 1788. These same settlers had the foresight to set aside the city's extensive prehistoric earthworks, which include the 680-foot Sacra Via, an elegant graded esplanade that leads from a large square mound, now a park, to the Muskingum River.

Although mounds were new to me, in the Ohio Valley they are part of local culture. Every town with a mound usually had a Mound Street or Mound Avenue, and of course, Moundsville, West Virginia, takes its name from the Grave Creek Mound. Police in Newark, Ohio, the site of a large Hopewell complex, have a likeness of a mound embroidered on their shoulder patches, and in Tiltonsville, a working community amid the steel mills on the upper Ohio River, the local Lions Club has taken on responsibility for maintaining the town's thirteen-foot-high Adena burial mound, which is located in one of the state's earliest cemeteries.

Not all mounds are original; a number have been rebuilt after being damaged by agriculture or commerce or even archeology. The thought that archeology could do harm surprised me when Martha Otto, curator of archeology at the Ohio Historical Society, first brought it up. "Any excavation is destructive," she said. "Any time you put a shovel in the ground, you are taking on a responsibility to observe carefully and to understand what you are looking at."

Mounds themselves, she explained, are no longer the central objects of archeological curiosity. Instead scientists are focusing on broader issues, like interaction between prehistoric cultures, diet (corn was once considered responsible for Hopewell achievements; now "we think it is much less important"), the relationship of prehistoric peoples to the environment, and "how they changed that environment." For example, the prairies that European settlers found when they arrived were not virgin terrain; they had been enhanced by the slash-and-burn practices of the Late Woodland people (A.D. 900–1500).

Not surprisingly, given prehistoric man's taste for choice real estate, many mounds now sport buildings. When I heard that there was an Indian mound in the parking lot of a Hardee's restaurant in the river town of Belpre, Ohio, I made a detour so I could see for myself. There, just as I had been told, a small mound rose like a miniature volcano out of the blacktop. In Newark, Ohio, a portion of the immense Newark Earthworks is now a country-club golf course; it has an observation tower for visitors, but those who want a close-up look at the walls risk being beaned by a golf ball. A small amusement park in Huntington, West Virginia, provides an even more unusual setting for a mound. It costs a dollar to get in, but it's probably the only place in the world where you can see a burial mound from a roller coaster.

After several days of traveling in mound country, I started to see prehistoric earthworks everywhere. Every undulation in a cornfield, every knoll, hillock, or protuberance became evidence of an ancient culture. Most of these I passed by, but south of Newark I braked my car when I glimpsed what I was sure a mound on a hillside. My guidebook confirmed that this time I was not imagining; this was an Adena burial mound, about fifteen feet high, situated between the Fairmount Presbyterian Church and a graveyard.

In the late-afternoon light it was a pleasant sight, the church nestled by the side of the mound; the mound, like the cemetery, neatly mowed, the graves lined in neat rows down the hillside, ancient man and modern man buried together. If it weren't for that damned light pole sticking like a periscope out of the top of the mound, the picture would have been perfect.

Brad Lepper took the small arrowpoint I had found in a tobacco field and turned it over in his hand. I was surprised when he pronounced it "Late Archaic." Maslowski had said it was early Adena, but Lepper assured me that the two periods overlapped. And I was slightly irked when he described it as "clunky." I had been carrying the artifact with me for several days, and it had become, in my eyes, an object of beauty.

Lepper was until recently the curator of the Newark Earthworks, east of Columbus, Ohio, which he calls "the largest complex of geometric earthworks in the world." Although the earthworks once covered four square miles, they are now broken up into two major sites and two smaller ones spread about the city. In their 1848 work Ancient Monuments of the Mississippi Valley, Squier and Davis wrote that the Newark earthworks "are so complicated that it is impossible to give anything like a comprehensible description of them." This is even more true now that the complex has been overrun by civilization. A canal, a railroad, a fairground, and a racetrack all preceded today's golf course.

The widespread damage done to the earthworks, Lepper says, misled both professionals and the public into assuming that "there is nothing left here." That is far from true, he insists. A recent cultural-resource survey turned up evidence of a prehistoric habitation site just outside the earthworks. "I am constantly surprised by back-yard finds. It proves that you can destroy a site but you can't obliterate all information."

The headquarters of the complex, which includes a museum, is located in the twenty-six acres known as the Great Circle Earthworks, enclosed by an earthen wall eight to fourteen feet high and twelve hundred feet in diameter. (An unusual moat running along the inside of the wall reflects "principles of military science now lost or inexplicable," a puzzled observer wrote in 1839.) Two smaller, nearby sites—the six-foot-high Owen Mound and the Wright Earthworks, a surviving section of a large enclosure—are also part of the complex.

The second major section, the 120-acre Octagon State Memorial, includes the large earthen octagon covering 50 acres that is now part of the groomed golf course of the Mound Builders Country Club, which has held a lease from the Ohio Historical Society since 1933. Some years before that it was the site of a National Guard camp whose members damaged an embankment while practicing gunnery.

I met Lepper at his cubbyhole of an office in the museum at the Mound Builders State Memorial, but we were soon trudging our way through a cornfield headed for a distant thicket of trees and the remains of a walled highway that, Lepper is convinced, the Hopewell built from Newark straight to Chillicothe some sixty miles to the southwest.

Lepper warned me not to expect too much, and he was right: the remnants of the road's walls were hardly more than brush-covered irregularities in the surface of the ground. But these irregularities were eloquent to Lepper. "This is the first evidence we have of a great road in the eastern Woodlands. Not only is it monumental in size, it's older than any other we know about."

A walled roadway from the Newark earthworks to a creek about two and a half miles away appears on early maps, like the one Squier and Davis published in 1848. In 1990 Lepper rediscovered an unpublished map from 1862 that took the road another three miles toward Chillicothe. When he first saw the map, Lepper says, "It was as if I had gotten into a time machine and been transported back to 1862." Beyond that, aerial photographs and physical evidence of the wall have convinced him of that thoroughfare's reality.

Building a straight road is not that difficult—"Three men holding sticks could do that," says Lepper—but the fact that this one appears to go straight to a destination sixty miles away is astonishing. If the road can be confirmed, it will throw a new light on the Hopewell culture, says Bob Petersen, an archeologist at the Hopewell Culture National Historical Park, a burial-mound grouping in Chillicothe at the other end of the putative highway. "It will show a greater commitment of time and energy than we thought them capable of and greater engineering skills than we thought they had."

Lepper describes the Newark earthworks as "monumental architecture that we usually associate with kings and queens." But there is no evidence that the Hopewell had a nobility or that the common people were coerced to build the earthworks, so it is possible that the architecture is the result of a common goal and vision shared by the populace over a span of generations. This is a difficult concept for us to grasp today, Lepper says, "when we can't seem to sustain a national vision for more than the four or eight years of a Presidency.

"There seems to be a message here from the past. We can work together."

For nearly two centuries Chillicothe has been the pre-eminent place to go to see mounds; it has a number of its own, and it is at the geographic center of mound country. Most of the other sites I visited, even those in West Virginia, lie within a hundred miles of it.

Chillicothe also has a firm place in the history of American archeology. The names archeologists have given to two principal prehistoric cultures come from there: Hopewell from the farm of Capt. M. C. Hopewell, where three dozen mounds were found in and around a 110-acre enclosure, and Adena from the estate of the same name belonging to Thomas Worthington, Ohio's governor from 1814 to 1818. With the excavation of a large mound on Worthington's estate in 1901, the Adena and the Hopewell began to emerge as clearly separate cultures.

Chillicothe was also home to the young newspaper editor Ephraim George Squier and his physician-collaborator Edwin Hamilton Davis, authors of that influential 1848 work *Ancient Monuments of the Mississippi Valley*. The team did extensive work right in their own back yard, at twenty-three Hopewell burial mounds grouped in thirteen walled acres that today form the largest concentration of mounds in the Ohio Valley. The National Park Service, owner of the site, recently renamed it the Hopewell Culture National Historical Park, but it is still usually called by its previous name, Mound City. Badly damaged when the U.S. Army put a World War I training camp there, the site was extensively rebuilt and restored after it became a national monument in 1923.

Death Mask Mound, the largest at the site, was the only mound untouched during the war. When excavated, it yielded up the remains of thirteen individuals and an unusual ceremonial headpiece—or death mask—made from fragments of human skull. A cutaway section of the Mica Grave Mound reveals the burial site of four cremations and provides a glimpse into how the mound was constructed: the burials, a layer of earth over the cremated remains, then a layer of sand covered by sheets of mica, and then more earth. And so the mound grew.

When Squier and Davis explored the site in the 1840s, they struck archeological pay dirt. A single mound, now called Mound of the Pipes, contained "not far from two hundred pipes, carved in stone. . . . The bowls of most of the pipes are carved in miniature figures of animals, birds, reptiles, etc. All of them are executed with strict fidelity to nature and with exquisite skill." Earlier in my trip, during a stop at the Ohio Historical Society in Columbus, Martha Otto explained that it was public dismay over the loss of the pipes to the British Museum that had led to the founding of the society, then called the Ohio State Historical and Archaeological Society.

The entire thirteen-acre Mound City complex can be seen from a balcony at the visitors' center. As archeological sites go, it is not large. But as Bob Petersen told me, its twenty-three mounds, compared with the two or three found elsewhere, "clearly indicate that something special was going on here." From my vantage point on the balcony I could see what he meant. In the haze of a hot June morning the well-groomed mounds rising from the earth lay mystical and beckoning.

Before being excavated in the twenties, Seip Mound, fourteen miles southwest of Chillicothe, was—at 240 feet long, 160 feet wide, and 30 feet high—the second-largest Hopewell mound in existence. Standing on top of it, N'omi Greber pointed out the full extent of the walled enclosure, which once consisted of two connected circles and a large square. She guesses that the Hopewell built two large buildings, whose size can be determined from the size and depth of the postholes found on the site, then mounded them over with earth and added a wall around the complex. Seip is a place Greber knows well, having camped out there with students on field trips. At dusk, she says, Seip becomes "theatrical with the sun going down, the moon coming up, fireflies blinking, clouds hovering around the tops of the mountains. If you wanted a place for a ceremony, this would be it."

As at other sites, archeology produced more questions than answers. How many people did it take to build the mound? How was it used? Where did the Hopewell people live? Who was buried in there? Where was everybody else buried?

Greber, a mathematician before she became an archeologist, admits she is not one given to speculation. (When I showed her my arrowpoint, she declined to classify it, but she did suggest that a slight curve on one edge might indicate that it was a small knife rather than part of an arrow.) Still, she is fairly sure that a mound like Seip could be built by two hundred to two hundred and fifty people —"not the thousands that people associate with the Egyptian pyramids.

"It is generally assumed that you need a strong leader to do all these things, but I don't think that is true," she continues. "I think they were very autonomous. They probably had important people, but not as the basis of the social organization. The Europeans came here and imposed the concept of chiefs on what they saw, because that is what they understood. But not all societies are like that. There are more possibilities of how people arrange themselves than we think."

I left Greber in Chillicothe and the next day made some quick stops at sites I had missed: Story Mound, a large Adena burial mound owned by the Ohio Historical Society and located in a residential section of Chillicothe; Fort Hill, a hilltop enclosure southwest of Chillicothe, where, on a trail deep in the woods, I came across a man hunting wild rosemary—just like the hunter-gatherers of old, I thought. And finally the spectacular effigy Serpent Mound, near Locust Grove, the seven curves of its body covering nearly a quarter of a mile. Visitors can get an overview of the serpent from an observation tower, but how the Adena—or maybe the later Fort Ancient people—were able to achieve its faultless proportions is a mystery.

As I headed home, I thought about what Greber had said about how people "arranged themselves"—maybe in ways that we know nothing about—and what Lepper had said about their ability to cooperate without compulsion and how this could be a "message from the past."

I had to admit that the message seemed faint, but then, to me, messages from the past often are. More to the point, I thought, was a story Susan Yoho told me about a farmer who went out daily to his fields to look for prehistoric artifacts. Every day his wife would say to him, "Honey, I don't know what you're looking for, but I hope you find it."

Well, I thought, I didn't know what I was looking for in the Ohio Valley, but I had found it aplenty. I had gotten in my mind a vivid picture of what a nineteenth-century traveler called "the great monuments and pyramids . . . of the ancient nations of N. America" and, in my pocket, an arrowpoint from a tobacco field in West Virginia that I at least found beautiful.

2

The Renegade

Steven Rinella

Living in the English-speaking United States in the twenty-first century, it is easy to forget that Frenchmen played a large role in the settling of North America. Following the 1608 establishment of a colony at Quebec in present Canada, French voyageurs *continued their exploration up the St. Lawrence River, establishing ties with Native Americans and discovering the Great Lakes. By the end of the seventeenth century, French explorers had moved from the St. Lawrence drainage to the waters that flowed into the Mississippi River and emptied into the Gulf of Mexico. Claiming the entire territory between the Appalachian Mountains and the Rocky Mountains for France, these explorers named the region Louisiana after their great king, Louis XIV. This article looks at one of these forgotten French explorers and his exploits among the Indians of the St. Lawrence River and the Great Lakes.*

Growing up in the Great Lakes region of North America, I developed an early appreciation for the European explorers who had long ago traveled the waterways of my home. I read all the books I could find about adventurers like Champlain, Jolliet, Marquette, and Nicolet, and they defined what I thought I should be as a young man: tough, brave, single-minded, and born a couple of hundred years earlier. When I got older, though, I realized that my affection for these men was not shared by everyone. I started college in 1992, seemingly at the height of the so-called revisionist historians' attempts to convert the old pioneering heroes into the new societal enemies.

This new line of thinking certainly rubbed off on me, and I had to admit that greatness was something more than the resolute desire to mow down everything and everyone in your path in the name of God and country. It was kind of heartbreaking, though, because I had enjoyed loving the Great Lakes explorers, and now it seemed both unfashionable and unconscionable to do so. But just when I was thinking that I would have to continue my reading with the dry, uninspired analysis of a historian, I was saved by a man named Etienne Brulé, a French explorer turned pagan traitor who was killed and eaten by the Huron Indians in the winter of 1632.

I first got turned on to Brulé when it occurred to me that if the current templates of thinking made the pioneer heroes look like villains, maybe the old pioneering villains should be re-examined for heroic attributes. This idea was spurred on by *Champlain: The Life of Fortitude*, Morris Bishop's admiring 1948 biography of the French explorer and founder of Quebec, Samuel de Champlain. Brulé weaves in and out of the narrative for 25 years, from his arrival in the New World as a boy of 15 under the service of Champlain to the winter of his death. Toward the end of the book, Bishop borrows an epitaph for Brulé that was originally offered by the Recollect du Creux, a French missionary order: "Long a transgressor of the laws of God and man, he spent . . . his wretched life in vile intemperance, such as no Christian should exhibit among heathen. He died by treachery, perhaps only that he might perish in his sins." But following this quote, almost as if he had anticipated the revisionist movement, Bishop writes, "Let any who wish rehabilitate the memory of this extraordinary discoverer."

Nothing is known of Brulé's existence prior to the day in April 1608 when he set sail for the New World with Champlain, King Henry IV's royal geographer and the governor-to-be of New France. Champlain had made several previous trips to the Americas, but the scope of the French territory was vague, ranging along the Atlantic seaboard from northern New England to the Gulf of the St. Lawrence and perhaps beyond. Nobody had a clear idea what lay inland, but it was generally agreed that the inventory included the Western Sea, with its passage to the Orient, lost souls to be converted to Catholicism, the lost souls' beaver pelts to be converted into French currency, and the potential for self-supporting colonies.

The French saw the St. Lawrence River as the gateway to the interior, so that was where Champlain concentrated his efforts and resources. For years, Indians of the St. Lawrence Basin had traveled down to its mouth to trade furs with European fishermen and independent traders, but Champlain wanted to push far up the river and intercept the commerce. He also had plans for further involvement with the Indians, and that was where Brulé came in.

Years before, while Champlain was exploring up and down the Atlantic coast of America, he had realized that adolescent crewmen had a particular facility both for learning the natives' languages and for surviving the winters, so he had developed a plan to introduce French youths to the allied Indian tribes of the St. Lawrence. Once living with them full-time, Champlain figured, these boys could learn their languages and customs and serve as valuable assets to the fur trade. Brulé was to be the exemplar of this plan, the continent's first exchange student.

He quickly proved his mettle on the front line of wilderness imperialism by being one of only 8 out of 24 Frenchmen to survive the first winter in newly founded Quebec. To Champlain's pleasure, Brulé spent the winter hunting moose in the deep snows and fishing through the ice around the fort with the local Montagnais Indians, whose difficult language he picked up. After another year, in 1610, Champlain felt enough confidence in his experiment to send his charge into the unknown. Brulé was about 17 years old. Champlain decided that the boy should spend the winter with Chief Iroquet of the Algonquin Indians, who had come down to Quebec to trade furs. Iroquet's village was on the upper Ottawa River, probably in what today is Ontario, a place no white man had ever seen. At first, Iroquet resisted Champlain's request, fearing the wrath of the French should the boy die. Champlain told him not to worry, accidents could happen to anyone.

It's hard to fathom the amount of legal release forms you would have to sign in order to make a trip like that today. It brings to mind the dog that the Russians sent into orbit, ignorant of its fate, attached to feelers and sensors to gather information for the betterment of another's cause. Brulé's chance of survival wouldn't have been much better. Not only were the Algonquins involved in an ancient, nasty war with the Iroquois nation to the south, they were rarely able to stockpile enough food to last the entire winter. But Brulé had yet another problem: He was entirely dependent on the Algonquins' goodwill at the same time he was a liability to them, a helpless piece of baggage for their canoes that could easily bring trouble.

And these canoes must have been pure misery. Accounts by, Champlain and the Recollect missionary Gabriel Sagard give a good picture of what Brulé must have gone through. While on the move during warmer weather, his new companions, traveling naked or in loincloths, endured hunger and insects and physical hardships that would have killed most Frenchmen. To avoid stopping, they used their wooden food bowls as chamber pots in the boat. Their diet was radically different from that of the French, comprising dried fish, parched corn, and whatever the forest or river provided. At times, they ate their human enemies. They would load quartered corpses into the bow of a canoe or carry prisoners live to be consumed later. With every bend in the river, Brulé probably thought less about Champlain's imperial desires and more about his own safety.

One of history's great missing stories is what happened that winter with Brulé. All that is really known is that he survived and learned the language, "very well" as Champlain wrote in his journal the following summer. Champlain's journals are the best available device for tracking Brulé, but they are sparse with relevant details. The Champlain Society would cringe, but I'd happily trade information about his own lavishly recorded doings for more coverage of Brulé's.

When Brulé's first winter with the Algonquins, away from other white men, was over, he came down the Ottowa River to the St. Lawrence with 200 Indians to meet with the French for what had become an annual trading fair below the Lachine Rapids near Montreal. It was June 13, 1611. They swapped beaver pelts for knives and kettles and hatchets, and Brulé served as the interpreter for Chief Iroquet, who now showed complete trust in him.

At the close of the trading season, Brulé asked to go spend the year with the Huron Indians, who lived near what is now known as Lake Huron's Georgian Bay. His desires happened to coincide with those of Champlain, who still didn't have an interpreter for the Hurons, a wealthy and powerful people. So plans were made for the boy to go visit the land where, in about 20 years, without a friend or a nation, he would die.

Champlain justified his decision to send a boy into so very different a culture by claiming he would demonstrate Christian principles to the savages. This was certainly a gesture to the church, which saw Champlain's journals as dispatches from the war with the devil. Without church support, Champlain was sunk (as was anyone in government), yet even the most pious should have doubted the logic of planting a single adolescent male into another Culture in the belief that he'd come out as a shining representative of his society's values. But the single-minded Champlain felt he needed every advantage he could get in the fur trade, no matter the cost.

When Brulé left with the Hurons in 1611, he disappeared from the record for four years. With this trip he knew what he was getting into, so it must have been far different from the one he had taken a year before with Chief Iroquet. Surely he couldn't have cared much about Champlain's financial interests; it's likely he had his own reasons for wanting the life he was pursuing. In France he could be executed for hunting one of the king's rabbits, but here was an endless expanse of land on which to hunt deer, bear, and moose. The Hurons had greater reverence for personal autonomy; respect and power were earned by acts, not by birth. Coming from a country where you could be dealt a bad hand before you even knew what the game was called, this must have been invigorating. What a system the Hurons had! A young man sent to live with them stood a better chance at getting respect and equality than he did among his own countrymen. I can see Brulé paddling hard, carrying more than his weight.

When he re-emerged in Champlain's journals, four years later, he was completely transformed. He was dressed fully in skins and participated in the open promiscuity of the Huron youth. This resembles remarkably the mating strategy of my generation of college-educated twenty-somethings. In both, a young woman would go through any number of male suitors, sleeping with them at will under no pretenses about commitment, before eventually settling down with her favorite.

Champlain and the Jesuit and Recollect fathers who would become open critics of Brulé probably started to form their nasty opinions of him around this time. Still, the boy brought back with him a great haul of news and rumors, including tales of a northern sea above and west of Lake Huron. Plus, the interpreter now knew many dialects and could speak with almost anyone in the eastern Great Lakes watershed. Just what Champlain needed, too, because in 1615 he was planning an expedition into New York to slaughter a village of Iroquois, and he wanted to assemble an allied force.

Forays against the Iroquois were a sort of summer hobby for Champlain. These residents of present-day upstate New York were primarily farmers, but their raids into the St. Lawrence Valley for fur and captives had gained them the bitter enmity of the Hurons and Algonquins. Every beaver pelt that made it into an Iroquois canoe was bound for Dutch merchants to the south, not for the French, so the Iroquois inadvertently picked up some terrible foes. Twice Champlain had ventured to the Iroquois homeland with his muskets and his Indian allies, annihilating forces of Iroquois. For some of these people, the first firearm they ever saw had Champlain's eyeball staring down its barrel.

The 1615 expedition was bound for a village along Onondaga Lake, in central New York, and Brulé was in the party, along with several hundred Hurons. The plan was for Brulé and 12 of the Hurons to split off at Lake Simcoe and head down through enemy territory to gather a force of 500 Andaste warriors who lived to the south along the Susquehanna River near what is now Elmira, New York. Then they all would meet at the Iroquois village and raze it together.

On September 8, Brulé departed with the Hurons on his mission. Champlain wouldn't see him again for three years. With the 12 Hurons, Brulé traveled south from Lake Simcoe, becoming the first white man to see Lake Ontario and Lake Erie, and then headed to the Andaste village. The Andastes agreed to send the 500 men, but they wasted five days on pre-war partying. When they did get around to making the three-day journey north, they were too late. Champlain had already been defeated and wounded by the Iroquois and had left for the north.

Brulé went back with the Andastes. To kill time over the winter, he traveled down the Susquehanna River to Chesapeake Bay and the Atlantic Ocean, perhaps near Baltimore, racking up several more firsts for

European explorers. He somehow passed unscathed through the lands of many enemies of the French. When his journey south was over, he went back to the Andastes for a while, then left with six men to travel up to the Hurons' country. On the way, the group was attacked by a party of Iroquois and scattered. Brulé wandered for days. Lost and starving, he found a path and followed it to three Iroquois who were returning to their village with a load of fish. They fed him and took him home with them. At their village, Brulé denied being French and said he came from another, better nation that loved the Iroquois. They knew he was lying, so they began the long, torturous murder process obsessively described by many Frenchmen. They ripped out his fingernails and pulled out his beard and burned him with hot sticks. The ritual was interrupted only when Brulé, in desperation, threatened them with the wrath of God just as the clear sky turned cloudy and broke out in a great thunderstorm. This scared them so badly that he became a figure of much importance in the village of his former enemies.

Brother Sagard, a Recollect du Creux lay brother, who had no problem believing in miracles, found this story of Brulé's a little curious. He would later say of it, "God works his marvels often through the worst persons." People familiar with Brulé said that the explorer did not even know his prayers and that he commonly offered tobacco to inanimate objects in the belief that he would then receive safe passage. Also, it seems a bit odd that a people who lived so very directly in the natural world would be astounded by a sudden change in the weather. Champlain did later witness the physical evidence of Brulé's mishandling, and the Iroquois weren't ones to take sudden pity on someone after starting in on him. Whatever really happened that day is a mystery. Perhaps Brulé had simply charmed them.

In the summer of 1618, he left his new Iroquois friends, vowing another visit. He returned to the Hurons, then made a short journey with them down to Quebec. There, he explained his three-year delay to Champlain, and then he left again with the Hurons.

About 1620, he crossed Lake Ontario, heading west, and then traversed the land north of Lake Huron. There are few known details about this trip, only that he was checking on the rumor of the Great Western Sea. He made the first ascent by a European up the rapids at what is now Sault Ste. Marie, was the first to set foot on Michigan soil, and became the first to enter Lake Superior. Somewhere along the way in Lake Superior, perhaps all the way to Isle Royale, he came across an ingot of copper, which he later showed to the French on the St. Lawrence. Many years later, the retrieval of that copper from its source would physically transform the northern Great Lakes more than all previous events, more than the missionaries and wars and fur trading that followed closely in Brulé's steps.

His trip up to Lake Superior and northern Michigan would be the last history he would make as an explorer of never-before-seen places. He took to spending much of his time in Huronia, along the eastern shore of Lake Huron near Georgian Bay. By now, his countrymen considered Brulé a total pagan, unashamed of his defection to Indian life.

In 1623 Brother Sagard went to Huronia to minister to the people there. While Brulé helped guide him around a little, he ultimately tried to block the missionary's efforts. Sagard's interpreters struck a deal among themselves that no one should teach the missionary to master the Huron language. Instead, they taught him obscenities so that if he tried to explain the Trinity, he would be talking about something else altogether. Sagard later complained to Champlain that Brulé did not want the Indians to settle down and lead moral lives. He also reported that Brulé was "much addicted to women."

It's odd that no one ever discusses Brulé as an early force against globalization, a person defending an indigenous way of life that was fading. Instead, his actions are regarded just as Champlain described them, as the willy-nilly workings of a lunatic. But his efforts didn't stop with his sabotage as an interpreter.

In 1629 a war between France and England had spilled across the Atlantic, and an English general, Thomas Kirke, had put Quebec under siege. His ship was the largest ever to sail up the St. Lawrence, which could be tough to navigate. No problem, though, for he had a skillful pilot to take him upstream. When Champlain surrendered the fort without a fight, he was surprised to see the pilot among the captors: It was Brulé. Champlain wrote down the lecture he gave to his sometime protégé that day, and it was prophetic: "You will be pointed at with scorn on all sides, wherever you may be." Brulé returned to Huronia.

In no time at all, the French regained their territory. No sooner had Kirke taken Quebec than word of a treaty between France and England spread to the New World, and all recent conquests were off. Trade with the Indians continued, and every year they came downriver in greater numbers. In the summer of 1633, 140 canoe loads of Hurons came down. The Indians were somewhat tense because over the winter they had killed and eaten Etienne Brulé after a quarrel, and they feared French retaliation. Champlain told them to forget it. The man had no nationality, so his life was of no concern to the French; don't let it spoil the trading fair.

Brulé would have been boiled in a kettle or hollow log, not roasted, and eaten without salt; we know that. What we don't know is why it happened. Champlain suggests it was because of a woman. According to the Recollect du Creux, Brulé's trip to the judgment seat was expedited so that he might sooner be made to answer for his life of sin. The missionaries' attempts to demonstrate something better to the Hurons didn't do them much good. By 1649 they had been annihilated by the Iroquois in their villages. Hundreds were led away as slaves or food. Eight Jesuits were killed in all, several of them tortured to death.

As far as the history books go, getting killed by the Hurons was one of Brulé's greatest accomplishments. The very few authors that ever mention him always point that out. Seeing the name in print was too much for Champlain. In 1633 he revised his journals, removing Brulé's name in the discussion of that explorer's greatest adventures.

3

How Self-sufficient
Was Early America?

Carole Shammas

Traditionally, historians have looked to urban communities to draw conclusions about consumer culture in early America. The rural household and village, on the other hand, have been portrayed as self-sufficient units, standing as both an ethical and economic counter-image to city life in the colonies. Historian Carole Shammas demonstrates that rural populations were just as active participants as urban communities in England's "empire of goods," and were also participants in a more regional market of services (milling, baking, brewing, weaving, tailoring, shoemaking, etc.). The specialized skills and equipment needed for the production of cost-effective goods and services necessitated the "outsourcing" of certain activities that originally had been part of the local or household economy. The myth of familial/communal self-sufficiency was used by later generations of Americans to celebrate the Spartan republican virtues of their forefathers. Thus, this myth was to inspire American audiences in the late-eighteenth, nineteenth, and twentieth centuries to once again embrace self-reliance and liberate themselves from their frivolous, slavish and dangerous dependence on the Market (which remained a predominantly British market for over a century after American independence). Shammas does not argue that assumptions about economic self-sufficiency were simply invented for political and ethical purposes; rather, she suggests that these assumptions were a product of historians' lack of familiarity with women's work in the early-modern household. Either way, her evidence and conclusions belie the notion of a golden age of self-reliance and demonstrate that American colonists were never immune to the fever of consumerism.

> At this time my farm gave me and my whole family a good living on the produce of it; and left me one year with another one hundred and fifty silver dollars, for I never spent more than ten dollars a year, which was for salt, nails, and the like. Nothing to wear, eat, or drink, was purchased...

So reads one of the most frequently cited passages in early American history. The idea that pre-industrial households practiced self-sufficiency has been a powerful one, and the vision of the past evoked in the quotation has enjoyed widespread popularity for some time. To conservatives, it highlights the self-reliance and frugality of the good old days, whereas to the Left, it illustrates the purity and simplicity of life before capitalists and industrialists botched things up.[1]

There is some question, though, about how accurate a reflection of the past this image is since few specialists on the colonial economy ascribe to it, and about how much historical material can be mustered in its support. The excerpt that is quoted above, for example, turns out to be a rather flimsy piece of evidence. The lines appeared in a letter from "A Farmer," published by the *American Museum,* a Philadelphia magazine, in 1787. The writer goes on for about a page and a half discussing the virtues of self-sufficiency, bemoaning his own and his country-men's sad departure from that happy condition, and vowing a return to his former state before he is ruined financially. In the process of relating his plight, he gives us his life story. Born to poor parents, he married at twenty-two and rented a forty-acre farm. Through his own industry and that of his wife ("and a very good working young woman she was"), he managed to purchase a 120-acre farm as well as considerable outlands for his children when they reached maturity. All went smoothly, and he saved $150 a year, which he put to interest or invested in cattle. When his eldest daughter married, he gave her husband, a "clever lad," 100 acres and told her, a "dutiful working girl," that she could take the best of his wool and flax and spin herself gowns, coats, stockings, and shifts. He even allowed her to buy some cotton that she then fashioned into sheets.[2]

---

[1] See, for example, Alice Morse Earle, *Home Life in Colonial Days* (New York, 1945; orig. pub. 1898), 158; Rolla Milton Tryon, *Household Manufactures in the United States* (Chicago, 1917), 126–127; Lawrence K. Frank, "Social Change and the Family," *Annals of the American Academy of Political and Social Science,* CLX (1932), 95; Margaret G. Reid, *Economics of Household Production* (New York, 1934), 43; Stuart Ewen, *Captains of Consciousness* (New York, 1976), 114.

[2] *American Museum,* I (1787), 11–13.

Unfortunately, life changed. The "good working young woman" that he married turned into a scheming Eve who tempted him with the forbidden fruit of consumer goods. When his second daughter prepared her trousseau, his wife insisted that the girl be furnished with store-bought goods—a calico gown, stoneware tea cups, pewter spoons, and so forth. Although the farmer protested that homespun was good enough, he gave his wife the money. Upon the marriage of the next daughter, his wife again demanded money and this time she bought silk and china. From that point on, no money could be saved because all of the profits went for market commodities. Aside from their expenses, these luxuries wasted time. "Breakfast, which used to take ten minutes, when we were satisfied with milk, or pottage made of it, now takes my whole family an hour at tea or coffee." At age sixty-five, after twenty years of such slothful practices, the farmer swore he would return to the simple ways: "no one thing to eat, drink, or wear shall come into my house which is not raised on my farm, or in the parish, or in the country except salt and iron-work, for repairing my buildings and tools—no tea, sugar, coffee, or rum. The tea-kettle shall be sold."

There are several curious things about the letter from this self-described "honest farmer." First it is difficult to locate him in time and place. In 1787 the *American Museum* was not publishing original pieces but was picking up items from journals and newspapers, some originally printed at the time of the Revolution. In addition the farmer dated his self-sufficiency period twenty years prior to the time when he wrote the letter. That would place it in the 1760s, if he wrote in 1787, and even earlier, if the letter actually had been composed before. Nor is it certain where he lived. Historians have identified him variously as a Pennsylvania farmer and a New Englander, but he mentions no residence in the letter and refers only to his rural "parish," an administrative unit that did not exist in either place.

In fact, it is conceivable that the farmer, his "spendthrift" wife, and luxury-loving daughters never existed at all. Letters from alleged "farmers" complaining about societal vice and luxury crowded the pages of the early American press. The authors of these letters tended to be rich gentlemen, deeply involved in politics, who assumed the classical literary persona of a humble farmer to attest to their love of simplicity and lack of guile. At the end of this particular letter, when the farmer makes a vow to return to self-sufficiency, it is not household self-sufficiency about which he exhibits the most concern, but that of the community. He states that he will not use anything that had not been produced on his farm *or* in his parish *or* his country.

It was probably no coincidence that the article following this letter in the *American Museum* concerned the ways in which a nation flourished by producing its own manufactures and exporting them into other lands, and that the next article related to the propriety of giving a congress the power to regulate the trade of the states in the union. The magazine became known for its Federalist sympathies, and the farmer's letter adhered to that line. His logic, then, closely paralleled the reasoning contained in much of the popular political economy of the time. The hardworking Yankee farmer who lived in snug self-sufficiency in the wilderness became a source of national pride, and early textbook writers adopted him as a symbol of America's superiority over decadent Europe.[3]

Even if the letter were genuine, the economics of the situation related therein seem implausible and suggest that the farmer's memory might have been faulty. To begin with, he had a rather incredible savings ratio, $150 dollars a year out of $160, or 94 percent. The $150 in profits came from the sale of farm produce and cattle as well as money at interest, indicating that the farmer might not have been buying on the market. But obviously somebody was if he could earn those dividends.

The farmer referred to his wife as a "very good working woman" when he married her. As the mother of seven children and the manufacturer of all the food, drink, and apparel on the farm for twenty years, she would have had to have been. Women, with the assistance of children old enough to work, carried on almost all the food and clothing production in the home, aside from the cultivation of the grain and the supervision of the livestock. How complicated and arduous some of those tasks could be will be discussed in more detail below. Considering these circumstances, it follows that it would have been the wife who finally insisted that the farmer put some of his money into consumer goods. It is interesting that he viewed the purchase of iron tools to aid him in his field work a legitimate expenditure, but the buying of clothing and eating utensils that might have made his spouse's life easier and more pleasant he judged a needless luxury. Indeed, the virtues of saving 94 percent of one's profits and spending ten minutes for breakfast may escape some of us, just as others might be perplexed about the evils of a tea kettle.

What *would a* 120-acre farm have to produce to make a nine-person household, such as our legendary farmer's, self-sufficient? A study does exist that estimates the production on a holding about the same size (125 acres) as his—a farm in Lancaster county, Pennsylvania, in the post-1760 period. When prices from inventories

---

[3] Frances FitzGerald, *America Revised* (New York, 1977), 74.

are added to the production figures, some idea can be obtained of profits made from any surplus.[4]

Table 1 lists the commodities raised on such a farm to provide a family with grain, vegetables, fruit, cider, dairy products, meat, wool, and linen clothing. I have assumed that a small number of essentials—salt, sugar, spices, buttons, and so forth—would have to have been bought. Fuel is not listed, but a number of acres remained forested so that wood could have been gathered free. What can plainly be seen from the table is that the farmer planted and raised a little of this and a little of that, and almost all of it was either consumed by the household or by animals. It is calculated that the latter devoured 215 bushels of grain, 30 tons of hay, and numerous bushels of potatoes yearly. Some of the crop also had to be put aside for the next year's seeding. All I could discover in terms of what the farmer would have had left to sell amounted to a little wheat and rye, some flax and flax seed, and apples, which presumably would be converted into cider for sale. Total sales come to £14 sterling (1760–1774 prices) or $63 and the costs of marketing and transporting the various products would have to be subtracted before a profit could be derived. Also, the meat, dairy, and wool portions per person were low and probably would have to have been supplemented with commodities bought on the market. Clearly, the sum fell far short of the $160 that the letter-writer claimed to have cleared each year. Of course, he might have achieved higher yields on his land, put a higher proportion of acres under cultivation than normal, or done any number of things that might have boosted the total.

Whether the farmer, by doing one thing or another, might have gained an additional dollar or so is really beside the point. It is obvious from the long list in the commodities column of Table 1 that the costs of self-sufficiency would have exceeded the resources available to many households. To buy the land, livestock, seed, and equipment (including plow and field tools, dairy utensils, a cider mill, equipment to manufacture apparel, soap and candlemaking utensils, and carpenter and cooper tools) involved an outlay of around £145 sterling, a considerable investment for the ordinary person. The equipment, although crude and not of great value by modern standards, could not be fully utilized, for self-sufficient farms could not take much advantage of economies of scale. We now know that in prime agricultural areas usually from one third to one half or more of

---

[4] James T. Lemon, *The Best Poor Man's Country* (Baltimore, 1976).

Table 1 Annual Production and Consumption on a 125-Acre Pennsylvania Farm[a]

Commodity	Quantity	Amount produced	Consumed at home	Sold on market
Wheat	8 acres	80 bushels	91% (8 bu. seed; 65 bu. for food)	9% 7 bu. at 5s. ea. = £1.75
Rye	2 acres	25 bushels	24% (2 bu. seed; 4 bu. food)	76% 19 bu. at 3s. = £2.85
Oats	4 acres	60 bushels	100% (3 bu. seed; rest for animals)	
Barley	2 acres	30 bushels	100% (3 bu. seed; rest for animals)	
Buckwheat	2 acres	30 bushels	100% (3 bu. seed; rest for animals)	
Indian corn	8 acres	120 bushels	100% (12 bu. seed; 9 bu. food; rest for animal feed)	
Hay	20 acres	30 tons	100% (animal feed)	
Root vegs.	3 acres	300 bushels	100% (291 bu. animal feed; 9 bu. food)	
Fruit (apples)	2 acres	800 bushels	50% (400 bu. food)	50% = 400 bu. = 25 barrels cider at 10s. ea. = £12.5
Flax	2 acres	300 bushels 10 bushels seed	43% (130 lbs. family cloth) 20% (2 bu.)	57% 170 lbs. at 6d. = £4.25 80% 8 bu. at 6s. = £2.4
Sheep	10	30 lbs. wool	100% (family cloth)	
Cattle	3 cows with calves; 1 steer	450 lbs. meat; 300 gallons milk	100% (food) 100% (food)	
Swine	8	550 lbs. meat	100% (food)	

£23.75 Pennsylvania currency = £14 pounds sterling = $63

SOURCES: Lemon, *Best Poor Man's Country,* 150–183 Alice Hanson Jones, *American Colonial Wealth* (New York, 1977), I, 69–329; Percy Wells Bidwell and John I. Falconer, *History of Agriculture in the Northern United States, 1620–1860* (Washington, D.C., 1925). 71; Stevenson Whitcomb Fletcher, *Pennsylvania Agriculture and Country Life, 1640–1840* (Harrisburg, 1950); Lemon, "Household Consumption in Eighteenth-Century America and its Relationship to Production and Trade: The Situation among Farmers in Southeastern Pennsylvania," *Agricultural History,* XLI (1967), *59–70;* Max George Schumacher, *The Northern Farmer and his Markets during the Late Colonial Period* (New York, 1975).

[a] Assuming: the "farmer's" nine family members of whom four eat an adult diet

	Per Child	Per Adult		Per Child	Per Adult
wheat	5 bu.	10 bu.	flax	10 lbs.	20 lbs.
rye	1 bu.	1 bu.	wool	2 lbs.	5 lbs.
corn	1 bu.	1 bu.	pork	50 lbs.	75 lbs.
potatoes	1 bu.	1 bu.	beef	50 lbs.	50 lbs.
apples/cider	24 bu.	60 bu.	milk	20 gallons	50 gallons

Animals require 215 bushels of grain and 30 tons of hay.

the farmers were tenants who owned little in the way of livestock or tools.[5]

In addition, self-sufficient households demanded a bewildering number of skills from their members, especially from women. Although males had charge of most, though not all, of the production of the raw materials—what might be called the primary processes involved in making apparel, food, drink, and other goods for household consumption—female labor performed practically all of the intermediary and final ones. Thus the house-wife who made everything from scratch had to possess the knowledge of the flax spinster, wool spinster, weaver, dyer, fuller, tailor, knitter, miller, baker, gardener, dairy maid, chandler, and soapmaker. Women, traditionally, malted the barley and brewed the beer too, but in America, where cider had largely displaced beer as the favored homemade beverage, men apparently devoted themselves more to the making of drink. Women's home production had to be squeezed into a schedule that included dressing and supervising small children, preparing meals, and so forth. Moreover, if her creations were to compare favorably with what could be bought on the market, she had not only to make these goods but also to be skillful in this labor. The female side of farm production, however, has received relatively little attention from agricultural historians who, traditionally, have fixed their gaze upon the cultivation of field crops.

Exactly what tasks would self-sufficient households have to perform and what necessities were early American families most likely to manufacture themselves? Much is known about cloth production. Linens, fashioned from flax or hemp, and woolens constituted the two primary materials of standard Western dress. In addition, most colonials possessed articles made from cotton and silk which, in most instances, they would have had to purchase. For simplicity's sake, however, we will assume that linen and woolen would have satisfied the wants of a provincial family.

---

[5] *Investment in Self-Sufficiency* (amounts in pounds sterling 1760–1774; to convert to Pennsylvania currency multiply by 1.7).

Farm of 125 acres (26 acres grain; 20 acres meadow; 20 acres pasture; 7 acres flax, potatoes, fruit; 2 acres house and garden; so acres fallow and woodlands) 12s. an acre = £75.

Livestock (7 cattle £10); 4 horses £23.5; 10 sheep £2; 8 swine £3; bees and poultry £1.5) = £40.

Seed = £5.

Equipment (plow and field tools £10; dairy utensils £2.5; cider-making utensils £3; wheels, looms, etc., £5; soap and candlemaking utensils £1; carpenter and cooper tools £1.75; misc. equipment £1.75) = £25.

For sources see Table I. I discuss the recent work on tenancy in "The Rise of the Colonial Tenant," *Reviews in American History*, VI (1978), 490–495.

Historians of colonial home life have described the processes involved in the production of the two textiles. Although the household required only a patch of land (a quarter to half an acre) in order to cultivate flax, what it demanded in the way of labor was considerable. After pulling the grown plant and drying it, it could be dressed, which meant separating the woody part of the plant from the fiber by beating it with blunt instruments. Then came the hackling, a winding of the fiber through a comb to take out the tow, the coarser element used in making rope. The more combing, the finer the cloth. Spinning came next, and then the yarn had to be bleached, which meant that a worker had to soak it in warm water, for several days— constantly changing the water and wringing out the yarn—rinse it in clear water, pour ashes and hot water on it, and then place it in more clear water for a week. After that more seething, ringing, beating, washing, and drying ensued. Finally the weaver received the product, but afterwards the bleaching process began all over again. According to one nineteenth-century source, who cited her mother as the authority, "to bring the fine linen for shirts to the required degree of showiness no less than thirty and sometimes forty bleachings were necessary." Although not everyone's standards might have been as high as this anonymous parent's, manufacturing linen was clearly a time-consuming process. Commonly sixteen months would elapse between the sowing of flax and the finishing of the cloth.[6]

Wool also involved an elaborate processing. After shearing, the fleece had to be cleaned, greased, carded (a combing procedure), and spun. Woolen yarn for weaving, as opposed to knitting yarn, had to be spun twice. Women stood while spinning wool, and it has been estimated that the daily backward and forward motions made in order to guide the yarn through the wheel amounted to twenty miles of walking. After the weaving came the fulling to remove the grease and other impurities as well as to soften the cloth. When done at home instead of in a fulling mill, the cloth was wet, beaten with sticks,

---

[6] See Earle, *Home Life*, 166–251, for the best description of home manufacture of textiles. Also see Tryon, *Household Manufactures*, 206–216; Alice Clark, *Working Life of Women in the Seventeenth Century* (New York, 1920), 97ff. English husbandry books of the sixteenth and early seventeenth centuries list the cultivation of flax and hemp under the duties of the housewife: Master Fitzherbert (ed. Walter W. Skeat), *The Book of Husbandry* (London, 1882; based on 1534 ed.), 96; Thomas Tusser, *Five Hundred Points of Good Husbandry* (London, 1812; collation of 1571, 1580, 1581 eds.), 153; G[ervase] M[arkham], *Countrey Contentments or the English Huswife* (London, 1623), 162–165. Earle, in *Home Life*, 168–169), when discussing eighteenth-century colonial practices, however, assumes men will do some of the flax field work; Tryon, *Household Manufactures*, 207–208, assumes men will do it all. See also *ibid.*, 213; Earle, *Home Life*, 235.

rinsed, and wrung out to dry. Somewhere along the way the wool, yarn, or cloth had to be dyed. The materials for home-produced dyes would have to have been gathered from the garden or the woods: hickory and sassafras bark, peach leaves, horse laurel, barberry root, or the petals of Jerusalem artichokes provided yellows; iris petals furnished purple; cedar berries created plunket shades, and so on. The final steps were the cutting out of the material and the sewing.[7]

Although people did not expect many changes of garb, the size to which some households grew—our letter-writing farmer, for example, claimed seven children—the increasing use of table and bed linens, and the need for cloth to perform everyday household chores, meant that impressive amounts of fabric must have been consumed.

What we want to know is how many pre-industrial households in America actually produced all of their own cloth and apparel. Conventional wisdom has held that every colonial woman spun and knitted, but recent research has challenged that assumption. In seventeenth-century settlements, particularly those with plantation economies, the labor force concentrated its energy on producing staple crops and few households owned spinning wheels or other clothmaking equipment. For example, in Virginia from 1660 to 1676, only 1 percent of the inventories contained a reference to a spinning wheel.[8]

As the colonies matured, it became desirable to manufacture cheap cloth used for everyday purposes and to produce other types of fabric during wartime when trade was disrupted. Yet many women, especially those in towns, still grew up without developing the skills of spinning and knitting. The Non-Importation Acts gave an additional boost to homespun, and colonial spinning probably reached a high point on the eve of the Revolution when owning a wheel,

---

[7] *Ibid.*, 198.

[8] *Ibid.*, 167–168, for the conventional wisdom. Newer research is by Lois Green Carr and Lorena S. Walsh, "The Planter's Wife: The Experience of White Women in Seventeenth-Century Maryland," *William and Mary Quarterly*, XXIV (1977), 542–571; Linda R. Baumgarten, "The Textile Trade in Boston, 1650–1700," in Ian M. G. Quimby (ed.), *Arts of the Anglo-American Community in the Seventeenth Century* (Charlottesville, 1975), 219–273; Laurel Thatcher Ulrich, "A Friendly Neighbor: Social Dimensions of Daily Work in Northern Colonial New England," *Feminist Studies*, VI (1980), 392—405; Mary Beth Norton, *Liberty's Daughters: The Revolutionary Experience of American Women, 1750—1800* (Boston, 1980), 15–20, 155—167. For a description of the sample from Virginia, see Shammas, "The Determinants of Wealth in Seventeenth-Century England and America," *Journal of Economic History*, XXXVII (1977), 679–680.

whether it received much use or not, demonstrated a love for one's native soil.[9]

Probate inventories—those lists of the goods of decedents required by law in the early modern period—enumerate the contents of rooms as well as livestock holdings and outdoor equipment. Thus, if a household owned a spinning wheel or other clothmaking tools, they should appear somewhere in the document. Although it could not be expected that every inventory would include clothmaking equipment because some decedents lived with other people, the vast majority of cases pertained to householders, however humble, as the estates of wives, minors, apprentices, indentured servants, and slaves normally were not probated.

Table 2 shows the distribution of spinning wheels in inventories from pre-Revolutionary Massachusetts. These documents are among the 900 or so copied verbatim by Jones and printed in *American Colonial Wealth*. They comprise all of the inventories proved in the Massachusetts counties of Suffolk, Essex, Plymouth, Hampshire, and Worcester during the year 1774. The five counties had very different kinds of economies. Suffolk contained the metropolis and major port of Boston. Essex and Plymouth, also situated on the coast, mixed farming with maritime activity. Although located far inland and heavily agricultural, Hampshire in the Connecticut River Valley had been settled in the mid-seventeenth century, whereas Worcester developed later and more of its inhabitants lived in a frontier environment.[10]

Table 2 Percentage of 1774 Massachusetts Inventories Containing Materials and Equipment for Cloth Production

County	N	% with Spinning Wheel(s)	% with Linen and Woolen Wheels, Loom, Sheep, Flax
Suffolk	95	27.4%	2.1%
Essex	98	49.0	6.1
Plymouth	25	64.0	8.0
Worcester	39	74.3	5.1
Hampshire	27	74.1	14.8
Total	284	48.9%	5.7%

SOURCE: Data set created from Massachusetts inventories printed in Jones, *American Colonial Wealth*

[9] Gary B. Nash, "The Failure of Female Factory Labor in Colonial Boston," *Labor History,* XX (1979), 173.

[10] Alice Hanson Jones, *American Colonial Wealth* (New York, 1977), 3 v.

The inventories reveal that almost half of the decedents' estates contained a spinning wheel for linen or wool, although in Suffolk County (where Boston was located) only about one in four listed the implement. It was in the more thinly populated western portions of the colony, in Worcester and Hampshire counties, that the proportions were highest: about three fourths of the inventories included them. When it came actually to stocking all of the primary materials and equipment necessary to be self-sufficient in woolen and linen cloth production, however, a very small percentage in every county possessed the two spinning wheels, the loom, the sheep, and the flax patch for such activity—only 15 percent in Hampshire and a mere one in fifty in densely settled Suffolk. These figures correspond closely to those obtained in another study of New England (Essex County and Maine) inventories from the period 1670 to 1730, when 40 percent of decedents had spinning wheels and 7 percent owned looms. Probably much of the yarn spun at home was used for knitting stockings and caps."[11]

Households in the more sparsely populated areas where households occasionally had looms would not always weave material themselves. Itinerants often came to do the work and that, it seems, is why the inventories of these artisans often did not contain looms. Instead they used the implements provided by a customer. It also seems that New England had a primitive putting out system in operation, although its dimensions are still unclear. Women sold yarn to storekeepers, who in turn put it out to knitters or weavers and then paid to have it whitened or fulled.[12]

Many households did not find it economical to engage in their own cloth production. Investments in flax patches and sheep were made primarily by richer farmers, and it is, therefore, no surprise that plantation owners with their large slave labor force were the only ones, in the long term, who threw themselves wholeheartedly into the home production of cloth. Whereas in the early years of settlement the plantation colonies exhibited the lowest percentage of inventories with spinning wheels, Maryland and Virginia in 1774 had 71 percent coverage, and by the end of the eighteenth century the manufacture of cloth by slaves for home use had become commonplace."[13]

---

[11] Ulrich, "Friendly Neighbor," 395.

[12] Margaret E. Martin, "Merchants and Trade of the Connecticut River Valley, 1750–1820," *Smith College Studies*, XXIV (1938–1939), 95, 156.

[13] On who were the flax growers in New England, see Robert A. Gross, "Change in the Countryside: The Transformation of Concord, 1750–1850," paper delivered at the Conference on Economic Growth and Social Change in the Early Republic, 1775–1860 (1980). Virginia and Maryland 1774 figures calculated from inventories published in Jones, *American Colonial Wealth.*

Making cloth at home did not preclude buying large amounts of it on the market too. One way to test the importance of homespun in the total outlay for textiles made by households would be to measure the effect of spinning wheels on linen and apparel investment. Presumably, the presence of spinning wheels would lower the amount invested if the families relied heavily upon homespun to satisfy their clothing needs. Statistical analysis (see Appendix 1) of eighteenth-century Massachusetts inventories indicates that possession of wheels had no influence upon how much decedents invested in clothes and bed or table cloths. One is led to conclude that in America only a fraction of what people wore or put on their tables and beds had been spun at home.

Clothing accessories, such as hats and stockings, had been mass produced in England since the sixteenth century, and Americans imported large quantities of these items (see below). Farm inventories in Massachusetts did contain more references to shoe-makers' tools than can be found in England, yet home production did not impede the development of the shoe industry in the colony where, by 1768, the cottage laborers in one of its towns, Lynn, allegedly manufactured 80,000 pairs of shoes annually.[14]

Besides apparel, a self-sufficient household would have to have produced all of its own food, or at least its own bread, vegetables, drink, dairy goods, and meat. By the eighteenth century an Americanization of the traditional English diet had occurred that theoretically should have facilitated self-sufficiency, as products more easily grown in North America and requiring less complex processing were frequently substituted for the old nutritional staples. At the same time, however, more specialization in food crops developed, making home production for home consumption even less likely.[15]

In their breads and porridges, the colonists often replaced wheat, oats, and barley with corn, which they could cultivate more easily than any other grain. Still, wheat became a specialized agricultural commodity and continued to find a ready market throughout the colonies. In Massachusetts, for example, the amount of bread, flour, and grain imported annually from other colonies in the 1760s would have been enough to furnish over one fifth of the colony's population with the requisite allotment of cereals. Considering that not all shipments entered the ports legally and that the New England farmers grew some grains for sale themselves, it is difficult to imagine that a

---

[14] Alan Dawley, *Class and Community: The Industrial Revolution in Lynn* (Cambridge, 1976), 14.

[15] On the changes in diet, see Sarah F. McMahon, "'Provisions Laid Up for the Family': Toward a History of Diet in New England, 1650–1850," *Historical Methods,* XIV (1981), 4–21.

majority of house-holds produced all of their own bread. Even in the countryside, researchers have found that no more than half of the *taxpayers* had a team of oxen for plowing the arable land.[16]

New England soil was notoriously poor, so it is not surprising that households failed to furnish all of their own grain. But what about the other major areas of the diet? Although we can assume that families in small towns and rural areas all cultivated vegetable gardens, the extent of home production of drink, dairy products, and meat demands further scrutiny. Table 3 indicates the percentage of inventories from the Massachusetts countryside, the major towns (those with over 500 families), and Boston that contained goods and livestock used in the production of essential foods: equipment for making cider, beer, or spirits; milk cows and butter or cheese implements for dairy products; and pigs for meat.

The first column of Table 3 shows that only 5 percent of the inventories included implements to make any kind of drink, whether it be cider, beer, or hard liquor—not too much higher than the proportion of people engaged in the beverage trade as their primary occupation. As part of the Americanization process colonists favored cider and rum over beer. Rum, coming either from the West Indies or New England distilleries, was almost exclusively a market commodity, but cider has been often identified as a completely home produced good. These Massachusetts inventories, however, suggest differently.

Dairying appears to have been more ubiquitous. Nearly three quarters of the decedents from the countryside possessed at least one milk cow. Milk, butter, and especially cheese played a crucial role in the early modern diet, being the major source of fat and protein among poorer individuals. The work of the dairy fell to the female and required considerable skill if the products were to be any good. The churning of butter and the processing of cheese were labor intensive. It took two to three gallons of milk to make a pound of butter and one gallon for a pound of cheese. One or two pounds of one or the other was the likely amount eaten weekly per person, meaning that the housewife in a six-person family would have to have

---

[16] Schumacher, *The Northern Farmer,* 152, furnishes figures for Massachusetts' annual net imports (re-exports and exports subtracted) for bread, flour, wheat, and corn based upon customs records. The average annual net amount of bread/flour imported (1768–1772) was 3,262 tons. Dividing by 300 lbs., the average amount consumed annually per capita, the needs of 24,356 could be met. Corn and wheat net imports amounted to 232,402 bushels, and figuring to bushels per capita, 23,240 could be fed. Altogether that makes 47,596 out of a 1770 population in Massachusetts of 235,308, or 20.2%. Because some of the flour and grains subtracted from imports to get net imports were Massachusetts produced and not re-exports, this 20% figure is an underestimation. Gross, "Change in the Countryside."

manufactured from 300 to 600 lbs. a year. According to one description of cheesemaking, "it was an unending care from the time the milk was set over the fire to warm and then to curdle; through the breaking of the curds and the cheese-basket; through shaping into cheese and pressing in the cheese-press, placing them on the cheese-ladders, and constantly turning and rubbing them." Despite all of this work, the end product might be rather unpalatable unless the woman knew what she was doing.[17]

Table 3 Percentage of Inventories Containing Selected Home Production Goods (Massachusetts 1774)

	N	Cider/Brewing/ Distilling Equipment	Pigs	Milk Cows	Cheese/ Butter Equipment
Countryside	161	5.6%	58.6	71.4	44.1
Major Towns[a]	64	1.5	32.8	39.1	17.2
Boston	50	2.0	0.0	8.0	0.0
Total	275	5.1	42.0	52.4	29.8

SOURCE: see Table 2.
[a]Towns include Bridgewater, Gloucester, Ipswich, Marblehead, Newbury, Newburyport, and Salem.

Although most of the sample households, outside of those in Boston, owned a cow, it is unclear how many families were actually self-sufficient in dairy production. To meet the minimum requirement of a pound of cheese a week and some milk for a family of six, the household had to have possessed three of the scrawny pre-industrial beasts; yet only a quarter of the Massachusetts inventories mentioned this amount or more. Also, as Table 3 shows, over two thirds of the sample inventories lacked equipment to manufacture butter or cheese. Both of these facts suggest that the mere ownership of a cow did not mean self-sufficiency in dairy products.[18]

Finally, we come to the home production of meat. If people raised livestock for this purpose, the most affordable animal would have been the pig, so the Massachusetts inventories were checked for the presence of hogs. Although Boston households apparently did not normally have a prospective flitch of bacon foraging in the backyard,

---

[17] Earle, *Home Life,* 150. Lemon, *Poor Man's Country,* 154, has the information about gallons of milk required for butter and cheese.

[18] See George E. Fussell (ed.), *Robert Loder's Farm Accounts, 1610–1620* (London, 1936), xii, for a note concerning the low milk production of cows in the early modern era. Ulrich, "Friendly Neighbor," *395,* finds that in the period 1670–1730 in Essex County, Massachusetts, and Maine most decedents had cows but less than one quarter had dairy equipment.

nearly 60 percent of those living in the countryside did. Yet only one fifth of those had three or more animals enumerated, indicating that many rural households bought a pig or two to fatten but did not raise livestock for self-sufficiency.

Statistical analysis of the characteristics of those decedents who owned both milk cows and pigs (see Appendix 2) shows that wealth encouraged the possession of the former more than the latter and household size made more difference with pigs. Gentlemen, merchants, and professionals, all other things equal, shied away from the ownership of both animals, and widows, although as likely as others to have a milk cow, seemed less inclined to keep swine.

So far we have dealt solely with the plausibility or implausibility of household self-sufficiency, but what about *local* self-sufficiency? A richly textured literature exists portraying early American communities as one big happy family where neighborhood reciprocity rather than the cash nexus kept the seamless web all in one piece. The strength of this work is that it draws attention to the fact that different material circumstances produce different attitudes and expectations. Thus the options and priorities of modern men and women are not necessarily those of people in the past.[19]

The major weakness of this viewpoint is the assumption that specie-poor early Americans who conducted their transactions in kind or by performing labor services lived in a world uninfluenced by the capitalist marketplace. Even in the seventeenth century the accounts of farmers and shopkeepers routinely listed a price after a receipt or disbursement regardless of the form in which the payment had been made. If, for example, grain was the medium of payment, the price per bushel would be stated, and if the sum exceeded the amount needed then the purchase would have a credit—even though it might only be a penny. Thus in 1661 Thomas Minor of Stonington, Connecticut, agreed to pay a local shoemaker "in pease or Indian Coren 3s. p bushel wheat at 4s. p bushell, butter and good merchatabell cheese at 6d. p pound if the cheese be all new milk if not at 5 pence p pound." The amounts and quality were all spelled out in the price.[20]

---

[19] Recent examples of this viewpoint are Michael Merrill, "Cash is Good to Eat: Self-Sufficiency and Exchange in the Rural Economy of the United States," *Radical History Review*, III (1977), 42–71; James Henretta, "Families and Farms: *Mentalité* in Pre-Industrial America," *William and Mary Quarterly*, XXXV (1978), 3–32; Christopher Clark, "Household Economy, Market Exchange, and the Rise of Capitalism in the Connecticut Valley, 1800–1860," *Journal of Social History*, XIII (1979), 170–189.

[20] Disney H. Miner and George D. Stanton, Jr. (eds.), *Diary of Thomas Minor 1653 to 1684* (New London, 1899), 54–55, 106.

Larger transactions were conducted with the resident "great man," who most often was a big landowner, or a general store proprietor. These middlemen collected the staples in the area and sent them on to a marketing center or major port. Their accounts contained precise valuations. Rather than being unconcerned with monetary values, colonists seemed more interested in them than people today, perhaps because they owned less. The careful, item by item appraisals of estates carried out by neighbors, not professionals, for probate purposes is another illustration of the average person's knowledge of market prices. Whether they liked it or not, early Americans had to operate in an environment where prices were attached to their labor and goods, and usually these prices had been affected by regional, continental, and international markets.[21]

It is common for local studies to ignore the participation of colonists in the worldwide commercial system or to deal only with their role as exporters of staple crops. Americans, however, were consumers too, and records exist that indicate the scale of that participation. Because of the revenue that it generated, over-seas trade became the first area of the economy for which the British Crown collected annual statistics. Figures for English imports into the thirteen colonies begin in 1697. Table 4 shows the per capita unadjusted value of legal imports from England *only*. The table indicates that, despite the growth of colonial crafts and manufactures, the full-scale entry of the Scots into American commerce, and the series of trade disrupting wars in the eighteenth century, the unadjusted per capita value of imports did not exhibit a downward trend.

---

[21] See for example "Account Book of Major John Pynchon, 1664–1667," Univ. of Pennsylvania microfilm of transcript in the Connecticut Valley Historical Museum. A later example can be found in the John Harris of Harrisburg account books, Historical Society of Pennsylvania. Only with the Indians, primarily Indian women selling grain, did the shopkeepers omit prices, and one suspects that this omission did not work to the advantage of Native Americans. Winifred B. Rothenberg, "The Market and Massachusetts Farmers, 1750–1855," *Journal of Economic History*, XLI (1981), 3100–3112, finds a synchronization of prices in Massachusetts, Philadelphia, and New York from at least 1750 on.

Table 4 Per Capita Unadjusted "Official" Value of Imports from England into the Thirteen Colonies (average annual figures)[a]

Years	
1701–10	£ .92
1711–20	.86
1721–30	.86
1731–40	.84
1741–50	.82
1751–60	1.14
1761–70	.96

SOURCE: Bureau of the Census. *Historical Statistics of the United States* (Washington, D.C., 1975), 1168, 1174.

[a] Note that the imports into the colonies arc only those from England and include goods of English and Irish manufacture as well as re-exported commodities such as tea. The average annual import value was divided by an average of the population at the start of a decade and at the end.

But these unadjusted figures cannot be used in their raw form to indicate actual per capita expenditure. For one thing the official values only cover imports from England, both goods of English manufacture or re-exports. For many of the provinces those imports made up 85 percent or more of the total commodities brought in legally, but by the time of the Revolution, they comprised only about 75 percent of the imports into the Middle Colonies and two thirds of those into New England. The colonies could also receive goods from Scotland, the West Indies, and southern Europe, and those imports also have to be added as well as some average figure for the trade among the thirteen colonies themselves.

Another problem arises from the fact that smuggling flourished in the Land of the Free: ships regularly brought in goods such as sugar, molasses, tea, cloth, and wine from European nations and their possessions even though the Navigation Acts forbade this direct trade. Finally, there are difficulties with the official values themselves. The figures are wholesale, not retail, prices that exclude merchants' profits, some distribution costs, and customs and excise taxes.[22]

---

[22] The following discussion about the problems with the trade statistics is based upon Trevor H. Ashton's introduction to Elizabeth Boody Schumpeter, *English Overseas Trade Statistics, 1697–1808* (Oxford, 196o), 1–14; James F. Shepherd and Gary M. Walton, *Shipping, Maritime Trade, and the Economic Development of Colonial North America* (Cambridge, 1972), Appendix II; George N. Clark, *Guide to English Commercial Statistics, 1696–1782* (London, 1938); Thomas C. Barrow, *Trade and Empire: The British Customs Service in Colonial America, 1660–1775* (Cambridge, Mass., 1967), 134–150; John J. McCusker, "The Current Value of English Exports, 1697 to 1800," *William and Mary Quarterly*, XXVIII (1970), 607–628.

With the details of the adjustments relegated to a footnote, I arrived at the figure of £3.3 5 for the average annual per capita expenditure on imported goods by colonists during the decade prior to the Revolution, 1761 to 1770.[23] Jones has estimated per capita

[23] I have estimated that the average annual expenditure per capita for the thirteen colonies from 1761 to 1970 amounted to £3.35. In order to arrive at this figure, I made the following assumptions:

a.   The pound sterling value of legal imports per capita from
   1.   England = £.96 (from Table 4).
   2.   Scotland = £.12. This is the average of 1761–1770 from Scotland in Bureau of the Census. *Historical Statistics,* 1177, as corrected by Jacob Price in "Communication," *William and Mary Quarterly,* XXXIV (1977), 517.
   3.   West Indies and southern Europe = £.48. Shepherd and Walton, *Shipping, Maritime Trade,* 228–230, estimate the West Indies and southern European imports in 1772 as £817,776 and £71,689 respectively, and I used that year's figures because they seemed the most complete.
   4.   Coastal American trade = £.22. Using the figures provided by Shepherd and Samuel Williamson, "The Coastal Trade of the British North American Colonies, 1768–1772," *Journal of Economic History, XXXII* (1972), 783–811, the average annual value of the imports from the intra-mainland colonial trade from 1768 to 1772 came to £616,000 or £.33 per capita with perhaps two thirds or £.22 being the actual amount after adjusting for duplications (e.g. molasses imported from the West Indies to New England and thus already being counted under West Indies imports counted once again upon re-export from New England to the Middle Colonies).
b.   Smuggling—I have estimated that the amounts under a., totaling £1.78, should be increased by 25% to account for illegal trade. In 1768 the colonies were supposedly paying duties on enumerated articles shipped from one colony to another: wines, foreign sugar and indigo, molasses, coffee, glass, paper, painters' colors, lead, and tea. In 1770, the repeal of the Townshend Duties still left duties on tobacco, wine, sugar, molasses, and tea. The last commodity was certainly the star of the pre-Revolutionary contraband trade, as molasses had been earlier. In 1768, roughly £170,000 legally entered the colonies from Great Britain. It has been estimated that as much as 90% of the tea drunk was foreign and smuggled in. If we assume a lower figure of 75%, the value of illegal tea still would amount to about 18.5% of total imports from all places into the colonies. No wonder the colonists failed to appreciate the favor that the British Parliament claimed to be doing them by passing the Tea Act in 1773. As some allowance also has to be made for the smuggling of wine and other commodities, I arrived at the 25% figure. Adding 25% to £1.78 produces a sum of £2.23.
c.   Merchant mark-ups—Considering that the English commission merchants often added something to the price of items aside from their 2.5% fee and thus raised prices above the official values; that colonial merchants marked up the goods by 20% or more to cover costs of freight, insurance, and factorage, and to make a profit; and that shopkeepers or peddlers who usually sold the goods to the consumer also had to make a profit and cover the costs of inland transportation, a 50% mark-up seems sufficiently conservative and results in a total average annual expenditure

income in 1774 to have been in the range of £10.7 to £12.5. Assuming a figure of £12, which is on the higher end of the range, then the average American spent over one quarter (27.5 percent) of his or her budget on imports from outside his or her colony of residence. (A 1758 estimate by a storekeeper in Cape May, New Jersey, of the consumption of foreign goods in his county was £4 a person.)[24]

What makes the sizable percentage of expenditures lavished upon imports so relevant to the issue of self-sufficiency and home production is that consumer goods constituted the bulk of the items flowing in. Table 5 lists the most important commodities legally imported into America during the sample year, 1768. The three major sources of legal imports for the mainland colonies were Great Britain, the West Indies, and southern Europe. The primary goods being brought in were diet and dress items: tea, sugar and its by-products, wine, woolens, linen, and cotton, both cloth and garments. For example, the colonies at one point imported annually enough men's worsted stockings from England to put a pair on every adult male in America. As for the other types of goods, wrought iron could mean nails and tools, but it also included housewares. "Goods of several sorts" and the "Other" categories covered paper, silks, glassware, cotton, calico, pottery, brass, and furniture. It appears, then, that 75 percent and probably more of total imports entering the colonies legally went to meet consumer needs. In addition, the major categories of goods smuggled in—sugar, molasses, spirits, and tea—were all consumer commodities.

---

per capita of £3.35. On merchant mark-ups see Price, *Capital and Credit in British Overseas Trade: The View from the Chesapeake, 1700–1776* (Cambridge, Mass., 1980), 149–150; Martin, *Merchants and Trade*, 138–139; Arthur Jensen, *The Maritime Commerce of Colonial Philadelphia* (Madison, 1964), 103–106. Jensen's book contains complaints by colonists about English commission merchants raising the prices of the goods that they bought from wholesalers. If the wholesaler or retailer in America had to offer credit to his customer, as he often did, then the mark-up would be higher and some commodities provided a larger margin of profit than others. Total mark-ups then could be as high as 100%. Shepherd and Walton, *Shipping, Maritime Trade, 58–59,* suggest that the distribution costs from the British manufacturer to the colonial consumer declined substantially during the century.

[24] Jones, *Wealth of a Nation to Be* (New York, 1980), 62–63. Robert Gallman's estimates, £11 to £12.5, are very similar to Jones; see Shepherd and Walton, *Shipping, Maritime Trade,* 29–30. Schumacher, *Northern Farmer,* 141.

Table 5 Most Important Commodities Imported Legally into the American Colonies, 1768

	Percentage of Total Value
Commodities Imported from Great Britain = £2,198,000	
Woolens	19.7
Linens—domestic and foreign	15.9
Tea	7.7
Wrought Iron	6.0
Goods of "several sorts"—paper, glass, etc.	12.6
Other	38.1
	100.0[a]
Commodities Imported from the West Indies = £482,731	
Rum	42.9
Molasses	32.4
Sugar	13.3
Cotton	4.6
Other	6.8
	100.0
Commodities Imported from Southern Europe = £70,494	
Wine	70.1
Salt	29.9
	100.0

SOURCES: Information contained in Shepherd and Walton, *Shipping, Maritime Trade,* 180–186, 228–230; Brian R. Mitchell, *Abstract of British Historical Statistics* (Cambridge, 1971), 310.

[a] Percentage is of total official value of exports from Great Britain to the thirteen American colonies in 1768.

The idea that colonial households functioned in a similar way to the household of the legendary farmer mentioned at the beginning of this article, and that they produced all of their own goods, seems highly unlikely. Rather, what the Massachusetts inventories show is the inclination of rural households to perform one or two steps in the production process—spin the flax, grow corn, milk the cow, or fatten the pig—and then rely on craftsmen for the rest of the processing. In addition, they supplemented homegrown products with textiles, flour, butter, and meat bought from tradesmen, peddlers, and neighboring producers. With some products, such as drink, almost no one except those engaged in the trade possessed the equipment to make it properly. Finally, in Boston and the major towns of the province, decedents frequently did not possess the livestock or implements needed to make the apparel or the food required for self-sufficiency.

The standard response to the discovery that colonial households lacked the means to meet their own consumption needs is that they relied on neighborhood reciprocity, and thus they existed in a state of *local* self-sufficiency. Yet how can communities that spent a quarter of per capita income on goods imported from outside the *colony* be described as practicing local self-sufficiency? The growth of the colonial population, European Atlantic ports, the British shipping industry, indentured servitude, and chattel slavery all stand as testimony to the voracious appetite of Western consumers for new market commodities, and there is no evidence that Americans did not fully participate in that commercial world.

APPENDIX 1 Determinants of Linen and Apparel Investment in Inventories (Massachusetts 1774)

Investment in Linen (Ln)		*Investment in Apparel (Ln)*	
N = 251	R^2 = 469	N = 264	R^2 = .525
Constant	−.040	Constant	−2.150
Wealth[1] (In)	.479[a]	Wealth (In)	.726[a]
	(.083)[b]		(.057)
Household size[2]	.178[a]	Spinning Wheels	−.027
	(.028)		(.143)
Spinning Wheels?	.247	Occupational status	
	(.194)	gent., merc., prof.	.184
Occupational status			(.214)
gent., mere., prof.	.287	crafts, trades, dual occ.	.066
	(.291)		(.175)
crafts, trades, dual occ.	.282	husbandmen	.205
	(.238)		(.234)
husbandmen, farmers	.372	laborers	.419
	(.318)		(.242)
laborers, mariners	.639[a]	women	.840[a]
	(.311)		(.270)
women	.656	Urban location	
	(3.50)	major towns	−.091
Urban location			(.166)
major towns[4]	.798[a]	Boston	.066
	(.219)		(.098)
Boston	−.123	Books	.311[a]
	(.270)		(.149)
Age			
25 and below	.333		
	(.428)		
26 to 45	−.115		
	(.177)		
Books[5]	.314		
	(.197)		

SOURCE: see Table 2.
[1] Wealth excludes real estate.
[2] Household size = two times the number of beds with zero beds coded as one person.
[3] Reference categories for dummy variables: spinning wheels = none; occupational status = yeomen; urban location = rural area; age = over 45; and books = none.
[4] Major towns include Salem, Ipswich, Marblehead, Newburyport, Newbury, Gloucester, and Bridgewater, all with over 500 families in the 1764 census.
[5] Books are a proxy for education.
[a] Significant at the .05 level or better.
[b] Figures in parentheses are standard errors.

Explanation The hypothesis behind these two regressions is that the possession of a spinning wheel should lower the pound sterling investment in linen and apparel if it were used continually to produce large amounts of cloth at home for the family, homespun cloth being, generally, cheaper than storebought cloth. Neither of the coefficients for spinning wheels (.247 or –.027), however, was different from zero at a statistically significant level, indicating that the ownership of the implement did not necessarily mean that the household produced much homemade cloth. I transformed the two dependent variables and wealth into natural logs (ln) to tone down the effect of outliers and make the variables more normally distributed. As might be expected, wealth was an important determinant in both regressions. Since household size is based upon the number of beds, linen would be influenced strongly by the number, even more strongly than would probably be the case if we knew directly the number in the household. Household size is not included in the apparel regression because only the dress of the decedent was usually included in the enumeration. Laborers, wealth held constant, had greater amounts invested in linen, largely because such a small proportion of their wealth was in producer goods. For the same reason women had high investment in apparel. Why major towns, but not Boston, had higher linen investment than rural areas or why those owning books had more money in apparel requires further investigation before explanations can be offered.

APPENDIX 2 Determinants of the Number of Milk Cows and Pigs Listed in Massachusetts 1774 Inventories

N = 257	$R^2 = .380$	$R^2 = .221$
Independent Variables	Number of Milk Cows	Number of Pigs
Constant	−.135	−.399
Wealth[1] (ln)	.451[a]	.264[a]
	(.089)[b]	(.122)
Household size	.073[a]	.127[a]
	(.034)	(.046)
Urban location[c]		
Major towns	−.997[a]	−1.016[a]
	(.263)	(.360)
Boston	−1.890[a]	−1.980[a]
	(.288)	(.396)
Occupational status[c]		
Gent., prof., merchant	−.960[a]	−1.044[a]
	(.345)	(.473)
Craftsmen, tradesmen	−.552	−.492
	(.284)	(.389)
Husbands, farmers	−.143	-2.95
	(.399)	(.547)
Laborers, mariners	−.479	−.752
	(.378)	(.518)
Women	−.165	−1.212[a]
	(.430)	(.590)
Age		
25 or under	−.750	.379
	(.519)	(.713)
26–45	−.233	.058
	(.216)	(.297)

SOURCE: see Table 2.

[1] Wealth *includes* realty. Other variables are the same as in Appendix 1.

[a] Significant at the .05 level or better.

[b] Figures in parentheses are standard errors.

[c] Reference categories for dummy variables: occupational status = yeomen; urban location = rural area; age = over 45.

Explanation These two regressions show that, in addition to the positive effect of wealth and household size on the number of cows and pigs owned, urban location had a strongly negative impact. Living in Boston rather than in a rural area reduced the number of cows (−1.89) and pigs (−1.98) owned by nearly two, whereas living in a major town such as Salem or Newbury eliminated one cow (−.997) and pig (−1.016). The mean for cows and pigs owned was 1.48 and 1.39, respectively. Being a gentleman, etc., depressed the dependent variables as well (–.96 and – 1.044). The other occupational categories are not significantly different from the reference category of yeomen except for women's ownership of pigs, another negative relationship.

4

The Scotch-Irish

James G. Leyburn

America is a nation of immigrants. Native Americans' ancestors were immigrants to the New World just as were the forebears of every other national and ethnic strain that has contributed to the creation of an "American culture." In historic times, the Scotch-Irish were one of the many groups of peoples who sought refuge and relief in America. The "Scotch-Irish" came into being in the early seventeenth century when the English government, anxious to rule Ireland, transplanted Lowland Scots as colonists to the county of Ulster in northern Ireland. For about a century the Scotch-Irish eked out a living in Ireland, but in the early part of the eighteenth century their economic condition suffered a series of disastrous reversals. As a consequence, a wave of perhaps five thousand Scotch-Irish immigrated to America in 1717. By the end of the eighteenth century four more waves of Scotch-Irish departed Ireland for America and several hundred thousand "Ulstermen" settled in nearly every section of the English colonies. Proud, Presbyterian, and turbulent, the Scotch-Irish profoundly affected the regions they occupied. They were a colorful group of people who helped to manufacture our national character.

Millions of Americans have Scotch-Irish ancestors, for when this country gained its independence perhaps one out of every ten persons was Scotch-Irish. Few descendants among these millions, however, know much about their ancestors—about what the hyphenated name implies, where the original Scotch-Irishmen came from and why, or what part this vigorous folk played in early American history.

Because the thirteen original American colonies were English, with government in English hands and the population predominantly from England, the tendency of our history books has been to make us see colonial history as the product of transplanted Englishmen. Every American child learns about Jamestown, Pilgrims and Puritans, Tidewater planters, landed proprietors and gentry—all English; but few schoolbooks make a child aware of the non-English "first Americans." In quite recent years our attention has been insistently called to the blacks who made up one sixth of our first census in 1790; and the very names of German, Dutch, Portuguese Jewish, and French Huguenot elements tell us who these early Americans were. But who were the Scotch-Irish?

Next to the English they were the most numerous of all colonists, with settlements from Maine to Georgia. Some historians suggest that they were "archetypal" Americans, in the sense that their ideals and attitudes, limitations and prepossessions, virtues and vices, proved to be common national characteristics of nineteenth-century Americans. If such a claim has any validity, the people themselves deserve to be more than a vague name.

To English colonists who were their neighbors from 1717 to 1775 any idea that immigrants from northern Ireland might presage future American character would have been startling if not dismaying. Few of the settled colonists had kind words for the newcomers in those days. Pennsylvania received the largest numbers of them, and James Logan, secretary to the Penn family and an Irishman himself, lamented that "the settlement of five families of [Scotch-Irishmen] gives me more trouble than fifty of any other people." When they continued to pour into the colony, Logan, fearing that the decent Quaker element might be submerged, fumed: "It is strange that they thus crowd where they are not wanted." Cotton Mather in Massachusetts was more forthright; he fulminated against their presence as one of "the formidable attempts of Satan and his Sons to Unsettle us." On the eve of the Revolution a loyal English colonist declared the Scotch-Irish to be, with few exceptions, "the most God-provoking democrats on this side of Hell."

Such initial hostility toward a wave of foreigners was to become commonplace during the next century, when America received some thirty million immigrants from Europe. By comparison with these late-comers, however, the Scotch-Irish were fortunate, since they experienced active hostility for only a brief time. Practically all of them pushed as quickly as possible to the cheap lands of the back country, where, out of sight, they no longer offended the sensibilities of English colonists by their "oddities."

In many ways the Scotch-Irish pioneers were indeed an augury of Americans-to-be. They were probably the first settlers to identify themselves as Americans—not as Pennsylvanians or Virginians or citizens of some other colony, nor as Englishmen or Germans or any

European nationality. Their daily experience of living on the outer fringe of settlement, of making small farms in the forests, of facing the danger of Native American attack and fighting back, called for qualities of self-reliance, ingenuity, and improvisation that Americans have ranked high as virtues. They were inaugurators of the heroic myth of the winning of the West that was to dominate our nineteenth-century history. Their Presbyterian Church, with its tradition of formality in worship and its insistence upon an educated ministry, was the first denomination to make tentative, if reluctant, adjustments to the realities of frontier life. Social mixing and intermarriage with their neighbors, irrespective of national background, made any such qualifier as Scotch-Irish (or northern Irish or Ulsterman) disappear within a generation.

When the Revolutionary War came, Scotch-Irishmen were the most wholehearted supporters of the American cause in each of the thirteen colonies. If before 1775 they were still regarded as aliens and immigrants, their zeal as patriots and soldiers changed all that. At home and abroad they were credited with playing a vital part in the struggle for independence. A Hessian captain wrote in 1778, "Call this war by whatever name you may, only call it not an American rebellion; it is nothing more or less than a Scotch Irish Presbyterian rebellion." King George was reported to have characterized the Revolution as "a Presbyterian war," and Horace Walpole told Parliament that "there is no use crying about it. Cousin America has run off with a Presbyterian parson, and that is the end of it." A representative of Lord Dartmouth wrote from New York in 1776 that "Presbyterianism is really at the Bottom of this whole Conspiracy, has supplied it with Vigour, and will never rest, till something is decided upon it." Such testimony to enthusiasm for the American cause was not given to any other group of immigrants.

Upon the conclusion of the war, when the great Ohio and Mississippi valleys were opened up and the rush westward began, sons and daughters of the original Scotch-Irishmen led the way across the mountains to the new frontiers. Theodore Roosevelt is not the only historian who suggests that the institutions, attitudes, and characteristics of these trans-Allegheny pioneers constituted the practical middle ground into which the diversities of easterners and southerners might merge into something new—American culture.

The hyphenated term "Scotch-Irish" is an Americanism, generally unknown in Scotland and Ireland and rarely used by British historians. In American usage it refers to people of Scottish descent who, having lived for a time in the north of Ireland, migrated in considerable numbers to the American colonies during the half century before the Revolutionary War. Perhaps 250,000 of them actually crossed the sea to America, and they bred rapidly; their sons, like later arrivals from Ulster, constantly extended settlements westward to the Appalachians. The mountains then sent the flow of newcomers north and especially south from Pennsylvania until they constituted a dominant element in many colonies.

Only occasionally were these people then called Scotch-Irish; the usual designation was simply "Irish." "Scotch-Irish" is accurate, yet many Irish-American critics assert that it is an appellation born of snobbish pride and prejudice. They are not entirely wrong. During the years of immigration, from 1717 to 1775, none of the newcomers seem to have insisted upon the "Scotch" part of the name; this insistence developed only among their descendants, and for interesting reasons.

As is well known, after the potato famines of 1845 and 1846 the Irish began to pour into the United States. These people were desperately poor; they were Roman Catholics coming to a Protestant-dominated country; they were mostly illiterate, often uncouth by American standards, and they were very visible in their concentration in Eastern cities. Prejudice against the "shanty Irish" was rampant for decades. In these very decades, antiquarian interest was quickening among Americans; local historical societies burgeoned; people looked for distinguished ancestors among their colonial forefathers. Descendants of the people from Ulster, whose grandparents had not objected to being called Irish, now preferred the hyphenated name Scotch-Irish—all the more enthusiastically because Sir Walter Scott had beguiled the nation with his romantic picture of Scots and of Scotland. A Scotch-Irish Society was founded, and its annual meetings, like its publications, boasted of notable ancestors and important contributions to the United States.[1]

The ostentatious pride of these later Scotch-Irish, and their boasts of importance to America, aroused first the anger of many Irish-Americans and then their sarcastic wit. The newly invented hyphenated name was called a cant phrase, a shibboleth, a mongrel absurdity, a delusion; and the Scotch-Irish Society was proclaimed "an organized humbug." One Irish-American, in a waggish poem

---

[1] One typical list of distinguished Americans whose forebears were Scotch-Irish was published in 1920. It included the names (listed alphabetically) of Thomas Hart Benton, James G. Blaine, John C. Calhoun, John G. Carlisle, Andrew Carnegie, George Rogers Clark, Jefferson Davis, Ulysses S. Grant, Horace Greeley, Alexander Hamilton, Mark Hanna, Samuel Houston, Andrew Jackson, Thomas Jonathan "Stonewall" Jackson, John Paul Jones, George B. McClellan, William McKinley, Oliver Hazard Perry, John D. Rockefeller, Edward Rutledge, Winfield Scott, Zachary Taylor, Matthew Thornton, Anthony Wayne, and Woodrow Wilson.

entitled "The Gathering of the Scotch-Irish Clans," lampooned the false pretenses of Irishmen who would not admit their true origins:

> Are ye gangin' to the meetin', to the meetin' o' the clans
> With your tartans and your pibrochs and your bonnets and brogans?
> There are Neeleys from New Hampshire and Mulligans from Maine,
> McCarthys from Missouri and a Tennessee McShane.

There follows a succession of straight Irish names, and the satire ends:

> We'll sit upon the pint-stoup and we'll talk of auld lang syne
> As we quaff the flowing haggis to our lasses' bonnie eyne.
> And we'll join the jubilation for the thing that we are not;
> For we say we aren't Irish, and God knows we aren't Scot!

(The members of the Scotch-Irish Society might have informed the satirist that one does not "quaff" haggis, a formidable pudding made with a sheep's viscera.)

Yet for all the implicit snobbishness in the double name, it directs attention to geographical, historical, and cultural facts in the background of the Scotch-Irish people. The persistence of ancestral traits of character can be exaggerated and even given a mystical quality; but there is no doubt that tradition, ancient "sets" of mind, religious convictions, limitations of outlook, and abiding prejudices gave the Scotch-Irish qualities of personality and character that affected their life in America.

The people who began to come to America in 1717 were not Scots, and certainly they were not Irish: already they were Scotch-Irish, even though this name was rarely given them. The hyphen bespeaks two centuries of historical events, many of them tragic ("dark and drublie" was the Scottish phrase), some of them heroic. The ancestors of these people had come, in the century after 1610, from the Lowlands of Scotland across the twenty-mile channel to the northern province of Ireland (Ulster) as a result of a political experiment undertaken by England. It was called the Plantation of Ulster, and it was simply one of England's many attempts to solve "the Irish problem."

For five centuries, ever since the time of Henry II (1133–89), England had tried to rule Ireland, but the Irish refused to become docile subjects. Their resistance was intensified into bitterness when England became Protestant and tried to extirpate the Roman Catholic religion in Ireland. Finally, in Queen Elizabeth's closing years, Irish earls in the north, after a desperate struggle, were defeated and exiled, and the Crown confiscated all their lands. James I, who followed Elizabeth in 1603, proposed (at the suggestion of Edmund Spenser and others of his counsellors) to settle this region with loyal English and Scottish Protestants who, in return for cheap land, would keep the Irish under control. Since the king had been James VI of Scotland before succeeding to the English crown, he was successful in persuading thousands of his Scottish subjects to cross to Ulster and start a new life there under advantageous economic circumstances.

Only a vivid modern imagination can conceive the squalor, indeed the near savagery, of the northern Irish counties around 1600. Queen Elizabeth called the inhabitants "the wild Irish." She and her advisers looked upon them much as Victorians did African natives and other "lesser breeds without the law." These Irishmen had no cities, no education, no refinements; they lived from hand to mouth at a primitive level (maintained, of course, by centuries of guerrilla fighting against the English). Their Catholic religion, a patriotic rallying point and a blessed solace, had acquired many elements of magic and superstition. Almost utter demoralization had ensued upon the defeat and exile of their leaders in the 1590s.

The Scots who were invited (along with English Protestants) by King James to settle Ulster and subdue its natives were thus the first Scotch-Irishmen. They came from the Lowlands, that region nearest the English border and longest in contact with English ways, language, and ideas. They were not the romantic Highland figures of Scott's novels. They were not clansmen who wore kilts and who marched, complete with dirk, sporran, brooch, and bonnet, to the skirling of bagpipes in the glens. On the contrary, they were farmers who eked out a bare living on thin soil as tenants of a laird. Three words best characterize them: they were poor, Presbyterian, and pertinacious.

Their farming methods were primitive. Crops were not rotated, and the yield was meager; starvation was always imminent in the long winters, for both man and beast. King James's offer of a new start in Ireland on larger farms whose land had lain fallow was, therefore, very appealing, all the more because lairds in the Lowlands had recently demanded higher rents and contracts that made farmers feel a loss of traditional rights and dignity.

The first Scotsmen to pioneer in Ulster succeeded well enough to allure other thousands of Lowlanders, and when, in mid-century, troubles arose with the English king and his church, the exodus increased. The new Ulstermen ran the gamut of character, as pioneers do. Their motives for migration—desire for a better living, escape from problems and debts—indicate ambition and initiative. Some of the adventurers proved to be shiftless; others had qualities needing only opportunity to bring them to full flower. Most of the "planters" took their families with them, thus proclaiming their intention to stay and establish themselves. Socially, they were generally humble folk (aristocrats rarely migrate), but with tenacious qualities indispensable for pioneers.

They were Presbyterians to a man, and Scottish Presbyterianism was unique in its intensity, even in those religious days. The Reformation in Scotland, led by John Knox, had achieved immediate and almost universal success among Lowlanders. Their Calvinist "kirk" became the Church of Scotland, a nationalist symbol for the people, who supported it all the more loyally because of the initial struggle against "popery" and the subsequent resistance against royal efforts to make it Anglican. A notable aspect of the Reformation in Scotland was the enthusiastic commitment of the people to education, not only for ministers but also for laymen. It was as if a dormant ideal had suddenly and permanently come to flower. The highest aspiration of a Lowland family was that a son might attend a university and become a minister or dominie. The passion for education carried over to northern Ireland and to America, with far-reaching results in the colonies.

It is likely that the quality of the Lowlanders that made the king most hopeful of their success in the Ulster Plantation was their well-known stubbornness and dourness ("dour" and "durable" are linguistically related). He counted on these traits to hold them in Ulster even when things went badly, and to make them keep the "wild Irish" in tow, and his confidence proved justified. Had not an elder of the kirk besought the Lord that he might always be right, "for Thou knowest, Lord, that I am unco' hard to turn"?

In the century between 1610 and 1717 perhaps as many as one hundred thousand Lowlanders came across from Scotland, and by the latter date there were some five Scots to every three Irishmen and one Englishman in Ulster. The English planters represented the Establishment: high civil officials, Anglican churchmen, businessmen, and the Army; but the preponderant Scots set the tone of the new culture of northern Ireland. It is a culture that, as the recent troubles there have painfully shown, is still self-consciously different from that of the rest of the island.

The Ulster experience was a fitting preparation for pioneering in America. The farmers had constantly to be on guard against native Irish uprisings. Agricultural methods decidedly improved under English example. Feudalism, which still existed in Scotland, simply disappeared in Ulster, for farmers were no longer subject to an overlord or attached to one locality. The Presbyterian Church, with its members "straitly" watched over and disciplined by the session of each parish kirk, stiffened the moral fiber of the people, and with its own presbyteries, not subject to the Scottish Kirk, gave the members experience in self-government.

In one respect, however, the Scotch-Irish seemed to be deficient. The Renaissance did not reach Scotland until the eighteenth century, many years after the Lowlanders had left. From the moment of their arrival in northern Ireland comment was made by Englishmen on the apparently complete lack of aesthetic sensibility on the part of these Scots. As one observer remarked, if a Scotsman in Ulster "builds a cottage, it is a prison in miniature; if he has a lawn, it is only grass; the fence of his grounds is a stone wall, seldom a hedge. He has a sluggish imagination: it may be awakened by the gloomy or terrific, but seldom revels in the beautiful." The same limitations apparently characterized the Scotch-Irish in America.

In the very decades when at last the Ulster Plantation seemed to be achieving its purpose, with the Irish subdued, Protestantism dominant, English rule secured, and prosperity imminent, the great migration to America got under way. As usually happens when thousands of people undertake so hazardous an enterprise as crossing an ocean to find a new home, there was both a push from the old country and a pull from the new.

Paradoxically, Ulster's growing prosperity was one cause of the first wave of migration. A lucrative woolen and linen industry, developing since the 1690s, alarmed the English Parliament and led to the passage of a series of crippling protective acts whose results were resentment on the part of Ulstermen, economic depression, and recurrent unemployment. A second cause touched men personally and turned many thoughts to migration: this was the hated practice of rack-renting. The term referred to a landlord's raising rent when a long lease on his land expired—and in the decade after 1710 hundreds of leases came up for renewal. To us, such a practice seems normal; but Ulster farmers felt it to be a violation of tradition, a moral injury, because a tenant was treated impersonally. If the farmer could not or would not pay the higher rent, he had only two practical alternatives: a return to the poverty of Scotland, or migration to the New World.

Still other causes stimulated emigration. Six years in succession after 1714 brought dire drought, with depression in the flax industry and soaring costs of food. In 1716 sheep were afflicted with a destructive disease; severe frosts throughout the decade discouraged farmers; a smallpox epidemic scourged Ulster. In addition there was a goad from the Anglican religious establishment. Deserting the tolerant policy of William III, the High-Church party, ascendant during the reign of Queen Anne (1702–14), secured the passage of a Test Act, requiring all office-holders in Ireland to take the sacrament according to prescriptions of the Church of England. Although aimed at Irish Catholics, the weight of this requirement fell heavily upon substantial Presbyterians who held magistracies and other civil posts. By extension, Presbyterian ministers could no longer perform legal marriages or even bury the dead, nor could "dissenters" teach school. This unwise law, though not everywhere rigidly enforced, caused resentment among the stubborn Scots, intensified by the fact that they had been loyal to the Crown and had proved a bulwark of defense against the rampageous Irish.

For all these reasons some five thousand Ulster Scots went to America in 1717 and 1718. After that initial migration, the pull of America began to exert more effect than the push from northern Ireland. Reports coming from the colonies were highly favorable, especially from Pennsylvania. Land was cheap and plentiful, authorities were well disposed, the soil was fertile beyond all imagination, and opportunities were boundless. Only two drawbacks loomed: the perils of an ocean crossing, and the expense of the passage. The former was very real in those days; but optimism persuaded young people that the nightmare of several weeks on a tiny, overcrowded ship, with much illness, was rarely fatal and that grim memories would soon fade. As for passage money, the practice of indenture had long been a familiar device. Few who had made up their minds to go would be deterred by having to work for a master in America for a period of years to pay off their passage fee, for then came freedom and a new life in a country which, according to some, resembled paradise.

Five great waves brought a quarter million Ulster Scots to America, turned them into Scotch-Irish Americans, depressed the economy of Ulster, and depopulated parts of that province. The tides ebbed and flowed partly with conditions in Ulster, partly with upsurges of what was called migration fever. The chief waves were those of 1717–18, 1725–29, 1740–41, 1754–55, and 1771–75; and each benefited particular colonies. The first two helped fill up the back country of Pennsylvania and soon began spilling over into the Shenandoah Valley of Virginia. The third further peopled the Shenandoah Valley and spread into the piedmont and upcountry of North Carolina. That colony and South Carolina drew most of the people in the fourth wave, while the final group, coming just before the Revolutionary War, spread out widely from New York to Georgia.

In each wave, other colonies also drew settlers. Because the Delaware River early proved the favorite entryway, the colonies of New Jersey, Delaware, and Maryland soon had many Ulstermen. Massachusetts reluctantly admitted a few but so disliked their uncongenial ways that later arrivals in Boston went on to New Hampshire or Maine.

Two facts about the migration are significant for American history. First, there was almost no further influx from northern Ireland after the Revolutionary War; thus, there was no addition to the Scotch-Irish element from abroad nor any inducement to maintain sentimental ties or a "national" identity with a country ruled by England. Second, the concentration of Scotch-Irishmen in the geographically central colonies of Pennsylvania and Virginia made a kind of reservoir from which the people spread north and south through all other colonies; moreover, their farms just east of the Alleghenies were nearest the Great West when that vast territory opened up after 1783. Scotch-Irishmen were thus the vanguard of the trans-Allegheny pioneers.

It has already been observed that no other immigrants were so patriotically unanimous in support of the American cause as the Scotch-Irish. One group of patriotic settlers in Mecklenburg County, North Carolina, drew up a set of resolutions on May 20, 1775, declaring the people of that county free and independent of the British Crown. This predominantly Scotch-Irish assemblage thus anticipated by more than a year the Declaration of Independence. The Revolutionary War might not have been won without Scotch-Irish fighting men.

With independence gained, the Scotch-Irish almost everywhere exerted a unifying, an *American,* influence, favoring a central government of truly united states. The very fact of their recent arrival in the country and their spread through all thirteen colonies had prevented the growth of strong ties to a particular colony and therefore of an insistent demand for states' rights. In Pennsylvania and Virginia support by the Scotch-Irish may have been decisive in shaping state constitutions that were extraordinarily liberal for the times. In Pennsylvania power was wrested from the Philadelphia Quakers and given to the majority of the people, thanks to the combined efforts of Scotch-Irish, German, and non-Quaker English settlers in the western regions. In Virginia also, the Scotch-Irish of the Shenandoah Valley strongly supported a constitution remarkable for its break with tradition—one that abolished quitrents, entails, primogeniture, and the slave trade, and guaranteed religious liberty. (It must be noted, however, that leadership for all these liberal measures came from Jefferson, Madison, and other English Virginians.)

Scotch-Irishmen struck a real blow for religious liberty in this country. In 1738 the royal governor of Virginia and the Tidewater planters actively sought to persuade newcomers to the Pennsylvania frontier to leave that crowded region and settle in the Shenandoah

Valley. An ancestor of John C. Calhoun presented to Governor William Gooch a memorial drawn up by the Presbyterian Synod of Philadelphia requiring religious toleration as a prerequisite for settlement. Gooch acceded to the demand, to the benefit of Virginia and of later American freedom.

From the first, Scotch-Irishmen took an active part in politics. They were elected to office in their communities, became effective lawyers, and in significantly large numbers served in legislatures, on high courts, and as governors—though hardly because their ancestors had come from Scotland and northern Ireland. With the election of Andrew Jackson as President, the descendants of the Scotch-Irish had attained the highest office in the land, and most of them had by then ceased to emphasize their ancestry.

In education and religion it may be asserted that many American ideals and standards derive from the happy agreement of two self-assured colonial groups, the Scotch-Irish and the New England Yankees. Alone, neither people might have been weighty enough or (in the case of the Yankees) unprovincial enough to have prevailed; but their common Calvinism and earnestness gave America its first commitment to general education as well as its tendency to identify religion with upright moral character.

For both people, schools followed churches as the first institutions to be formed. The Word of God must be expounded by educated ministers, and colonists could not send their sons abroad for training. The connection between church and school, going back to the Reformation, was to remain close for descendants of both Presbyterians and Puritans until the present century. Ministers were schoolmasters as well as preachers. Curricula in Scotch-Irish log schools on the frontier resembled those of the town schools in earlier New England, with training in the three R's, the Bible, and the catechisms, while higher education was directed toward training for the ministry. The Puritans founded Harvard and Yale well before the Presbyterians established Princeton and Hampden-Sydney and Dickinson; but from these first colleges came a host of others, whose students were not wholly ministerial. Until the Civil War the great majority of colleges in the country were founded by religious denominations and still remained under their control. (The state's responsibility for higher education had not yet been widely claimed.) Of the 207 permanent colleges founded before 1861, well over half were established by Presbyterians and New Englanders; and many of them were notable as "mothers" of still other colleges.

The distinctive religious influence of the Scotch-Irish and New Englanders was not in their common Calvinism, though certainly Calvinist theology has had its effect upon America: it was rather in persuading millions of Americans that religion and character are synonyms. In most other parts of the world religion is likely to mean ritual observance, adherence to a creed, customary pious acts, or some combination of these; but when an American says that a person is deeply religious he is likely to mean first of all that he is upright and highly moral. Both Puritans and Scotch-Irish insisted upon rectitude of life and behavior, stubborn adherence to principle, scorn of compromise, and a stern severity that could be as hard upon others as upon self. Neither people could accept the idea that a man's religious duty consisted only of acts performed on Sunday or of doctrinal orthodoxy. Since America quickly became pluralistic in religion, there could never have been agreement upon ritual, creed, or observances to unify us religiously; but all Americans could agree on admirable character and high moral rectitude. What the Puritans and Scotch-Irish made of religion was immensely reinforced when the Baptist and Methodist movements, rising to ascendancy in the nineteenth century, taught the same ideas.

In certain ways the Presbyterian Church of the Scotch-Irish was the first important denomination to become "Americanized" and broadly "American." In log churches on a frontier, with a congregation of pioneer farmers, many formal traditions of the dignified Presbyterian Church quietly vanished—the Geneva gown and stock, the separate pulpit, the attendance of the minister by a beadle, the set prayers. Many of the colonial Presbyterian ministers experimented with unconventional, direct methods of evangelism, in order to speak clearly to a people losing interest in dignity for the sake of tradition. (The approval of the presbyteries for this informality was not won, however; and because the dynamic Methodists and Baptists felt free to adopt resourceful methods of evangelism, they drew thousands of adherents among descendants of the Scotch-Irish.)

The Church of England was the established religion in six colonies and the Congregational faith in three others; both, then, were identified with the upper-class English Establishment; but the Presbyterian Church was nowhere official, elite, or English. Moreover, these other two dominant churches were regional, strong only in the Tidewater and in New England; but the Presbyterian Church, like the Scotch-Irish people, was present in every colony. Its ministers were supported not by legally exacted tithes but by free contributions of members; these ministers in their work moved freely from one region to another. The organization of the church was controlled by presbyteries that ranged from New York to the South. The "federal" structure of the church of the Scotch-Irish seemed congenial to

American conditions and exerted a unifying influence in our early history.

If we of the twentieth century wish to admire the Scotch-Irish as representative prototypes of later Americans, we must ruefully note that their Ulster forefathers' neglect of things aesthetic was carried over to the new country. European visitors and critics in the nineteenth century, indeed, considered all Americans deficient in such matters; but we now know how wrong they were, for our museums are full of beautiful early American art and artifacts from New England, from the Tidewater, from German farmlands, and from many other regions and districts—but not from Scotch-Irish settlements. Nothing in the background of these people in either Scotland or northern Ireland had attracted them to painting, sculpture, architecture, music, and literature, and nothing in their way of life in the colonies apparently changed their attitude. They liked what was practical and seemed indifferent to whether it was beautiful. The lists of distinguished scions of the Scotch-Irish in nineteenth-century America include no names of artists and poets.

By 1800 the young United States was growing strong and self-confident, with a continent to win. Already the authority of the thirteen original states was losing its hold over the rising generation. If a farsighted historian of the time had been inclined to identify representative types of inhabitants who would probably become the most characteristic Americans of the new century, he might well have named the restless frontiersman and the rising middle-class townsman. The former was rapidly winning the West, clearing the wilderness, exploiting America's fabulous wealth, adding romance to the American myth; the latter was establishing law and order, building industry, adding comfort to utility, and treasuring respectability and responsibility. If the same historian had sought to find the embodiment of each of his representative types, he could have pointed immediately to the descendants of the vigorous Scotch-Irish, now thoroughly American, with no further accretions from abroad. Most of them had even forgotten the adjective formerly applied to them. The daily life of being an American was too absorbing to permit adulation of one's ancestors, even though these had been the admirable Scotch-Irish.

5

The Case of John Peter Zenger

Lincoln Barnett

Twentieth-century Americans see a free press as essential to the ordering of their society, and even though they support the notion, they often are unaware of the struggles that have been fought to establish such a principle. The quarrel between Governor William Cosby of New York colony and a fairly obscure printer named John Peter Zenger became a landmark battle in early American history.

Cosby was a vain, greedy, and foolish man who was ill-equipped to serve as New York's governor. As he repeatedly blundered in the performance of his duties as governor, Cosby was attacked by his opponents who used the press as one means to popularize their opposition to his policies. As the governor and the radical political faction clashed, John Peter Zenger, who was not much more than a pawn in the conflict, became locally famous as a symbol of a struggle to establish a free press in colonial New York. Zenger's trial did not forever set free the press in colonial America, but it was an important milestone in that direction.

On the morning of August 4, 1735, a cross section of New York's ten thousand citizens clustered outside the city hall at the corner of Wall and Nassau streets. English and Dutch, men of all classes and trades, waited and argued tensely. Carts bounced over the paving blocks. The mid-summer morning light slanted down on white sails in the harbor and on the spire of Trinity Church a block away. Here and there in the crowd readers scanned the pages of a four-page paper entitled *The New-York Weekly Journal, Containing the freshest Advices, Foreign, and Domestick.*

In a few moments, in a courtroom inside the hall, the publisher of that controversial weekly would go on trial for his freedom. It was not only those in the immediate assembly who sensed the drama of the contest that was about to unfold. Throughout New England, from Boston to Philadelphia, and even in London, men of awareness had long discussed the political and intellectual issues that now were about to collide as the government sought to imprison a little known German-born printer: the right of citizens to criticize their rulers versus the claims of public order and safety. It was a tense moment in the unending battle for freedom of speech and press that is by no means quiescent today.

For more than eight months the thirty-eight-year-old John Peter Zenger (whose family had left the Upper Palatinate when he was thirteen) had been held in jail on charges of seditious libel stemming from his publication in the *Journal* of criticisms of the current colonial administration in New York. These were embodied in editorials and letters to the editor, sometimes scholarly in tone, sometimes satirical, composed by a few of the colony's most highly literate, erudite, and articulate citizens. And they had continued to appear and to sting the authorities throughout his long incarceration. For Zenger was allowed visits from his wife, Anna, and his two oldest sons; and while they cocked their ears against a hole in the door of his cell, he relayed to them muffled instructions for printing the work of his contributors. Except for the first week following his arrest, the *Journal* did not miss a single issue.

Meanwhile, the tensions created by this first major confrontation in America between government and the press had kept growing, dividing public opinion not only in New York but in other colonies as well. New York, however, was the storm center. Zenger's paper was the voice of a faction in the colony's politics. On his side were most middle-class New Yorkers, most residents of Quaker or Dutch extraction, and most long-established freeholders—independent owners of land and property. Hostile to him were members of the so-called Court Party—wealthy merchants whose interests lay in trade with England, colonial bureaucrats, and peripheral followers of the incumbent governor of New York, William Cosby. It was this official's personality and behavior that had thrown the city into turmoil.

When Cosby arrived in New York to assume the office of governor by appointment of King George II on August 1, 1732, he ignited the fuse of events that exploded at the Zenger trial three years later. Prior to his coming, the mood of the colony was so tranquil that one of the city's most distinguished lawyers, James Alexander, predicted that Cosby would enjoy an easier administration than any previous governor of New York. People knew that he was an Anglo-Irish aristocrat, a close friend of the Duke of Newcastle, an army colonel, and brother-in-law to the Earl of Halifax. These facts had preceded him during the year that elapsed between his appointment and his actual disembarkation in New York Harbor. The cause of the delay, as he let it be known, was his protracted fight to procure the defeat of a sugar bill that would favor southern plantation owners at the expense of the middle colonies. So a trusting and grateful populace was there to welcome him warmly as he set foot ashore.

It did not take long, however, for Cosby to reveal his offensive characteristics. The first to emerge were his unbridled temper and arrogance. The day after his arrival he ordered his coachman to horsewhip a farmer who was driving a loaded wagon with his wife seated beside him, because the man did not yield the right of way to Cosby's carriage with instant, deferential speed.

The prime force that smouldered within this essentially rather stupid and only half-educated man, however, was avarice. What New Yorkers did not know at first was that in his last post as governor of the Mediterranean island of Minorca he had ruthlessly confiscated the property of a Spanish merchant, sold the property at auction, retained the proceeds, secreted the papers to cover his theft, and denied the injured merchant his right of appeal. News of the affair eventually got back to England, and despite Cosby's powerful connections, his crime was too flagrant to be ignored. He was ordered to reimburse his victim, fined £10,000 for his misconduct, and removed from his post in Minorca. Yet Cosby somehow managed to obtain other appointments, culminating in his important post as governor of New York, which he avowedly looked upon as an opportunity to "repair his fortunes."

Only a few knew of the Minorca episode, however, and in the first days of Cosby's administration the New York assembly voted him a salary of £1,500, plus a special gratuity of £750 for his alleged services in obtaining repeal of the sugar bill. When news of the assembly's appropriation was reported to Cosby, he flared in fury at what he considered the frugality of the award (though by the King's instructions he was forbidden to accept any gifts from the assembly) and roared violently, "Damn them! Why did they not add the shillings and pence!" Meekly the assembly raised the amount of the gift to £1,000.

Repeatedly, Cosby took arbitrary action without asking for the assembly's authorization or advice; he practiced nepotism (appointing his son to a sinecure office as "Secretary of the Jerseys" at an annual stipend of £450); he sold various local jobs at his disposal, attempted to rig elections, ignored instructions from London, and eventually, as will be seen, tampered with the courts.

The many diffuse antagonisms Cosby had built up congealed suddenly in a single, concrete clash over the issue of "Van Dam's salary." Between the death of the governor who preceded Cosby and the time of the new appointee's arrival, the powers of the office were in the hands of Rip Van Dam, senior member of the provincial council. Van Dam, who came from an old Dutch family, had served capably and honestly, and the grateful council had awarded him the full gubernatorial salary for his service. In the past, some—but not all—such acting governors had given half of their salaries to the official incumbent for whom they were substituting. Cosby demanded that Van Dam follow this uncertain precedent. But the old gentleman refused, unless compelled by due course of law.

Cosby at once sought just such compulsion. But no jury in New York was likely to find in favor of the unpopular governor. So he resorted to a bit of complex legal chicanery that would altogether eliminate the presence of jurors. He decreed that the three-justice supreme court of the colony should sit on the case as "Barons of the Exchequer," a court of equity. The verdicts of such courts were given by judges alone. Van Dam's attorneys, two of the ablest lawyers in New York, at once prepared to defy Cosby and challenge the jurisdiction of the reconstructed court. James Alexander and William Smith, long-time friends and political allies, were both legal scholars and forceful, articulate men. Alexander owned the largest law library in the American colonies and was a founder of the American Philosophical Society. Smith held both Bachelor's and Master's degrees from Yale (where he had distinguished himself in the classics) and was a founder of Princeton College.

When the Van Dam case came up for argument before the supreme court in April, 1733, the presiding justice was Lewis Morris, a man of great intellectual power, an owner of extensive lands in what is now part of the Bronx, and one of the most respected and politically powerful personages in America. He had served as chief justice since 1715 and later would become the first governor of New Jersey. In the litigation now before him, Morris ruled in favor of Van Dam, denying that the supreme court had jurisdiction in equity cases and attacking the propriety and legality of Cosby's maneuver. The two other judges were James De Lancey and Frederick Philipse. Both were young and inexperienced, sons of self-made businessmen who represented the powerful mercantile clique in New York's assembly, and both refused to concur with Morris.

Outraged by such upstart opposition, the senior justice promptly rebuked the two, left the courtroom, and, in an unusual step, released the text of his opinion for publication, together with some comments on Cosby's public character. And thus the battle lines were drawn.

Cosby swiftly wrote to London accusing the chief justice of bias, intemperate drinking, unreliability, and all-round inefficiency. Then, in August, he summarily dismissed Morris from the supreme court. In his place the governor appointed the callow but tractable Justice De Lancey.

Morris became, overnight, leader of an anti-Cosby faction that embraced many of the freeholders and professional people in the colony, among them such distinguished men as Gerardus Stuyvesant, Philip Livingston, and Cadwallader Colden. Their allies extended up the Hudson Valley as far as Albany. When, in the autumn of 1733, Morris and his son ran for the assembly, both were elected by strong majorities. Moreover, in October of 1734, Morrisite candidates were to win every seat but one in New York City's common council.

Secure in their political base, Morris and his supporters began an all-out war, by pamphlet and oratory, to effect the recall of Cosby, whom they assailed as an unprincipled and corrupt tyrant. And then they sought out a relatively new medium, a facade behind which a writer could discreetly remain anonymous, namely, a newspaper. But New York's only newspaper at that time was the *New York Gazette,* owned by William Bradford, and Bradford, who held an official monopoly as public printer, was not disposed to lose it by publishing criticisms of the administration.

But John Peter Zenger was a printer, too. He had, in fact, been indentured to Bradford as an apprentice, and after a journeyman's sojourn in Maryland, had been Bradford's partner for a year. In 1726 he had set up his own small, struggling printshop in Smith Street, near Maiden Lane. His spelling, syntax, and grammar were unreliable, and his typography left much to be desired. Nevertheless, he did own a working printing press, and this asset, whose value was quite evident to the Morris supporters, led them to back Zenger in the founding of *The New-York Weekly Journal,* referred to by historian Stanley N. Katz, an authority on Zenger, as "America's first party newspaper."

Issue No. 1 of the *Journal* appeared on November 5, 1733, bearing Zenger's imprimatur. It featured as its main story the election of Lewis Morris and his son to the assembly against the opposition of Cosby, whose appointed sheriff had used every device to disqualify pro-Morris voters. From its debut the *Journal* enchanted a readership accustomed only to the bland columns of the *Gazette,* for its anonymous writers—Alexander, Smith, and the Morrises—wielded the sharpest and most erudite pens in the province. Although it provided some foreign news (with a dateline about ten weeks old) and reported ship arrivals and departures, the *Journal* regularly devoted its first two pages to a "letter" addressed to Mr. Zenger that was in essence an editorial on local affairs.

It was Alexander, Van Dam's gifted attorney, who gave Zenger's paper its basic tone. He and his fellow contributors dipped into the past, quoted from the classics, cited the essays of Addison and Steele, and composed original diatribes against Cosby and his so-called Court Party. Some weeks they applied a touch of sly, ironic innuendo, as in one article that discussed the cabalistic significance of certain letters of the alphabet. It pointed out that the letter C appeared to bring bad luck to New York as well as to England, as demonstrated in history by Charles I, Cromwell, Charles II, and Lord Cornbury, a predecessor of Cosby's whose governorship had thrown the colony of New York into turmoil.

Colored by sharp criticism and outspoken dissent, the *Journal* pursued a course that was bold, indeed reckless, in the light of contemporary libel laws—so rigorous that any printed comment casting disfavor on the government, whether justified or not, could subject both author and publisher to fine and imprisonment.

It cannot be proved in retrospect that the *Journal* was preparing a challenge, a test of freedom of the press. But it did address the issue at once. In its second and third issues it ran "letters" emphasizing the value of free criticism of government officials. A bad minister was an "impudent Monster in Iniquity," declared one of these, who might not "immediately be come at by ordinary justice." But "let him yet receive the Lash of Satyr . . . and if he has no Conscience, rouse his Fear . . . sting him with the Dread of Punishment, cover him with Shame, and render his Actions odious to all honest Minds," and he might be brought down. At the least, such exposures of highly placed administrators would make them cautious, and this alone made "Liberty of the Press not only consistent with, but a necessary Part of the Constitution itself." (The author's reference was to the unwritten constitution of England.)

The *Journal* went on to assert that not only were truthful attacks on wicked officials indispensable to good government, but even the possibility that a free press would give currency to false accusations was to be accepted as risk of freedom. " . . . very few good Ministers can be hurt by Falsehood, but many wicked Ones by seasonable Truth." The "mischief" that a few might meet with by calumny was nothing to what king and people might suffer "by a shameful, cowardly Silence under the Tyranny of an insolent, rapacious, infamous Minister." Mere inconvenience was rather to be endured than total destruction. For, "The Loss of Liberty in general would soon follow the Suppression of the Liberty of the Press.... "

As weeks passed, the *Journal* subtly veered from these bold but general statements to specific and only slightly veiled assaults on Cosby and his cronies. Its writers employed three forms—satire, reportage of facts, and comment. Within the framework of its time the *Journal* was unusually daring. Other publications often prudently sought advance clearance for their content, although this was not strictly necessary, since the custom of precensorship—of requiring a printer to secure approval and a license before he could set material in type—had expired in England in 1695 and was almost never used in the colonies.

This freedom from advance clearance, in fact, was what an eighteenth-century Englishman understood "freedom of the press" to mean. But it was a limited liberty, since the printer was still liable to prosecution for seditious libel, namely, criticism that tended, in the words of English Chief Justice Holt in *Rex v. Tutchin* in 1704, "to beget an ill opinion" of the government or its officers. Such prosecutions were not uncommon and could carry drastic penalties. But the *Journal* disdained precautionary measures and went an independent way, reporting what it chose. In January, 1734, the *Journal* cast discretion to the winds and openly called Cosby a "rogue Governour"—one who did "a thousand Things for which a small Rogue would have deserved a halter."

The rising tempo of attack did not go unnoticed, and in that same month Chief Justice De Lancey tried to persuade a grand jury to return an indictment against Zenger and his writers for seditious libel, but the jury declined to act. In September, however, when a city election brought resounding defeat to a ticket of Cosby supporters, printed pamphlets from Zenger's press fluttered through the streets, broadcasting effusive ballads celebrating the returns. It was the dissemination of these verses, each set to a popular tune of the time, that triggered the Zenger trial. The sound of sedition is virtually inaudible today, but in Cosby's domain it rang loud and clear. For example:

> To you good lads that dare oppose all lawless power and might,
>
> You are the theme that we have chose, and to your praise we write:
>
> You dar'd to shew your faces brave In spight of every abject slave;
>
> with a fa la la... .

Such ballads, climaxing weeks of constant, impudent dissent in the columns of the *Journal,* seemed to provide Cosby with the final evidence of seditious libel. Under the law Zenger, as printer of the offensive doggerel, threatened provincial security, divided public opinion, and cast doubt on the credibility of the administration. Cosby decided to silence Zenger and the Morrisites once and for all.

Hence, when the October grand jury convened a few days after the rain of ballads, De Lancey once again asked for a libel action, observing, "Sometimes heavy, half-witted Men get a knack of Rhyming, but it is Time to break them of it, when they grow Abusive, Insolent and Mischievous with it." Once again the jurors demurred, protesting that they found it impossible to identify the author or publisher of the objectionable material.

Cosby now brought his personal power into play. He decreed a public burning of the ballads and, at a later date, of several especially obnoxious numbers of the *Journal* and ordered the mayor and all city magistrates to be witnesses. The magistrates not only refused to attend but denied Cosby the services of the common hangman, whom he had named as chief incinerator. As a consequence, the immolation of the four offending issues was performed on November 6 by the sheriff's Negro slave in the lonely presence of the recorder and a handful of officers from the British garrison. Then Cosby struck at the printer himself.

On Sunday, November 17, 1734, Zenger was summarily arrested by the sheriff and locked in the common jail on the third floor of city hall. The charge specified that his paper, the *Journal*, contained many things "tending to raise Factions and Tumults, among the People of this Province, inflaming their Minds with Contempt of His Majesty's Government, and greatly disturbing the Peace thereof."

Held incommunicado at first, Zenger was unable to get out an issue of the *Journal* that week. This threatened Cosby's foes with the loss of their journalistic voice. Even though Zenger was able to resume publication, there was a chance of his being permanently silenced. Lewis Morris took off for London to argue Zenger's case before officials of the Crown. James Alexander and William Smith applied on November 23 for a writ of habeas corpus to free Zenger on moderate bail, noting that the defendant had sworn he was not worth more than £40, excepting only the "tools of his trade and his wife and children's wearing apparel." Ignoring the arguments and affidavits, Chief Justice De Lancey harshly set bail at £400 plus two "sureties" (guarantors) who had to pledge £200 each, though no precedent in New York history sustained such judicial extortion. Unable to produce this, Zenger was remanded to jail. The question has been raised many times: Why did affluent men like Morris, Alexander, Smith, and Van Dam not come to the rescue of the printer who had served their cause so well? One speculation is that Zenger's patrons decided that by letting him remain incarcerated, he would be seen as a martyr and symbolic victim of the tyranny they opposed.

As the court calendar crept leisurely through winter and spring, Zenger continued to hold weekly conversations with his wife and sons, and the *Journal* continued to appear under the direction of Alexander and Smith without interruption and without change in its editorial attitudes. At the opening of the supreme court's spring term on April 15, Zenger's lawyers made an audacious move by questioning on technical grounds the right of Justices De Lancey and Philipse to preside over a case on which their views were notoriously predisposed. For on signing the warrant for Zenger's arrest in November, De Lancey had publicly and imprudently announced to spectators that "if a jury found Zenger Not Guilty, they would be perjured." De Lancey not only refused to allow the exceptions, but on April 16 he disbarred Alexander and Smith from further law practice in New York.

Zenger's predicament had now become grave indeed. There were few lawyers in New York and none so able as Alexander and Smith. A prisoner without counsel, Zenger had no recourse but to petition the court to assign an attorney for his defense. De Lancey responded by naming John Chambers, a young man relatively competent but relatively inexperienced and a member of the Court Party. He pleaded Not Guilty for Zenger and requested an adjournment until the summer term in order to prepare his case. It was granted and Zenger stayed in jail.

When the trial finally opened on that August morning of 1735, few present expected an acquittal. As the crowd surged into the hearing room, there was only one bright element amid the general pessimism of the Zenger supporters. Overturning a bit of Cosbyite chicanery that would have packed the jury with men indebted to the Governor, they had induced Chambers to select a friendly jury. All were simple artisans, moreover, and apt to be opposed to Cosby's aristocratic faction. Zenger's friends knew that if the halfhearted defense counsel could develop any possible basis for acquittal, the jurors would thankfully seize it.

To open the trial the prosecutor, Attorney General Richard Bradley, cited passages from the *Journal* that had been deemed false, scandalous, malicious, and seditious at the time of Zenger's arrest in November. Two particular issues had been singled out—those of January 28 and April 8, 1734. The earlier one had declared, in the italics and capitals that colonial printers delighted in using for emphasis: *"The People of this City and Province . . . think, as Matters now stand, that their* LIBERTIES *and* PROPERTIES *are precarious, and that* SLAVERY *is like to be entailed on them and their Posterity, if some past Things be not amended."* The second cited the remark of an anonymous citizen who was fleeing to Pennsylvania: "I *think the Law itself is at an End"* - and, in an explosion of capitals, "WE SEE MENS DEEDS DESTROYED, JUDGES ARBITRARILY *displaced, new courts erected*

without consent of the legislature . . . BY WHICH, IT SEEMS TO ME, TRIALS BY
JURIES ARE TAKEN AWAY WHEN A GOVERNOUR PLEASES ... [and] MEN OF
KNOWN ESTATES DENIED THEIR VOTES. . . . "

Bradley then informed the jurors of their duty under a strict but
solidly acceptable construction of the law. Their sole function was to
determine whether John Peter Zenger had published the offensive
quotations. The question of libellousness, he said, was for the judges
to determine. In legal parlance, the jury could find only as to the
facts, but not the law.

When Bradley had concluded, Chambers arose and delivered a
gentle and general disquisition on the nature of libel, expressing
doubt that the prosecution could prove that a single individual had
been libelled. In his presentation there was no hint of an aggressive
defense of his client, but rather a plea of nolo contendere—of not
disputing the accusation, but not acknowledging guilt.

As Chambers uttered the last syllables of his mild peroration, an
elderly and imposing gentleman rose dramatically from a bench at the
rear of the courtroom and announced that he wished to participate in
Zenger's defense. An ember of hope and excitement glowed in the
bloc of Zenger supporters. Members of the Court Party looked
questioningly toward the bench. Unknown to all, including Zenger,
Alexander and Smith had communicated, after their disqualification,
with perhaps the best legal mind in America: Andrew Hamilton,
former attorney general of Philadelphia, former speaker of the
Pennsylvania assembly, former vice-admiralty judge, a member of
London's Gray's Inn, an independent in politics and religion, and
versatile enough to have been one of the architects of Independence
Hall. In the later colonial period, the term "Philadelphia lawyer"
would be a high compliment to a member of the bar, and it is
possible, though not provable, that Hamilton was the prototype and
that the phrase originated with the Zenger case.

When he walked down the aisle of the courtroom to defend
Zenger, Hamilton seemed a strong and dominant figure in comparison
with the startled young justices on the bench. Some years later the
son of William Smith recalled, in a history of New York, "He had art,
eloquence, vivacity, and humor, was ambitious of fame, negligent of
nothing to ensure success, and possessed a confidence which no
terrors could awe."

Like many lawyers, Hamilton had perhaps a bit of the actor in
him, and it may have been this trait, combined with a touch of gout,
that caused him to limp down the aisle and disarm the uncertain
judges with an air of overpowering venerability. The Zenger case had
appealed to his own political disposition. He had been a friend of

Alexander's; and when he received a call for help, he agreed without hesitation to make the long trip to New York.

Upon his unexpected appearance, Cosby supporters waited expectantly for De Lancey to expel Hamilton from the chamber, as he had disbarred Alexander and Smith. But Hamilton's prestige and assurance of manner may have disconcerted the young chief justice. He conferred briefly with his associate justice, Philipse, and then rapped for the hearing to begin.

Attorney General Bradley was about to call his first witness to testify that Zenger and no other man had published the libellous papers when Hamilton interceded and astonished the court by an amiable declaration. "I'll save Mr. Attorney the Trouble of examining his Witnesses to that Point; and I do (for my Client) confess, that he both printed and published the two News Papers set forth in the Information, and I hope in so doing he has committed no crime."[1]

Quite probably taken aback by Hamilton's concession, the attorney general, after a moment of hesitation, turned to the bench and said, "Then, if Your Honor pleases, since Mr. *Hamilton* has confessed the Fact, I think our Witnesses may be discharged; we have no further Occasion for them."

"If you brought them here," said Hamilton, "only to prove the Printing and Publishing of these News Papers, we have acknowledged that, and shall abide by it."

At this point Zenger's journeyman and two sons, and a few other witnesses subpoenaed by Bradley, were discharged and there was silence in the courtroom for some time.

"Well Mr. Attorney," De Lancey finally said, "will you proceed?"

"Indeed, Sir," responded the prosecutor, "as Mr. *Hamilton* has confessed the Printing and Publishing these Libels, I think the jury must find a Verdict for the King; for supposing they were true, the Law says that they are not the less libellous for that; nay indeed the Law says that their being true is an Aggravation of the Crime."

Hamilton instantly demurred. "Not so neither, Mr. Attorney," he exclaimed, "there are two Words to that Bargain. I hope it is not our bare Printing and Publishing a Paper that will make it a Libel: You will have something more to do, before you make my Client a libeller; for the Words themselves must be libellous, that is, *false, scandalous,* and *seditious* or else we are not guilty."

---

[1] Hamilton's remarks at the trial, as well as those of other participants, are not derived from a court transcript but are taken from A *Brief Narrative of the Case and Trial of John Peter Zenger (1736),* prepared by James Alexander and Andrew Hamilton a few months after the trial. This work, often reprinted, was one of the most renowned American publications in the eighteenth century.

The adjectives touched off a semantic and legal debate. For if the only restraint on the press was not prior licensing but the law of libel, that law was strict. It was designed to prohibit what an English judge, in a later case *(Dean of St. Asaph's* case, 1784) had called "written censure upon public men for their conduct as such, or upon the laws, or upon the institutions of the country." Nor did it matter whether the words were true or false. In short, any man could say or write what he chose, but he could be penalized if his words were judged, under the broad umbrella, to be libellous. In England the common law courts of King's Bench had taken over such cases by 1735, and in New York, where English common law was binding, criticism of Governor Cosby could theoretically be punished as severely as criticism of King George II in England.

That was Bradley's line of argument. Quoting from the specimens of political comment in the *journal* that, by earlier English precedents, were clearly libellous, the attorney general added that he did not know what could be said in defense of a man who had so notoriously scandalized the governor and other officers of the government, when all knew that government was entitled to "great regard and reverence . . . both under the law and the gospel." If this was not libel, he added, he did not know what it was.

To this Hamilton replied, "May it please Your Honor, I agree with Mr. Attorney, that Government is a sacred Thing, but I differ very widely from him when he would insinuate, that the just Complaints of a Number of Men, who suffer under a bad Administration, is libelling that Administration. Had I believed that to be Law, I should not have given the Court the Trouble of hearing any Thing that I could say in this cause."

Hamilton then began his assault on the major precedent, cited by both Chief Justice De Lancey and Bradley. In 1606, during the oppressive reign of James I, the Court of Star Chamber, composed of Crown-appointed judges who sat in secret, held, in the case of *de Libellis Famosis*, that statements could be libellous even if true. This thesis had prevailed on both sides of the Atlantic for more than a century, and it was Hamilton's determination to shoot it down. His opening salvo was directed at Bradley's selection of supportive cases from the hated Star Chamber tribunal, abolished in 1641.

"I was in hopes," said Hamilton, "as that terrible Court, where those dreadful judgments were given, and that Law established, which Mr. Attorney has produced for Authorities to support this Cause, was long ago laid aside, as the most dangerous Court to the Liberties of the People of *England* that ever was known in that Kingdom that Mr. Attorney . . . would not have attempted . . . to make their judgments a Precedent to us. For it is well known, that what would have been judg'd Treason in those Days for a Man to speak, I think, has since, not only been practiced as lawful, but the contrary Doctrine has been held to be Law."

Declining to argue the merits of Star Chamber precedent, the attorney general went back to what he insisted was the nub of the matter. "The Case before the Court is, whether Mr. *Zenger is* guilty of *Libelling* His Excellency the Governor of *New-York*, and indeed the whole Administration of the Government? Mr. *Hamilton* has confessed the Printing and Publishing, and I think nothing is plainer, than that the Words in the Information are *scandalous, and tend to sedition, and to disquiet the minds of the People of this Province.* And if such Papers are not Libels, I think it may be said, there can be no such Thing as libel."

Hamilton at once leaped on a significant omission. "May it please Your Honour; I cannot agree with Mr. Attorney. For tho' I freely acknowledge, that there are such Things as Libels, yet I insist at the same Time that what my Client is charged with, is not a Libel; and I observed just now, that Mr. Attorney in defining a Libel made use of the Words, *scandalous, seditious, and tend to disquiet the people*; but (whether with Design or not I will not say) he omitted the Word *false.*"

Bradley brushed this aside. "I think I did not omit the Word *false,*" he declared. "But it has been said already, that it may be a Libel notwithstanding it may be true." That was precisely what Hamilton wanted to dispute, and the debate crackled briskly for a few moments.

HAMILTON: "In this I must still differ with Mr. Attorney . . . [for] we are charged with Printing and publishing *a certain false, malicious, seditious and scandalous libel.* This Word *false* must have some Meaning, or else how came it there? . . . No the Falsehood makes the Scandal, and both make the Libel. And to shew the Court that I am in good Earnest, and to save the Court's Time, and Mr. Attorney's Trouble, I will agree, that if he can prove the Facts charged upon us to be *false,* I'll own them to be *scandalous, seditious and a Libel.* So the Work seems now to be pretty much shortened, and Mr. Attorney has now only to prove the Words *false,* in order to make us Guilty."

BRADLEY *(refusing to be drawn in):* "We have nothing to prove; you have confessed the Printing and Publishing; but if it was necessary (as I insist it is not) how can we prove a Negative? . . .

HAMILTON: "I did expect to hear, That a Negative cannot be proved; but every body knows there are many Exceptions to that general

Rule: For if a Man is charged with killing another, or stealing his neighbour's horse, if he is innocent in the one Case, he may prove the Man said to be killed, to be really alive; and the Horse said to be stolen, never to have been out of his Master's Stable, and this, I think, is proving a Negative. But we will save Mr. Attorney the Trouble of proving a Negative, and take the *Onus probandi* upon ourselves, and prove those very papers that are called Libels to be *true.*"

That was enough to bring in Chief Justice De Lancey to reiterate the law. "You cannot be admitted, Mr. *Hamilton,* to give the Truth of a Libel in Evidence. A Libel is not to be justified; for it is nevertheless a Libel that is true."

Hamilton was ready with a long list of citations and an argument that ridiculed the idea of "the greater the truth, the greater the libel": "I know it is said, *That Truth makes a Libel the more provoking, and therefore the Offense is the greater, and consequently the judgment should be the heavier.* Well, suppose it were so, and let us agree for once, *That Truth is a greater Sin than Falsehood;* Yet as the Offenses are not equal . . . is it not absolutely necessary that [the judges] should know, whether the Libel is *true* or *false,* that they may by that Means be able to proportion the Punishment? For, would it not be a sad Case, if the judges, for want of a due Information, should chance to give as severe a judgment against a Man for writing or publishing a Lie, as for writing or publishing a Truth? And yet this . . . as monstrous and ridiculous as it may seem to be, is the natural Consequence of Mr. Attorney's Doctrine, *That Truth makes a worse Libel than Falsehood,* and must follow from his not proving our papers to be *false,* or not suffering us to prove them to be *true.*"

De Lancey not only remained unmoved but resorted to judicial fiat, and, it may be guessed from the words used, some exasperation. Once more he announced: "Mr. Hamilton, the Court is of the Opinion, you ought not to be permitted to prove the Facts in the Papers," and read the supporting citation from a law book before him. When Hamilton tried to persist, he was brusquely cut down.

HAMILTON: "These are Star Chamber Cases, and I was in Hopes that Practice had been dead with the Court."

DE LANCEY: "Mr. *Hamilton,* the Court have delivered their Opinion, and we expect you will use us with good Manners; you are not to be permitted to argue against the Opinion of the Court."

HAMILTON: "With Submission, I have seen the Practice in very great Courts, and never heard it deemed unmannerly t o — "

DE LANCEY: "After the Court have declared their Opinion, it is not good Manners to insist upon a Point in which you are overruled."

HAMILTON: "I will say no more at this Time; the Court I see is against us in this Point; and that I hope I may be allowed to say."

DE LANCEY: "Use the Court with good Manners, and you shall be allowed all the Liberty you can reasonably desire."

Zenger's supporters felt their spirits wane. It seemed clear that the great lawyer's effort had failed. Stripped of power to distinguish truth from falsehood, the jury could return no other verdict than Guilty. Yet Hamilton showed no sign of chagrin. He had one more maneuver to try—unprecedented, hazardous, one that might possibly lead to disbarment, possibly prison.

Calmly, he said: "I thank Your Honour," and turned to the jurors. "Then, Gentlemen of the jury, it is to you we must now appeal, for Witness, to the Truth of the Facts we have offered and are denied the Liberty to prove; and let it not seem strange, that I apply myself to you in this Manner, I am warranted so to do both by Law and Reason. . . . were you to find a Verdict against my client, you must take upon you to say, the Papers referred to in the Information, and which we acknowledge we printed and published, are *false, scandalous and seditious;* but of this I can have no Apprehension. You are citizens of *New-York; you* are really what the Law supposes you to be, *honest and lawful men....* And as we are denied the Liberty of giving Evidence, to prove the Truth of what we have published, I will beg Leave to lay it down as a standing Rule in such cases, *That the suppressing of Evidence ought always to be taken for the strongest Evidence.*"

What Hamilton was now doing was to appeal over the heads of the chief justice and the attorney general and urge the jury to ignore the court's order, determine the truth of the *Journal's* charges, and find Zenger innocent of libel if indeed the accusations had merit. After a few more verbal exchanges with Bradley, this became clear. For when De Lancey repeated once more: "No, Mr. Hamilton; the jury may find that Zenger printed and published those Papers, and leave it to the Court to judge whether they are libelous," Hamilton was almost blunt: "I know, may it please Your Honor, the jury may do so; but I do likewise know they may do otherwise. I know they have the Right beyond all Dispute to determine both the Law and the Fact, and where they do not doubt Of the Law, they ought to do so. This of leaving it to the Judgment of the Court, *whether the Words are libellous or not* in Effect renders Juries useless. . . ." And as he swept onward in his argument, Hamilton went beyond the issues of Cosby and his enemies. He moved toward a general defense of freedom of speech. He declared that "all the high Things that are said in Favor of Rulers, and of Dignities, and upon the side of Power, will not be able to stop People's Mouths when they feel themselves oppressed. . . ." And he even harked back to the English revolt against the Stuarts, quoting "a great and good Man" whom he did not name, to the effect that *the Practice of Informations* [prosecutions without grand-jury indictments] *for Libels is a Sword in the Hands of a wicked King and an arrant Coward to cut down and destroy the Innocent.*"

That was enough to bring Bradley up sharp. "Pray Mr. Hamilton," he warned, "have a Care what you say, don't go too far neither, I don't like those Liberties." Blandly Hamilton backed away: "Sure, Mr. Attorney, you won't make any Applications; all Men agree we are governed by the best of Kings." And smoothly, he moved into a lengthy, moving, and still painfully timely discourse in defense of "a Right which all Freemen claim . . . they have a right publickly to remonstrate the Abuses of Power in the strongest Terms, to put their neighbors upon their Guard against the Craft or open Violence of Men in Authority, and to assert with Courage the Sense they have of the Blessings of Liberty, the Value they put upon it, and their Resolution at all Hazards to preserve it as one of the greatest Blessings Heaven can bestow."

De Lancey and Bradley apparently sat without interruption as the powerful attorney eloquently developed his theme of the ineluctable necessity of free speech, while ranging easily for examples through recent British and ancient Roman history.

Two centuries ago, he noted, heretics were burned at the stake for uttering unorthodox theological doctrines, but in 1735 a man could criticize the church with impunity. " . . . it is pretty clear," said Hamilton with deliberate irony, "That in *New-York* a Man may make very free with his God, but he must take special Care what he says of his Governor." The Attorney General, he continued, seemed to feel that *"Government is a sacred Thing; That it is to be supported and reverenced; It is Government that protects our Persons and Estates; That prevents Treasons, Murders, Robberies, Riots, and all the Train of Evils that overturns Kingdoms and States, and ruins particular Persons;* and if those in the Administration, especially the *Supream Magistrate, must have all their Conduct censured by private Men, Government cannot subsist. This is called a Licentiousness not to be tolerated. It is said, That it brings the Rulers of the People into Contempt, and their Authority not to be regarded, and so in the End the Laws cannot be put into Execution.*"

Throwing all caution aside, Hamilton approached the end of his plea by advising the jurors that earlier English cases established that *"the Judges, how great soever they be, have no Right to Fine, imprison, or punish a Jury for not finding a Verdict according to the Direction of the Court.* And this I hope is sufficient to prove, That Jurymen are to see with their own Eyes, to hear with their own ears, and to make use of their own Consciences and Understandings, in judging of the Lives, Liberties or Estates of their fellow Subjects. . . . Gentlemen the danger is great. . . . A proper Confidence in a Court is commendable; but as the Verdict (whatever it is) will be yours, you ought to refer no Part of your Duty to the Discretion of other Persons. If you should be of Opinion, that there is no Falsehood in Mr. *Zenger's* Papers, you will, nay (pardon me for the Expression) you ought to say so. . . . It is your Right to do so, and there is much depending upon your Resolution, as well as upon your Integrity."

"Power," the Philadelphia attorney said (or later recalled saying), "may justly be compared to a great River, while kept within its due Bounds . . . both beautiful and useful; but when it overflows its Banks, it is then too impetuous to be stemmed, it bears down All before it and brings Destruction and Desolation wherever it comes. If then this is the Nature of Power, let us at least do our Duty, and like wise Men (who value Freedom) use our utmost Care to support Liberty, the only bulwark against lawless Power." Drawing on a reserve of histrionic ability, he alluded to his age, his "weight of many years" and "great infirmities of body," yet declared that he was ready to go anywhere to combat efforts to "deprive a People of the Right of remonstrating. . . [against] the arbitrary Attempts of Men in Power." Undoubtedly having the jurors in his spell at that point, he launched into a historic and deservedly much-quoted finale.

". . . the question before the Court and you Gentlemen of the jury, is not of small nor private Concern; it is not the Cause of the poor Printer, nor of *New-York* alone, which you are now trying: No! It may in it's Consequence, affect every Freeman that lives under a British Government on the main of *America*. It is the best Cause. It is the Cause of Liberty; and I make no Doubt but your upright Conduct, this Day, will not only entitle you to the Love and Esteem of your Fellow-Citizens; but every Man who prefers Freedom to a life of slavery will bless and honor You, as Men who have baffled the Attempt of Tyranny; and by an impartial and uncorrupt Verdict, have laid a noble Foundation for securing to ourselves, our Posterity, and our Neighbors, That, to which Nature and the Laws of our Country have given us a Right,—the Liberty—both of exposing and opposing arbitrary Power (in these Parts of the World, at least) by speaking and writing Truth."

Andrew Hamilton bowed, returned to his bench, and sat down. Angry and almost inarticulate, De Lancey addressed the jury. "The great pains Mr. *Hamilton* has taken to show how little Regard Juries are to Pay to the Opinion of the Judges . . . is done, no doubt, with a Design that you should take but very little Notice of what I might say upon this Occasion." Nevertheless, it was all quite clear. "The only Thing that can come in Question before you is, whether the Words as set forth in the Information make a Lybel. And that is a Matter of Law, no Doubt, and which you may leave to the Court." A moment later, when De Lancey had concluded, Hamilton rose to humbly beg pardon: "I am very much misapprehended, if you suppose what I said was so designed." Hamilton had no wish to be in contempt of court. He may also, as he settled back to wait for the verdict, have realized that he had brilliantly achieved his task—to get around the law, which was plainly against Zenger, and mobilize the jury's hostility to Cosby.

The jurors retired. In ten minutes they announced that they had reached a verdict. The court was recalled to order. Justice De Lancey may well have looked pleased, obviously convinced that the jurymen had wasted no time discussing complexities of free speech and the libel code. Hamilton's lengthy discourse on the power and duty of juries to evolve new interpretations of the law had been wasted rhetoric.

The clerk faced the jury and asked if the defendant, John Peter Zenger, had been guilty of publishing the libels as charged. The foreman, one Thomas Hunt, a mariner, rose to his feet and announced the verdict: "Not Guilty."

An eruption of cheers and laughter shook the crowded courtroom. The initial chaotic outburst was quickly coordinated into three united huzzas for the defendant, three for Hamilton, three for the jury. Reactions to the outburst varied with the political orientation of the observer. One conservative historian reported that two justices on the bench turned pale with terror at the clamor. The record shows that De Lancey pounded his gavel for order and rebuked the crowd for its demonstration.

From the back benches an audacious voice retorted. It was a young naval officer, Captain Matthew Norris, Lewis Morris' son-in-law. "Cheers," he drawled impudently, "are customary on such occasions." Again shouts and huzzas rattled the windowpanes. The judges gathered their robes about them and swirled out in a vortex of juridical wrath.

That night forty prominent New Yorkers gave a dinner at the Black Horse Tavern on Smith Street in honor of Andrew Hamilton, the Philadelphia lawyer who had defeated the Governor's design. It was a noisy and intemperate evening for a man of his years, for ahead of him lay the long and rigorous journey down New York Harbor to Amboy, through the New Jersey forests, and thence down the

Delaware River to the green, shady city of the Quakers. But there was one acid drop in the celebration. For John Peter Zenger, the protagonist, was not present to join the festivities. The city government refused to release him until the jail had been reimbursed for the expense of his maintenance during the eight and a half months of his confinement. It was not until the next day that his friends raised the money to pay the bill and Zenger emerged a free man.

Meanwhile, Hamilton embarked at the Battery to the cheers of admiring New Yorkers and the salvos of guns from sloops anchored at the mouth of the Hudson. As his ship vanished down the bay in the warm summer breeze and the last triumphant cannon rumbled to silence over the salt marshes of New Jersey, John Peter Zenger, probably paler and thinner, walked out of jail and returned to his forms and ink pots in the *Journal* office.

Zenger also returned to the controversies, which had continued to rage during his incarceration. Public hostility toward Cosby persisted and did not abate until his death almost a year later. Alexander and Smith were petitioning for readmission to the bar and finally won a quiet reinstatement. Through the remainder of 1735 and 1736, Zenger's *Journal* remained the storm center of political conflict. But in the summer of 1737, Zenger's friendship with Lewis Morris, Jr., son of the former chief justice and now speaker of the New York assembly, won him the appointment of public printer for the province of New York. And in the following year, when the elder Morris became governor of New Jersey, Zenger was awarded a similar commission for that province.

A forgetful and fickle public, however, allowed the *Journal's* circulation and advertising revenues slowly to decline. On August 4, 1746, a relatively recently begun paper called the *New York Evening Post* printed a small obituary notice.

> On Monday evening last, departed this Life, *Mr. John Peter Zenger* Printer, in the 49th Year of his Age. He has left a Wife and six Children behind, he was a loving Husband, and a tender Father, and his Death is much lamented by his Family and Relations.

For five difficult years Zenger's widow and oldest son, John, Jr., did their best to carry on the paper. Periodic notices appeared, requesting subscribers who were unable to pay bills in cash to meet their obligations with hams, butter, cheese, or poultry. Finally, on March 18, 1751, the *Journal* lapsed into silence. It was an unspectacular end for a paper that had served so well the press of a republic still unborn.

Some historians say that the Zenger case cannot truly be seen as establishing a legal precedent, inasmuch as trials and convictions for seditious libel continued to occur on both sides of the Atlantic until the end of the eighteenth century. And it has also been observed that Hamilton's defense of Zenger was not good law. And indeed it was not. He defied existing law and came perilously close to contempt of court; a more experienced judge than De Lancey might have so ruled. But Hamilton was not practicing the law of his era, he was presaging the law of the future. As Professor Zechariah Chaffee, Jr., of the Harvard Law School, has written: "The victories of liberty of speech must be won in the mind before they are won in the courts."

The two great principles set forth by Hamilton—the validity of truth as a defense of libel and the right of the jury to decide libellousness—did eventually become universal in the English-speaking world. In the United States they were embodied, curiously enough, in the anti-libertarian Sedition Act of 1798. When that measure died, the federal government went out of the business of prosecuting libels altogether, but Hamilton's principles were gradually extended to apply to the States. In England the final incorporation of truth as a defense and the jury's right to judge libellousness did not come until Lord Campbell's Act of 1843.

Yet despite the lag in the law, the fact remains that Alexander's account of the trial and Hamilton's eloquent peroration to the jury were printed widely throughout the intervening years and caused a furor wherever thoughtful men met—from Barbados to the Inns of Court. They went through fourteen editions in this country alone before 1791. And the Zenger trial was referred to repeatedly during the drafting of the First Amendment to the Constitution. As early as 1738 an English barrister, quoted by a correspondent in Benjamin Franklin's Pennsylvania Gazette, declared, "If it is not law it is better than law, it ought to be law, and will always be law wherever justice prevails."

Quite apart from Hamilton's brilliant victory, it should not be overlooked that John Peter Zenger, the humble printer, inarticulate and merely a mechanical aide to his intellectual contributors—the virtually unseen eye of the storm of political and philosophical controversy that raged around him—had also established a precedent of great importance by his silence, his refusal to divulge the identities of the men whose words he published. Ever since, journalists have looked back upon Zenger as the father of their most cherished and inviolable privilege—the right to protect the sources of their information, a right they must constantly fight for to this day.

The importance of the Zenger trial was not underestimated by the Founding Fathers in 1776. In the words of Gouverneur Morris: "The trial of Zenger in 1735 was the germ of American freedom, the morning star of that liberty which subsequently revolutionized America."

6

The Spirit of '54

Richard M. Ketchum

On the eve of the outbreak of the French and Indian War in 1754, delegates from seven of the thirteen English North American mainland colonies met in Albany, New York to discuss the situation concerning the French in Canada and the Indians of the Iroquois Confederacy. Led by Benjamin Franklin of Pennsylvania, the delegates devised a Plan of Union which proposed that the colonies send delegates to a continental assembly that would assume responsibility for all western affairs: trade, Indian policy, and defense. But the proposed union, which was to be presided over by a royal governor, never materialized because the provincial assemblies wanted to preserve the authority and the imperial government feared the consequences of convoking the great assembly. Despite its failure, the Albany Plan of Union helped lay the foundation for the Articles of Confederation of 1777 as well as for the Constitution of 1787.

More than two decades before the Revolution broke out, a group of Americans voted on a scheme to unite the colonies. For the rest of his life, Benjamin Franklin thought it could have prevented the war. It didn't—but it did give us our Constitution. By Richard M. Ketchum

Improbable it may seem, but an industrious, aquatic, fur-bearing rodent deserves a share of the credit for the first real effort at unifying Britain's American colonies. Just as we tend to forget that the Americas were discovered as a byproduct of the search for pepper, the reason the beaver's contribution has gone unsung all these years is, in the words of the journalist Henry Hobhouse, "Men *have* always liked to believe in their own influence."

Almost from the beginning, the colonials engaged in the fur trade, which was centered in Albany, New York, and managed by Dutch traders, who relied for their supply of pelts on the Mohawk, Seneca, Cayuga, Oneida, Onondaga, and, later, Tuscarora Indians: the League, or Six Nations, of the Iroquois. Those Native Americans occupied an enormous area south and east of Lake Ontario, but the insatiable demand for furs so reduced the population of fur-bearing animals that a Canadian governor wrote as early as 1671 that "they experience the greatest difficulty in finding a single beaver there." Responding to this challenge, the Iroquois expanded their hunting grounds into lands across Lake Ontario and began to function as middlemen for the transfer of furs from Western tribes to Albany.

At the same time, hundreds of Pennsylvania and Virginia traders and land speculators were pushing deeper into the Great Lakes region and the Ohio Valley. Naturally, that alarmed the French in Canada, whose ties to the Western Indians were as strong as those of the English with the Iroquois. They reacted by building forts on the Niagara River and on Lake Champlain and by sending some 200 troops into the Ohio Valley to warn potential trespassers that the land on both sides of the river and all streams flowing into it belonged to France. To further thwart British actions, the French began cutting a trail to the headwaters of the Ohio and constructed Forts Presque Isle, Le Boeuf, and Venango to cover the approaches to the Allegheny River.

Now it was the Iroquois' turn to worry, and in the spring of 1753 the Mohawk sachem Theyanoguin, or Tiyanoga—known to the Dutch as Hendrick—led a tribal delegation to Manhattan to voice their concerns. Hendrick was a commanding figure, revered for his wisdom and courage in battle, from which he bore a hideous tomahawk scar running from his mouth to near his left ear. He informed the Governor's Council that had the British not reneged on their commitments in the last war the Mohawks would have "torn the Frenchman's heart out." Now that the English were doing nothing to halt the theft of his nation's lands, the colonials had left the Indians defenseless against French attack, and his patience and respect for them were exhausted.

"So, brother," he said, "you are not to expect to hear of me any more, and, brother, we desire to hear no more of you!" With that he stalked out, followed by his angry braves, effectively dissolving the century-old covenant between the English and the Iroquois League.

When that shocking news reached London weeks later, the Board of Trade and Plantations, the effective governing body of the colonies, wrote the governor of New York, directing him to summon representatives of the other colonies to a meeting. They were to negotiate a treaty with the Indians, improve the handling of Indian affairs, and see to it that all lands purchased thenceforth from the Indians be bought in the King's name.

Lt. Gov. James De Lancey, acting governor when the letter arrived, soon dispatched invitations to Massachusetts, New Hampshire, New Jersey, Pennsylvania, Maryland, and Virginia, requesting that they send delegates to discuss the crisis in Indian affairs and, above all, repair the vital Iroquois alliance.

The Board of Trade and Plantations, in London, despite its distance from the scene, its customary focus on the bottom line, and the fact that they had neither spoken with nor laid eyes on the Native Americans, proved to have a remarkably accurate and sensitive perception of how the Iroquois alliance had gone wrong. In their letter to the governor, the Lords laid the blame squarely on officials of the province of New York for being "so inattentive to the general interest of his Majesty's subjects in America, as well as to their own particular security" in ignoring complaints made by the Indians. Then, referring to the angry departure of Chief Hendrick and the Mohawks from their meeting with the governor, they condemned "the dissatisfactory answers given to the Indians" and the inexcusable failure to redress their grievances.

The instructions from the Lords of Trade made it clear to De Lancey that it was up to him to restore the alliance with the Six Nations, which was crucial to "all his Majesty's Colonies and Plantations in America in general, as well as to New York in particular." He was told to select delegates well acquainted with the Indians and their customs and interpreters who were men of ability and integrity, versed in the Indian language. Since it was customary to give the Indians "presents" at these affairs, he was to be generous, affording them every reason for "burying the hatchet and renewing the covenant chain."

Further instructions stipulated that delegates to the congress must be scrupulous in examining the Indians' complaints of having been defrauded of their lands, take legal steps to redress their grievances, and make reasonable reimbursement for lands "unwarrantably taken from them." In the future any land the natives decided to sell was to be bought from them in the name of the King and with public funds. This was a tall order, and whether De Lancey could bring it off would depend on the diplomatic skills he and the other men brought to the table.

As it happened, several of those invited to the conference had an idea in mind that went well beyond holding yet another powwow with Indians. It was apparent to them that the overriding problem of the colonies—a problem that militated against successfully combating the French and Indian menace to the frontiers, as well as forming a common front in pressing their case in London—was a lack of unity.

Benjamin Franklin, who was one of the Pennsylvania delegates, had been thinking about a union of the colonies since 1751, and before leaving Philadelphia he published in his *Pennsylvania Gazette* of May 9 what may be the first American cartoon—which he probably drew— showing a snake *in* eight pieces. One piece was "NE" to represent the New England colonies. The others bore the initials of New York, New Jersey, Pennsylvania, Maryland, Virginia, North Carolina, and South Carolina, and it ran with the caption JOIN, OR DIE. En route to Albany he stopped off in New York to visit Archibald Kennedy and James Alexander, two members of the governor's council, and he wrote out for them what he called "Short Hints Towards a Scheme for Uniting the Northern Colonies."

Getting to Albany was easier said than done. Although winter and the mud season were only memories now, the journey was long and arduous for almost all the envoys, and it was a wonder that so many completed the trip. The Boston contingent, for instance, took 12 days to get there, while the delegates from Maryland and Pennsylvania spent three days on the road from Philadelphia to New York, where they boarded schooners for the trip up the Hudson knowing that depending on the winds and tides, anywhere from three days to two weeks might pass before they reached Albany. For that upriver community the opportunity to play host to a congress ordered by the Lords of Trade was of course a major event, and the local militia company turned out to give De Lancey and the New York delegation a proper salute. To those from the other colonies their first encounter with the little Dutch town must have seemed like a visit to a foreign land.

The commissioners, as the delegates were called, discovered that they were in for several disappointments. First they were told that New Jersey's assembly had refused to authorize the appointment of commissioners on the grounds that the province had never negotiated treaties with the Six Nations or traded with them and had no wish to do so now. Virginia, which probably had the most to gain from a united front among the colonies, turned down the invitation because its lieutenant governor had scheduled a meeting with several Southern Indian tribes, and the House of Burgesses rebelled at the prospect of paying to send delegates to two conferences. Worse, it turned out that the Indians, who were, after all, the reason everyone had traveled so far, were very poorly represented. The Mohawks, the most influential nation, had not shown up at all, and no one knew if they would.

All the delegates except those from New York were officially commissioned. The reason New York's had no such authorization may have been De Lancey's hope of keeping control of them in his hands. He had no enthusiasm for the idea of union, and it seems significant that three New York councilors who did not attend (all of them political foes of De Lancey)—James Alexander, Cadwallader Colden, and Archibald Kennedy—were known to support Franklin's Plan of Union.

After Thomas Hutchinson arrived from Massachusetts, he surveyed his colleagues and observed rather immodestly, considering he was one of them, that the assembly "was the most deserving of respect of any which had ever been convened in America, whether we consider the Colonies which were rep-resented, the rank and characters of the delegates, or the purposes for which it was convened." Boastful or not, he was quite right. In fact, as Hutchinson appreciated, the meeting was going to be one of the true landmarks of America's colonial era, attended by a group of un-paralleled distinction.

Hutchinson, one of five Massachusetts representatives, was the former speaker of his colony's House of Representatives and later would be its chief justice and governor. Meshech Weare was a justice of New Hampshire's superior court and later president of the state. Stephen Hopkins of Rhode Island, former speaker of that province's assembly, went on to become presiding judge of its Superior Court, governor, and signer of the Declaration of Independence. Connecticut' sent William Pitkin, its deputy governor, the former governor Roger Wolcott, and the president of Yale, Elisha Williams. Pennsylvania's delegation included Benjamin Franklin, John Penn—a grandson of William and later the lieutenant governor of the colony—and Richard Peters, the provincial secretary. From Maryland came Benjamin Tasker, a member of the provincial council.

Twenty-four envoys were present when the first session convened in the courthouse at 10:00 A.M. on June 19, 1754, and for the first few days they sat wherever there was an empty chair until someone complained about this haphazard arrangement. Then the New York councilors, as hosts, sat at the head of the table and the others took positions according to the location of their province from north to south, starting with Massachusetts (whose District of Maine was the northernmost of all the colonies) and ending with Maryland. That, he declared, would "avoid all disputes about the precedency of the Colonies."

It was probably fortunate that so few of the Iroquois put in an early appearance, because not until June 27 was the draft of a welcoming speech to them finally agreed on. In the meantime, however, the delegates voted on a most significant and unusual subject: "whether a Union of all the Colonies is not at present absolutely necessary for their security and defence." When the question passed unanimously, a committee consisting of one representative from each colony was appointed to receive and study various schemes and settle on a single plan.

The appointed business was with the Indians, of course, and such periodic conferences with the Iroquois Nations had already evolved into highly ritualistic affairs. The meetings were calm and at the same time prolix—calm because the very idea behind them was to achieve the unanimity demanded by the Iroquois for a binding solution, prolix because eloquent oratory was the equivalent of Iroquois literature. Because Iroquois society had no written language, ornate figures of speech and cadences, repeated again and again, were essential elements of what became an oral history to be remembered and handed down. In lieu of pieces of paper, belts, or woven strings of elongated beads made from seashells, constituted the records of what transpired.

It was June 28 before Hendrick and his tribesmen arrived, and on June 29 De Lancey delivered his opening address to the assembled natives. That was followed by nine days of speeches and exchanges of belts, which were mostly fashioned of dark purple wampum. On them the Indians' castles, or lodges, were represented by square figures made of white beads. Alliances were symbolized by "human figures holding a chain of friendship, each figure representing a nation." The belts varied in size according to the importance of the subject under discussion. A belt was "thrown" by a speaker before a new topic was introduced and was kept on display while that subject was under consideration. Once a decision had been reached, the belt was stored away, to be retrieved if the subject came up again at a future meeting.

After the torrent of words and the throwing of hundreds of belts, it was time for the presentation of traditional gifts—400 firearms, bars of lead, 50 barrels of powder, and 10,000 flints from the King, plus a contribution from each colony, altogether enough to fill 30 wagons. As the last native disappeared from view, the commissioners congratulated themselves on a job well done: The Indians, they felt, had had plenty of opportunity to air their complaints, and despite their manifold grievances, they had departed in fairly good spirits. And at that the conferees turned to the question of colonial union.

Although most of the delegates lacked instructions concerning a plan of union and exceeded their powers by undertaking to establish one, several schemes were broached and discussed both in committees and in plenary sessions, and it was evident that Franklin's proposal was the one preferred by all. Wisely, the delegates recognized that what lay at the heart of the problem with the French was the disunity of the colonies and their failure to act together. The congress noted bitterly that France's affairs on the North American continent, by contrast with those of England, "are under one direction," emanating from the court at Versailles.

Against the ever-growing menace to the colonies' frontiers, a system based on voluntary contribution of men and money had not worked in the past, nor was it likely to in the future. As Franklin was to write: "the colonies cost England nothing in forts, citadels, garrisons, or armies to keep them in subjugation. They were governed at the expense of a little pen, ink, and paper." Given the likelihood that this predicament would continue, what was essential for the colonies' mutual defense was confederation, and the question before the representatives was how best to bring this about.

It was a tricky business, and as Franklin and James Alexander had already concluded in New York, its ultimate success would hinge on whether a union could be structured without "affecting our liberties on the one hand, or being ineffectual on the other." On the basis of what he had heard over the years, Franklin greatly admired the Iroquois League and believed that the system of government they had devised could serve as a model. He wrote to Archibald Kennedy, "It would be a strange thing if Six Nations of ignorant savages should be capable of forming a scheme for such an union, and be able to execute it in such a manner as . . . has subsisted [for] ages and appears indissoluble; and yet . . . a like union should be impracticable for ten or a dozen English colonies, to whom it is *more* necessary and must be more advantageous, and who cannot be sup-posed to want an equal understanding of their interests."

It may be hoped that the Philadelphian revised his opinion of the Six Nations as "ignorant savages" after seeing them and hearing their eloquent speeches in Albany. In any event, he was asked on July 9 to prepare a draft of the plan "as now concluded upon," and the next day his draft was adopted by the assembly and ordered transmitted to the seven colonies represented at the congress, plus New Jersey, Virginia, and the Carolinas.

In the give-and-take of debate, Franklin's "Short Hints" underwent changes, but he accepted them in order to carry his main point. It was essential, he successfully insisted, that the proposed government be established by act of Parliament, not by Americans. (Franklin was a realist and saw no hope of achieving union through some sort of voluntary association.) According to his scheme, the government was to have an executive and legislative branch. The chief executive, to be appointed and paid by the Crown and known as the president-general, was to have the power to make treaties with the Indians and declare war and peace, with the advice and consent of the legislative body. The legislature, to be known as the grand council, would consist of members chosen every three years by the assemblies of the colonies in numbers proportional to the taxes they paid into the union treasury. Placing power in the hands of provincial assemblies rather than the more aristocratic and conservative governor's councils was a decidedly democratic innovation.

All in all it was a bold, novel proposal that would create a central government with the power to *levy* taxes and make laws concerning matters within its jurisdiction, even though these would have to be submitted to the King in Council for approval. The new government would also deal with the many problems of defense, raising and supporting armies, building forts and ships, and regulating the Indians. Significantly, the delegates resolved to limit the power of the colonies over Western lands, stipulating that all land purchases from the Indians be made in the name of the Crown and that the boundaries of some colonies be "reduced to more convenient dimensions." (Virginia, for instance, claimed a swath of land as deep as the colony's north to south borders, extending across the continent to the Pacific.)

Because of its central location, Philadelphia was chosen as *the* place where the union was to be organized. The Plan would permit members to select a different meeting place every year, but Franklin predicted that Philadelphia would remain their choice except in time of war, when they would gather in the colony nearest to the hostilities.

The records aren't wholly clear, but the only delegates who seem to have objected to the Plan were those from Connecticut, mostly on the grounds that the land area involved was too large to administer and the population growing too fast to be governed under a single executive. They also quarreled with giving the president-general the right to veto measures of the grand council, and they opposed the taxing power as contrary to the rights of Englishmen. Yet Franklin and Thomas Hutchinson stated that the Plan was adopted unanimously, although with "a great deal of Disputation about it, almost every article being contested," according to the former. This suggests that the Connecticut delegation, despite its reservations, may have refrained from casting a negative vote. Two other delegates recalled that every member of the congress approved the Plan except James De Lancey.

The delegates' enthusiasm and support reveal a great deal about the mind-set of the group. Franklin and the others were American colonials, but they thought of themselves as Englishmen. That attitude was at the heart of the "Short Hints" Franklin took to Albany in 1754, which he and his colleagues refined until they had a highly original conception of the American colonies' place within the British Empire. They understood that the colonies must think of themselves not individually but as a whole, a whole that was an integral part of the empire and whose only separation from the mother country happened to be the ocean between them.

Although no one at the congress could have known it, on the same day that James De Lancey delivered his speech to the Indians, fate took a hand some 350 miles to the southwest, where George Washington and a party of Virginians were overwhelmingly defeated by a French and Indian force at Fort Necessity. That event prompted James Alexander to write to Cadwallader Colden saying that he hoped the recommendations of the Albany Congress would "prevail on King & Parliament . . . to unite the force of the Colonies, and [do so] at the first meeting of parliament, for a Delay of it may be fatal, as there's nothing to hinder the french at this very time to make a Conquest of the Colonies, and put it then out of our power to hurt them by our intended union."

Despite Fort Necessity's dramatic warning of the colonies' urgent need to unite, the Plan of Union was opposed or ignored by every provincial assembly that considered it except New York. In fact, the efforts of the commissioners, prominent as they were, were received with outright scorn by the very provincial governments that had deputized them. However surprising that seemed, what it came down to was that in 1754 no colonial legislature was willing to yield any of its powers to a grand council and an executive appointed and paid by the Crown.

The delegates had, assumed that the provincial assemblies would comment on the Plan of Union and then it would be sent to London. But De Lancey ignored their wishes and sent a copy of the proceedings straight to the Lords of Trade, who passed it on to George II without comment. When nothing favorable was heard from the colonies, no action was taken in England, and the ambitious project died.

In December of that year, Franklin, in Boston, spoke at length with Gov. William Shirley, who had his own ideas about how a colonial union should function. Shirley believed that the colonies should have little power and should get the money they needed for defense from taxes levied on them by Parliament. Franklin disagreed, and he expanded on his views in three letters to Shirley that contained all the ingredients of the arguments the colonies would make two decades later.

He maintained that it was patently unfair to tax the colonists unless they were represented in Parliament and had a say in the matter. People in the colonies, not members of Parliament, were the proper judges of how much money was needed for defense and how it should be spent. He hammered the point home, insisting that it is "an undoubted right of Englishmen not to be taxed but by their own consent given through their representatives." Forcing them to do so without their agreement "would be rather like raising contributions in an enemy's country than taxing of Englishmen for their own public benefit."

Think of the situation this way, he said. An empire's frontiers must be defended at public expense. The American colonies bordering on Canada were Britain's frontiers and were already contributing to the cost of their defense through the indirect taxes they paid to England. Not only did Britain restrain their trade with other countries, it forbade most manufacturing in the colonies. These restrictions not only amounted to secondary taxes on colonials, they also enabled British merchants and manufacturers to pay their own taxes out of the pockets of Americans.

In Franklin's opinion it was in England's self-interest to promote colonial manufacturing, and he explained it this way: Since there were already about a million people in North America ("though 'tis thought scarce 80,000 have been brought over seas"), and since that population could be expected to double every 20 years (marriages being more frequent in America than in Europe), he foresaw the day, a century thence, when the people of the colonies would outnumber those in England. "The greatest number of Englishmen will be on this side of the water."

In fact, Franklin took insufficient account of the thousands of English, Scots, Welsh, Swiss, Germans, French Huguenots, and Ulster Presbyterians who were pouring into the colonies, in addition to involuntary black slave and indentured white immigration. He knew, of course, that although these new arrivals would concentrate initially in coastal areas, they would soon move into the vast interior, which would take ages to fill. As they struck out for new land, they would set up their own trades, so labor would never be cheap in the colonies. A growing America was a growing market for manufactures, whether British or American, and Britain should not restrain these enterprises. "A wise and good mother will not do it. To distress is to weaken, and weakening the children weakens the whole family."

At the end of December 1754 Franklin wrote his friend Peter Collinson in England: "Every Body cries, a Union is absolutely necessary; but when they come to the Manner and Form of the Union, their weak Noodles are presently distracted."

Some 30 years later Franklin offered an explanation of why his scheme had been rejected on both sides of the Atlantic. The colonial assemblies, he asserted, turned it down fearing that there was too much "prerogative" in it—that it would benefit a privileged few. And England, he said, failed to adopt it because it was too democratic. All of which led him to suspect that his plan "was really the true medium; and I am still of [the] opinion that it would have been happy for both sides of the water if it had been adopted." But, he added, "such mistakes are not new; history is full of the errors of states and princes . . . Those who govern, having much business on their hands, do not generally like to take the trouble of considering and carrying into execution new projects."

By then he could be philosophical about this major failure of British-American statesmanship, one of the great might-have-beens of American history. The Albany Plan of Union, which was his more than any other man's, had been rejected, but it was far from forgotten. It became the basis of the form of governance that initially took effect with the First Continental Congress in 1774. The Articles of Confederation embodied a number of ideas included in the Plan, notably federal control of Western lands, which was established by the Northwest Ordinance of 1787.

The ultimate recognition of Franklin's vision came in 1787, when the Constitutional Convention adopted the essence of the Plan of Union, merely substituting a president for the president-general and adding a second house to the legislature. The Constitution granted Congress all the same powers as were to be given the grand council, except for the power to purchase Indian lands and make new colonies of them.

Writing in 1789, when the new federal government of the United States of America was functioning, Franklin indulged in speculation about what might have been had the Plan of Union been adopted: "On reflection, it now seems possible, that, if the foregoing plan, or something like it, had been adopted and carried into execution, the subsequent separation of the colonies from the mother country might not so soon have happened, nor the mischiefs suffered on both sides have occurred, perhaps, during another century. For the colonies, if so united, would have really been, as they then thought themselves, sufficient to their own defense: and, being trusted with it, as by the plan, an army from Britain, for that purpose, would have been unnecessary. The pretences for framing the Stamp Act would then not have existed, nor the other projects for drawing a revenue from America to Britain by acts of Parliament, which were the cause of the breach, and attended with such terrible expense of blood and treasure: so that the different parts of the empire might still have remained in peace and union."

7

Why Benedict Arnold Did It

Willard Sterne Randall

Although Benedict Arnold is the most famous traitor in American history—in fact, his name is virtually synonymous with treason—most people do not know the reasons behind his actions. What would cause a man who was born into an elite New England family and performed so heroically in the Revolutionary War that he rose to be the third-highest-ranking general in the American army to switch sides and desert to the enemy in the middle of the conflict? The following article traces the life and career of Benedict Arnold and shows how he felt himself betrayed by the Continental Congress and the Continental Army and, therefore, fully justified in switching his allegiance to the British. While one might not condone Arnold's actions, the article provides a more complete explanation of the complex motives of perhaps the most vilified character in American history.

Shortly after noon on Thursday, April 20, 1775, a weary postrider swung out of the saddle at Hunt's Tavern in New Haven, Connecticut, with an urgent message from the Massachusetts Committee of Correspondence. At dawn the day before, British light infantry had killed six militiamen on Lexington Green. Anxious New Haven citizens crowded into an emergency town meeting and voted to maintain a policy of neutrality despite Massachusetts's plea for troops and supplies.

Nevertheless, Benedict Arnold, the thirty-four-year-old captain of New Haven's elite 2d Company of Governor's Footguards and head of the town's Sons of Liberty, mustered his men and prepared to march on Boston. First, though, he led his company of militia, several of them Yale undergraduates, to Hunt's Tavern, where the community's selectmen were deliberating, and demanded keys to the town's powder magazine.

David Wooster, a colonel in the militia and also New Haven's justice of the peace, refused. Arnold, he said, would have to wait for regular orders from the colonial legislature in Hartford. "Regular orders be damned!" Arnold retorted; a war had begun. Again Wooster refused, but Arnold's band of radicals threatened to tear down the doors to the powder magazine. "None but Almighty God shall prevent my marching," shouted Arnold. Wooster handed him the keys.

Benedict Arnold's confrontation with the New Haven authorities and his quick march to Boston were typical of a stormy military career that culminated in the most celebrated betrayal in American history. In the seven clamorous years between 1775 and 1782, Arnold may well have won a greater number of important battles than any other officer on either side. He rose to be the third-highest-ranking American general before deserting to the British. Many historians have believed Arnold turned traitor simply for money, but like the man himself, the motives were complex.

A RESTLESS APPRENTICE

The man whose name is the very eponym for treason was born in Norwich, Connecticut, on January 14, 1741, a fifth-generation New Englander whose great-grandfather, also named Benedict Arnold, had been the first governor of Rhode Island. He lived with his pious Puritan mother and his devoted sister in a big gambrel-roofed white frame house on the outskirts of town. Arnold's father, who had owned and sailed ships in the Caribbean trade, was an alcoholic. As his father's business slipped toward bankruptcy, Benedict was sent off at eleven to a relative's church school, where he learned Greek and Latin. At thirteen, after his father's arrest for public drunkenness, he was yanked out of school and briefly roamed the Norwich waterfront, distinguishing himself for feats of strength and public pranks. Five feet ten, barrel-chested and muscular, with dark hair and gray eyes, proud despite his father's disgrace—and perhaps the fiercer because of it—Arnold was often in trouble until, in 1754, he was consigned to an eight-year apprenticeship with his mother's cousin, Dr. Daniel Lathrop.

Lathrop, a Yale graduate trained in medicine in London, operated the only apothecary shop between Boston and New York City. He was a cultivated man who lived opulently in a mansion surrounded by formal gardens, owned liveried slaves, and sent his young apprentice on errands in a fancy yellow carriage. He also taught Arnold about gardening, growing herbs, breeding horses, sailing, hunting, accounting, literature, and music, but he could not quench the apprentice's restlessness.

Benedict twice ran away to join the militia in the French and Indian War. Both times he was hauled back, and by the age of eighteen he had become Lathrop's trusted chief clerk, sailing to England, Canada, and the West Indies on buying and selling trips. When Dr. Lathrop landed the lucrative contract to provide medical supplies for the British Northern Army, it was Arnold who delivered them to British forces besieging Quebec. He learned that businessmen could make huge—and perfectly legal—profits in wartime.

When his apprenticeship ended in 1762, Arnold turned down Dr. Lathrop's offer to remain in his business but accepted his generous gift of five hundred pounds to set up his own apothecary shop in New Haven. It was more like a general store, offering books for students across the green at Yale College and cosmetics, jewelry, and what Arnold called "a very elegant assortment of Metzotinto Pictures, Prints, Maps, Stationery-Ware and Paper-Hangings for rooms." Arnold had a knack for selling. He soon opened a larger shop overlooking the harbor and bought a sloop. By the time he was twenty-six, Arnold had three ships trading lumber and "large, fat, genteel horses" he bought from Canada for sugar and cotton from the Caribbean.

As Americans began to resist British imperial trade regulations, Arnold emerged as New Haven's leading smuggler of rum, sugar, and molasses. He also became its leading patriot but from the outset was an outsider in Revolutionary politics. Considered an interloper by New Haven's landed society, Arnold was also excluded from the upper echelons of Connecticut politics by the Revolutionary clique around Gov. Jonathan Trumbull that governed the colony from Hartford. All his life an outsider, he became more and more a maverick in business and politics.

TICONDEROGA

Leading his column of scarlet-coated footguards—a slash of color against the pale green of a New England spring—Capt. Benedict Arnold marched north toward Boston on April 22, 1775. He had scarcely left New Haven before he came upon Samuel Holden Parsons, a New London lawyer and land speculator who had led his company to Boston at the Lexington alarm and who was now on his way back to Connecticut to raise troops. Parsons told Arnold that the patriot army assembling around Boston had neither supplies nor ammunition and, worst of all, no cannon to besiege the heavily armed British. Arnold told Parsons that there were hundreds of good cannon at the dilapidated and weakly held British forts at Ticonderoga and Crown Point at the southern end of Lake Champlain, on the northern New York frontier.

A few days after Arnold and his men arrived at the American camp at Cambridge, he told the same story to the Massachusetts Committee of

Safety, and on May 3 the full Provincial Congress of Massachusetts approved Arnold's appointment as colonel and commissioned him to raise a regiment of four hundred men in the Berkshires, then seize the forts at Ticonderoga and Crown Point. Issued ten horses and a meager hundred-pound war chest to buy provisions, Arnold and six of his foot-guards left that night with cartridges in their saddlebags, horses sagging under casks of gunpowder. It took a maddening three days for the party to struggle 110 miles west over sodden roads in heavy spring rains to Williamstown, where Arnold learned that Samuel Parsons had beaten him to the punch; after their meeting Parsons had taken Arnold's idea to the Connecticut authorities and had organized a rival expedition that was now under the command of Ethan Allen. Furious at what he saw as Parsons's opportunism, Arnold left behind his recruits and dashed northwest with only an orderly sergeant to overtake Allen and assert his command.

At Shoreham, fifty miles north of Bennington, Arnold found Allen. Marching directly up to the green-uniformed Allen, Arnold presented his written orders and said his rival officer had no legitimate authority. Daunted, Allen told his men that Arnold would lead them, but they would still receive their two-dollars-a-day pay. "Damn the pay," someone muttered, and several announced they would walk home if they couldn't serve under their own officers. Eager to press the attack, Arnold offered a compromise: Allen would be in charge of his Green Mountain Boys, Arnold of all the Massachusetts troops he could raise. They would lead the first American offensive of the Revolution in a joint command.

That night, 230 men, including 50 from Massachusetts, gathered in the woods across the lake from Ticonderoga, but by the time dawn broke on May 10, 1775, only two 30-foot scows had arrived and the initial attack was made by 83 men. Arnold and Allen led the troops, mostly veterans of the French and Indian War, to the south side of Fort Ticonderoga, where the wall lay ruptured and the main gate would no longer close tight. Just inside, a single sentry dozed. Arnold, on the left, sprinted ahead of Allen and squeezed through the narrow opening and, sword drawn, rushed the guard. The startled redcoat woke, aimed, pulled the trigger; his damp gunpowder misfired. Americans surged into the fort, and four years later, when he published his memoirs, Allen claimed he and he alone had captured the works "in the name of the Great Jehovah and the Continental Congress."

Four hundred more Green Mountain Boys arrived from across the cove to crowd into the fort, and Arnold reported to the Massachusetts Provincial Congress that "the greatest confusion and anarchy" broke out. The Boys found a cellar housing ninety gallons of rum, then set about "destroying and plundering private property, committing every enormity and paying no attention to public service." When Arnold protested, an infuriated Ethan Allen stripped him of his joint command at gunpoint.

Confining himself to the officers' quarters, Arnold wrote to Massachusetts authorities that inasmuch as he had been "the first person who entered and took possession of the Fort, I shall keep it, at every hazard." For four days, "often insulted by Allen and his officers and often threatened with my life," Arnold coolly studied the fort, surveyed its guns—nearly eighty usable cannon, six mortars, three howitzers—and waited for more of his own men.

On May 14 Arnold's regiment arrived with a schooner commandeered at nearby Skenesboro. Arnold named it *Liberty*, fitted it with four carriage and six swivel guns, and, leaving Ethan Allen and his troops behind, sailed north with fifty Massachusetts men to attack the British base at St. Johns (present-day St. Jean), on the Richelieu River just inside Quebec Province. In a matter of days he took St. Johns, scuttled five British vessels, and came home with four others; he now commanded the first American naval squadron. Arnold's raid made impossible a British counterattack in 1776 and left him master of the hundred-mile lake.

For six weeks Arnold held Lake Champlain and the New York-Vermont frontier until thousands of reinforcements were sent in by the Continental Congress—and then he was brushed aside. Cutting off money, supplies, and men, Congress and the New England revolutionary governments sent Arnold conflicting orders and then repudiated them. According to his recently discovered expense accounts, Arnold financed the defense of the frontier after the meager hundred-pound war chest was gone, borrowing money and pledging slightly less than fourteen hundred pounds of his own cash as he pleaded with Congress to allow him to attack Canada and bring it into the Continental Union before the British had time to reinforce.

Meanwhile, as Ethan Allen and his friends worked to discredit Arnold in Congress, a committee of the Massachusetts Provincial Congress headed by Dr. Benjamin Church (a Cambridge physician soon to be court-martialed for treason) was scrutinizing Arnold's orders, expenditures, and general bookkeeping at Ticonderoga. Disgusted with his treatment, Arnold resigned his commission, "not being able," he wrote, "to hold it longer with honor." Six weeks after storming Ticonderoga, the first significant American military success of the Revolution, Benedict Arnold disbanded his Massachusetts regiment under a cloud of accusations of overstepping his orders and misappropriating money. Stunned and bitter, he headed home, learning on the way that his wife had died.

THE ATTACK ON CANADA

Just three weeks later he was back in the fight. Before leaving Ticonderoga, Arnold had proposed an invasion of Canada. Congress soon formed a Northern Department under Maj. Gen. Philip Schuyler to achieve that very goal, and Arnold was offered the post of adjutant general. But Arnold wanted a field commission and went instead to Massachusetts to clean up his accounts and offer his services to the Continental Army's new commander in chief, George Washington. In his saddlebags he carried a detailed plan for a two-pronged invasion of Quebec Province.

In early August 1775 Arnold met Washington and proposed an attack on Quebec City as a diversion in force while Schuyler struck at Montreal. The British, Arnold pointed out, had only six hundred men to hold vast Quebec Province. Schuyler's attack from the south would draw them to the New York border, allowing Arnold, leading a small army along the old Indian route up the Kennebec River through Maine and down the Chaudière, to take the Canadian capital by surprise. A thousand shock troops appearing suddenly outside an undefended Quebec, Arnold believed, would inspire Canadians already sympathetic to the American cause.

Washington endorsed Arnold's plan and offered him his pick of eleven hundred men from the Continental Army but also told him to wait for Schuyler's concurrence before moving ahead. It took two weeks, until almost the end of the short Canadian summer, before Schuyler's approval came. Meanwhile, Arnold planned every detail of the invasion and traveled to Watertown to unravel his accounts with the Massachusetts Congress.

In an all-day hearing at Watertown, Arnold presented an account of regimental expenditures, arguing that having been so far from Boston, he had had to make decisions on behalf of the state and pay prevailing wages and prices. The Church Committee objected most to his personal expenses, especially "1 Sorrel horse rec'd by order of the Committee—valued at cost when bought 16," and finally allowed him only three pounds. It also refused nearly forty pounds in wages Arnold had given a wheelwright to make gun carriages to transport cannon. Arnold, Church declared, should have used soldiers as carpenters. Challenges ranged from the petty (paying an officer's small out-of-pocket expenses without obtaining a proper receipt) to the more serious (the committee objected to Arnold's acting as his own commissary and charging the customary 10 percent broker's fee). In all, the committee refused more than half of Arnold's claims. Months later, after Church's arrest for treason, Washington stepped in and asked Congress to clear the account, but by that time Arnold was far north in the Canadian wilderness and had need of more than acquittal.

On August 30, 1775, in Cambridge, the newly commissioned Continental Army colonel Benedict Arnold began to pick his men. Washington and his staff rode the lines with Arnold on that dusty gray Sunday morning. Chaplain William Emerson recalled that "the whole army was paraded in continued line of companies" with "one continued roll of drums." When his choices reported to Cambridge Common the next day, Arnold and his adjutants asked each man about his experience in the wilderness and at sea. Farmers who had never been in a boat but were bored with camp life lied to get in on the fighting, and by dusk Arnold had 1,050 men he thought could survive a wilderness march. But Washington's staff had to prepare orders, and not until September 15 did Arnold shake hands with the general and ride north. At Newburyport, where Arnold gathered eleven ships, three more days slipped away before the wind was favorable. Departing the harbor, the overloaded troop transport *Swallow* ran aground. A storm at sea hid the convoy from British blockades but scattered Arnold's ships on the 125-mile passage to the mouth of the Kennebec. "Our voyage has been very troublesome indeed," Arnold wrote back.

The troubles were just beginning. At Gardinerstown on the lower Kennebec, he found the two hundred lightweight bateaux he had ordered only three weeks earlier, but they were built from uncaulked green wood, and each weighed about four hundred pounds. Loaded with gear, they would be half a ton, terribly heavy for four men to carry over long portages. But with winter hard on the heels of fall, there wasn't time to rebuild. Continuing north on September 22, Arnold's men pulled and poled up the Kennebec to Fort Western. The boats proved to be "very leaky" and took a beating from river-bottom rocks exposed by a long drought. Moving slowly, the inexperienced soldiers had to carry the waterlogged bateaux up the slippery and almost perpendicular hundred-foot-high slopes beside Ticonic Falls near Skowhegan. "You would have taken the men for amphibious animals," Arnold wrote to Washington, "as they were a great part of the time under water."

Arnold had estimated the distance through the wilderness at two hundred miles. Actually it was nearly double that. By the beginning of October men who had thrashed through foaming rapids all day slept on the ground in clothing "frozen a pane of glass thick." On October 3 Arnold, inspecting the boats, found cracked barrels of beef swarming with maggots, rotted fish, and containers of flour and peas turned into putty. By now the army had reached the Dead River and was bogged down in nightmarish swamps.

Toward the end of the month, a hurricane struck the troops at four in the morning, driving a twelve-foot wall of water down the Dead River and scattering food, guns, and boats over two miles. One division after another became lost in the flooded swamps, wading all night through raging cold water. When rain turned to six inches of wet snow, the rear-guard division, under Col. Roger Enos of Connecticut, decided to go home, taking most of the remaining food, ammunition, and medical supplies. Arnold left his army behind and made a dash for the first settlement in Canada to find food. He "paddled on briskly," sending back three Maine guides—maps provided for the march by an unsuspected Loyalist surveyor had proved treacherously inaccurate—and orders to jettison the heavy boats and to cram all food and gunpowder into knapsacks. The army was down to eating roots and bark and broth from boiling shoes, candles, cartridge boxes.

Six days after Arnold's departure, the forward troops spotted "men and horses and cattle making toward us" as they staggered along beside the Chaudière into Canada. Arnold had reached the French settlement at St. Georges, Quebec, bought all the available livestock, and sent it back. Fifty-one days after swinging out of Cambridge, the American army, 40 percent of it lost to death or desertion, stumbled into the huts of St. Georges. When word of Arnold's survival reached Washington, he hailed Arnold as an officer of "great merit and trust." In the Continental Congress a North Carolina delegate praised "that little army" as equal to "Hannibal's over the Alps."

THE SIEGE OF QUEBEC

Arnold could not salvage enough equipment or men from the wreckage to make an immediate attack on Quebec. Not one of the two hundred bateaux remained, and all the gunpowder was ruined. With the help of Native Americans he was able to round up enough birchbark canoes to face the fast-moving mile-wide St. Lawrence, whipped into whitecaps by a winter storm. Through three days of snow squalls, Arnold waited for a moonless night, when his men could slip past British patrol boats. During that wait tough Loyalist veterans of the French and Indian War who made up the Royal Highland Emigrants marched into Quebec, fortifying the city's defenses. Arnold was too late.

Outnumbered by more than two to one, and without artillery, Arnold had to wait until reinforcements arrived. The Americans did not attack until New Year's Eve. On the last day of American enlistments, Arnold led the main push on the Lower Town while Brig. Gen. Richard Montgomery stormed the barricades below Cape Diamond in a blinding blizzard, his column of three hundred New Yorkers slithering over great chunks of river ice for an hour just to get there. Arriving at the first palisades, they sawed off timbers, and Montgomery stepped through a gap, leading his officers toward a silent two-story blockhouse. When he was within forty feet, three cannons fired at once, killing Montgomery and several of his officers. His second-in-command led a precipitous retreat of the entire

New York division, freeing the Quebec garrison to pour "a tremendous fire of musketry" into Arnold's thin column as it snaked through deep snow toward the Lower Town.

Arnold led the charge up to a log barricade, where he ordered Capt. Daniel Morgan and his riflemen to jam their rifles into gun slits and fire pointblank at the defenders. As Arnold waved his men over the barricade, he felt his right leg go numb. He tried to run on but pitched forward into the snow. He got up and hopped through volley after volley from houses close in on both sides. The bullet had missed Arnold's boot top, ricocheting from the shin onto the inner bone of his leg and then lodging in the Achilles' tendon. Dragged to a hospital, where a surgeon probed his leg, he learned the grim news: Morgan had taken over Arnold's 500-man force and kept fighting house-to-house for another three hours. About 80 men were killed or wounded, and 426 had been forced to surrender. Of the 300 men who had survived the trip up the Kennebec, 100 remained.

Arnold and his remnant of an army besieged Quebec for four more months. By sham and bluff, with the help of French-Canadian volunteers, he menaced Quebec from snow-and-ice forts. "I have no thoughts of leaving this proud town until I first enter it in triumph," he wrote to his sister. But on May 6, 1776, a British fleet arrived in the St. Lawrence with ten thousand reinforcements, raising the siege and forcing the Americans to retreat. In the weeks that followed, a series of American generals—David Wooster, John Thomas, John Sullivan—were promoted over Arnold's head, but all of them failed to stem the British counteroffensive. Leading the rear guard, Arnold escaped toward St. Johns with the enemy in sight. Along the way, to slow the British, he burned towns, forts, bridges, ships, and shipyards and successfully evacuated thousands of the sick and wounded. Hotly pursued by British grenadiers, Arnold barely made it into the last boat to leave Canada.

SAVING THE REVOLUTION

On July 7, 1776, the American generals defending New York and the New England backcountry against the British counteroffensive rendezvoused in the ruins of the old British fort at Crown Point for an emergency council of war. Already, Native Americans and British light infantry were probing southward through the forests along the shores, attempting to cut off the military roads leading east to the New England coast and south to New York City. At the lake's northern tip British troops were refitting.

In the holds and lashed to the decks of British warships anchored off Quebec in the St. Lawrence were the planks and masts, guns, rigging, and sails for one hundred landing barges, three men-of-war, one heavy-artillery bomb ketch, and twenty gunboats—an entire fleet prefabricated in England and then disassembled and shipped across an ocean to fight on a mountain lake. Each of the pre-cut men-of-war was bigger than any vessel that had ever sailed on Lake Champlain. With this elite force, Sir Guy Carleton was poised to carry out the British ministry's strategy to divide and conquer America and extinguish its year-old rebellion.

Carleton's Northern Army was to plunge down the lake, down Lake George, and on down the Hudson River to Albany to link up with the main thirty-four-thousand-man British force moving northward from New York City. Of the American officers gathered at Crown Point to figure out how to cope with this ambitious offensive, only Benedict Arnold had combat command experience. Although he was pessimistic—his army, he believed, had been "neglected by Congress" and "distressed by the smallpox, want of generals and discipline"—he vowed "one more bout for the honour of Americans."

Arnold went into the meeting with a bold plan. The only chance to stop the British, he said, was to delay them until the northern winter forced them to halt their operations. With no roads to travel south on, Carleton would have to strike across Lake Champlain, nearly impossible in the fierce winds and heavy seas of winter. Arnold proposed building a fleet to attack the open troop transports as they came across that fall: eight row galleys, thirty gondolas, and a thirty-six-gun frigate. The side that had the larger man-of-war would control the lake, he argued.

To carry out his plan, Arnold needed a thousand workmen—five hundred experienced shipwrights and ship carpenters and five hundred axmen to cut timber. Most of all, he needed nine hundred experienced seamen. Horatio Gates, in command at Ticonderoga and Arnold's immediate superior, wrote Washington: "General Arnold, who is perfectly skilled in maritime affairs, has nobly undertaken to command our fleet upon the lake. . . . I have committed the whole of that department to his care, convinced that he will thereby, add to that brilliant reputation."

The race was on. "Ship carpenters, gangs of fifteen each," Arnold sent off to the main shipyard at Skenesboro to expand the barracks and stocks, while others felled thousands of trees to feed the two sawmills that snarled day and night. Arnold also appointed officers to lead them without consulting Gates, overstepping his authority and antagonizing his commanding officer in the opening round of a feud that worsened for two years and earned Arnold many enemies. For his part, Gates wrote a report to Congress that took full credit for all of Arnold's efforts.

More than two hundred carpenters, armorers, and blacksmiths converged on Skenesboro that first week. They rose early and worked seven days a week despite a brief rebellion by New Englanders against Sunday labor. But nowhere near enough men answered the call for crews to man the fighting ships, and Arnold again refused to work through the proper channels. In a letter to Washington he appealed over Gates's head for crews. "Without a larger number of seamen, our navigation will be useless." Arnold also enclosed the first of many lists of supplies he could not obtain from Gates at Ticonderoga and then sent his own purchasing agents and recruiters to Connecticut; Gates hauled them back and sent his own.

The dragnet for men and munitions moved slowly, but by July 24, 1776, 150 more ship carpenters had marched into Skenesboro, tool bags slung over their shoulders. An exhilarated Arnold sent them to work. In a week six row galleys were on the stocks.

Arnold's personal enemies were busy too. In the midst of his naval preparation, he found himself facing a hostile court of inquiry at Ticonderoga investigating charges of looting in Canada. During the siege of Quebec, Loyalist merchants and captured British officers had been robbed. In fact, it was Arnold who had discovered the thefts, complained about them to the congressional commissioners in Canada, and received their permission to punish several looters severely. There was no evidence that Arnold was guilty of any wrongdoing; nonetheless, the court-martial, run by friends of Ethan Allen, dragged on. Arnold's anger boiled over. He entered a formal protest on the court record and appealed to Congress for a hearing. Then he challenged each officer on the court to a duel.

Nevertheless, on August 24, just seven weeks after the emergency council of war at Crown Point, Arnold sailed north with the ten small ships of his naval squadron, their new-made sails fluttering and filling, sunlight glinting on their barn-red sides. Two schooners, two sloops, and six gondolas crowded with untrained men headed up the lake to face a formidable enemy that had also been building ships at an amazing rate. Carleton already had a fleet equal the size of Arnold's on the stocks at St. Johns, plus a full-rigged eighteen-gun three-masted sloop of war, the *Inflexible.*

October 11 dawned with Arnold's fleet—now fifteen strong—drawn up in an arc in the narrows between Valcour Island and the New York shore, five miles south of present-day Plattsburgh. The British fleet had to sail into the wind to engage the American squadron. In a brutal seven-hour battle, Arnold sank two British gunboats and crippled the schooner *Carleton,* while losing his own largest craft, the schooner *Royal Savage,* and one gondola, the *Philadelphia.*

Almost out of ammunition, Arnold escaped that night by sailing silently through the British fleet, making it halfway down the lake with his badly damaged squadron before the British overtook him on October 13. After a second fight, which lasted five hours and permitted five ships to escape, Arnold scuttled his rear guard of five vessels, their rattlesnake flags flying as they sank, then led his men on a nightlong twenty-mile march through the forests to Ticonderoga, carrying the wounded in sails and twice eluding Native American ambushes.

Benedict Arnold's makeshift navy had ruined the invaders' plans to divide and conquer America in 1776. Winter had set in, and the British expeditionary force had to return to Canada, giving the Americans another year. With troops freed from the northern frontier, Arnold and Gates rushed reinforcements to the beleaguered Washington, making possible the crucial surprise attack at Trenton. More than a century passed before the most influential of all American naval historians gave Arnold proper credit for keeping the Revolution alive. "Save for Arnold's flotilla," wrote Alfred Thayer Mahan, the British would have "settled the business. The little American navy was wiped out, but never had any force, big or small, lived to better purpose."

ARNOLD, OUR EVIL GENIUS

At the time, few people could see the importance of Arnold's efforts in Canada and on Lake Champlain. The British praised him in dispatches, but many Americans saw Arnold simply as the man who had engineered a disastrous defeat in Canada and overseen the destruction of the first American fleet. Gen. William Maxwell wrote from Ticonderoga to New Jersey's governor, William Livingston, to explain that "Arnold, our evil genius to the north, has, with a good deal of industry, got us clear of all our fine fleet." From Congress, Richard Henry Lee of Virginia, member of the Marine Committee, decried Arnold to Gov. Thomas Jefferson as "fiery, hot and impetuous [and] without discretion." At Ticonderoga, Ethan Allen's former aide Maj. John Brown demanded that Gates arrest Arnold for thirteen "crimes" adding up to "great misconduct" in Canada.

Arnold soon found that Ethan Allen's friends had petitioned Congress for a court of inquiry into his affairs, but it was becoming more difficult for Arnold to defend himself: Witnesses were scattered, and many of his records and private papers had been burned or lost at Valcour Bay and during the retreat from Quebec. Now found, the papers include his missing accounts with French-Canadian and revolutionary Canadian commissaries who bought supplies from him in the winter of 1775-76, documents that could have saved Arnold endless trouble and that might even have prevented his treason. As one Canadian historian put it, "To give the invading devil his due, he paid his way."

It was Washington who intervened on Arnold's behalf, sending him to Rhode Island absence, on February 19, 1777, the Continental Congress issued Arnold the rebuff that almost certainly touched off the long fuse of bitterness that led to his defection. Without consulting Washington, Congress promoted five officers over Arnold's head to major general, all of them junior to him in both length of service and distinction. Arnold wrote Washington that Congress must have intended passing him over as "a very civil way of requesting my resignation." Despite Washington's urging that he remain in the service, Arnold resigned.

On May 2, 1777, Congress finally relented after a yearlong struggle with Washington and his generals over promotions and gave Arnold a new commission as major general. In the meantime, despite his growing hatred of revolutionary politicians, Arnold had raised a militia to fight the two thousand British regulars and Connecticut Loyalists attempting to destroy the huge Danbury munitions depot.

Washington sent his new major general to do what he did best—raise, train, and lead militia—to meet another invasion. As the British again invaded from Canada, the man who had shocked them into withdrawing twice before now led a relief expedition up the Mohawk River that raised the siege of Fort Stanwix, ending the threat to the American rear. Rejoining the main force, which had lost Ticonderoga and retreated almost all the way to Albany, Arnold found it in the command of Horatio Gates, whom he disliked and who promptly stripped him of his divisional command and barred him from staff meetings.

Instead of leaving or staying in his tent, Arnold defied Gates during the second Battle of Saratoga; he led the crucial charge that broke Breymann Redoubt, precipitating Gen. John Burgoyne's surrender and leaving Arnold critically wounded again, his right thigh shattered. "I wish it had been my heart," Arnold told an officer bending over him before he lost consciousness.

Although Gates, like Ethan Allen, omitted Arnold's name from official reports of the decisive victory at Saratoga, Washington learned of his bravery and honored him with a gold epaulet and sword knot. And Congress, finally forced to acknowledge Arnold's contribution to the revolutionary cause, resolved that Washington should adjust his date of rank and restore his seniority. Benedict Arnold's slate seemed clean.

"A CRIPPLE IN THE SERVICE OF MY COUNTRY"

Seven months later, in May 1778, at the end of the Continental Army's brutal winter at Valley Forge, Benedict Arnold, his leg only partially healed, was helped from a carriage at Washington's headquarters west of Philadelphia. No longer able to ride a horse, Arnold hobbled inside, wearing a built-up boot and leaning on a cane. Washington urged Arnold to take more time to mend but was eventually persuaded to assign him what was supposed to be a safe rear-area command as military governor of Philadelphia, with orders to reclaim the capital after the British evacuation. Philadelphia proved the stormiest post of Arnold's stormy career.

As governor, Arnold was considered haughty, arbitrary, and inflexible by rival Pennsylvania politicians, led by Joseph Reed, who became president of the Supreme Executive Council at a time when it was stronger than the Continental Confederation government. Reed, who was purging hundreds of suspected Loyalists, found Arnold's open friendship with Loyalists and his public courtship of Peggy Shippen, daughter of a purportedly Loyalist judge, especially objectionable.

As the capital city's presiding officer, Arnold insisted on asserting the federal prerogative and the prestige of the Continental Army in ways small, large, and invariably controversial. He closed the city's shops while he took an inventory of all captured goods and decided which should be requisitioned by army quartermasters, a move that earned him the enmity of many influential revolutionaries, who insinuated that, as at Montreal, he did so to line his own pockets. Later he was to insist that he stocked the basement of his headquarters in the Penn mansion only to provide for the governor's table, but there were lingering accusations that with the collusion of the clothier general, James Mease, and his deputy, William West, Arnold pillaged the shops for a week and then made a fortune on the black market. The mere closing of the shops created shortages and drove up prices in a technique known as engrossing, a practice despised by George Washington.

Arnold's actions brought him into open confrontation with Philadelphia revolutionaries in October 1778, when he issued orders for the army's wagon master general to take twelve military wagons to Chestnut Neck, New Jersey, which was inside his jurisdiction, and haul a large quantity of goods to safety in Philadelphia. Arnold later tried to pay the man £553 for his services, but after the goods went on sale in a Philadelphia storefront, Pennsylvania authorities alleged that Arnold's private use of army wagons was an abuse of power.

When Arnold bankrolled a Connecticut captain and his privateering crew in a lawsuit against the state, he pushed the Pennsylvania authorities to their limit. The sloop *Active* had been captured by the British, recaptured by its own crew, and then captured again by Pennsylvania privateers. Arnold considered the Connecticut sailors his countrymen and fed and housed them and paid their legal fees in a long battle with Pennsylvania authorities; had they won, he would have pocketed half the forty-five-thousand-pound value of the ship and cargo.

Beginning in November 1778, anonymous Pennsylvania radicals vilified Arnold almost weekly in the *Pennsylvania Packet*. Arnold repeatedly counterattacked in print, and in February 1779 the Council of Pennsylvania brought eight charges against him, alleging abuse of power, misuse of military authority, and self-aggrandizing business dealings. Some charges were petty; others raised constitutional questions. He was accused of malfeasance in office for forcing shop closures and of misappropriating military property by using army wagons to haul private goods to Philadelphia.

Angered, Arnold wrote to Washington on May 5, 1779: "If your Excellency thinks me criminal, for heaven's sake let me be immediately tried and, if found guilty, executed." He despaired, he said, of ever receiving justice from Congress or the Pennsylvania Council, a "set of artful, unprincipled men" who had come to power and "misrepresent the most innocent actions." He had, he reminded Washington, "made every sacrifice of fortune and blood, and become a cripple in the service of my country." He had "little expected to meet the ungrateful returns I have received from my countrymen."

"WHOM CAN WE TRUST NOW?"

In April 1779 Arnold married Peggy Shippen, who, at nineteen, was exactly half his age. A month later he sent word secretly through a Philadelphia Loyalist that he was ready to go over to the British army, and on May 10 he opened negotiations with Henry Clinton, the British commander in chief. That summer Arnold resigned as military governor and with his new wife moved into a smaller house owned by his father-in-law. In late December 1779 Arnold faced a court-martial at Dickerson's Tavern in Morristown, New Jersey. He indignantly denied all charges and opened his own defense with an impassioned speech.

"When the present necessary war against Great Britain commenced," he said, "I was in easy circumstances and enjoyed a fair prospect of improving them. I was happy in domestic connections and blessed with a rising family, who claimed my care and attention. . . . I sacrificed domestic ease and happiness to the service of my country, and in her service I sacrificed a great part of a handsome fortune. I was one of the first who appeared in the field and, from that time to the present hour, have not abandoned her service." Insisting that he was being persecuted by Pennsylvania authorities for his open associations with accused Loyalists, he argued, "It is enough for me to contend with men on the field."

Although there were those on the court-martial board who thought that Arnold should be cashiered from the army—and although documents discovered years later owed him to have been considerably more dishonest than the authorities suspected—its presiding officer, Maj. Gen. Robert Howe, who himself had clashed with revolutionary civilians as the military governor of Charleston, concluded that there was insufficient evidence on most counts. Arnold was convicted of only two misdemeanors: granting an illegal pass for the cargo vessel *Charming Nancy* and misappropriating public wagons. The board further recommended that Congress instruct Washington officially to reprimand Arnold.

The commander in chief did rebuke Arnold, characterizing his conduct in the *Charming Nancy* affair as "peculiarly reprehensible," but in fact, Washington's chiding was as mild as it could be without openly insulting the court-martial board, and he did not exclude Arnold from his plans for the coming campaign. Washington would soon offer Arnold a post of honor, command of the left wing of the main Continental Army. Arnold, however, was angry and dispirited.

Two more blows came almost immediately from Congress. On April 27, 1780, two weeks after Arnold's official reprimand, the Board of Treasury ruled that, despite the fact that Arnold had never been paid as a Continental officer and that he had pressed for his back wages for more than a year, he owed Congress more than three thousand pounds.

One month later, in May 1780, Arnold's request to be appointed to a naval command in the Caribbean was discouraged by Washington and rejected by Congress. Meanwhile, Arnold's negotiations with the British had broken down when Clinton refused to pay him a flat fee of ten thousand pounds no matter what services Arnold was to render. Now he resumed his secret correspondence, filling coded letters with military intelligence and with predictions that the Revolution would soon collapse because Congress had ruined the economy. He noted the rapid depreciation of Continental currency and scarcities of such basic commodities as flour as well as Congress's failure to obtain vital loans because "their time is taken up in trifles."

Arnold now asked Clinton for command of a Loyalist army as well as for financial compensation for the losses he said he had sustained as a result of Congress's refusal to settle his accounts. He also suggested a way to bring about the surrender of the vital American fortress at West Point. By mid June 1780, when he rode north to join Washington on the Hudson, Arnold wrote to Maj. John André, Clinton's adjutant general and head of his secret service, "I expect soon to command West Point."

Never losing faith in his troublesome field officer, Washington was perplexed by Arnold's reluctance to accept his left wing but nevertheless changed his command assignments and gave Arnold West Point, augmenting it with responsibility for all works and men between Albany and New York City.

From his new headquarters on the Hudson, Benedict Arnold began systematically to weaken West Point's defenses. On September 16 he learned that Washington, the Marquis de Lafayette, Henry Knox, and their combined staffs would be crossing the Hudson at Peekskill en route to Hartford for secret talks with the French command. "I shall be at Peekskill on Sunday evening," Washington wrote confidentially to Arnold. Arnold was to handpick fifty guards and forty spare horses to escort them. "You will keep this to yourself, as I want to make my journey a secret." Arnold knew how rarely Washington traveled without his army and how vulnerable he would be. At once he sent off his most trusted courier to Clinton under an illegal flag of truce. If the message arrived in time and the British chose to move quickly, they could easily capture

Washington as he crossed the Hudson on September 18. Arnold also informed Clinton that Washington would be spending the night at an inn at Peekskill within an easy ride of the nearest British dragoons.

Although Arnold personally led his handpicked guards to meet Washington on the eighteenth, ostensibly to deliver a memo on conditions at West Point, his message did not reach Clinton in time, and the British raid never came. Instead, a solitary vessel, the three-masted sloop of war *Vulture*, arrived in Haverstraw Bay, twelve miles south of West Point. Aboard was Maj. John André, Arnold's inexperienced twenty-nine-year-old spymaster, who, like Arnold, had insisted to Clinton that a face-to-face meeting between Arnold and André was needed to confirm Arnold's identity and to plan in detail the surrender of the key American stronghold. The British commander had reluctantly acquiesced to sending André on the mission, and he had given three orders intended to safeguard the young officer: He was not to go behind enemy lines; he was not to disguise himself but was to wear his British uniform; and he was to carry no compromising papers. If he violated any of these rules of war, he could be hanged as a spy.

André violated all three. Shortly after midnight on September 23, he landed at the foot of Long Clove Mountain, two miles below Haverstraw and well behind American lines. He concealed his British uniform under a dark caped coat. After talking with Arnold until first light, André left carrying Arnold's pass, made out under a false identity, "John Anderson," and five documents in Arnold's undisguised handwriting, among them a summary of the American army's strength and displacement and a report of the troops and ordnance at West Point and their weak spots. Concealing the messages between a sock and a conspicuously English boot, he changed his uniform for an old claret coat, a yellow waistcoat, and breeches.

Arnold then made arrangements for André to be rowed back to the *Vulture*, but the oarsman, up all night and increasingly suspicious, refused to take him, and André wound up riding south through the American lines and hiding for the night in a farmhouse. The next morning, as he approached a British outpost near Tarrytown, André mistook three men who sprang out into his path as Loyalists; one of them wore a captured green and red Hessian uniform. André identified himself as a British officer and then foolishly presented Arnold's pass, which said he was a civilian. The three American militiamen, who were absent without leave from their unit and had intended to rob him, now searched the oddly dressed spy and found the compromising documents.

They decided they would receive a reward if they turned their captive over to the nearest American outpost.

At nearby North Castle, John Jameson, the American colonel in charge, had earlier received instructions from Arnold that a John

Anderson might cross the lines from New York City. But although he did not recognize the handwriting, Jameson was puzzled by the papers "Anderson" carried and by the fact that he had been found *behind* the lines. He rushed word to Arnold of André's capture but dispatched the confiscated papers, which he characterized as being of "a very dangerous tendency," to Washington. The messenger, unable to find the general that night, returned to North Castle. Only Jameson's unintentional warning allowed Arnold to escape in his barge to the *Vulture*.

When Washington arrived from Hartford at Arnold's headquarters the next morning, September 25, he went upstairs with Lafayette to the rooms reserved for them to await the noonday meal. After they had inspected the defenses, Jameson's messenger arrived after riding all night with a packet for the commander in chief. As Washington broke open the seal and paged through the documents in Arnold's handwriting, the incredible truth struck him: Benedict Arnold had gone over to the British.

Remarkably clear-headed under fire, Washington was the only one at West Point that day to act calmly. He immediately ordered Alexander Hamilton and James McHenry to go after Arnold. Amid shouted orders Lafayette came into the dressing room where Washington was sitting, head down, hand trembling with its sheaf of treasonous papers, murmuring to Henry Knox, "Arnold has betrayed me. Whom can we trust now?"

THE FRUITS OF TREASON

Arnold's price for changing sides and turning over the Americans at West Point (including some of the very men who had followed him to Quebec) was twenty thousand pounds, about the amount he reckoned he had lost from Congress, from property he could not sell, and from debts a traitor could not collect. He received less than a third of it, but he was still a wealthy man; he had been transferring money to New York and London and on a brigadier general's modest pay was able to rent a mansion at 2 Broadway, right next door to British headquarters in New York City. More lucrative than his payment for changing sides was his new post as the ranking general of Loyalist troops, including his own new unit, the American Legion, made up entirely of deserters from the Continental Army.

Clinton unleashed Arnold on two bloody raids of plunder that severely damaged the American war effort and further enriched Arnold. In January 1781 he devastated Virginia at the head of a Loyalist army, sacking and burning the capital at Richmond. According to his own count, his troops destroyed a cannon foundry and arms warehouses and seized "thirty to forty ships loaded with tobacco, West Indies goods, wines, sailcloth." Arnold's share of the prize money was two thousand pounds. His second raid was on his native Thames Valley of Connecticut. In an attack on New London, a privateer base that had captured some five hundred British ships during the war, Arnold took ten richly laden prize ships in an assault that was so bloody that Clinton decided he could not afford any more such victories. Arnold's 1,732-man Loyalist army, according to his own meticulous records, destroyed 143 buildings but sustained casualties of almost 25 percent, one of the heaviest British tolls of the war.

Arnold's new compatriots never really warmed to him or trusted him fully. When he proposed an attack on Philadelphia to capture Congress and destroy military targets, Clinton turned him down. In December 1781 Arnold left the United States on the same ship as Earl Cornwallis, recently vanquished at Yorktown. Arnold finished the war as a retired British colonel on a half-pay pension, living out his life in exile in England, Canada, and the West Indies. He died heavily in debt in 1801.

Arnold never returned to the United States during his twenty-year exile, and he rarely spoke of it. He never ceased to see himself as a hero, but he was content, he wrote a friend shortly before his death, with obscurity in exile; contentment was "the greatest happiness to be expected in the world." In England, he concluded, he was "comfortable but not sufficiently elevated to be the object of envy and distinction."

8

Shays' Rebellion

Alden T. Vaughan

The 1780s were marked by a series of events that have fascinated historians for generations. In the first part of the decade the nation successfully concluded its revolution against Great Britain and launched a new government defined by the Articles of Confederation and Perpetual Union. Each event in its own right was an amazing feat. Then finally, in the latter part of the decade, the United States of America cast aside the loosely confederated government established under the Articles of Confederation and replaced it with a new and drastically different form of union. The 1780s were clearly a time of courage, experimentation, and change.

Alden T. Vaughan discusses the armed insurrection in Massachusetts that was one of the several events helping to undermine the Confederation and to promote the writing of a new constitution. When the delegates to the Constitutional Convention assembled in Philadelphia to serve in that fateful assembly, all were aware of the implied dangers in the disorders that had occurred in Massachusetts, and Daniel Shays and his compatriots certainly influenced their deliberations. Except for the Civil War, Shays' Rebellion was the nation's most significant domestic disorder, and its impact was profound.

OCTOBER, 1786: "Are your people . . . mad?" thundered the usually calm George Washington to a Massachusetts correspondent. Recent events in the Bay State had convinced the General, who was living the life of a country squire at Mount Vernon, that the United States was "fast verging to anarchy and confusion!" Would the nation that had so recently humbled the British Empire now succumb to internal dissension and die in its infancy? To many Americans in the fall of 1786 it seemed quite possible, for while Washington was writing frantic notes to his friends, several thousand insurgents under the nominal leadership of a Revolutionary War veteran named Daniel Shays were closing courts with impunity, defying the state militia, and threatening to revamp the state government.

The uprising in Massachusetts was serious in itself, but more frightening was the prospect that it could spread to the other states. It had, in fact, already tainted Rhode Island, Vermont, and New Hampshire, and it showed some danger of infecting Connecticut and New York as well. By the spring of 1787, American spokesmen from Maine to Georgia were alarmed, Congress had been induced to raise troops for possible deployment against the rebels, and observers on both sides of the Atlantic voiced concern for the future of the nation. Even John Adams in London and Thomas Jefferson in Paris took time from their critical diplomatic duties to comment—the former, as might be expected, pessimistically; the latter with his usual optimism—on the causes and consequences of Shays' Rebellion. And well they might: the Massachusetts uprising of 1786–1787 was to make a lasting contribution to the future of the United States by magnifying the demand for a stronger central government to replace the one created by the Articles of Confederation—a demand that reached fruition in the drafting and ratification of the Constitution in 1787–88. From the vantage point of the twentieth century, the rebellion of Daniel Shays stands—with the exception of the Civil War—as the nation's most famous and most important domestic revolt.

The root of the trouble in Massachusetts lay in the economic chaos that accompanied political independence. The successful war against Great Britain had left the thirteen former colonies free to rule themselves, but it had also left them without the commercial ties that had done so much to promote colonial prosperity. While American producers, merchants, and shippers scurried after new goods and new markets to replace the old, the ill effects of economic independence crept across the nation.

Of all the American states, perhaps none felt the postwar slump so grievously as did Massachusetts. Its $14 million debt was staggering, as was its shortage of specie. Bay Staters once again swapped wheat for shoes, and cordwood for help with the plowing. They suffered too from the ruinous inflation that afflicted the entire nation as the value of Continental currency fell in the three years after 1777 to a ridiculous low of four thousand dollars in paper money to one dollar in silver or gold. But in addition, Massachusetts caught the full brunt of England's decision—vengeful, the Americans considered it—to curtail trade between the United States and the British West Indies. To New Englanders, more than half of whom lived in Massachusetts, the new British policy threatened economic disaster. Gone was their dominance of the carrying trade, gone the booms in shipbuilding, in distilling, in food and lumber exporting, and in the slave trade. Gone too was New England's chief source of hard cash, for the West Indies had been the one place with which New England merchants enjoyed a favorable balance of trade.

Most residents of Massachusetts were probably unaware of the seriousness of their plight until it came close to home. By the early 1780s the signs were unmistakable. Men in debt—and debt was epidemic in the late seventies and eighties—saw their farms confiscated by the state and sold for as little as a third of what they considered to be the true values. Others, less fortunate, found themselves in the dark and filthy county jails, waiting helplessly for sympathetic friends or embarrassed relatives to bail them out of debtors' prison. As the economic crisis worsened, a gloomy pessimism spread among the farmers and tradesmen in the central and western parts of the state.

The economic problems of Massachusetts were difficult, but probably not insoluble. At least they could have been lessened by a wise and considerate state government. Unfortunately for the Bay Staters, good government was as scarce as good money in the early 1780s. After creating a fundamentally sound framework of government in the state constitution of 1780, the voters of Massachusetts failed to staff it with far-sighted and dedicated servants of the people. "Thieves, knaves, and robbers," snorted one disgruntled citizen. With mounting grievances and apathetic legislators, the people increasingly took matters into their own hands.

As early as February, 1782, trouble broke out in Pittsfield in the Berkshires, and before the year was over, mob actions had disrupted the tranquillity of several other towns in the western part of the state. The immediate target of the Pittsfield agitators was the local court, which they temporarily closed by barring the door to members of the bench. A court that did not sit could not process foreclosures, pass judgments on debts, or confiscate property for defaulted taxes. In April, violence broke out at Northampton, where a former Connecticut clergyman named Samuel Ely—branded by one early historian as "a vehement, brazen-faced declaimer, abounding in hypocritical pretensions to piety, and an industrious sower of discord"—led the attack on the judges. Ely harangued a Northampton crowd to "go to the woodpile and get clubs enough, and knock their grey wigs off, and sent them out of the world in an instant." Ely was promptly arrested and sentenced to six months in prison, but a mob soon freed him from the Springfield jail. The ex-parson found refuge in Vermont.

Instead of recognizing the validity of such protests, the Massachusetts legislature countered with a temporary suspension of habeas corpus and imposed new and higher court costs as well. And while the government did bend to the extent of authorizing certain foodstuffs and lumber to be used in lieu of money, the net effect of its measures was to rub salt into wounds already smarting. Currency remained dear, foreclosures mounted, the shadow of debtor's prison continued to cast a pall, and the state's legal system remained unduly complicated and expensive. Many citizens of eastern Massachusetts now began to question the benefits of independence; a few even concluded that the patriot leaders of 1776 had deluded them, and cheers for King George III were heard once again in towns that a few years before had cursed his name. And unrest continued to spread. In May, 1783, a mob tried to prevent the opening of the spring session of the Hampshire County Court at Springfield.

Perhaps the major outbreak of 1786 would have occurred a year or so sooner had it not been for a fortuitous combination of events that made the years 1784 and 1785 relatively easy to bear. In 1784 came news that a final peace had been signed with England; in 1785 Massachusetts farmers enjoyed their best harvest in several years, while the legislature, in one of its conciliatory if vagrant moods, refrained from levying a state tax. Although tempers continued to simmer, no serious outbreaks marred the period from early 1783 to midsummer 1786.

The episodes of 1782–83 and those that followed held a particular appeal for veterans of the revolution. Even more than their civilian neighbors, the former soldiers nursed grievances that they could attribute to incompetent, if not dishonest, government. They had left their farms and shops to fight the hated redcoats, but they could not even depend on the paltry sums their services had earned for them. Inflation had made their Continental currency almost worthless, and now the government set up by the Articles of Confederation was delaying payment of over-due wages and retracting its promises of lifetime pensions to officers.

One lesson of the Revolution not lost on the Massachusetts veterans was that in times of necessity the people could reform an insensitive government by force of arms, and many of them still had in their possession the weapons they had used so effectively against the British and Hessian troops. Old habits and old weapons increasingly took on new meaning to the men of Massachusetts as the economic and political crisis of the 1780s deepened. The veterans of the Bay State knew where to find leadership, too, for among those hard-pressed by the economic problems of the decade were many who had served as officers during the War of Independence.

By 1786 several of these officers had emerged as acknowledged leaders in their own localities, although not until the final stages of the rebellion would any single commander claim the allegiance of more than a few hundred men at most.

In the eastern part of the state the most prominent leader was Captain Job Shattuck of Groton, a veteran of the French and Indian War as well as of the Revolution. Now in his fifties, Shattuck had been protesting vehemently, and sometimes violently, since 1781. His principal lieutenant in Middlesex County was Nathan Smith of Shirley, a tough veteran of both wartime and peacetime conflict—with a patch over one eye as testimony of his involvement in the latter. It was the burly Smith who on one occasion gave his hearers the unhappy choice of joining his band or being run out of town.

Farther west the rebels looked to other leaders. In Springfield and neighboring towns it was to Luke Day, said by some to be "the master spirit of the insurrection." A former brevet major in the Continental Army, Day seems to have had the inclination as well as the experience necessary to command a rebellion. In the dismal eighties he was often found grumbling his discontent in West Springfield's Old Stebbin's Tavern or drilling his followers on the town common.

But it was not upon Shattuck or Smith or Day that the final leadership devolved, with its mixed portions of glory and infamy, but on Captain Daniel Shays of Pelham. In some respects Shays was an improbable leader for a popular revolt, for he seems to have been a reluctant rebel in the first place; as late as the fall of 1786 he insisted: "I at their head! I am not." And even after he had assumed command of the bulk of the rebel army, he expressed eagerness to accept a pardon. But at the same time, Shays had attributes that made him a likely prospect for gaining the loyalty of the insurgents. Unlike the others, Shays presented a calm moderation that inspired confidence and respect. He also had a penchant for military courtesy and protocol, a quality that would have undoubtedly been repugnant to the veterans if overdone, but one that was essential if the "mobbers," as they were often called, were to acquire the discipline and organization necessary to resist the forces of government.

Daniel Shays also attracted confidence through his impressive Revolutionary War record. Joining the Continental Army at the outbreak of hostilities, he fought bravely at Bunker Hill (where his courage earned him a promotion to sergeant), served under Ethan Allen at Ticonderoga, helped thwart Gentleman Johnny Burgoyne at Saratoga, and stormed Stony Point with Mad Anthony Wayne. For recruiting a company of volunteers in Massachusetts Shays ultimately received a commission as their captain, a position he seems to have filled adequately if not outstandingly. And before leaving the service, Shays suffered at least one wound in battle.

Shays resigned from the army in 1780 and turned his hand to farming in the small town of Pelham, a few miles east of the Connecticut River. There his popularity, undoubtedly enhanced by his military reputation, won him election to various local offices. At the same time, Shays learned

at first hand the problems that can beset a returned veteran. He had
already sold for cash the handsome ceremonial sword that the Marquis de
Lafayette had presented to him in honor of the victory at Saratoga. On
long winter evenings at Conkey's Tavern, Daniel Shays listed to his
neighbors' tales of distress. In 1784 he was himself sued for a debt of
twelve dollars; by 1786 he was deeply involved in the insurrection. Like
so many other men in western and central Massachusetts, Shays had been
maneuvered by events of the post-war period into actions that he would
hardly have contemplated a few years earlier.

The relative calm that followed the outbreaks of 1782-83 was abruptly
shattered in 1786. To make up for the low revenue of the previous year,
the legislature in the spring of 1786 imposed unusually heavy poll and
property taxes, amounting to one third of the total income of the people.
In 1774 taxes had been fifteen cents per capita; in 1786 they leaped to
$1.75—a hefty sum for heads of families in frontier areas where a skilled
laborer earned thirty to fifty cents a day. Protested one poor cobbler,
"The constable keeps at us for rates, rates, rates!" Besides, the new tax
schedule was notorious for its inequity, placing heavy duties on land
without regard for its value—a palpable discrimination against the poorest
farmers. The new schedule also worked injury on the least affluent classes
by seeking almost forty per cent of its revenue through a head tax, asking
equal amounts from pauper and merchant prince. As court and jail
records poignantly testify, many people in the central and western parts
of the state could not pay both the new taxes and their old debts.
Worcester County, for example, had four thousand suits for debts in
1785–86 (double the total of the preceding two years), and the number of
persons imprisoned for debt jumped from seven to seventy-two during
that period. In 1786 debtors outnumbered all other criminals in Worcester
County prisons 3 to 1.

The new taxes would probably have caused considerable anger by
themselves, but when added to old grievances they were sure to bring
trouble. During the summer of 1786, conventions met in several western
counties—in Worcester, in Hampshire, in Berkshire—and even as far east
as Middlesex, only a few miles from Boston. From these quasi-legal
meetings came resolutions to the Massachusetts legislature calling for a
variety of reforms; reduction of court and lawyers' fees, reduction of
salaries for state officials, issuance of paper money, removal of the state
capital from Boston (where it was deemed too susceptible to the influence
of eastern commercial interests), reduction of taxes, redistribution of the
tax load, and many similar changes. A few protests called for still more
drastic reforms, such as abolition of the state senate and curtailment of
the governor's appointive power, while some petitioners insisted on a
state-wide convention to amend the constitution of 1780, now barely six
years old. But on the whole the petitions demanded evolution, not

revolution. This was a tempered and healthy challenge to an administration that had shown itself insensitive and incompetent.

In the protests about the government, two categories of citizens were singled out for criticism by the petitioners. First were the merchants and professional men, who enjoyed an unfair advantage within the tax system. Second were the lawyers, who seemed to be conspiring with judges and creditors to force the debtor still further into obligation. Perhaps not all lawyers were so harshly judged, but the condemnation was certainly meant to apply to those whom John Adams called "the dirty dabblers in the law," men who often created more litigation than they resolved. In contrast to the turbulent days before the Revolution, the new era in Massachusetts did not find lawyers in the vanguard of the movement for reform.

But in one respect, at least, the 1780s bore resemblance to the years before Lexington: peaceful protest soon gave way to more forceful action. In late August, following a Hampshire County convention at Hatfield, a mob of 1,500 men "armed with guns, swords, and other deadly weapons, and with drums beating and fifes playing" took command of the county courthouse at Northampton and forced the judges of the Court of Common Pleas and General Sessions of the Peace to adjourn sine die. During the next few months, similar conventions with similar results took place in Middlesex, Bristol, and Worcester counties. By early fall, mobs armed with muskets or hickory clubs and often sporting sprigs of hemlock in their hats as a sign of allegiance to the rebel cause moved at will through the interior counties.

The rebels did not go unopposed. In each county there were some citizens who looked askance at the growing anarchy and did their best to thwart it. In Worcester, seat of Worcester County, Judge Artemas Ward showed the mettle of those who would not succumb to mob rule. When on the fifth of September two hundred armed men blocked his path to the courthouse, the aging but still impressive ex-general defied the bayonets that pierced his judicial robes and for two hours lectured the crowd on the dangers of anarchy and the meaning of treason. A heavy downpour finally silenced the judge, though not until he had intoned a timely plea that "the sun never shine on rebellion in Massachusetts." But neither rain nor words had got the judge and his colleagues into the courthouse.

Elsewhere the story was much the same: a few citizens tried to stem the tide of rebellion but in the end were swept aside. At Great Barrington, in Berkshire County, a mob of 800 stopped the court, broke open the jail and released its prisoners, and abused the judges who protested. At Springfield, Daniel Shays and Luke Day made sure that the courthouse doors remained shut, while at Concord, less than twenty miles from Boston, Job Shattuck, aided by Nathan Smith and his brother Sylvanus, prevented the sitting of the Middlesex County court. Only at

Taunton, in Bristol County, did a sizable mob meet its match. There Chief Justice (and former general) David Cobb was ready with a field piece, thirty volunteers, and a determination to "sit as a judge or die as a general." The Bristol court met as scheduled.

Governor James Bowdoin and the legislature responded to the latest outbreaks with a confusing mixture of sternness, concession, and indecision. In early September, the Governor issued his first proclamation, condemning the mobbers' flirtation with "riot, anarchy and confusion." In October the legislature suspended habeas corpus, but it also authorized some categories of goods as legal tender for specified kinds of public and private debts, and it offered full pardon to all rebels who would take an oath of allegiance before the end of the year. Yet the government failed to find solutions to the major complaints. No significant reforms were made in court procedures, the tax load was not reduced, officials' salaries were not lowered, the capital was not moved, and no curbs were placed on lawyers' machinations.

As mob violence continued through the fall of 1786, spokesmen in the Bay State and elsewhere voiced a growing fear that the anarchy of Massachusetts might infect the entire nation. Several months earlier John Jay had predicted a crisis—"something I cannot foresee or conjecture. I am uneasy and apprehensive; more so than during the war." Now Secretary of War Henry Knox, Massachusetts statesman Rufus King, and others began to have similar apprehensions. They wrote frantic letters to one another, asking for news and predicting disaster. Abigail Adams, then in London, bristled at the "ignorant and wrestless desperadoes," while reports of the uprising helped prod her husband John into writing his ponderous *Defence of the Constitutions*. Even General Washington lost his equanimity. "[For] God's sake, tell me," he wrote to his former aide-de-camp, David Humphreys, in October, "what is the cause of all these commotions? Do they proceed from licentiousness, British influence disseminated by the Tories, or real grievances which admit of redress? If the latter, why were they delayed 'till the public mind had been so much agitated? If the former, why are not the powers of Government tried at once?"

Fearful that the powers of state government would not be sufficient to thwart the rebellion, Governor Bowdoin and Secretary of War Knox hatched a scheme for employing federal troops should the need arise. Knox discussed the matter with Congress: the outcome was a call for 1,340 volunteers for the federal army (which then numbered only 700), most of them to be raised in Massachusetts and Connecticut. The additional troops were ostensibly to be used against the Native Americans of the Northwest, but in secret session Congress acknowledged the possibility that they might be sent instead against the self-styled "regulators" in New England, and that they might be needed to protect the federal arsenal in Springfied—a likely target for the rebellious veterans. Meanwhile the Massachusetts Council authorized a state army of 4,400 men and four regiments of artillery, to be drawn largely from the militia of the eastern counties.

Command of the state forces fell to Major General Benjamin Lincoln, a battle-tested veteran of the Revolution, and a man of tact and humanity as well as martial vigor. But before taking the field, Lincoln served a brief stint as fund-raiser for his own army, for the cost of a thirty-day campaign had been calculated at about £5,000, or about $20,000, and the impoverished state treasury could offer nothing but promises of eventual reimbursement to any who would lend cash to the government. In less than twenty-four hours General Lincoln collected contributions from 130 of Boston's wealthy citizens, including £250 from Governor Bowdoin.

By the time Lincoln's army was equipped for action, the rebellion was over in eastern Massachusetts. It had never been strong there, but in November of 1786 a mob tried to halt the Middlesex County court. This time the militia was alert. After a brief skirmish in which Job Shattuck received a crippling wound, the Groton leader and two of his lieutenants were captured. While Shattuck languished in the Boston jail, his followers drifted west to join other rebel groups.

The situation now grew alarming in Worcester, where the Supreme Court was scheduled to meet on December 5; by late November, mobs of armed men drifting into town had closed the Court of Common Pleas and made it obvious that no court could meet without an army to back it up. Local officials looked on helplessly. Even bold Sheriff Greenleaf, who offered to help alleviate the high court costs by hanging every rebel free of charge, was powerless in the face of such numbers, and he became a laughingstock to boot when he strode away from the courthouse one day unaware that someone had adorned his hat with the symbolic hemlock tuft.

At first the rebels at Worcester suffered from lack of a universally recognized leader. Then in early December Daniel Shays rode in from Pelham, mounted on a white horse and followed by 350 men. He had not come to do battle if he could avoid it; to a friend he confided: "For God's sake, have matters settled peaceably; it was against my inclinations I undertook this business; importunity was used which I could not withstand, but I heartily wish it was well over." Still, as a showdown with the judges approached, Shays increasingly assumed the role of spokesman for the disparate forces. And it was just as well; with milling crowds of disgruntled veterans and a frightened and divided populace, violence might well have erupted. Instead, choosing wisdom as the better part of valor, the rebels put their energies into drafting a petition to the legislature for a redress of grievances and into several wordy defenses of their own actions. Violence was scrupulously avoided. And their immediate point, after all, had been won; the Worcester court gathered weekly in the Sun Tavern and adjourned until January 23. The insurgents then gave way before the more impressive force of winter blizzards and dispersed to the west. Friends of the rebels were not greatly heartened, however, for the basic grievances remained. Friends of the government rejoiced at the retreat of the rebels, and chanted:

> Says sober Bill, "Well Shays has fled,
> And peace returns to bless our days!"

> "Indeed," cries Ned, "I always said
> He'd prove at last a fall-back Shays,

> And those turned over and undone
> Call him a worthless Shays, to run!"

But Shays was only running to a new scene of action. The Hampshire County court, scheduled to meet in Springfield in late January, should be stopped. Besides, the federal arsenal in that town had the only cache of arms the rebels could hope to capture, and without weapons the rebellion must collapse.

General Lincoln was preparing to defend the January session of the Worcester court when news reached him of the crisis in Springfield. The arsenal there boasted a garrison of some 1,100 militia under General William Shepard, but surrounding the troops were three rebel forces: Daniel Shays commanded 1,200 men at Wilbraham, eight miles to the east; Eli Parson had 400 at Chicopee, three miles to the north; Luke Day led another 400 at West Springfield, just across the Connecticut River to the west. There was every reason to believe they could overwhelm Shepard's garrison if they were willing to risk some bloodshed. General Lincoln headed for Springfield on the double.

Had Shays and his cohorts carried out their original plan they would in all likelihood have had possession of the arsenal before Lincoln arrived with reinforcements. The attack had been set for January 25: Shays was to have led a frontal assault from the southeast while Day directed a flanking movement from the west. But at the last minute Day decided to wait until the twenty-sixth, and his note informing Shays of the change was intercepted by Shepard's men. When Shays moved forward on the afternoon of the twenty-fifth, Shepard confidently grouped his full strength against the lone attack. But not much strength was needed. Shepard fired only three cannon shots. When two warning volleys failed to turn back the rebels, Shepard aimed the third into their midst. Three insurgents fell dead in the snow, a fourth lay mortally wounded. The remainder fled in confusion. It was a shattered band that Shays succeeded in regrouping a few miles from the scene of conflict.

At this point General Lincoln arrived and took position between Day and Shays. Both rebel armies at once broke camp and headed for safer territory—Day's men so hastily that they left pork and beans baking in their ovens and discarded knapsacks strewn along their route. The main force, under Shays, beat a rapid retreat to the northeast, passing through Ludlow, South Hadley, Amherst, and Pelham. Lincoln followed in close pursuit, moving overland after Shays, while General Shepard marched up the frozen Connecticut River to prevent a reunion of the rebel army's eastern and western wings.

At Hadley, General Lincoln halted his pursuit long enough to discuss surrender proposals with Shays. The rebel leader was willing to negotiate, but his insistence on an unconditional pardon for himself and his men was more than General Lincoln was authorized to grant. With no agreement likely, Shays suddenly shifted his men to the relative security of Petersham, a center of regulator sentiment which lay in terrain easier to defend. It was midwinter—an unusually cold and stormy winter—and deep snow blanketed the Connecticut Valley. Perhaps the militia would not bother to follow.

But Shays reckoned without General Lincoln. Ever since 1780, when he had surrendered Charleston, South Carolina, and its garrison of 5,400 men to the British in the most costly American defeat of the Revolution, Benjamin Lincoln had had to endure charges of cowardice and indecision. Although he had been officially exonerated, a few critics persisted; in a vigorous suppression of the Shaysites General Lincoln could perhaps fully restore himself in the public's esteem. With superb stamina and determination, Lincoln marched his men the thirty miles from Hadley to Petersham through a blinding snowstorm on the night of Saturday, February 3, arriving at Petersham early the next morning. Taken completely by surprise, the insurgents were routed: some 150 were captured; the rest, including Shays, escaped to the north. Lincoln then moved across the Connecticut River to disperse rebel nests in the Berkshires. By the end of February only scattered resistance remained. What the legislature had recently condemned as a "horrid and unnatural Rebellion and War . . . traitorously raised and levied against this Commonwealth" had come to an inglorious end.

While the militia crushed the remnants of rebellion, the state government drafted a series of regulations for punishing the insurgents. In mid-February, two weeks after Shays' dispersal at Petersham, it issued a stiff Disqualifying Act, offering pardons to privates and noncommissioned officers, but denying them for three years the right to vote, to serve on juries, and to be employed as schoolteachers, innkeepers, or liquor retailers. Massachusetts citizens would thus be shielded from the baneful influence of the Shaysites. Not included in the partial amnesty were the insurgent officers, citizens of other states who had joined the

Massachusetts uprising, former state officers or members of the state legislature who had aided the rebels, and persons who had attended regulator conventions. Men in those categories would be tried for treason.

The government's vindictive measures aroused widespread protest, not only from those who had sympathized with the rebel cause but from many of its active opponents as well. General Lincoln, among others, believed that such harsh reprisals would further alienate the discontented, and he observed to General Washington that the disfranchisement of so many people would wholly deprive some towns of their representation in the legislature. New outbreaks, he argued, would then occur in areas that had no other way to voice their grievances. In token concession to its critics, the legislature in March, 1787, appointed a special commission of three men to determine the fate of rebels not covered by the Disqualifying Act. General Lincoln served on the commission, and under his moderating influence it eventually extended pardons to 790 persons. But in the meantime, county courts apprehended and tried whatever rebel leaders they could find. In Hampshire County, with Robert Treat Paine serving as prosecuting attorney, six men were sentenced to death and many others incurred fines or imprisonment. In Berkshire County eight men were sentenced to die for their part in the uprising.

Had the government of 1786–1787 remained in office, more than a dozen lives would have been lost to the hangman, hundreds of other men would have suffered disqualifications, and the fundamental causes of Shays' Rebellion might have lingered on to trigger new outbreaks. But however strongly the regulators might complain of the legislative and judicial shortcomings of Massachusetts, they had cause to be thankful that its constitution required annual elections and that the franchise was broad enough to let popular sentiment determine the tenor of government. The result of the April election revealed the breadth and depth of the sympathy in which the regulators were held by the citizens and the extent of popular revulsion at the ineptitude of the government. In the gubernatorial contest, popular John Hancock, recently recovered from an illness that had caused him to resign the governorship early in 1785, overwhelmingly defeated Governor Bowdoin. Only 62 of the 222 members of the legislature and 11 members of the 24-man senate were returned to their seats. In some instances the voters chose men who had actively participated in the rebellion, including Josiah Whitney, who had recently served sixteen days in the Worcester jail.

Within the next few months the new legislature sharply mitigated both the causes of unrest and the punishments assigned to the rebels. It repealed the Disqualifying Act, reprieved all men under sentence of death—some on the very steps of the gallows—and by the following summer it had pardoned even Daniel Shays, though he and a few other leaders were still precluded from holding civil and military offices in the state. Equally important, it enacted long-range reform—extending the law that permitted the use of certain personal and real property in payment of debts, imposing a lower and more equitable tax schedule, and releasing most debtors from prison.

Now in truth the rebellion was over. Peace, and soon prosperity, returned to the Massachusetts countryside. Differences of opinion still lingered, of course, as was made clear one Sunday when the church at Whately christened two infants—one named after Daniel Shays, the other after Benjamin Lincoln. But the Shaysites made no further trouble for Bay State authorities, and Daniel Shays, the reluctant leader, soon moved on to New York State, where he eked out a skimpy existence on his Revolutionary War pension until his death in 1825.

Americans of the 1780s drew various lessons from the affair in Massachusetts. Some, like Washington and Madison, appear to have misinterpreted the event and ascribed to the rebels a more drastic program than the majority of them had ever advocated. Others, like Mercy Warren, the historian, and Joseph Hawley, the Massachusetts patriot, detected the hand of Great Britain behind the uprising. Still others sensed that the true causes of Shays' Rebellion were local in origin and primarily the fault of the state government. Baron von Steuben had correctly surmised that "when a whole people complains . . . something must be wrong," while Thomas Jefferson, then American Minister to France, thought the rebellion of no dangerous importance and preferred to set it in a broader perspective than had most Americans. "We have had," wrote Jefferson, "13 states independent 11 years. There has been one rebellion. That comes to one rebellion in a century and a half for each state. What country before ever existed a century and a half without a rebellion? And what country can preserve its liberties if their rulers are not warned from time to time that the people preserve the spirit of resistance? . . . The tree of liberty, must be refreshed from time to time with the blood of patriots and tyrants." But while observers were drawing these diverse conclusions from the episode in Massachusetts, an increasing number of Americans were concerned with how to make sure it would never happen again.

On May 25, 1787, less than four months after the rout at Petersham, the Constitutional Convention began its deliberations at Independence Hall, Philadelphia. Through a long hot summer the delegates proposed, argued, and compromised as they sought to construct a new and better form of government for the American nation. And among the knottiest problems they faced were several recently emphasized by Shays' Rebellion: problems of currency regulation, of debts and contracts, and of ways to thwart domestic insurrection. As the records of the federal Convention reveal, the recent uprising in Massachusetts lay heavily on the minds of the delegates. Although it is impossible to pinpoint the exact phrases in the final document that owed their wording to the fear of similar revolts, there is no doubt that the Constitution reflected the determination of the Founding Fathers to do all they could to prevent future rebellions and to make it easier for the new government to suppress them if they did occur. Significantly, the new polity forbade the states to issue paper money, strengthened the military powers of the executive branch, and authorized Congress to call up state militiamen to "suppress Insurrections" and enforce the laws of the land. Jefferson's first glimpse of the Constitution convinced him that "our Convention has been too much impressed by the insurrection of Massachusetts. . . ." Jefferson exaggerated, but it is clear that the movement for a stronger central government had gained immense momentum from the "horrid and unnatural Rebellion" of Daniel Shays.

By the summer of 1788 the requisite nine states had ratified the new Constitution, and in the following spring General Washington took the oath of office as President. In the prosperous and dynamic years that followed, the passions generated by the insurrection in Massachusetts were gradually extinguished. But the lesson and the impact of Shays' Rebellion are still with us. Because of it, important changes were made in the government of Massachusetts as well as in the government of the nation, changes that have stood the test of time. Perhaps this episode lends some ironic credence to Thomas Jefferson's suggestion that "the spirit of resistance to government is . . . valuable on certain occasions."

9

Alexander Hamilton's Alternative: Technology Piracy and the Report on Manufactures

Doron Ben-Atar

Alexander Hamilton has been accused by his opponents and by some historians of being so dazzled by the dominance of Great Britain and its aristocratic elite as to have become a British agent in Washington's cabinet. Thus, the economic programs sponsored by Hamilton's Treasury Department have been portrayed as initiatives designed to undermine American interests and enhance British control of the American economy. Hamilton's goal for the United States, according to these observers, was to ride Britain's coat tails, creating an Anglo-American commercial empire controlling a global economy. Historian Doron Ben-Atar challenges this assessment by calling attention to a crucial element in Hamilton's range of economic programs—the Treasury Department's active support for industrial espionage and piracy against Great Britain. This initiative, according to Ben-Atar, indicates that Hamilton's economic programs represented an effort to emulate Britain's economic ascendance and to inherit Britain's commercial and industrial power.

Hamilton was convinced that technological backwardness, a lack of skilled workers and the high wages in the United States made American products more expensive and of lower quality than European goods. Not a believer in the "invisible hand of the free market," Hamilton wanted to commit the Federal Government to attracting skilled workers and modern technology from Britain by offering financial incentives and issuing American patents for stolen technology. Other Treasury Department proposals were designed to propel Americans and new immigrants to American cities, increasing competition for manufacturing jobs, thereby lowering wages.

What is striking about Hamilton's various economic, commercial and industrial programs—his vision of the United States as a commercial and manufacturing rival to Great Britain—is that the United States in the 1790s was a thoroughly agrarian society. Some, indeed, have argued that the Federalists disappeared so quickly from American political life because their vision and policies were out of touch with reality.

On March 24, 1791, an announcement appeared in the Philadelphia *Federal Gazette.* One George Parkinson, of that city, advertised that he had recently obtained a United States patent for spinning flax, hemp, and combed wool by methods that represented "improvements upon the mill or machinery of Kendrew and Porthouse of the town of Darlington in Great Britain." Why had Parkinson, an English weaver who later worked for the Society for Establishing Useful Manufactures (SEUM) in Paterson, New Jersey, been granted a patent monopoly even though his version of Richard Arkwright's flax-spinning machine only marginally improved on the original? Parkinson's announcement provided the answer. It was because this "machinery, with the original mechanism . . . [was] of the utmost value to the United States."[1] By granting a patent to an "introducer" of a machine that was protected under Britain's intellectual property laws the United States patent office rewarded technology piracy.[2]

Prohibitions on the emigration of artisans and the export of machinery from the British empire had been in effect throughout the eighteenth century. In the period following American Independence, growing anxiety in Britain over industrial piracy prompted stronger legislation and stricter enforcement.

---

[1] *Federal Gazette, Mar.* 24, 1791. Parkinson initially argued his was an "entire new invention" that would be "of general utility to the United States"; Parkinson to Benjamin Franklin, Dec. 22, 1789, Franklin Papers, American Philosophical Society (APS), Philadelphia. His American partner, Tench Coxe, made no such claims. He explained that he and Parkinson were "not the inventors, but the introducers, there being no model or drawing of these invaluable movements in the United States," and that they considered Arkwright "the inventor and ourselves the introducers." Coxe to George Clymer, Jan. 17, 1790, Tench Coxe Papers, Historical Society of Pennsylvania (HSP), Philadelphia, Pa. See also Jacob E. Cooke, "Tench Coxe, Alexander Hamilton, and the Encouragement of American Manufactures," *William and Mary Quarterly,* 3d Ser., 32 (1975), 381.

[2] I use the term "piracy" strictly in the modern sense of the word to describe "3. an unauthorized appropriation and reproduction of anothe's production, invention, or conception esp. in infringement of a copyright"; *Webster's Third New International Dictionary* (Springfield, Mass., 1961), 1723. *The William and Mary Quarterly,* 3d Series, Vol. LII, No. 3, July 1995

Under the new laws, illegal emigrant artisans forfeited their nationality and property and could be convicted of treason. Recruiting agents could be fined £500 and imprisoned for twelve months for each emigrant they enticed. A £200 fine, forfeiture of equipment, and twelve months' imprisonment (or a £500 fine and forfeiture in the case of textile machinery) were laid down for the export or attempted export of industrial machinery. Ships' captains were required to submit lists detailing passenger occupations to customs officials at British ports before departing, and in at least one instance the Royal Navy seized an illegal emigrant on an American ship, the *Union*, as it left Liverpool. British consular officials in America were instructed to report on British artisans and machinery in the United States.[3]

In 1791, Secretary of State Thomas Jefferson was in charge of American patents. In that official capacity, Jefferson approved Parkinson's patent application and helped arrange the migration of Parkinson's family to the United States.[4] He thus sanctioned an overt violation of British restrictions on the diffusion of industrial technology. But Jefferson, staunch foe of Great Britain that he was, held conflicting views about technology piracy.[5] He lent a hand to Parkinson's family but not to Parkinson himself; as Julian P. Boyd writes, he "took no part in aiding the immigration of British artisans because it was forbidden by law." A year earlier, Jefferson had been reluctant to support William Pollard's application for a patent monopoly of another version of Arkwright's machine.[6]

---

[3] David J. Jeremy, "Damming the Flood: British Government Efforts to Check the Outflow of Technicians and Machinery, 1780–1843," *Business History Review*, 51 (1977), 1–34; John R. Harris, "Industrial Espionage in the Eighteenth Century," *Industrial Archeology Review*, 7 (Spring 1985), 128–29; A. E. Musson, "The 'Manchester School' and Exportation of Machinery," *Business History*, 14 (1972), 20–21.

[4] Tench Coxe to Jefferson, Mar. 14, 1791, Jefferson to James Maury, May 1, 1791, in Julian *Boyd* et al., eds., *The Papers of Thomas Jefferson*, 25 vols. to date (Princeton, 1950–), XIX, 553, XX, 339 (hereafter *Jefferson Papers*).

[5] Only a few weeks earlier, Jefferson had submitted to Congress reports on the state of American fisheries and on Gouverneur Morris's mission to London that blasted English policy and proposed aggressive retaliatory economic diplomacy. Vernon G. Setser, *The Commercial Reciprocity Polity of the United States*, 1774–1829 (Philadelphia, 1937), 100–13; Alexander DeConde, *Entangling Alliance: Politics and Diplomacy under George Washington* (Durham, N. C., 1958), 75–79; Doron S. Ben-Atar, *The Origins of Jeffersonian Commercial Policy and Diplomacy* (New York, 1993), 108–12.

[6] Boyd et al., eds., *Jefferson Papers*, XX, 340. Jefferson was lukewarm toward Pollard, sensing "the delicate condition of American relations with England at the time," as Anthony F. C. Wallace and David J. Jeremy explain in "William Pollard and the Arkwright Patents," *WMQ*, 3d Ser., 34 (1977), 409. On the other hand,

Treasury secretary Alexander Hamilton, on the other hand, wholeheartedly supported technology piracy. Parkinson was a partner of Tench Coxe, Hamilton's trusted assistant. Coxe had contracted with Parkinson to build a mill based on the latter's claim of detailed knowledge of the secret Arkwright machine. Hamilton thought the experiment merited a forty-eight-dollar Treasury subsidy to cover Parkinson's living expenses in the spring of 1791.[7] This episode was one of many instances in which Hamilton's Treasury Department organized and supported raids on Britain's industrial preeminence. Such projects strained Anglo-American relations because, as Anthony F. C. Wallace and David J. Jeremy explain, for "some of the highest officials of the American government to reward the violation of British law by issuing a patent for stolen invention—and thus to encourage similar adventures by other industrial spies—would hardly be considered a friendly act."[8]

Hamilton's efforts to undermine British technological supremacy seem out of character for a statesman whom historians often depict as something between a traitor and an obsessive Anglophile. Boyd long ago charged that Hamilton acted as a British operative in George Washington's cabinet and that his deceptions and betrayals undermined the independent diplomacy Jefferson was trying to orchestrate.[9] Albert Bowman similarly argues that in conceiving American interests "exclusively in terms of a close connection with England," Hamilton's diplomacy grossly misread "the American tradition . . . the American spirit and . . . the American promise."[10] Richard Buel, Jr., holds that Hamilton remained throughout the 1790s "committed to Anglo-American collaboration, even though worsening relations with France eventually made a formal alliance with Britain no longer necessary or even

---

while serving as U. S. minister to the court of Louis XVI, Jefferson participated in attempts to pirate Arkwright's inventions by acquiring carding and spinning machinery built by immigrant English artisans in France. William Bingham to Jefferson, Apr. 16, 1789, Jefferson to Bingham, Sept. 25, 1789, in Boyd et al., eds., *Jefferson Papers*, XV, 55–56, 476–77.

[7] Receipt from Parkinson, July 20, 1791, in Harold C. Syrett et al., eds., *The Papers of Alexander Hamilton*, 27 vols. (New York, 1961–1987), VIII, 588 (hereafter *Hamilton Papers*). Jefferson's and Hamilton's basic agreement in this case is in line with Lawrence S. Kaplan's claim that the Jefferson-Hamilton diplomatic dispute prior to the wars of the French Revolution has been overblown by historians and that "most of the evidence that suggest[s] otherwise belongs to a later stage of the Hamilton Jefferson rivalry," in *Entangling Alliances with None: American Foreign Policy in the Age of Jefferson* (Kent, Ohio, 1987), 77.

[8] Wallace and Jeremy, "William Pollard and the Arkwright Patents," 409.

[9] Boyd, *Number 7: Alexander Hamilton's Secret Attempts to Control American Foreign Policy* (Princeton, 1964), passim.

[10] Bowman, "Jefferson, Hamilton, and American Foreign Policy," *Political Science Quarterly*, 71 (1956), 21, 19.

particularly advantageous."[11] Bradford Perkins writes that Hamilton acted as a double agent in the Washington cabinet, "betraying information" to British representatives and subverting American interests by being "indiscreet, or disloyal."[12] Critics of American diplomacy concur. William Appleman Williams sees Hamilton committed to "an American-British empire embracing most of the world."[13] Jerald A. Combs vilifies Hamilton as a ruthless imperialist, obsessed with heroism, glory, and power, who, to serve his personal ambition, mortgaged American independence to Britain's political and economic interests.[14] And Alexander DeConde has recently portrayed Hamilton as "an ardent Anglophile" intent on frustrating the anti-British initiatives of Jefferson.[15]

Hamilton has always had defenders. From nineteenth-century writers such as Richard Hildreth and John Bach McMaster through twentieth-century analysts such as Samuel Flagg Bemis and Forrest McDonald to Stanley Elkins and Eric McKitrick, scholars have rejected the portrayal of Hamilton as an English dupe and preferred instead a depiction of a highly gifted man who decided it was in the young nation's best interest to throw in its lot with Great Britain. Yet even those who do not rush to condemn Hamilton's policies explain those policies in terms of realistic acquiescence to English superiority. Elkins and McKitrick, for example, declare that an "Anglophile position on virtually everything" is at the core of Hamiltonianism.[16]

In the following pages I take a fresh look at Hamilton's political economy from the perspective of international economic competition.[17] I argue that British and American leaders believed technological

---

[11] Buel, *Securing the Revolution: Ideology in American Politics, 1789–1815* (Ithaca, 1972), 32. John M. Murrin similarly does not distinguish between American diplomacy before and after the outbreak of the wars of the French Revolution, stating that all along it was orchestrated and executed by Hamilton in a pro-British manner, in "The Great Inversion, or Court versus Country: A Comparison of the Revolutionary Settlements in England (1688–1721) and America (1776–1816)," in J.G.A. Pocock, ed., *Three British Revolutions, 1641, 1688, 1776* (Princeton, 1980), 410.

[12] *The Cambridge History of American Foreign Relations,* vol. 1: Perkins, *The Creation of a Republican Empire, 1776–1865* (New York, 1993), 108 n. 22.

[13] Williams, *The Contours of American History* (Cleveland, 1961), 155.

[14] Combs, *The Jay Treaty: Political Battleground of the Founding Fathers* (Berkeley, 1970), 33–49.

[15] DeConde, *Ethnicity, Race, and American Foreign Policy: A History* (Boston, 1992), 18.

[16] Elkins and McKitrick, *The Age of Federalism* (New York, 1993), 128. See also Paul A. Varg, *Foreign Policies of the Founding Fathers,* 2d ed. (Baltimore, 1970), 72.

[17] This general point of view is the core of Paul M. Kennedy's celebrated *The Rise And Fall of Great Powers: Economic Change and Military Conflict from 1500 to 2000* (New York, 1987), esp. 143–58.

competition played a crucial role in the international balance of power and that Hamilton's initiatives in the battle over manufacturing expertise threatened the perceived source of Britain's economic power—its industrial technology. I have stated elsewhere that Hamilton's commercial program "amounted to . . . acquiescence in British restrictions on American commerce."[18] His industrialization plan, on the other hand, challenged Britain's position as the premier industrial power in North America. He was willing, temporarily, to accept his country's skewed balance of trade with England; at the same time, he challenged Britain's industrial superiority by pirating British technology.[19] Hamilton was on the mark when he reflected in 1800: "I may at some time have suggested *a temporary* connection [with Great Britain] for the purpose of cooperating against France . . . but . . . I well remember that the expediency of the measure was always problematical in my mind, and that I have occasionally discouraged it."[20]

Contemporaries correctly pointed out, as have historians since, that Hamilton greatly admired Britain's economic and political power and wanted the United States to emulate it.[21] Yet constructing a British modeled political economy in America did not mean turning the United States into a British satellite. On the contrary. British political economy and economic diplomacy were founded on the assumption of a zero-sum game in which a gain for Britain meant a loss to other countries and vice versa. Transplanting this vision across the Atlantic did not mean that the

---

[18] Ben-Atar, *Origins of Jeffersonian Commercial Polity*, 93–94.

[19] On the impact of Britain's industrialization on its economic rivals see David S. Landes, *The Unbound Prometheus: Technological Change and Industrial Development in Western Europe from 1750 to the Present* (Cambridge, 1969), 124–42. John R. Nelson, Jr., argues that, by accepting the Anglo-American trade pattern, Hamilton "subordinated America to Britain, restricted commercial expansion, and retarded manufacturing," in *Liberty and Property: Political Economy and Policymaking in the New Nation, 1789–1812* (Baltimore, 1987), 165.

[20] Hamilton, "Concerning the Public Conduct and Character of John Adams, Esq.," Oct. 24, 1800, in Syrett et al., eds., *Hamilton Papers*, XXV, 230 n.

[2121] During the Philadelphia Convention, for example, Hamilton declared that the structure of the British government "was the best in the world" and implored the delegates to adopt much of it; "Speech on a Plan of Government," June 18, 1787, ibid., IV, 192. See also James Roger Sharp, *American Politics in the Early Republic: The New Nation in Crisis* (New Haven, 1993), 43. As Herbert Sloan points out, Hamilton's system of finances emulated the British one "only at a very high level of generalization. . . . In America the blank slate allowed Hamilton to begin largely anew, to take the best of contemporary European practices without the accompanying load of historical burdens and shape it to the needs of the new nation"; "'Whatsoever May Remain Unfinished in our System of Public Credit': Second Thoughts on Federalist Finance," in Ben-Atar and Barbara B. Oberg, eds., *Federalists Reconsidered* (forthcoming).

United States would become a weakened British crony but a strong egocentric competing power.[22]

Hamilton's commercial and industrial programs, in spite of their opposing international orientations, complemented one another. Like British neomercantilists of the late eighteenth century, who "combined economic liberalism with economic nationalism," Hamilton, "the preeminent neomercantilist in the United States," favored liberalization of trade, development of the domestic economy, and government sponsorship of home manufactures.[23] He believed that economic independence was inseparable from political independence and was dismayed by the American addiction to manufactured British imports. After securing the financial stability of the nation, Hamilton outlined his vision of government aid to industry. Close examination of Hamilton's supposed anglophilia in relation to his practice of technology piracy reveals a sophisticated and subtle plan of government sponsorship of manufactures that would challenge British industrial preeminence without risking United States involvement in a trade war it could not win.

The Report on Manufactures (ROM), unlike Hamilton's other two financial papers, did not address a specific or immediate fiscal problem. It dared to project the future, expressing the Hamiltonian vision at its fullest. Hamilton put forward a powerful theoretical argument in favor of the federal government's active promotion of manufacturing. He took on the antistatist political economists of the time, particularly Adam Smith and the Physiocrats, who had argued that "manufactures without the aid of government will grow up as soon and as fast, as the natural state of things and the interest of the community may require."[24] Submitted on

---

[22] French and British observers put little stock in Jeffersonian characterizations of the Hamiltonians as British agents. A disillusioned emigrant wrote that even the better informed of the Federalists "still retain a shyness against your countrymen," in *Emigration to America candidly considered in a series of letters, form a gentleman, resident there, to his friend in England* (London, 1798), 43–44. French consuls in America, who frequently warned their superiors that Anglo-American relations were warming up, were not alarmed by Hamilton's supposed bias; Peter P. Hill, *French Perceptions of the Early American Republic, 1783–1793* (Philadelphia, 1988), 35–36.

[23] John E. Crowley, Jr., *The Privileges of Independence: Neomercantilism and the American Revolution* (Baltimore, 1993), 77, 153. See also Harvey Flaumenhaft, *The Effective Republic: Administration and Constitution in the Thought of Alexander Hamilton* (Durham, N.C., 1992), 24–25.

[24] Hamilton, "Report on the Subject of Manufactures," Dec. 5, 1791, in Syrett et al., eds., *Hamilton Papers, X,* z66 (hereafter ROM. All citations to the ROM in this article are to the final draft unless specifically noted). Despite overwhelming scholarly examination that proves the contrary, writes Jacob Ernest Cooke in *Alexander Hamilton* (New York, t982), 99, the "notion that Hamilton was Smith's disciple dies hard." For an analysis of Hamilton's use of Smith's ideas in the ROM

December 5, 1791, the report failed to inspire Congressional legislation because it contained, as the editors of Hamilton's papers note, "few, if any, specific proposals."[25] The report therefore has been evaluated primarily as a theoretical presentation.[26]

On January 15, 1790, the House of Representatives had asked the secretary of the Treasury to prepare a report on the state of American manufactures and devise a plan for their encouragement. Hamilton turned to manufacturing societies that had appeared in many cities in the 1780s for information. The responses had much in common. They described growing industrial activities and at the same time elaborated on the obstacles to manufacturing in the United States.

Overcoming technological backwardness was seen as the key to success. Correspondents from states unable to attract foreign workers, such as South Carolina, blamed their industrial underdevelopment on the shortage of skilled labor.[27] One Connecticut industrialist complained that the price of hats had fallen significantly in the past few months because of "bad Work done which goes to Market & has injured the Credit of

---

see Robert James Parks, *European Origins of the Economic Ideas of Alexander Hamilton* (New York, 1977), chap. 5.

[25] Editorial note, in Syrett et al., eds., *Hamilton Papers*, X, 1. The minimal legislative applicability of the ROM is best exemplified by Hamilton's decision not to recommend high tariffs to protect the infant American industries. See also John F. Kasson, *Civilizing the Machine: Technology and Republican Values in America, 1776-1900* (New York 1977), 35–36.

[26] Attitudes toward the ROM range from ridicule to admiration. Historians who see in the ROM a reflection of a plan for "a systematic fostering of industry by government" include Elkins and McKitrick, *Age of Federalism*, 258; Richard B. Morris, ed., *Alexander Hamilton and the Founding of the Nation* (New York, 1957), 360; Curtis P. Nettels, *The Emergence of a National Economy, 1775-1815* (New York, 1962), 125; Broach's Mitchell, *Alexander Hamilton*, 2 vols. (New York, 1957–1961), II, 143; John C. Miller, *Alexander Hamilton: Portrait in Paradox* (New York, 1959), 283; Forrest McDonald, *Alexander Hamilton: A Biography* (New York, 1979), 233–36; Joseph Dorfman, *The Economic Mind in American Civilization*, 5 vols. (New York, 1946–1959), I, 410; and Samuel Rezneck, "The Rise and Early Development of Industrial Consciousness in the United States, 1760-1830," *Journal of Economic and Business History*, 4 (1932). 790, 797. Studies questioning Hamilton's commitment to manufacturing, arguing that his rhetoric merely masked his preference for monetary manipulations and commercial circles, include Williams, *Contours of American History*, 163; Nelson, *Liberty and Property*, 37–51; and Nelson, "Alexander Hamilton and American Manufacturing: A Reexamination," *Journal of American History*, 65 (1979), 971–95.

[27] Memo to Daniel Stevens from Charleston, S. C., leather manufacturers, Oct. 1791, in Arthur H. Cole, ed., *Industrial and Commercial Correspondence of Alexander Hamilton, Anticipating His Report on Manufactures* (Chicago, 1928), 90. This volume contains the responses to Hamilton's queries.

American Hats very much, & must in time ruin it entirely."[28] Glass manufacturing in Massachusetts was said to be handicapped because entrepreneurs "wait only for Workmen which are engaged & probably on their passage, to commence making Sheet and other Glass."[29] Textile manufacturing in Massachusetts was "destitute of the necessary information," as local investors were "misled by every pretender to knowledge."[30]

Naturally, Hamilton consulted manufacturers who had successfully established factories. These men did not hide the fact that their success depended on their ability to pirate British technology, primarily by enticing skilled British artisans to emigrate. Button production in New Haven, noted a report from John Mix, Jr., received a boost from the arrival of an English worker who "has the Skill perfectly who is a Gentleman who is able and has Engaged to Instruct and teach us every thing Necessary in the making of them."[31] Elisha Colt, manager of the Hartford Woolen Manufactory, emphasized the crucial role played by British artisans in the success of his factory. 'When the company was first established, "We were at that period not only totally unacquainted with the various parts or subdivisions of the Labour; but equally destitute of every kind of Machinery and Labourers for executing such a project—But the news of this infant attempt to establish so usefull a Manufacture soon collected a number of Workmen about us, who had been bred to different branches of the Woolen & Worsted Business in England."[32] Colt boasted that "every part or branch of the Business is managed in the same manner as practised in England." From Providence, Moses Brown wrote that repeated technological failures had halted his attempt to introduce textile manufacturing to Rhode Island until an operator who had worked in English factories came. Brown felt lucky to be approached by "a young

---

[28] O. Burr and Co. to John Chester, Sept. 12, 1791, ibid., 22.

[29] Samuel Breck to Hamilton, Sept. 3, 1791, ibid., 61.

[30] George Cabot to Hamilton, Sept. 6, 1791, ibid., 62. The technological difficulties that led to the downfall of the Pennsylvania Society for the Encouragement of Manufactures and the Useful Arts must also have been known to Hamilton by the time he prepared his report. The society's inferior machinery and untrained laborers produced coarse cloth that was no match for the superior and cheaper British imports. Despite legislative and financial support from the Pennsylvania legislature the factory closed its doors following a fire early in 1790; William R. Bagnall, *The Textile Industries of the United States . . .* , 2 vols. (Cambridge, Mass., 1893), I, 77–79, 84–86.

[31] Mix to Chester, Oct. 7, 1791, in Cole, ed., *Industrial and Commercial Correspondence*, 51–52.

[32] Colt to Chester, Aug. 20, 1791, ibid., 7–8, 9. As Ian Inkster explains, "technology may be organisational rather than mechanical, procedural rather than chemical"; *Science and Technology in History: An Approach to Industrial Development* (New Brunswick, N. J., 1991), 2.

Man then lately Arived at Newyork from Arkwrights works in England."
Brown had to pay a price. The young man, Samuel Slater, demanded and
got complete control of the mill's operation. All the same, the success of
the venture became evident to Brown as early as the summer of 1791.[33]

Among the respondents was the secretary of the Pennsylvania Society
for the Encouragement of Manufactures and the Useful Arts (PSEMUA),
Tench Coxe, who, according to his biographer, was "among the nation's
best-known and most active advocates of manufactures."[34] Coxe had
come out publicly for state and federal support of industrial piracy as
early as 1787.[35] He made sure that the technological deficiencies of
American industry were on the minds of the men who convened in
Philadelphia to frame the new constitution in the summer of that year. On
May 11, three days before the delegates were scheduled to begin
deliberations, Coxe addressed the need for government-sponsored
industrialization in a passionate talk at the home of Benjamin Franklin.
Then, while the convention was in session, on August 9, he called for
importing technology in a public address to the PSEMUA.

The new national government, he told the men gathered at Franklin's,
must support industrialization to provide employment to the *many* who
"will probably emigrate from Europe, who will chuse to continue at their
trades."[36] Artisans would cross the Atlantic because tyranny,

---

[33] Brown to John Dexter, July 22, 1791, in Cole, ed., *Industrial and Commercial
Correspondence*, 73. Slater, Americas most famous industrial recruit, had decided to
leave for the U. S. alter hearing of the premiums and rewards offered to migrating
artisans; George S. White, *Memoir of Samuel Slater, the Father of American
Manufactures Connected with a History of the Rise and Progress of the Cotton
Manufacture in England and America with Remarks on the Moral Influence of
Manufactures in the United States* (Philadelphia, 1831), 37. See also Barbara M.
Tucker, *Samuel Slater and the Origins of the American Textile Industry, 1790–1860*
(Ithaca, 1984).

[34] Cooke, *Tench Coxe and the Early Republic* (Chapel Hill, 1978), 183. Cooke points
out that Hamilton asked for Coxe's assistance in the matter on Oct. 26, 1789, almost
two months before the House of Representatives requested the report. See also
Joseph Stancliffe Davis, *Essays in the Earlier History of American Corporations*, 2
vols. (Cambridge, Mass., 1917), I, 354–57, and Leo Marx, *The Machine in the
Garden: Technology and the Pastoral Ideal in America* (New York, 1964), 151–66.

[35] Coxe was by *no* means the first to advocate such policies. Robert Styrettel Jones,
in an oration delivered in Mar. 1777 at the College of Philadelphia, warned that "if
America is to be wholly indebted to any foreign loom, we may be allowed to
exclaim—adieu to the religion! farewell the liberties of our country"; *American
Museum*, 5 (Mar. 1789), 265.

[36] Coxe, *An Enquiry into the Principles on which a Commercial System for the
United States Should be Founded* (Philadelphia, 1787), 19. A month later, while the
convention was in session, Coxe explained that "there is another grand source from
which supplies of manufacturers may be obtained—Emigration from foreign
countries" — and implored Franklin to persuade his convention colleagues to include

unemployment, low wages, and civil wars in Europe, contrasted with freedom and opportunity in America, "will bring many manufacturers to this asylum for mankind. Ours will be their industry, and, what is of still more consequence, ours will be their skill."[37] America's industrial virginity would work in its favor for, if Europeans continued to improve their machinery, "their people must be driven to us for want of employment, and if, on the other hand, they should return to manual labour, we shall underwork them by these invaluable engines." It was time for the young nation, he declared, to "borrow some of their inventions."[38]

Coxe urged that his listeners and the men who were about to devise the new form of federal government "carefully examine the conduct of Other countries in order to possess ourselves of their methods of encouraging manufactories." He made two specific proposals: grant federally protected exclusive rights over inventions to introducers of technology and make land grants to skilled Europeans who introduce European machinery to the United States.[39] Coxe did not confine himself to words. In the summer of 1787, he recruited Andrew Mitchell to return to England and pirate English textile technology. The scheme was discovered, British officials seized the trunk containing the illegally obtained models and drawings, and Mitchell fled to safe haven at Copenhagen.[40] In the same year, Coxe entered into partnership with a Philadelphia clock maker, Robert Leslie, who was known as a collector of "every model, drawing or description" of European machinery.[41] In 1788, Coxe, together with John Kaighan, reported that the process of coloring leather, although attempted in America, "has not yet been obtained here." They published the process "as communicated by Mr. Philippo, a native of Armenia, who received from the society for the encouragements of arts in London, one hundred pounds sterling, and also the gold medal of the society, as a reward for discovering this secret."[42] Americans "heartily rejoice," declared Coxe in Mathew Carey's *American Museum*,

---

immigration-inducing clauses in the plan for the new government; Coxe to Franklin, June 22, 1786, Franklin Papers.

[37] Coxe; *An Address to an Assembly of the Friends of American Manufactures. Convened for the Purpose of Establishing a Society for the Encouragement of Manufactures and the Useful Arts* (Philadelphia, 1787), 13.

[38] Ibid., 11.

[39] Ibid., 20-22.

[40] Wallace and Jeremy, "William Pollard and Arkwright Patents," 409–10; Cooke, *Tench Coxe*, 107; White, *Memoir of Samuel Slater*, 71.

[41] *Pennsylvania Gazette,* May 27, 1785.

[42] "Extracts from the minutes of the board of managers of the Pennsylvania Society of Arts and Manufactures," *American Museum*, 5 (Jan. 1789), 51, 52.

"in the early success of our endeavours to obtain" Europe's industrial secrets.[43]

When Coxe wrote of technological rivalry, he had only 'Great Britain in mind.[44] During the colonial period, "it was the unvaried policy of Great Britain, to discourage manufactures," and after the separation Britain continued to block the westward flow of technology.[45] In England, Lord Sheffield's 1783 attack on Anglo-American economic reconciliation showed that Coxe was not off the mark. Sheffield held that it would "be a long time before the Americans can manufacture for themselves." The high cost of labor would discourage investors. Skilled immigrants, tempted by the affordability and availability of land, would abandon their trades: "they will not work at manufactures when they can get double the profit by farming."[46] Sheffield's views were backed by British agents in

---

[43] Coxe, "Address to the Friends of American Manufactures," Oct. 20, 1788, ibid., IV, 342. Coxe, together with Clymer, wrote that because the high cost of labor had hitherto delayed the development of American manufactures, the acquisition of machines must receive top priority; ibid., 407.

[44] Historians question England's technological superiority and leadership in the Industrial Revolution. Eugene S. Ferguson and Thomas C. Cochran have persuasively argued that the American jack-of-all-trades was technologically superior to the specialized British worker. John J. McCusker and Russell R. Menard believe that by the Revolution American industry was ready to take off independently of Great Britain. Ferguson, "The American-ness of American Technology," *Technology and Culture*, 20 (1979), 3–24; Cochran, *Frontiers of Change: Early Industrialization in America* (New York, 1981); McCusker and Menard, *The Economy of British America, 1607–1789* (Chapel Hill, 1985), 281. European historians conclude that British industrialization was gradual and that the industrialization of other European countries, most notably France, was more balanced and humane, though not technologically inferior. Rondo Cameron, "A New View of European Industrialization," *Economic History Review*, 2d Ser., 38 (1985), 1–23; Robert Aldrich, "Late-Corner or Early-Starter? New Views on French Economic History," *Journal of European Economic History*, 16 (1987), 89–100. I do not argue that England was or was not the leader or model of modern industrialization but that Hamilton, Coxe, and their contemporaries believed it to be so. As Harris writes, the extent of foreign espionage *effort* in England "testifies beyond doubt to the intensity with which the new English technology was desired." Contemporaries believed in the centrality of technology to the industrialization and consequently "had few scruples as to what they did to filch it away"; Harris, "Industrial Espionage in the Eighteenth Century," 137, 136.

[45] Coxe, "Address to the Friends of American Manufactures," 346.

[46] John Baker Holroyd, Lord Sheffield), *Observations on the Commerce of the American States with Europe and the West Indies . . .* (Philadelphia, 1783), 38, 39. Many others shared Sheffield's view. A customs official from Newry, Ire., for example, reported in Aug. 1783 that the passengers on the 3 ships that had just left for America were not the most skilled workers but the lower order of tradesmen." He added that immigrants were sending back reports that were "very discouraging,

the United States who labored to retard American technological development. Coxe pointed out that, in 1787, the British consul in Philadelphia, Phineas Bond, bought four carding and spinning machines that had been smuggled out of Britain and shipped them back to Liverpool. Such actions, Coxe hoped, would wake American industrialists to the "dictates of national and commercial rivalship" in the all-out battle for technology. He urged the several states to adopt a "prudential spirit of jealousy and circumspection" and imitate Pennsylvania, which, following the Bond incident, had enacted legislation "to prevent the exportation of machines, and enticing *away* artizans."[47]

Coxe's reply to the Treasury secretary's query in 1790 was upbeat. He expressed enthusiasm about the prospects of industrialization in the Philadelphia area; his main concern was the need for labor and industrial know-how.[48] Hamilton, doubtless impressed by Coxe's knowledge and connections, appointed him assistant secretary of the Treasury and entrusted him with organizing the data of the inquiry and preparing the first draft of the ROM. By the end of winter 1790-1791, Coxe had drafted the report.

Coxe repeated the themes he had elaborated in the 1780s American manufactures were plagued by labor problems. Labor was scarce, wages were high, and the United States did not have competent operators versed in modern techniques. Coxe proposed three remedies. First, the United States should import modern machinery that used fewer workers, thereby reducing competition for laborers and bringing wages under control. Second, women and children, who earned much lower wages, should do the unskilled work. Third, the United States government should campaign aggressively to persuade European artisans to emigrate.[49]

Inducing emigration was pivotal to the program's success. Yet how could a nonmanufacturing, capital-starved economy attract skilled workers? Coxe proposed setting apart "five hundred thousand acres, of a

---

and will probably continue to damp the spirit of emigration"; quoted by Maldwyn A. Jones, "Ulster Emigration, 1783-1815," in E.R.R. Green, ed., *Essays in Scotch-Irish History* (London, 1969), 51. British industrialist Henry Wansey, who toured the U. S. in the mid-1790s, was highly skeptical of its textile manufacturing potential; Jeremy, ed., *Henry Wansey and His American Journal* (Philadelphia, 1970),102–03.

[47] Coxe, "Address to the Friends of American Manufactures," 342. For Bond's account see Bond to Lord Carmarthen, Nov. 20, 1787, in J. Franklin Jameson, ed., "Letters of Phineas Bond, British Consul at Philadelphia, to the Foreign Office . . . , 1787, 1788, 1789," *American Historical Association Annual Report for the Year 1896*, 2 vols. (Washington, D. C., 1897), I, 552–55. The best secondary work on Bond is Joanne Loewe Neel, *Phineas Bond: A Study in Anglo-American Relations, 1786-1812* (Philadelphia, 1968).

[48] Coxe to Hamilton, Nov. 30, 1789, in Syrett et al., eds., *Hamilton Papers*, V, 569–70.

[49] Coxe's 2d draft of the ROM, ibid., XXVI, 636.

good quality and advantageously situated," to grant first introducers or establishers of new and useful manufactories, arts machines, & secrets not before possessed, known or carried on in the United States."[50] A fund under the direction of the president was to remunerate introducers of items or ideas that "will not yield an immediate or adequate benefit" in the market.[51] Persons who brought in "manufacturing Machinery and secrets of great value" should be rewarded with "such exclusive privileges for a term of years as would have been secured by patent had they been the inventors."[52] Coxe concluded the draft by explaining that "those great Instruments of Manufacture in the European Nations, labor-saving Machines," were crucial to American industrial development and that the present state of American manufacturing made governmental efforts to help secure such machines politically and economically prudent.[53]

Hamilton reworked and expanded Coxe's draft five times before submitting his report to Congress almost a year later.[54] He introduced new

---

[50] Ibid., 638–39.

[51] Paper "A," ibid., X, 18-19 n. 52.

[52] Coxe's 2d draft of the ROM, ibid., XXVI, 639.

[53] Ibid., 646–47.

[54] As Hamilton's best modern biographer puts it, "during the torrid summer of 1791, Hamilton stuck to his desk, turning out draft after draft," revising the original Coxe plan and taking on the philosophy of laissez faire; Cooke, *Alexander Hamilton*, 99. So different was the final product that Cooke and Nelson, the two authorities on the ROM, conclude that Hamilton added many theoretical arguments but eliminated Coxe's practical suggestions. The reason, they suggest, is that Coxe's program, fully carried out, would have cut down significantly the need for British imports and thus undermined Hamilton's financial plans, first, by reducing the government revenues Hamilton counted on to finance the public debt and, second, by checking the economic power of merchants trading with England, the very group whose allegiance to the national government Hamilton deemed crucial to its survival. Cooke and Nelson exonerate Coxe of any international partiality and place the responsibility for the plan's supposed anglophilic shortcomings at Hamilton's door. Cooke concludes that Hamilton saw nothing wrong with the nation's continuing dependence on English manufactured imports. Nelson even questions Hamilton's "commitment to the economic development of the United States," charging that he "acted in a manner unquestionably hostile to domestic manufacturers" and that he abandoned "domestic manufacturers to their British competitors." Cooke, *Tench Coxe*, 183; Nelson, *Liberty and Property*, 53, 37, 52. See also Marx, *Machine in the Garden*, 167–68, and Douglass Adair, "The Tenth *Federalist* Revisited," *WMQ*, 3d Ser., 8 (1951), 54. Nelson's contention that the ROM was actually an attempt to stall the development of American manufactures would have come as a surprise to con-temporaries like James Madison, who feared it planned to sacrifice the *interests* of the entire nation for the sake of developing manufactures. Madison to Henry Lee, Jan. 21, 1792, in William T. Hutchinson et at., eds., *The Papers of James Madison*, 17 vols. (Chicago, 1962–1977; Charlottesville, 1977–), XIV, 193–94. As Andrew

ideas, expanded some proposals, modified others, and did not endorse Coxe's call for protective tariffs.[55] His additions and subtractions did not affect the anti-British spirit of Coxe's draft.[56] Hamilton's report projected a powerful neomercantilist vision that maintained the challenge to England's industrial preeminence in North America.

Hamilton agreed that technological deficiencies accounted for the great disparity between American and European manufacturing and that the gap would be "diminished in proportion to the use which can be made of machinery."[57] With modern technology, American manufacturing would catch up. The process need not take long. The great technological

---

Shankman explains, Nelson fails to distinguish between support for manufacturers and support for manufacturing. Hamilton favored state-sponsored enterprises like the SEUM precisely because he doubted that small American manufacturers could compete with English industry; "Alexander Hamilton, Manufacturing, and the Transition to Capitalism in America" (unpublished paper). See also Edward C. Papenfuse's review of Nelson's *Liberty and Property* in *American Historical Review,* 94 (1989), 1170–71.

[55] Hamilton explained his hostility to tariffs in *Federalist No.* 35, writing that they bring about "the oppression of particular branches of industry, . . . an unequal distribution of the taxes," and "render other classes of the community tributary, in an improper degree, to the manufacturing classes, to whom *they* give a premature monopoly of the markets"; Madison, Hamilton, and John Jay, *The Federalist Papers,* ed. Isaac Kramnick (New York, 1987), 231. See also Crowley, *Privileges of Independence,* 148.

[56] The international implications of the technological campaign of the ROM have by and large been ignored by historians. Alan I. Marcus and Howard P. Segal note that the ROM "may have smacked of industrial espionage" but leave it at that, in *Technology in America: A Brief History* (New York, 1989), 45. Gilbert L. Lycan, who seeks to balance Hamilton's "bad press through the years," ignores the report on manufactures and its diplomatic ramifications, in *Alexander Hamilton and American Foreign Policy: A Design for Greatness* (Norman, Okla., 1970), viii. McDonald's biography of Hamilton mentions the call to circumvent English laws but fails to develop the issue; *Alexander Hamilton,* 231. Nor do Mitchell, *Alexander Hamilton,* II, 145; Helene Johnson Looze, *Alexander Hamilton and the British Orientation of American Foreign Policy, 1783–1803* (The Hague, 1969), 111; and Morton J. Frisch, *Alexander Hamilton and the Political Order: An Interpretation of His Political Thought and Practice* (Lanham, Md., 1991), 41-51. Gerald Stourzh, an exception, challenged those historians who were quick to judge Hamilton's "sometimes treasonable accommodation with Britain" to examine "how could a man bent on the constant appeasement of Britain devise the *Report on Manufactures* with its theory of the protection of infant industries?" in *Alexander Hamilton and the Idea of Republican Government* (Stanford, 1970), 198–99.

[57] Hamilton, ROM, in Syrett et al., eds., *Hamilton Papers,* X, 271. Hamilton pointed to the example of the Hartford woolen manufactory's heavy reliance on English technology as the model of American industrialization. See also Jeremy, *Transatlantic Industrial Revolution: The Diffusion of Textile Technologies between Britain and America* (Cambridge, Mass., 1981), 20.

advances of the preceding twenty years, for example, were responsible for "the immense progress" of British textile industrial output. The forward movement was all the more remarkable because it was achieved without drawing on the agricultural labor supply.[58]

Technology could be acquired by smuggling up-to-date machinery out of England and by inducing skilled workers to move to the United States and build the machines they had operated in Europe.[59] Hamilton believed that "Machinery forms an item of great importance in the general mass of national industry."[60] He warned that to "procure all such machines as are known in any part of Europe, can only require a proper provision and due pains." He explained that America had an advantage over Europe in its abundant supplies of raw materials and energy sources needed to construct and operate advanced machinery. Moreover, modern machinery required fewer operators, which was appropriate for a young country with a chronic labor shortage.[61]

Machine importation, however, was problematic. Americans could not build machines from European manuals because few inventions were ever published. Even those recorded in magazines were not translatable into actual machines because the descriptions and drawings lacked specificity and clarity.[62] In theory, patented English inventions could be examined by the public in the London patent office during the term of the patent, but the knowledge required to conduct an effective search rendered copying specifications all but impossible.[63] Moreover, seventeenth- and eighteenth-

---

[58] Hamilton, ROM, in Syrett et al., eds., *Hamilton Papers*, X, 252. Hamilton borrowed this example directly from Coxe, who used it first in 1787 in *An Address to an Assembly of the Friends of American Manufactures*, 13–14.

[59] Hamilton, ROM, in Syrett et al., eds., *Hamilton Papers*, X, 249.

[60] Ibid., 251.

[61] Ibid., 272. As H. J. Habakkuk has shown in *American and British Technology in the Nineteenth Century: The Search for Labour-Saving Inventions* (Cambridge, 1962), American labor shortages made American industries unusually willing to take risks and adopt modern machinery in hopes of replacing operators with machines.

[62] Harris, "Movements of Technology between Britain and Europe in the Eighteenth Century," in Jeremy, ed., *International Technology Transfer: Europe, Japan and the USA, 1700–1914* (Brookfield, Vt., 1991), 12–13; H. I. Dutton, *The Patent System and Inventive Activity during the Industrial Revolution, 1750–1852* (Manchester, Eng., 1984), 21. For an opposing view on the value of drawings to technology diffusion see Ferguson, "The Mind's Eye: Nonverbal Thought in Technology," *Science*, New Ser., 197 (1977), 827–36. Ferguson, however, agrees that drawings played a minimal role in the diffusion of knowledge in the early republic, in "Technology as Knowledge," in Edwin T. Layton, Jr., ed., *Technology and Social Change in America* (New York, 1973), 14.

[63] "Industrial espionage on site or the defection of workmen was much more likely to spring the secret than was anyone searching for the specification in Whitehall"; Christine MacLeod, "The Paradoxes of Patenting: Invention and Its Diffusion in

century technical improvements were "more of a 'knack' than an invention." When a machine was taken apart and sent to the United States, only those who had operated it in England could put it back together and make it work. Such was the case with the carding machines Bond had sent back to England. They sat idle in America for more than three years because no one knew how to reassemble them.[64] Successful acquisition of prohibited English industrial knowledge thus depended on the emigration of skilled operators and factory managers.[65]

Hamilton understood this. In order to compete with the British textile industry, he wrote in the SEUM prospectus, Americans must have a better-qualified work force, competitive pricing, and additional capital for investment. His two reports on public credit addressed these last two needs. Skilled workers were "an essential ingredient" of American industrialization, yet thus far efforts "employed have not generally been adequate to the purpose of procuring them from abroad."[66] In the ROM, Hamilton explained that "progress of particular manufactures has been much retarded by the want of skilful workmen." Leaving it to individual entrepreneurs to rectify this imbalance would not produce the desired results, because "the capitals employed here are not equal to the purposes of bringing from abroad workmen of a superior kind." The federal

---

18th- and 19th-Century Britain, France, and North America," *Technology and Culture*, 32 (1991), 898. Because registering a patent in England included no objective examination and "involved purely clerical acts," most of the patents registered were of dubious utility; John N. Adams and Gwen Averley, "The Patent Specification: The Role of *Liardet v. Johnson*," *Journal of Legal History*, 7 (Sept. 1986),159–60. On the other hand, many developments were not registered because of the cost involved in registration and protection of patents. See, for example, Allan A. Gomme, "Patent Practice in the 18th Century: The Diary of Samuel Taylor, Threadmaker and Inventor, 1722–1723," *Journal of the Patent Office Society*, 19 (Apr. 1937), 256-72.

[64] MacLeod, *Inventing the Industrial Revolution: The English Patent System, 1660–1800* (Cambridge, 1988), 108. As Jeremy explains, American mechanics had a hard time putting together the spinning mule Bond shipped back because it was a novel design combining the early Arkwright water frame and Hargreaves jenny. "Only a competent mechanic already acquainted with the machine could have made sense of a box of mule parts"; "British Textile Technology Transmission to the United States: The Philadelphia Region Experience, 1770–1820," *Business Hist. Rev.*, 47 (1973), 40.

[65] Peter Mathias, "Skills and the Diffusion of Innovations from Britain in the Eighteenth Century," *Transactions of the Royal Historical Society*, 5th Ser., 25 (1975), 93–113; Cochran, *Frontiers of Change*, 14; Jeremy, *Transatlantic Industrial Revolution*, 43–49; A. E. Musson and Eric Robinson, *Science and Technology in the Industrial Revolution* (Manchester, Eng., 1969), 85.

[66] Hamilton, "Prospectus of the Society for Establishing Useful Manufactures," Aug. 1791, in Syrett et al., eds., *Hamilton Papers*, IX, 146.

government through some "auxiliary agency" must manage this "source of valuable acquisitions to the country."[67]

There was no difference between Hamilton's and Coxe's views on the centrality of emigration. Both believed that enticing foreign—that is, British—workers to emigrate to the United States was the surest and quickest way to get the knowledge. Coxe came at the issues from the perspective of industrializing Philadelphia. Hamilton understood the larger domestic and international ramifications of an enticement program and used the public pages of the ROM to explain and advocate his position.

As Hamilton knew, the dominant agricultural sector would resist government sponsorship of competing employment in manufactures. Former physician-in-chief of the Continental army John Morgan, for example, wrote in 1789 that manufacturing was suited to a country "fully stocked with inhabitants." America's labor shortage meant to Morgan that industrialization would have to come at the expense of agriculture, which was the real source of national wealth.[68] To counter "dearness of labour" objections, Hamilton followed Coxe's lead and played on the national mood favoring population growth. He promised that manufactures "will have the strongest tendency to multiply the inducements" to foreign emigration.[69] He realized, however, that this promise would not *alleviate* the widespread fears that industrialization would further deplete the already labor-starved agricultural sector. He elaborated: the advantage of manufacturing is its "tendency to draw emigrants from foreign countries." Artisans would not come unless they could find employment in their familiar line of work because "men are commonly reluctant to quit one course of occupation and livelihood for another." And America had much to offer: higher wages, cheaper raw materials, and political liberty. European migrants, Hamilton promised, would industrialize America. They had already become a reliable source of labor and innovation. Go through the towns of America and see the large proportion of ingenious and valuable workmen, in different arts and trades, who, by expatriating from Europe, have improved their own condition, and added to the industry and wealth of the United States. It is a natural inference from the experience, we have already had, that as soon as the United States shall present the countenance of serious prosecution of Manufactures—as soon as foreign artists be made sensible that the state of things *here* affords a moral certainty of employment and encouragement—competent numbers

---

[67] Hamilton, ROM,   X, 339
[68] Morgan, "Whether it be most beneficial to the united states to promote agriculture, or to encourage the mechanic arts and manufactures," *American Museum*, 6 (July 1789), 73-74
[69] Hamilton, ROM, in Syrett et al., eds., *Hamilton Papers*, X, 271, 214. 800 also Coxe's 2d draft of the ROM, ibid., XXVI, 633.

of European workmen will transplant themselves, effectually to ensure the success of the design.

In sum, American manufactures would, "in a great measure trade upon a foreign Stock."[70] The agricultural and commercial sectors would also benefit, as this "fruitful mean of augmenting the population"[71] would result in higher prices for agricultural products without "deducting from the hands, which might otherwise be drawn to tillage."[72]

Why would a considerable number of skilled European artisans move to the United States? Hamilton's answer was that artisans would value higher wages, cheaper provisions, lighter taxes, and political and religious freedoms. Yet he did not wish to imply that the disparity, as Americans saw it, would be sufficient inducement. If that were the case, then Congress would not have to promote emigration. This delicate balancing act—predicting that America would naturally attract skilled emigrants *yet* not lulling Congress into inaction—made its way into the final version of the ROM, where Hamilton inserted a statement that immigration would flow "as soon as foreign artists shall be made sensible that the state of things here affords a moral certainty of employment and encouragement."[73] On the one hand, the workers would be drawn by objective conditions to cross the Atlantic of their own accord. On the other hand, active dissemination of the news of an aggressive industrialization effort in America was necessary to make sure that European workers would learn of the opportunities and be moved to migrate.

Hamilton endorsed many of Coxe's emigration-inducing proposals such as travel subsidies for artisans and customs exemption for their tools, implements of trade, and household furniture. Most important, he came out strongly in favor of granting an inventor monopoly to introducers of technology. That issue had surfaced the previous year during debate on the Patent Act the Congress passed in 1790. The president had asked Congress in his annual message of January of that year to enact legislation encouraging "the introduction of new and useful invention from

---

[70] Hamilton, 3d draft of the ROM, ibid., X, 82; Hamilton, ROM, ibid., 270–71; see similar reporting on the impact of immigrants on American manufactures in *Universal Asylum and Columbian Magazine,* 7 (Nov. 1791), 328.

[71] Hamilton, 3d draft of ROM, in Syrett et al., eds., *Hamilton Papers,* X. 82.

[72] Hamilton, ROM, ibid., 254. The opposition was not persuaded. James Logan charged that "under the *pretext* of serving *the agricultural interest,*" Hamilton asked Congress to "grant exclusive privileges, bounties, and premiums, *to a few monied men,* to encourage them to extensive manufactures, and to enable them import from Europe, necessary machines and workmen"; *American Museum,* 12 (Oct. 1792), 216–17.

[73] Hamilton, ROM, is Syrett et al., *eds., Hamilton Papers,* X, 270.

abroad."[74] The House of Representatives version of the bill followed English law in giving to the first importer of technology the monopoly privileges accorded to original inventors.[75] But the Senate amended the bill to grant patent monopolies only to inventors of machines "not before known or used" and deleted the location qualifier "within the United States."[76] In the ROM, Hamilton urged Congress to revise the Patent Act of 1790, explaining that the United States must employ the same methods "which have been employed with success in other Countries."[77]

Yet Hamilton did not actively campaign for modeling United States patent law on that of Britain. In his first draft, Hamilton revised Coxe's call for awarding patent privileges to introducers with the qualifying clause, "if within the compass of the powers of the government."[78] He realized that, far from indicating a sudden conversion to the doctrine of strict construction, the prohibition on patents of importation could be circumvented without changing the language of the law. Applicants could claim the rights of inventors by slightly improving European inventions. Parkinson and Pollard received patents under just such a pretext. And Hamilton supported the patent application of William Pearce, a British textile operator, even though he recognized that the latter's claim to originality was unfounded and that Pearce was merely introducing to America techniques already under monopoly protection in England.[79]

---

[74] Washington to Congress, Jan. 8,1790, in Walter Lowerie and Matthew St. Clair Clark. eds.. *American State Papers, Documents. Legislative and Executive*, 38 vols. (Washington, D.C., 1832–1861), Foreign Affairs, 1, 12.

[75] Pamela O. Long. "Invention, Authorship, 'Intellectual Property,' and the Origin of Patents: Notes toward a Conceptual History," *Technology and Culture*, 32 (1991). 877; Floyd L. Vaughan, *The United States Patent System: Legal and Economic Conflicts in American Patent History* (Norman, Okla., 1956), 13.

[76] Linda G. De Pauw et al., eds., *Documentary History of the First Federal Congress of the United States of America*, vol. I: *Senate Legislative Journal* (Baltimore, 1972), 271 n. 91; ibid., vol. 6: *Legislative Histories* (Baltimore, 1986), 1632–33. There is little record of public debate or opposition to the measure. Philadelphia iron worker Richard Wells had petitioned against patents of importation. But why did the Senate prefer Wells's position over the president's? "Richard Wells Petition," Mar. 2, 1790, and Wells to Henry Wynkoop, Mar. 3, 1790, Records of the U. S. House of Representatives, HR 1A-E1, National Archives, Washington, D.C. See also Steven Lubar, "The Transformation of Antebellum Patent Law," *Technology and Culture*, 32 (1991), 935·

[77] Hamilton, ROM, in Syrett et al., eds., *Hamilton Papers*, X, 296.

[78] Hamilton, 1st draft of the ROM, ibid., X, 37.

[79] Hamilton to the Directors of the SEUM, Dec. 7, 1791, ibid., 345. For an excellent summary of the Pearce episode see Boyd et al., eds., *Jefferson Papers*, XX, 315–22. Pearce, Parkinson, and Pollard competed over who would have the rights to Arkwright's technology in America. Pearce, unlike Pollard and Parkinson, did not receive a patent. All 3 were involved in failed enterprises whereas Slater, who did not petition for a federal patent, succeeded; Wallace and Jeremy, "William Pollard

Hamilton also agreed with Coxe that Congress should promote new under-takings and promise rewards to introducers of industrial secrets. Yet his first revision of Coxe's draft eliminated the idea of offering land as an inducement, noting that the manner of inducing such migration "will be submitted hereafter."[80] According to John R. Nelson, Jr., Hamilton scrapped the plan because such aggressive recruitment would develop American manufactures at the expense of Great Britain.[81] But the mechanics who might have responded to the promise of land would have been those inclined to change their trades.

While threatening to attract skilled artisans from Britain, the proposal would actually have limited American competitiveness by leading them to abandon their trades. If Hamilton really feared offending Great Britain, why did he retain introducer monopoly and travel subsidies? Those programs, after all, directly challenged British industrial supremacy.[82]

Hamilton omitted the land-grant proposal because he believed that men were naturally inclined to become farmers. He feared that immigrant artisans would yield to the temptation of bucolic life and not remain in urban centers to develop their trades. "The desire of being a proprietor of lands depends upon such strong principles in the human breast, that where the opportunity of acquiring is so easy as it is in the United States the proportion must be small of those, whose circumstances would

---

and the Arkwright Patents," 410. The evolving historical reputations of Slater and Arkwright offer a valuable insight into the differing cultural attitudes toward technological piracy in England and the U.S. Arkwright's prestige was damaged when his originality was challenged in the early 19th century. Slater's standing as the founder of America's industry was unaffected by his industrial piracy; Jeremy, "British and American Entrepreneurial Values in the Early Nineteenth-Century: A Parting of the Ways?" in Robert A. Burchell, ed., *The End of Anglo-America: Historical Essays in the Study of Cultural Divergence* (Manchester, Eng., 1991), 34–42. I thank David J. Jeremy for helping me sort out this thorny issue.

[80] Hamilton, 1st draft of the ROM, in Syrert et al., eds., *Hamilton Papers*, X, 36–37.

[81] Nelson, *Liberty and Property*, 46–47.

[82] Madison thought that Coxe's "idea of appropriating a district of territory to the encouragement of imported inventions is new and worthy of consideration." But Madison feared that the plan could not be enacted under the Constitution because "Congress seem to be tied down to the single mode of encouraging inventions by granting the exclusive benefit of them for a limited time, and therefore to have no more power to give a further encouragement out of a fund of land than a fund of money." Madison explained to Coxe that he had proposed a clause to this effect in Philadelphia, but his proposal was "expressly rejected"; Madison to Coxe, Mar. 28, 1790, in Hutchinson et al., eds., *Madison Papers*, XIII, 128. Hamilton was not a strict constructionist, and I do not believe he rejected the program on these constitutional grounds.

otherwise lead to it, that would be diverted from the pursuit toward manufactures."[83]

Population and migration patterns in the second half of the eighteenth century lend some credence to Hamilton's observation. The South and Southwest were growing so rapidly by immigration that North Carolina, for example, which around 1760 had roughly the same number of people as New York, twenty years later had gone ahead by about sixty thousand.[84] Contemporaries assumed that the trend would continue and that immigrants, even skilled artisans, would become farmers. In eliminating the land-grant program Hamilton was not driven by a reluctance to confront Great Britain. Rather, he did not share Coxe's confidence in the natural superiority and attraction of manufacturing, and he feared that skilled immigrants would flow to the fields of the South and Southwest without sharing their precious trade secrets with their new countrymen.[85]

In his fourth draft, Hamilton expanded upon another one of Coxe's suggestions. He proposed a federally funded board, similar to the PSEMUA, which would "defray the expences of the emigration of Artists and Manufacturers in particular branches of extraordinary importance" and promote "the prosecution and introduction of useful discoveries, inventions & improvements by proportionate rewards judiciously held out and applied." American manufacturing, he repeated, was hampered by "the want of skilful workmen," and the federal government should subsidize the numerous "workmen, in every branch, who are prevented from emigrating solely by the want of means." The very same fund could

---

[83] Hamilton, 3d draft of the ROM, in Syrett et al., eds., *Hamilton Papers*, X, 91. For the final version see ibid., 250-51 Franklin similarly commented in 1784 that "the cheapness of land [in America was] inclining *many* to leave trades for agriculture." "Information for those who would wish to remove to America," *American Museum*, 2 (Sept. 1787), 214. See also Richard L. Bushman, "Freedom and Prosperity in the American Revolution," in Larry R. Gerlach, James A. Dolph, and Michael L. Nicholls, eds., *Legacies of the American Revolution* (Logan, Utah, 1978), 61-83.

[84] Drew R. McCoy, "James Madison and Visions of American Nationality in the Confederation Period: A Regional Perspective," in Richard Beeman, Stephen Botein and Edward C. Carter II, eds., *Beyond Confederation: Origins of the Constitution and American National Identity* (Chapel Hill, 1987), 230-32.

[85] Hamilton, ROM, in Syrett et al., eds., *Hamilton Papers*, X, 254, 270-71. To the extent that historians of early national occupational and geographical mobility have been able to track individuals through time, they confirm Hamilton's fears. See, for example, Wallace, *Rockdale: The Growth of an American Village in the Early Industrial Revolution* (New York, 1978), 63-65. This geographical tilt is all the more important in light of, as David Brion Davis has recently suggested, Hamilton's intention to "liberate the northern states from dependence on slave systems"; "The Triumph of the Country," *New York Review of Books, 41* (May 12, 1994), 28.

also be used to "procure and import foreign improvements"—that is, machines.[86]

This idea was so central to his vision that Hamilton made it the conclusion of the ROM. He explained that societies like the PSEMUA were "truly invaluable"; "there is scarcely any thing," he wrote, "which has been devised, better calculated to excite a general spirit of improvement." But the funds of such local voluntary associations "have been too contracted" to launch an adequate incentive campaign. The United States could not wait for patriotic private entrepreneurs to undertake the costly effort of bringing over machines and artisans from Europe.[87] The "public purse must supply the deficiency of private resources." What is more useful, Hamilton concluded, than "prompting and improving the efforts of industry?"[88]

Promotion of legal and illegal emigration was as old as British New World colonization.[89] As Bernard Bailyn has shown, anxiety over depopulation of the countryside became pronounced in England in the 1760s.[90] But Hamilton's proposed industrialization program went farther than the pre-Revolutionary recruiting of farmers and indentured servants.

---

[86] Hamilton, 4th draft of the ROM, in Syrett et al., eds., *Hamilton Papers*, X, 228-29.

[87] Hamilton, ROM, ibid., 339-40.

[88] Ibid., 340. As Peter F. Drucker has explained, Hamilton rejected the prevailing economic view of the 18th century that assumed that economic resources were limited and unlikely to grow significantly. Thus the U.S., which appeared in 1790 to be a conglomerate of sections and interests about to explode, survived all those crises, save slavery, with economic growth the glue; "On the 'Economic Basis' of American Politics," *The Public Interest, No.* 10 (1968), 35. J.G.A Pocock writes that "Hamilton can be said to have added a fourth term to the triad of Montesquieu, showing that if virtue is the principle of republics, interest is that of empires, so that a nonclassical federalism is necessary if the republic is to be also an empire," in *The Machiavellian Moment: Florentine Political Thought and the Atlantic Republican Tradition* (Princeton, 1975), 530. Cecelia Kenyon, on the other hand, argued that Hamilton *was* inspired by the idealism of the collective over the egoism of the natural rights theory of Jefferson and Madison. His view "of the public good was the older, corporate one . . . in which the corporate element, though still present, had given ground to individualism," in "Alexander Hamilton: Rousseau of the Right," *Political Science Quarterly*, 73 (1958), 175

[89] For example, one William Cunningham, who was executed in London on Aug. 10, 1791, in confessing his criminal past, recalled that in the 1770s he worked at enticing English mechanics "to ship themselves for America, on promises of great advantage, and then, artfully getting an indenture upon them; in consequence of which, on their arrival in America they are sold or obliged to serve a term of years for the passage"; *American Apollo*, 1(1792), 68-69.

[90] Bailyn, *Voyagers to the West: A Passage in the Peopling of America on the Eve of the Revolution* (New York, 1986), 29-66. See also Mildred Campbell, "English Emigration on the Eve of the American Revolution," *American Historical Review*, 61(1955),1–20.

It targeted the men the British most desired to keep. The government resented such unabashed, state-sanctioned flouting of British law. On a less principled level, officials and manufacturers feared the economic consequences of skilled workers' emigration and growing foreign competition.

The ROM was shelved in America, but in Britain it took on a life of its own. The SEUM founders counted on circulating the report in England to attract industrial immigrants.[91] Thomas Digges, accused double agent, embezzler, and industrial spy, had 1,000 copies printed in Dublin in 1792 and circulated among the manufacturing societies of Britain and Ireland.[92] He believed the report would "induce artists to move towards a Country so likely to very soon give them ample employ & domestic ease."[93] The Dublin edition was "destributed & Sold cheap," reported Edinburgh bookseller Samuel Paterson. Yet the ROM's encouragement to "the poor distressed Subjects of these States to flock to America" antagonized "the great people & Landed Interest [who] discourage Emigrations to America, as Well as governments."[94]

In the 1780s and early 1790s, British representatives in the United States kept their London superiors informed about American appropriation of British technology. Phineas Bond dedicated much of his official correspondence to it. Major George Beckwith, who discussed the possibility of an Anglo-American alliance with Hamilton in 1790, alarmingly reported the arrival of a model of Arkwright's machine in America. When the ROM and the SEUM plan became public, British officials immediately understood their explosiveness. As David J. Jeremy has explained, if Hamilton's industrialization program had proved as successful as his stabilization of American finances, Britain could have lost much of its export trade—worth more than $15 million in 1791 alone—to the United States.[95] Bond urged vigorous prosecution of laws "against seducing manufacturers and conveying away implements of

---

[91] Davis, *Essays*, 1, 489.

[92] William Bell Clark, "In Defense of Thomas Digges," *Pennsylvania Magazine of History and Biography*, 77 (1953). 381–438; Carroll W. Pursell, Jr., "Thomas Digges and William Pearce: An Example of the Transit of Technology," *WMQ* 3d Ser., 21 (1964), 551–60; Lynn Hudson Parsons, "The Mysterious Mr. Digges," ibid., 22 (1965), 486–92.

[93] Digges to Hamilton, Apr. 6, 1792, in Syrett et al., eds., *Hamilton Papers*, XI, 242.

[94] Paterson to Hamilton, Feb. 16, 1793, ibid., XIV, 87. Paterson then repeated a suggestion he made two years earlier "to give Some Encouragement to Ships bringing over Passengers of Certain Descriptions."

[95] Jeremy, *Henry Wansey*, 30. On the centrality of the American markets to British manufactures see also Nelson, *Liberty and Property*, 54; Combs, *Jay Treaty*, 25; and Samuel Flagg Bemis, *Jay's Treaty: A Study in Commerce and Diplomacy*, rev. ed. (New Haven, 1962), 49.

manufacturing."[96] The British minister in Philadelphia, George Hammond, expected the federal government to support fully the proposed program because "Mr. Hamilton's reputation is so materially involved in the result of the experiment."[97] England must now energetically enforce the prohibitions on technology export, he wrote to Grenville, "to prevent the emigration and exportation of machines necessary to the different branches of manufactures."[98] Beckwith reported to the governor of Canada, Lord Dorchester, that Americans were copying protected English machinery. He was particularly alarmed by the report's support of the SEUM and warned of the enterprise's "ultimate effect upon the interests of The Empire."[99]

During 1791 Hamilton sought introducers of English technology by interviewing immigrants. He sent a Scottish stocking weaver back home to recruit men for a factory in America. English artisans heard of the secretary's interest in English technology and expected assistance upon arrival.[100] Roger Newberry, for example, believed Hamilton should help

[96] Bond to Grenville, Sept. to, 1791, in Jameson, ed., "Letters of Phineas Bond," 487.

[97] Hammond to Grenville, Oct. 3, 1792, cited by Herbert Heaton, "The Industrial Immigrant in the United States, 1783–1812," *Proceedings of the American Philosophical Society*, 95 (1951), 523. Other British writers criticized Hamilton's advocacy of child labor in the ROM; Thomas Cooper, *Some Information Respecting America* (London, 1794), 78. Such expressions support my contention that the ROM was widely known in British political and intellectual circles.

[98] Hammond to Grenville, Dec. 6, 1791, in Bernard Mayo, ed., "Instructions to the British Ministers to the United States, 1791–1812," *Annual Report of the American Historical Association for the Year 1936*, 3 vols. (Washington, D.C., 1941), III, 81 n. 12. Darwin H. Stapleton points out that, for all the British efforts to hide their technology, Americans "seldom had difficulty obtaining the information they sought. Occasional obstinacy was often overcome by more-or-less deliberate industrial espionage"; *Accounts of European Science, Technology, and Medicine by American Travelers Abroad, 1735-1860, in the Collection of the American Philosophical Society* (Philadelphia, 1985), 12.

[99] Quoted in Boyd et al., eds., *Jefferson Papers*, XVII, 387. The correspondence is Beckwith to Dorchester, July 27, 1790, Beckwith to Grenville, Aug. 10, 1790, and Beckwith to Dorchester a year later; ibid., 387n. Boyd speculates that Hamilton informed Beckwith of the existence of an Arkwright model in the State Department basement and later arranged to have the machine stolen for the Paterson mill of the SEUM. Why would Hamilton steal a model he could have obtained through the Arkwright artisans who offered to work for the SEUM? Why would Hamilton inform Beckwith of the affair if he intended to use the stolen technology in his prized venture? For an account of Beckwith's services see Frank T. Reuter, "'Petty Spy' or Effective Diplomat: The Role of George Beckwith," *Journal of the Early Republic, to* (1990), 471–92.

[100] Hamilton to Benjamin Walker, July II, 1792, in Syrett et al., eds., *Hamilton Papers*, XII, 26; Davis, *Essays*. I, 398–99; Jeremy, *Transatlantic Industrial*

him find a job in America because he possessed plans for two "most ingenious & *very beneficial*" new English textile machines.[101] In December, Hamilton reported his under-standing with one Mr. Mort, who agreed to "go to Europe, to bring over Workmen, at his own Expence in the first instance; but with the assurance of reimbursement and indemnification." The society's directors approved the agreement unanimously on December 9, 1791, and promised to "carry the same Effect on their part."[102]

European correspondents, such as Samuel Paterson of Edinburgh, aware of Hamilton's support for travel subsidies, reported that thousands of eager-to-emigrate skilled artisans were not coming because "they are Utterly unable to pay for a Passage to America." Paterson begged Hamilton "to procure a Grant of Some Bounty or Relaxation of the Duties, to European Shipping bringing over Poor Industrious workmen to America."[103] A year earlier, Congress had debated such a subsidy. A House committee recommended loaning John F. Amelung $8,000 to bring hundreds of European glass workers to America, reasoning that "a manufactory attended with so much difficulty in its commencement, so important in its consequences to the United States, and of such general utility to the whole Union, ought to receive the assistance and protection of the United States." Opponents of this subsidy ultimately prevailed.[104] Hamilton favored reversing the Amelung decision. In planning the SEUM he called for allocation of means "to procure from Europe skilful

---

Revolution, 79; Wallace and Jeremy, "William Pollard and the Arkwright Patents," 413 n. 30.

[101] Newberry to Hamilton, undated, in Syrett et al., eds., *Hamilton Papers*, XXVI, 828.

[102] Hamilton to Directors of the SEUM, Dec. 7, 1791, ibid., X, 346, 347. See also Hamilton to Benjamin Walker, July 11, 1792, ibid., XII, 26. Hamilton also signed with John Campbell, another smuggler of British machinery to America, to go to Scotland to acquire men and machinery for the SEUM; Agreement with John Campbell and Receipt from John Campbell, Nov. 9, 1792, ibid., XIII, 31–32. See also Davis, *Essays*, I, 485, and Wallace and Jeremy, "William Pollard and the Arkwright Patents," 407.

[103] Paterson to Hamilton, Feb. 10, 1791, in Cole, ed., *Industrial and Commercial Correspondence*, 110.

[104] "Loan to John F. Amelung," June 2, 1790, *American State Papers*, Finances, IX, 6z; *Annals of the Congress of the United States, 1789-1842*, 42. vols. (Washington, D. C., 1834–1856), II, 1630–1632. Neil Longley York, who examined the numerous petitions for congressional assistance in the first two sessions, found many who pleaded for transportation subsidies. Congress regularly turned them all away; York, *Mechanical Metamorphosis: Technological Change in Revolutionary America* (Westport, Conn., 1985), 174.

workmen and such machines and implements as cannot be had here in sufficient perfection."[105]

When Hamilton suggested defraying the expenses of artisans' emigration, he knew he was aiding in the violation of the central codes of English economic policy and hence challenging British power. His European correspondents informed him of both the prohibitions and the penalties of such activities. Paterson, for example, reported that in "Britain the Penalties are £500 Str & 6 Mo imprisonment for every person Indented to goe out of the Kings Dominions." He suggested that bounties for smuggling artisans be given to European shippers because the "Penalties & Forfeitures, are so very heavy & so easily incurred, that No person Unacquainted] with the Laws durst Venture upon Such a Measure—But the European Captain & owners know how to agree with Passengers so as to Escape the Penalties."[106] Another English correspondent, Thomas Marshall, who professed to have been trained by Arkwright, explained to Hamilton that he came to the United States without documentation of his skill due to the "Laws of England being very severe against the Emigration of Mechanic's." Marshall claimed he was "fully Acquainted with every modern Improvement"; he had worked with Arkwright since 1786 and had learned the most recent secrets of the trade.[107] Marshall's application earned him a position with the SEUM, which shows that Hamilton read this letter with sufficient attention to be impressed with Marshall's qualifications or name-dropping, or both. He could not have missed either Marshall's detailed account of the English laws or his defiance.[108] In the ROM Hamilton acknowledged that most manufacturing nations "prohibit, under severe penalties, the exportation of implements and machines, which they have either invented or improved." The United States government must circumvent the efforts of industrially advanced nations to frustrate and prohibit the international diffusion of industrial know-how.[109]

---

[105] Hamilton, "Prospectus of the SEUM," Aug. 1791, in Syrett et al., eds., *Hamilton Papers*, IX, 147.

[106] Paterson to Hamilton, Feb. 10, 1791, in Cole, ed., *Industrial and Commercial Correspondence*, 111.

[107] Marshall to Hamilton, July 19, 1791, ibid., 185.

[108] Shortly after he started working at the SEUM, Marshall wrote Hamilton about the lack of skill and professionalism. He feared that "unless God should send us saints for Workmen and angels to conduct them" the enterprise would falter. To avert such calamity the U.S. must capitalize on the European crisis and "Engage as *many* manufacturers in as *many* different Branches as possible to Emigrate to this country." In Apr. 1793, Marshall was promoted so that he could devote more time to training American workers; Marshall to Hamilton, Sept: Oct. 1791, in Syrett et al., eds., *Hamilton Papers*, IX, 251, 252; Davis, *Essays*, I, 490.

[109] Hamilton, ROM, in Syrett et al., eds., *Hamilton Papers*, X, 308.

Not all eighteenth-century statesmen defined knowledge and skill as property. Franklin, for example, believed "science must be an international pursuit" for "the improvement of humanity's estate."[110] He had actively sponsored the dissemination of European technology in America since the early 1750s and he shared his scientific findings and technological innovations with friends and rivals.[111] He never sought to profit from the implementations of useful inventions such as the lightning rod and the Franklin stove. But his position was rapidly becoming anachronistic. Invention was now taken to be the fruit of the labor of the inventor, and, by the time of the Revolution, the American consensus was that "only an individual's labor created property, and therefore the individual had sole right to possession and disposition of that property."[112]

Hamilton did not share Franklin's views, nor did he subscribe to Enlightenment ideas about universal access to knowledge. He was more swayed by William Barton's *The True Interest of the United States*, which declared that nations should "spare no expense in procuring the ablest masters in every branch of industry, nor any cost in making the first establishments; providing machines, and every other necessary or useful to make the under-taking succeed."[113] In the ROM, a few paragraphs after suggesting ways to bring knowledge across the Atlantic, Hamilton called for prohibiting Europe-bound transmission of American innovations by

---

[110] I. Bernard Cohen, *Benjamin Franklin's Science* (Cambridge, Mass., 1990), 185, 199. For a discussion of the evolution of Enlightenment thinking regarding science see the two classics, Ernst Cassirer, *The Philosophy of the Enlightenment,* trans. Fritz C. A. Koelln and James P. Pettegrove (Princeton, 1955), 37–92, and Peter Gay, *The Enlightenment: An Interpretation,* 2 vols. (New York, 1966–69), II, 57–83.

[111] Franklin, "Observations Concerning the Increase of Mankind," in Leonard W. Labaree et al., eds., *The Papers of Benjamin Franklin,* 30 vols. to date (New Haven, 1959–), IV, 225–34. See also Franklin to William Shipley, Nov. 27, 1755, ibid., VI, 275–76. This aspect of Franklin's activities is incompatible with the republican Franklin best depicted by McCoy, *The Elusive Republic Political Economy in Jeffersonian America* (Chapel Hill, 1980), 49–67. For my view of these issues see Ben-Atar, "Republicanism, Liberalism, and Radicalism in the American Founding," *Intellectual History Newsletter,* 14 (1992), 47–59·

[112] James L. Huston, "The American Revolutionaries, the Political Economy of Aristocracy, and the American Concept of the Distribution of Wealth, 1765–1900," *AHR,* 98 (1993), 1081. See also Kenneth J. Burchfiel, "Revising the 'Original' Patent Clause: Pseudohistory in Constitutional Construction," *Harvard Journal of Law and Technology,* 2 (Spring 1989), 179.

[113] Barton, *The True Interests of the United States, and particularly of Pennsylvania Considered* (Philadelphia, 1786), 28. On Barton's influence see Miller, *Alexander Hamilton,* 282n and editorial note on the ROM, in Syrett et at., eds., *Hamilton Papers,* X, 12. Note that Hamilton borrowed from Barton, whose "Francophilia ... was well known"; Peter Onuf and Nicholas Onuf, *Federal Union, Modern World: The Law of Nations in an Age of Revolutions, 1776–1814* (Madison, Wis., 1993), 203.

imposing stiff penalties against export of technology invented or acquired by Americans. While supporting a strong patent protection law in the United States, he openly campaigned for the violation of British patents. On the one hand, he saw nothing improper in stimulating the "introduction of useful improvements" from abroad.[114] On the other, he strongly supported regulations protecting American improvements from foreign competitors so as not to allow "foreign workmen to rival those of the nation."[115] In sum, Hamilton believed that intellectual property, like physical property, was confined to national boundaries. Accordingly, he had no reservations about orchestrating a mass violation of English laws.

Hamilton's position was in line with international law in the sense that such law was *"not* ordained by nature, but established through international behavior,"* most notably in treaties among nations.[116] Prohibitions on technology piracy were not defined in any international agreement until the nineteenth century. English patent law was originally conceived to encourage foreign artisans to come to England and teach apprentices their trade. The policy remained in effect well into the nineteenth century and was highly successful. Britain attracted artisans in sufficient numbers to change from a technologically debtor nation in 1700 to a creditor one just half a century later. It continued to draw on continental technology throughout the Industrial Revolution.[117] Rival states, in turn, spied on British innovations for their own industrialization efforts. Jacques Necker, Louis XVI's chief advisor, explained that acquisition and exploitation of foreign industrial technology was the surest way to national economic independence. Industrial espionage was practiced "on a very wide scale by all western countries of any industrial significance."[118]

---

[114] Hamilton, ROM, in Syrett et al., eds., *Hamilton Papers,* X, 339. See also Coxe's 2d draft of the ROM, ibid., XXVI, 643.

[115] Hamilton, ROM, ibid., X, 297. See also ibid., 308–09.

[116] Onuf and Onuf, *Federal Union, Modem World,* 147. I thank Peter Onuf for helping me explain the issue in its international law context.

[117] MacLeod, *Inventing the Industrial Revolution,* 10–11; Harris, "The Transfer of Technology between Britain and France and the French Revolution," in Ceri Crossly and Ian Small, eds., *The French Revolution and British Culture* (Oxford, 1989), 158–59; A. E. Musson, "Continental Influences on the Industrial Revolution in Great Britain," in Barrie M. Ratcliffe, ed., *Great Britain and Her World 1750–1914* (Manchester, Eng., 1975), 71–85.

[118] Necker, *A Treatise on the Administration of the Finance of France,* trans. Thomas Mortimer, 3 vols. (London, 1784), II, 475–76; Harris, "Industrial Espionage in the Eighteenth Century," 127. As Harris explains, French leaders recognized that France had to create its own Industrial Revolution; "Transfer of Technology between Britain and France," 182. France was not the only European power to spy on English technology in the 18th century. The diary of Swedish diplomat Bengt Ferrner, advisor to King Gustav III, demonstrates the intensity of that country's efforts to

Hamilton's actions, then, contravened English domestic prohibitions, not the law of nations. Other members of Washington's cabinet, however, felt the United States should avoid promoting direct violations of British laws. Jefferson and Attorney General Edmund Randolph advised the president early in 1791 not to support a proposed textile factory in Virginia because it would be equipped with machines feloniously imported from England. Washington agreed, explaining that "it certainly would not carry an aspect very favorable to the dignity of the United States for the President in a clandestine manner to entice the subjects of another Nation to violate its Laws."[119] Hamilton, for his part, denied that the United States was obliged to respect the British restrictions. Technology piracy, he wrote, did "not violate any positive right of another" country.[120]

Hamilton provided neither constitutional nor moral justification for technology piracy. His argument was utilitarian. "It is the right of every independent nation," he explained, "to pursue its own interest, in its own way."[121] He saw the early 1790s as an excellent time to plunder European technology because the "crisis of the affairs of certain parts of Europe" would dispose "the requisite workmen" to emigrate.[122] By offering inducements and developing opportunities for employment, Hamilton wrote in the ROM, the United States could immeasurably increase "the number and extent of valuable acquisitions to the population arts and industry. . . . To find pleasure in the calamities of other nations, would be criminal; but to benefit ourselves, by opening an asylum to those who suffer, in consequence of them, is as justifiable as it is politic."[123] And Hamilton voiced similar sentiments in his model of American industrialization. The SEUM was to be founded on Europe's distress.

On March 1, 1792, inspired by the ROM, Representative Hugh Williamson of North Carolina introduced a revised patent law that proposed to use fees paid by patent applicants to import useful inventions from abroad.[124] Later that month the Treasury secretary's vigorous efforts

---

acquire English industrial processes; A. P. Woolrich, trans., *Ferrier's Journal 1759/60, An Industrial Spy in Bath and Bristol* (Eindhoven, Neth., 1986). See also Landes, *Unbound Prometheus,* 28.

[119] Edmund Randolph to Washington, Jan. 10, 1791, and Washington to Beverley Randolph, Jan. 13, 1791, cited in Boyd et al., eds., *Jefferson Papers XVIII,* 124n.

[120] Hamilton, 2d draft of the ROM, in Syrett et al., eds., *Hamilton Papers,* X, 60; Ben-Atar *Origins of Jeffersonian Commercial Policy,* 87-12I.

[121] Hamilton, 2d draft of the *ROM,* in Syrett et al., eds., *Hamilton Papers,* X, 60. Hamilton did not include this reasoning in the report submitted to Congress. See Hamilton, *ROM,* ibid., 264.

[122] Hamilton, "Prospectus of the SEUM," ibid., IX, 147.

[123] Hamilton, ROM, ibid., X, 296.

[124] *Annals of Congress,* Mar. 1, 1792, II, 432; P. J. Federico, "Outline of the History of the United States Patent Office," *J. Patent Office Soc.,* 18 (July 1936), 79; Bruce

on behalf of American technology became an embarrassment. His own favorite creation, the SEUM, did his program in. The ROM was the theoretical expression of Hamilton's industrial vision, and the SEUM *was* its practical application. Hamilton's authorship of the *SEUM's* plan and his involvement in its operations were public knowledge. The revelations that the SEUM's directors had lost most of the company's funds in the financial crash of March 1792 discredited Hamilton's program. The panic that "helped wreck the SEUM also helped make Congress less inclined to adopt innovative measures" to remedy American technological deficiencies.[125]

As late as June 1793 Hamilton continued to promote efforts to acquire British technology.[126] Partial fulfillment of his prediction that the "disturbed state of Europe" would incline "its citizens to emigration" lessened the need for federal recruitment of industrial workers.[127] In summer 1793, James Currie of Liverpool advised Hamilton that the outbreak of war in Europe was "occasioning great emigrations from Britain to America," mostly "manufacturers, the most valuable part of our labourers. How this may affect your schemes for establishing manufactures in America," Currie wrote, "you will be able to judge."[128]

More generally, France's decision to export its revolution forced Hamilton to move away from programs that could adversely affect Anglo-American relations. The European war made Hamilton "absolutely

---

W. Bugbee, *Genesis of American Patent and Copyright Law* (Washington, D. C., 1967), 150. When a new patent law was adopted early in 1793, however, it did not include such a program. It voided patents if "the thing thus declared was not originally discovered by the patentee"; Richard Peters, ed., *The Public Statues at Large of the United States of America . . . , 1789-1873*, 17 vols. (Boston, 1850-1873), I, 318-23. For a discussion of the mounting criticism of the 1790 act that led to the 1793 reform see York, *Mechanical Metamorphosis*, 202.

[125] Cooke, *Alexander Hamilton*, 104. See also Davis, *Essays*, I, 370–75, 410–26; McDonald, *Alexander Hamilton*, 232; and Elkins and McKitrick, *Age of Federalism*, 262–63. Nelson interprets Hamilton's inaction as evidence of lack of real interest in developing American manufactures. The ROM was but a "jingle" for the SEUM. It was created only to "convince investors of the SEUM's viability," and once the company's stock began its climb, the Treasury secretary lost interest in American industrialization; *Liberty and Property, 48.*

[126] Hamilton to Walker, July 30, 1792; Hamilton to the Governor and Directors of the SEUM, Aug. 16, 1792; Hamilton to Nicholas Low, June 14, 1793; Coxe to Hamilton, Jan. 4, 1793, in Syrett et al., eds., *Hamilton Papers*, XII, 135–36, 216–18, XIV, 546, XIII, 467.

[127] Hamilton, ROM, ibid., X, 296.

[128] Currie to Hamilton, July 1793, ibid., XV, 153. Heaton, who examined the State Department's partial list of British immigrants living in America during the War of 1812, concludes that "there was a continuous and at times considerable influx of industrial workers between the Revolution and the War of 1812," in "The Industrial Immigrant," 527. See also Jeremy, *Transatlantic Industrial Revolution*, 141–75.

determined that nothing should be done which might directly benefit France."[129] While Jefferson thought that the "liberty of the whole earth was depending on the issue of the contest" and was willing to sacrifice "half the earth" for the French cause, Hamilton publicly denied that "the cause of France is the cause of liberty."[130] He believed that the revolution brought to power the "most cruel" social order in human history, which annihilated "the foundations of social order and true liberty." When the John Jay mission was launched in 1794, he advised Jay to work for an arrangement that would exempt America-bound industrial migrants from British emigration restrictions. Lord Grenville rejected the proposal. Although the *Jay Treaty* did not address the British restrictions on the movement of machinery and men across the Atlantic, Hamilton ignored this omission and campaigned energetically for the treaty's ratification.[131] The French Revolution had changed his priorities. United States technological deficiencies did not justify alienating the nation he believed was America's sole protector from France.

These later developments must not obscure the facts that, before the wars of the French Revolution, Hamilton publicly urged the United States government to sponsor large-scale violations of Britain's laws and that technology piracy threatened the perceived source of Britain's premier position in the world—its superior industrial base. Hamilton's challenges to British industrial power make him no more an enemy of Britain, however, than his opposition to commercial coercion makes him the

---

[129] Harry Ammon, *The Genet Mission* (New York, 1973), 47.

[130] Jefferson to William Short, Jan. 3, 1793, in Boyd et al., eds., *Jefferson Papers*, XXV, 14; Hamilton, "Pacificus, No. VI," July 17, 1793, in Syrett et al., eds., *Hamilton Papers*, XV, 102; Hamilton, "The French Revolution," ibid., XVII, 587.

[131] Edmund Randolph's instructions to Jay, May 6, 1794, *American State Papers*, Foreign Relations, 1, 472. Although Secretary of State Randolph was the official signer of the instructions, historians have long concluded that Hamilton by and large wrote them. See Syrett et al., eds., *Hamilton Papers*, XVI, 326; Bemis, *Jay's Treaty*, 291; and Elkins and McKitrick, *Age of Federalism*, 396-97. During the negotiations, Jay proposed free movement of production and manufactures between British and American territories, but Grenville turned it down, and the final treaty specifically noted that commercial intercourse between the two countries was confined to "all Goods and Merchandize whose Importation into the United States shall not be wholly prohibited"; jay to Grenville, Aug. 6, 1794, London, Public Record Office, Foreign Office Papers, *95/512;* Article 3, The Anglo-American *Treaty* of 1794, in Charles R. Ritcheson, *Aftermath of Revolution: British Policy toward the United States, 1783–1795* (Dallas, 1969), 388. Immigration and citizenship were discussed in relation to those residing in territories controlled by the soon to be evacuated northwest posts. Grenville's draft treaty, Aug. 30, 1794; Jay to Grenville, Sept. 6, 1794; Grenville to *Jay*, Sept. 7, 1794, F/O 95/512; Article 2, The Anglo-American Treaty of 1794, in Ritcheson, *Aftermath of Revolution*, 387. I thank Ene Sirvet for drawing my attention to this Jay/Grenville exchange.

double agent portrayed by historians from Boyd to Perkins and DeConde. The ROM was not an aberration. It was "an integral part of Hamilton's total design."[132] The Treasury secretary, whose career sprang from the American rejection of English colonial rule, had concluded that only through emulation of the English financial system and transfer of industrial expertise could American independence be made secure. Acquiring prohibited technology at the risk of alienating Britain and stabilizing the country's finances at the risk of alienating France were the twin sides of a neomercantilist plan to raise the United States to the rank of a great power.

Believing economic independence was inseparable from political freedom, Hamilton was alarmed by American dependence on British imports. He opposed commercial coercion, fearing that the young nation would be devastated by such a contest. His less confrontational design envisioned ridding the United States of British economic domination by developing American manufacturing. He concluded that American technological backwardness stood in the way of American manufactures and urged the federal government to launch an aggressive campaign to acquire England's protected industrial secrets. Congress and the country refused to go along with this subtle and sophisticated plan, opting instead to make no industrial policy. Inaction proved prophetic. European immigration and American ingenuity combined to overcome the technology gap. By the middle of the nineteenth century, the United States became the industrial model other nations sought to emulate.

Doron Ben-Atar is an assistant professor of history at Yale University. He is deeply indebted to his research assistants Greg Flynn and Rebecca Keith. He wishes to acknowledge James M. Banner, Jr., David A. Bell, Jacob E. Cooke, Carolyn C. Cooper, Arnon Gutfeld, David J. Jeremy, David Mattern, Peter S. Onuf, Eric Papenfuse, Ene Sirvet, and Herbert Sloan whose comments and suggestions improved the article. He also thanks the history faculty of Tel Aviv University and the members of the Philadelphia Center for Early American Studies for useful discussions of earlier versions.

---

[132] Elkins and McKitrick, *Age of Federalism*, 258. See also Cooke, *Alexander Hamilton*, 97; McDonald, *Alexander Hamilton*, 231; and Thomas K. McGraw, "The Strategic Vision of Alexander Hamilton," *American Scholar*, 63 (Winter 1994), 54.

10

'Immence Mountains to the West'
Lewis and Clark
Breach the Bitterroots

Stephen E. Ambrose

When the United States purchased the Louisiana Territory from France in 1803, most of the vast expanse of land—stretching from the mouth of the Mississippi River to the headwaters of the Missouri—had yet to be explored by Euroamericans. Therefore, Congress, at the urging of President Thomas Jefferson, authorized three expeditions to travel up western tributaries of the Mississippi to their sources in order to gain information about the new land's geography, flora, and fauna. Two of the expeditions, one which ascended the Red River and the other which traveled up the Arkansas, failed to achieve their goals.

The third expedition, however, led by Captains Meriwether Lewis and William Clark, proved to be a complete and astounding success. Leaving St. Louis in the spring of 1804 with nearly fifty men, the "Corps of Discovery" ascended the Missouri River to the Mandan Indian villages in modern North Dakota, where they spent the winter of 1804-05. The following year, they crossed the Rocky Mountains and descended the Columbia River to the Pacific Ocean. The expedition returned to St. Louis in 1806, having been gone nearly two and a half years. Lewis and Clark not only provided their countrymen with a wealth of information about the land they had traversed, they also staked a claim for the United States to the Oregon Territory, which would ultimately be annexed in 1846.

Much of the success of the expedition, in which only one man died, was due to the leadership capabilities of Captain Lewis. The following article, which details the problems the expedition faced as it attempted to cross the Rocky

Mountains in 1805, demonstrates Lewis's resourcefulness and confidence as he successfully overcame the series of challenges which con fronted him. Such examples of "undaunted courage" have deservedly earned the Lewis and Clark expedition the right to be ranked among the greatest achievements in American history.

On April 29, 1805, the Lewis and Clark Expedition entered Montana. It consisted of Captains Meriwether Lewis and William Clark, three sergeants, twenty-three privates, Clark's slave York, the Shoshone teenage girl Sacagawea, her husband Charbonneau (a French-Indian fur trader) and their infant son Baptiste. The captains and enlisted men were the first citizens of the United States to step foot in the state. Their objective was to explore the Missouri River to its source, cross the Rocky Mountains to the Columbia River drainage, and descend the Columbia to the Pacific Ocean.

This was the greatest exploration ever undertaken by Americans. Its objectives were many: to map the upper reaches of the Louisiana Purchase; to discover and describe the land and its people, flora, and fauna; to find the shortest route to the Pacific; to bring the various Indian tribes into an American fur-trade empire in the western portion of the continent; to establish an American claim to the Northwestern Empire (today's Idaho, Oregon, and Washington); and more. None of this could be accomplished without achieving the first objective—to get to the Pacific and return.

That goal required passing over the Rocky Mountains, whose extent, height, and difficulty were unknown. It was certain, however, that without the help of Indian horses the portage over those mountains would be difficult to impossible. It was therefore critical that the expedition meet and be able to trade with the Shoshones, who were known to live in the mountains and to have a multitude of horses. That was why Sacagawea was along—she was a Shoshone who had been captured at the Three Forks of the Missouri a few years earlier and sold to Charbonneau. Captains Lewis and Clark had met her in their winter camp at Fort Mandan (near today's Bismarck, North Dakota). She could translate Shoshone into Hidatsa, which Charbonneau could put into French, which a number of men could then put into English. With her help, the captains figured they could trade manufactured goods for horses.

Through May, June, and July the expedition made its way up the Missouri River. Its greatest challenge came at the Great Falls, where the portage required a full month. By early August it was past the Falls, the Gates of the Rocky Mountains (so named by Lewis), and the Three Forks. Captain Lewis's obsession now was to find the Shoshones. He set out with a party of three men in search of the

Shoshones, leaving Clark and the others to move the baggage up the Beaverhead River. On August 11, only a few miles short of the Continental Divide, he spotted a lone Indian on a horse. He approached cautiously, hoping not to frighten the man, but the Indian rode off anyway. Lewis and his party tried to follow his trail, assuming it would lead them to the tribe, but a heavy rain shower raised the grass and wiped out the track just before dusk. Lewis made camp.

On the morning of August 12, Lewis wrote in his journal, "we fell in with a large and plain Indian road. At a distance of 4 miles further the road took us to the most distant fountain of the waters of the mighty Missouri in search of which we have spent so many toilsome days and wristless nights."[1]

Lewis assessed the impact on himself: "Thus far I had accomplished one of those great objects on which my mind has been unalterably fixed for many years, judge then of the pleasure I felt in allying my thirst with this pure and ice cold water." Now was the moment to go to the top of the pass (Lemhi Pass, on today's Montana-Idaho border), to become the first American to look on Idaho and the great Northwestern Empire. Lewis described the moment: "We proceeded on to the top of the dividing ridge from which I discovered immence ranges of high mountains still to the West of us with their tops partially covered with snow."

To what degree Lewis was surprised or disheartened by the sight, he never said. John Logan Allen asks us to "imagine the shock and the surprise—for from the top of that ridge were to be seen neither the great river that had been promised nor the open plains extending to the shores of the South Sea." What Allen calls "the geography of hope" had to give way to "the geography of reality."[2] With Lewis's last step to the top of the Divide went decades of theory about the nature of the Rocky Mountains, shattered by a single glance from a single man. Equally shattered were Lewis's hopes for an easy portage to a major branch of the Columbia. Lewis was deep into Indian country with only three men, and his main body three or four days' march away. He had a few geegaws as his currency. He had a frightened Indian reporting back to the Shoshones that strangers were in the area. He had just been through enough experiences for an entire expedition, all in one day. He needed a good night's sleep, and lots of good luck in the morning.

---

[1] Meriwether Lewis quotations are from Gary E. Moulton, ed., *Journals of the Lewis and Clark Expedition* (8 vols., Lincoln: University of Nebraska Press, 1983–1993).
[2] John Logan Allen, "Summer of Decision: Lewis and Clark in Montana, 1805," *We Proceeded On*, 8 (Fall 1976), 10.

On Tuesday morning, August 13, 1805, Lewis set out early, headed west on a plain, heavily and recently used Indian trail that fell down a long, descending valley.

At nine miles Lewis saw two Indian women, a man, and some dogs. When he had arrived within half a mile of them, he ordered George Drouillard, the expedition's hunter and interpreter, and the two privates to halt, unslung his pack and rifle and put them on the ground, unfurled a flag, and advanced alone at a steady pace toward the Indians. The women retreated, but the man stayed in place until Lewis was within a hundred yards.

Lewis called out *"tab-ba-bone,"* loudly and frequently. The man "absconded." Sacagawea had told Lewis that the Shoshone word for white men was *"tab-ba-bone."* Actually the Shoshones had no word for "white men" as they had never seen one. *"Tab-ba-bone"* may have meant "stranger" or "enemy." If so it was the worst possible word for Lewis to use.

Lewis had his men join him and proceeded. After less than a mile, topping a rise, they came on three Indian women, one a twelve-year-old, one a teen, and the third elderly, only thirty yards away. At the first sight, Lewis laid down his rifle and advanced on the group. The teen ran off, but the old woman and the child remained. Seeing no chance to escape, they sat on the ground and held their heads down; to Lewis it looked as though they had reconciled themselves to die.

He approached and took the elderly woman by the hand, raised her up, said *"tab-ba-bone"* and rolled up his shirtsleeve to show her his white skin (his hands and face were so deeply tanned he might have been an Indian, and his clothes were entirely leather). Drouillard and the privates joined him. From their packs he gave the woman some beads, a few moccasin awls, a few mirrors, and some paint. His skin and the gifts, and his friendly attitude, were enough to calm her down.

Through Drouillard's sign language, he asked her to call the teen back, fearing that otherwise the girl might alarm the main body of Shoshones. The old woman did as asked, and the teen reappeared. When the Indians were composed, Lewis told them, through Drouillard, that he "wished them to conduct us to their camp that we wer anxious to become acquainted with the chiefs and warriors of their nation." They did as requested, and the group set off, the Indians leading.

After two miles, the long-anticipated and eagerly sought contact took place. Sixty warriors, mounted on excellent horses and armed for war with bows and arrows plus three inferior rifles, came on at full speed. When they saw Lewis's party, they halted.

This was the first time an American had ever seen a Shoshone war party, and the first time this band of Shoshones had ever seen an American. The Indians were overwhelmingly superior. It would have been the work of only a moment for them to overwhelm Lewis's party, and they would have more than doubled their firepower in rifles and gathered as loot more knives, awls, looking glasses, and other trinkets than any Rocky Mountain Indian band had ever seen.

But rather than assuming a defensive position, Lewis laid down his rifle, picked up his flag, told his party to stay in place, and, following the old woman who was guiding, advanced slowly toward he knew not what.

A man Lewis assumed was the chief rode in the lead. He halted to speak to the old woman. She told him that these were white men "and exultingly shewed the presents which had been given." This broke the tension. The chief and then the warriors dismounted.

The chief advanced. Saying *"ah-hi-e, ah-hi-e,"* which Lewis later learned meant "I am much pleased, I am much rejoiced," the chief put his left arm over Lewis's right shoulder and applied his left cheek to Lewis's right cheek, continuing "to frequently vociforate the word *ah-hi-e.*"

The warriors and Lewis's men then came on, "and we wer all carresed and besmeared with their grease and paint till I was heartily tired of the national hug."

This first meeting between Shoshones and Americans went better than Lewis could have dared to hope. The war party had ridden out in response to the alarm given by the man who had fled earlier that day. The Shoshones expected to find Blackfeet and might have attacked without pause save for the old woman. Had Lewis not met her, and had she not responded so positively to his appeals and gifts, there might well have been a firefight.

Instead there was a parlay. Lewis brought out his pipe and sat, indicating to the Indians that they should do the same.

Lewis lit and passed the pipe. After smoking several rounds, he distributed some presents. The Shoshones were "much pleased particularly with the blue beads and vermillion." Lewis learned that the chief's name was "Ca-me-ah-wait." Lewis told him that "the object of our visit was a friendly one," that after they reached Cameahwait's camp he would explain the expedition more fully, including "who we wer, from whence we had come and wither we were going."

Cameahwait spoke to his warriors, and soon the entire party set out for the main camp. He sent some youngsters ahead to inform the others to prepare for their arrival. When they reached the camp, on the east bank of the Lemhi River, about seven miles north of today's

Tendoy, Idaho, Lewis was ushered into an old leather tepee (the only one the band had left after the Blackfoot raid) and ceremoniously seated on great boughs and antelope skins.

After the ritual smoking, "I now explained to them the objects of our journey." How well the Shoshones could comprehend a trip across the continent—or if they could even conceive of the continent—Lewis did not say.

Women and children crowded around, eager to see these "children of the Great Spirit." Lewis distributed the presents he had left, to the delight of the Shoshones.[3]

By this time, it was growing dark. Lewis and his men had not eaten in twenty-four hours. He mentioned this to Cameahwait, who said he was sorry but the band had nothing but berries to eat. He gave the white men some cakes of serviceberries and chokecherries. "Of these I made a hearty meal," Lewis wrote.

He strolled down to the Lemhi River. Through Drouillard's signs, Lewis inquired about the course of the stream. Cameahwait replied that a half-day's march north it joined with another, twice as large, coming in from the southwest, forming today's Salmon River. On further questioning, Cameahwait said the river was "confined between inacessable mountains, was very rapid and rocky insomuch that it was impossible for us to pass either by land or water down this river to the great lake where the white men lived as he had been informed."

Cameahwait was referring to the traders who called at the mouth of the Columbia River. His description of the Salmon was as accurate as it was unwelcome. It confirmed what Lewis must have feared when he first gazed on the Bitterroots from Lemhi Pass—there was no all-water route, or anything remotely resembling it, across the continent. The distressing information about the Salmon was somewhat balanced for Lewis by the sight of "a great number of horses feeding in every direction around their camp." Assuming he could trade for an adequate number of horses, Lewis had "little doubt but we shall be enable to . . . transport our stores even if we are compelled to travel by land over these mountains." With contact made, Lewis now had to give Clark time to come up the Jefferson as far as the fork that marked the extreme limit of navigation—if that limit had not already been passed. Lewis decided to spend the morning of August 14 writing in his journal, the afternoon in procuring further information from Cameahwait about the country to the west. When Douillard returned from an unsuccesful morning's hunt, Lewis used his sign-language ability to ask Cameahwait "to instruct me with rispect to the

---

[3] James P. Ronda, *Lewis and Clark among the Indians* (Lincoln: University of Nebraska Press, 1984), 143.

geogrphy of his country." The chief repeated what he had said the previous day, with more details. After drawing a waving line on the ground to represent the river, he piled sand on each side of it to represent "the vast mountains of rock eternally covered with snow through which the river passed." He spoke of "perpendicular and even juting rocks so closely hemned in the river that there was no possibilyte of passing along the shore. . . . the whole surface of the river was beat into perfect foam as far as the eye could reach. That the mountains were also inaccessible to man or horse."

How, then, to cross those mountains? Cameahwait said he had never done it, but there was an old man in his band "who could probably give me some information of the country to the N.W." He added that "he had understood from the persed nosed Indians who inhabit this river below the rocky mountains that it ran a great way toward the seting sun and finally lost itself in a great lake of water which was illy taisted."

That sentence linked the continent. For the first time, a white man had a map, however imperfect and imprecise, to connect the great rivers of the western empire. Also for the first time, a white man heard of the Nez Percés, the major tribe living west of the mountains. Cameahwait added that the Nez Percés crossed to the Missouri River buffalo country to hunt each year.

What route did they use? Lewis asked. It was to the north the chief answered, "but added that the road was a very bad one as he had been informed by them and that they had suffered excessively with hunger on the rout being obliged to subsist for many days on berries alone as there was no game in that part of the mountains which were broken rockey and so thickly covered with timber that they could scarcely pass."

"My rout was instantly settled in my own mind," Lewis wrote. "I felt perfectly satisfyed, that if the Indians could pass these mountains with their women and Children, that we could also pass them."

This is a wonderful sentence. It shows his complete confidence in himself, Captain Clark, and the men. He is not boasting, or challenging, just being matter-of-fact about it. If they can, we can. Cameahwait had more information. He said there was no buffalo west of the mountains, that the Indians who lived there subsisted on salmon and roots. He complained about the Spanish policy of never selling guns to Indians, whereas the English sold guns to the Blackfeet, Hidatsas, and other enemies of the Shoshones. With that advantage in firepower, the Plains Indians were continually harassing the Shoshones, who were forced to hide in the interior of the mountains most of the year. But, Cameahwait added, "with his ferce eyes and lank jaws grown meager for the want of food, [such] would not be the case if we had guns, we could then live in the country of buffaloe and eat as our enimies do."

Here was the opening Lewis sought, here was the opportunity to make promises that would induce Cameahwait to help with the portage over the Continental Divide and to trade for horses that could get the expedition over the Bitterroots on the Nez Percé route. Lewis said that he had already induced the Hidatsas to promise that they would no longer raid against the Shoshones or make war on any of their neighbors (even though he knew that the Hidatsas had sent out a war party that spring), and that, when the expedition got to the Pacific and then returned to the United States, "whitemen would come to them [the Shoshones] with an abundance of guns and every other article necessary to their defence and comfort."

Lewis told Cameahwait that he wanted the band to cross Lemhi Pass with him in the morning, bringing thirty horses, to meet with Clark and the main party at the forks of Jefferson River and help bring the baggage over the pass and down to the Indian camp on the Lemhi River, where "we would then remain sometime among them and trade with them for horses." Lewis woke on the morning of Thursday, August 15, "as hungary as a wolf."

After breakfast, a crisis. The warriors would not move, despite Cameahwait's urging. Lewis asked after the cause and was told "that some foolish persons among them had suggested the idea that we were in league with the Pahkees [the Shoshone word for Atsinas] and had come on in order to decoy them into an ambuscade where their enemies were waiting to receive them."

Lewis told Cameahwait that he forgave the warriors their suspicion: "I knew they were not acquainted with whitemen . . . that among whitemen it was considered disgracefull to lye or entrap an enimy by falsehood." After that stretcher, Lewis threatened that, if the Shoshones did not help with the portage, no white man would come to bring them arms and ammunition.

Then he challenged their manhood, saying, "I still hope that there were some among them that were not affraid to die." Cameahwait mounted his horse and gave a speech to his people, saying he would go with the white men to convince himself of the truth of what Lewis said. He added that he hoped some at least of the warriors would join him. Six mounted their horses. The small party set out and soon another half-dozen men and three women joined them, making all together a party of sixteen Indians and four white men. They crossed Lemhi Pass and descended to Shoshone Cove, where they camped on the creek and had their second meal of the day: "I now cooked and among six of us eat the remaining pound of flour stired in a little boiling water." The Shoshones, save Cameahwait and an unnamed warrior, had nothing to eat that day.

The next morning, August 16, Lewis sent Drouillard and Shields out to kill some meat. He asked Cameahwait to keep his young men in camp so that they would not alarm the game. That was a mistake, for it reawakened the suspicions of the Shoshones. They feared the white men were trying to make contact with the Blackfeet, so two parties of warriors set out on each side of the valley to spy on Drouillard and Shields.

Lewis, McNeal, and the remainder of the Shoshones followed. After about an hour, "when we saw one of the spies comeing up the level plain under whip, the chief pawsed a little and seemed somewhat concerned. I felt a good deel so myself." Lewis's fear was that by "some unfortunate accedent" the Blackfeet really were in the neighborhood. But when the scout arrived, breathless, he had good news—Drouillard had killed a deer.

At the site of the kill, "the seen when I arrived was such that had I not have had a pretty keen appetite, myself I am confident I should not have taisted any part of the vension. . . . each [Indian] had a peice of some discription and all eating most ravenously. Some were eating the kidnies the melt [the spleen] and liver and the blood running from the corners of their mouths, others were in a similar situation with the paunch and guts.... I really did not untill now think that human nature ever presented itself in a shape so nearly allyed to the brute creation. I viewed these poor starved divils with pity and compassion."

However heartfelt, his pity and compassion did not extend far enough for him to note that, if the Indians appeared savage with the blood running down their cheeks, they had taken only the parts of the deer Drouillard had thrown away when he dressed the kill. They had not touched the meat.

Lewis saved a hindquarter for himself and his men and gave the balance to Cameahwait to divide among his people. As the party approached the forks, where Lewis had told the Indians they would meet Clark, Cameahwait stopped. With much ceremony, he put tippets such as the Shoshones were wearing around the necks of the white men. Lewis realized that the chief's suspicions were still strong, that he wanted to make the white men look like Indians in case it was Blackfeet and not Clark waiting at the forks. Realizing this, Lewis took off his cocked hat and put it on Cameahwait. The men followed his example, "and we were son completely metamorphosed."

The entire party moved downstream to the forks. Lewis had a warrior carry the flag, so that "our own party should know who we were." But when they got to within a couple of miles of the forks, "I discovered to my mortification" that Clark had not arrived.

Desperate, he gave Cameahwait his rifle and told him that if the Blackfeet were around he could use it to defend himself, "that for my own part I was not affraid to die and if I deceived him he might make what uce of the gun he thought proper or in other words that he might shoot me." Lewis had his men give up their rifles too, "which seemed to inspire them [the Indians] with more confidence."

This bold move bought Lewis enough time to think of a plan. Recalling that he had left a note for Clark at the forks, "I now had recource to a stratagem in which I thought myself justifyed by the occasion, but which I must confess set a little awkward." He sent Drouillard, accompanied by a warrior, to pick up the note. When Drouillard returned with the note and the warrior's confirmation that he had picked it up at the forks, Lewis told Cameahwait that Clark had written it and that it said he, Clark, was just below, coming on, and that Lewis should wait for him at the forks. To hold the Shoshones, Lewis told them that Sacagawea was with Clark, and that there was also a man with Clark "who was black and had short curling hair." The Indians expressed great eagerness to see such a curiosity.

Nevertheless, that night Lewis wrote in his journal, "my mind was in reality quite as gloomy . . . as the most affrighted indian but I affected cheerfullness." He lay down to sleep, Cameahwait beside him. "I slept but little as might be well expected, my mind dwelling on the state of the expedition which I have ever held in equal estimation with my own existence, and the fait of which appeared at this moment to depend in a great measure upon the caprice of a few savages who are ever as fickle as the wind."

In the morning, Lewis sent Drouillard and the warrior off at first light. At about 9:00 A.M., an Indian who had gone down the creek for a mile or so returned and reported "that the whitemen were coming." Shortly thereafter, Clark arrived, accompanied by Charbonneau and Sacagawea. Cameahwait gave Clark the national hug and festooned his hair with shells. In the midst of the excitement, one of the Shoshone women recognized Sacagawea. Her name, Jumping Fish, she had acquired on the day Sacagawea was taken prisoner, because of the way she had jumped through a stream in escaping the Hidatsas.[4] The reunited teens hugged and cried and talked, all at once.

Lewis had a camp set up just below the forks. (The site, known as Camp Fortunate, is now under the Clark Canyon Reservoir, south of Dillon, Montana.) He had a canopy formed from one of the large sails.

---

[4] Moulton, *Journals of the Lewis and Clark Expedition*, 5:116.

At 4:00 p.m., he called a conference. Dispensing with Drouillard and the sign language, he decided to use a translation chain that ran from Sacagawea, speaking Shoshone to the Indians and translating it into Hidatsa, to Charbonneau, who translated her Hidatsa into French, to Private Francis Labiche, who translated from French to English.

Scarcely had they begun the cumbersome process when Sacagawea began to stare at Cameahwait. Suddenly recognizing him as her brother, "she jumped up, ran & embraced him, & threw her blanket over him and cried profusely."[5]

What a piece of luck that was. No novelist would dare invent such a scene. As James Ronda writes, "the stars had danced for Lewis and Clark."[6]

Lewis wrote that the reunion was "really affecting." He wrote not a word to indicate that he was surprised by the show of so much emotion from Sacagawea, whom he had characterized a couple of weeks earlier as someone who never showed the slightest emotion.

When Sacagawea recovered herself, the council began—although it was frequently interrupted by her tears. The captains explained "the objects which had brought us into this distant part of the country," making it appear that the number-one object was to help the Shoshones by finding a more direct way to bring arms to them. In the process, "we made them sensible of their dependance on the will of our government for every species of merchandise as well for their defence & comfort." But this could not be accomplished without Shoshone horses, or without a guide to take them over the Nez Percé trail.

In reply, Cameahwait "declared his wish to serve us in every rispect; that he was sorry to find that it must yet be some time before they could be furnished with firearms but said they could live as they had done heretofore untill we brought them as we had promised." Even though he regarded Cameahwait as "a man of Influence Sence & easey & reserved manners, appears to possess a great deel of Cincerity," Clark wanted to see for himself before accepting Cameahwait's alarming description of the Salmon River route. He and Lewis conferred. Lewis agreed that in the morning Clark should set out with eleven men carrying axes and other necessary tools for making canoes. They would make a reconnaissance of the Salmon, accompanied by Charbonneau and Sacagawea.

If Clark found the river navigable, he would set to making canoes. Lewis, meanwhile, would bring on the remaining eighteen members of the party and the baggage to the Lemhi River. He figured the move

[5] Nicholas Biddle (prepared for press by Paul Allen) edition of the *Journals,* first published in 1814 by Thomas Bradford.
[6] Ronda, Lewis and Clark among the Indians, 147.

would take a week or more, enough time for Clark to make his reconnaissance and determine whether the expedition was to proceed by land or water. Whatever the route, Lewis had cause for satisfaction. The expedition was once more united and would soon be on the move. He slept better than the previous night.

In the morning, August 18, while Clark prepared for his reconnaissance, Lewis traded for some horses. He intended to provide Clark with two, to transport his baggage, and keep one for his hunters, to transport whatever meat they obtained. At 10:00 A.M., Clark set off, accompanied by all the Indians save the two lesser chiefs, Jumping Fish, and another woman.

Lewis prepared for the portage. Drouillard brought in a deer. One of the men caught a beaver. Lewis had a net arranged and set to catch some trout. He brought his journal up-to-date.

He concluded his August 18 journal entry with an oft-quoted passage of introspection and self-criticism. "This day I completed my thirty first year," he began. He figured he was halfway through his life's journey. "I reflected that I had as yet done but little, very little indeed, to further the hapiness of the human race, or to advance the information of the succeeding generation. I viewed with regret the many hours I have spent in indolence, and now soarly feel the want of that information which those hours would have given me had they been judiciously expended."

He shook the mood, writing that, since the past could not be recalled, "I dash from me the gloomy thought and resolved in future, to redouble my exertions and at least indeavour to promote those two primary objects of human existence, by giving them the aid of that portion of talents which nature and fortune have bestoed on me..." and here he seems to have lost his train of thought. Whatever the cause, he forgot to name those "two primary objects of human existence," and instead ended, "in future, to live for *mankind*, as I have heretofore lived *for myself*."

Much has been made of this remarkable passage, perhaps too much. It was not unusual for men of the Enlightenment to write such stuff—come to that, a thirtieth or thirty-first birthday leads to such thoughts for men of the late twentieth century—and Jefferson sometimes wrote in a similar mood and vein.

Among other things, the passage is a reminder of how young Lewis was to be carrying so heavy a burden of command. Physically tired and emotionally exhausted after the tension of the past few days, he was in what is still today one of the most remote places on the continent, with only eighteen enlisted men, Drouillard, and four Indians as companions. Lewis spent six days at Camp Fortunate. On August 22, an hour before noon, Cameahwait, Charbonneau,

Sacagawea, and some fifty Shoshone men accompanied by women and children arrived. After they set up camp, Lewis held a council. He distributed presents, especially to the second and third chiefs. Noting "these poor devils half starved," Lewis had the men prepare a meal of corn and beans, which he served after the council.

Cameahwait said he "wished that his nation could live in a country where they could provide such food." On the morning of August 24 Lewis was once again on the road, this time with eighteen of his own men, Charbonneau, Sacagawea, Drouillard, nine horses and a mule, and Cameahwait's band. But, notwithstanding future problems, he was happy, because "I had now the inexpressible satisfaction to find myself once more under way with all my baggage and party."

His joy didn't last long. On August 25 Charbonneau casually mentioned to Lewis that he expected to meet the whole of Cameahwait's band coming over Lemhi Pass on the way to the buffalo country.

Why? Lewis asked.

Charbonneau explained that Sacagawea had overheard Cameahwait say to some of his young men to tell the band to meet him the next day, so that together the reunited band could go to the Missouri River.

If that happened, Lewis and his men would be left literally high and dry, halfway up Lemhi Pass, with only a dozen or so horses, and no guide for the Nez Percé trail.

Another gut-tightening crisis. Lewis's temper flared, but he was too good a diplomat to direct it at the cause, Cameahwait. Instead he cussed Charbonneau, who had been in possession of the information for some hours before divulging it to Lewis. Then he called Cameahwait and the two lesser chiefs for a smoke and a talk.

"I asked them if they had not promised to assist me with my baggage to their camp.... They acknowledged that they had." Then why were they preparing to abandon him to go to the buffalo country? The Indians hung their heads.

Lewis said that, had they not promised to help with the portage, "I should not have attempted to pass the mountains but would have returned down the river and that in that case they would never have seen anymore white men in their country."

In truth, he was going to try to get over those mountains come hell or high water, a resolution he frequently put into his journal. Still, he took the high moral ground, instructing the chiefs that "they must never promis us anything which they did not mean to perform." He concluded by directing the chiefs to send a young man over the pass to the village to tell the people to stay where they were until Lewis, Cameahwait, and the others arrived.

The two lesser chiefs spoke up. They wanted to help and be as good as their word, they said, and it was not they who had instructed the band to cross to the Missouri River side of the Divide. Cameahwait had done it, and they had not approved.

"Cameahwait remained silent for some time," Lewis wrote; "at length he told me that he knew he had done wrong but that he had been induced to that measure from seeing all his people hungary, but as he had promised to give me his assistance he would not in future be worse than his word."

His people were starving. The buffalo country was not much more than a day's march away. Other bands of Shoshones were already meeting with Flathead villages to go on the hunt. But he had given his word, and Lewis shamed him into keeping it. A pity that Lewis never showed the slightest gratitude, or gave any indication that he understood what a difficult position Cameahwait was in. The evening of August 26, Lewis and his men and baggage made it to the camp on the Lemhi River. Private John Colter was already there, with a letter from Clark (who was in camp downstream) in which Clark described the Salmon River route as impassable.

Lewis was not surprised. He told Cameahwait that in the morning he wished to purchase twenty additional horses. Cameahwait pointed out that his people had lost a great number of their horses to the Blackfeet, but said he would see what he could do. He also said he thought the old man who had once crossed the mountains with the Nez Percé would be willing to guide Lewis and Clark.

"Matters being thus far arranged," Lewis ended his journal entry for the day, "I directed the fiddle to be played and the party danced very merily much to the amusement and gratification of the natives, though I must confess that the state of my own mind at this moment did not well accord with the prevailing mirth as I somewhat feared that the caprice of the indians might suddenly induce them to withhold their horses from us without which my hopes of prosicuting my voyage to advantage was lost."

The Indians were ready to sell, but the captains discovered over the next few days that the price had gone up considerably. The Shoshones had a captive, desperate market. It was clear to them that the white men had to have horses, come what may. On August 29 Clark found that he had to offer his pistol, a knife, and one hundred rounds of ammunition for one horse. The captains had tried to make it a strict rule never to reduce their arsenal, but now they had no choice.

Eventually, the captains bought twenty-nine horses, but, as James Ronda puts it, "The Shoshonis had proven to be better Yankee traders than the Americans." When Clark examined the horses in his corral, he found them to be "nearly all Sore Backs [and] several Pore, & young." The captains had bought the castoffs of the Shoshone herd.[7]

The party set out early on September 1, traveling cross-country over high, rugged hills, to today's North Fork of the Salmon River (Fish Creek to Lewis and Clark), following the Shoshone guide, whom the captains called Old Toby. They were headed almost due north and climbing toward the Continental Divide (on their right, to the east) in rough, seldom-traveled mountainous country, with no Indian trail or any other sign of human presence.

They were entering mountains far more difficult to pass than any American had ever attempted. The confusion of creeks and ravines cutting through the steep mountainsides has made the route the expedition used one of the most disputed of the entire journey. One expert, Harry Majors, calls the route "the single most obscure and enigmatic of the entire Lewis and Clark expedition."[8] On September 4 the party fell down a very steep descent to a north-flowing river that Lewis named "Clark's River" (present day Bitterroot River). There, at today's Ross's Hole, the captains encountered a band of some four hundred Salish Indians, with at least five hundred horses. The Salish were generous. Although their stock of provisions was as low as that of the expedition, they shared their berries and roots. And they traded for horses at much better prices than the Shoshones demanded, perhaps not aware of how desperate Lewis and Clark were. The captains bought thirteen horses for "a flew articles of merchendize," and the Salish were kind enough to exchange seven of the run-down Shoshone ponies for what Clark called "ellegant horses." The expedition now had approximately thirty-nine horses, three colts, and one mule—for packing, riding, or food in the last extreme.[9]

On the morning of September 6 the captains directed the men to lighten the loads on the Shoshone horses and pack the excess on the Salish horses. The expedition made ten miles and camped, with nothing to eat but two grouse and some berries. For the next three days, the descent of the wide and beautiful Bitterroot valley was relatively easy. But as they marched, the captains and their men kept looking to their left (west) at the snow-covered Bitterroot Mountains, described by Sergeant Patrick Gass as "the most terrible mountains I

---

[7] Ibid., 154.

[8] Harry M. Majors, "Lewis and Clark Enter the Rocky Mountains," Northwest Discovery, 7 (April-May 1986), 4–120, in Moulton, Journals of the Lewis and Clark Expedition, 5:186.

[9] Roy E. Appleman, *Lewis and Clark: Historic Places Associated with Their Trancontinental Exploration (1804–06)* (Washington, D.C.: National Park Service, 1975), 169. No matter how hungry, the Shoshones and the Salish never ate horsemeat. The Americans preferred not to but would if necessary.

ever beheld."[10] The barrier would have to be crossed; how, they could hardly imagine.

The party camped the night of September 9 at the junction of a stream coming in from the west (today's Lolo Creek, some ten miles south-southwest of Missoula). Lewis called the camp "Traveller's Rest." Old Toby informed Lewis that at this place the party would leave the Bitterroot River and head almost straight west up Lolo Creek, and then over the mountains. The ordeal that every man had dreaded every time he looked left was about to begin. Lewis wrote of "those unknown formidable snow clad Mountains," which the party was about to attempt "on the bare word of a Savage [Old Toby], while 99/100th of his Countrymen assured us that a passage was impracticable."[11]

Old Toby's countrymen were not far wrong. The expedition's passage over the Lolo Trail was fraught with danger and hardship. The men almost starved and managed to make it only by killing colts obtained from the Shoshones. They ran into a severe winter storm. They got lost. At no time in the twenty-eight-month journey were they in greater danger of perishing. Never were the captains' leadership abilities put to such a test. They had to get more out of the men than the men knew they had it in them to give.

Without those Shoshone horses to pack their baggage and carry them, they never would have made it.

They almost didn't anyway. On September 20, desperate, Clark went on ahead with a small party to force a way through the Bitterroots to the level country beyond. Lewis followed with the baggage and the main party. Clark killed one of his horses for food, leaving half of it hanging for Lewis's party. Clark and his group made it to a Nez Percé village; the Indians fed them roots. Clark sent one of the privates back to the Lewis party, with roots and dried fish. On September 22 Lewis finally came to the level country beyond the Rocky Mountains, where he met the private with the provisions and the good news that Clark had made friendly contact with the Nez Percé.

After eating, the party proceeded to a village of eighteen lodges, which it reached at 5:00 p.m. The expedition had made 160 miles since it left Traveler's Rest eleven days ago. It was one of the great forced marches in American history.

Lewis tried to describe his emotions: "the pleasure I now felt in having triumphed over the rocky Mountains and decending once more

---

[10] Quoted in Ronda, Lewis and Clark among the Indians, 157.

[11] Lewis made the comment in a letter of September 29, 1806, reprinted in Donald Jackson, ed., *Letters of the Lewis and Clark Expedition, with Related Documents, 1783–1854,* 2nd ed. (Urbana: University of Illinois Press, *1978), 339.*

to a level and fertile country where there was every rational hope of finding a comfortable subsistence for myself and party can be more readily conceived than expressed, nor was the flattering prospect of the final success of the expedition less pleasing."

Outstanding leadership made possible the triumph over the Rocky Mountains. Lewis and Clark had welded the Corps of Discovery into a tough, superbly disciplined family. They had built an unquestioning trust in themselves, and knew the strengths and skills of each of their men intimately. They had taken a calculated risk in trusting Old Toby, but their judgment that he knew what he was talking about (even though the talking was in sign language) proved to be justified.

Private Field told Lewis that Clark was at a second village, gathering information from the Nez Percé. At dark, Clark accompanied by Twisted Hair, a Nez Percé chief, returned and joined Lewis. "I found Capt Lewis & the party Encamped," he wrote, "much fatigued, & hungery, much rejoiced to find something to eate of which They appeared to partake plentifully." Clark's experience was that too many roots had made his hunters violently ill, so "I cautioned them of the Consequences of eateing too much & c," but they did, and consequently for over a week the expedition resembled a hospital ward for the critically ill more than it did a platoon of fighting men.

Herein lies one of the great stories of American history, even though it is a tale of what didn't happen rather than what did. It would have been the work of a few moments only for the Nez Percé to kill the white men and take for themselves all the expedition's goods. Had the Indians done so, they would have come into possession of by far the biggest arsenal not just west of the Rocky Mountains but west of the Mississippi River, along with priceless kettles, axes, hatchets, beads, and other trade items in quantities greater than any of them would ever see in their lifetimes.

Like the Shoshones, the Nez Percé had had no contact with whites, other than some cheap trade goods that had reached them from Columbia River tribes. They had only one or two inferior rifles. They were constantly harassed by their neighbors who did have guns, especially by the Blackfeet when the Nez Percé made their annual trip over the mountains to the buffalo country.

The Nez Percé were hardly oblivious to their once in-a-lifetime opportunity. According to their oral-history tradition, when they first met Clark and his six hunters—who had also gorged themselves on roots and fish and gotten dysentery—they considered killing them for their weapons. They were dissuaded by a woman named Watkuweis (meaning "Returned from a Far Country"). She had been captured by Blackfeet some six or seven years earlier, taken into Canada, and sold to a white trader. She lived with him, among other traders, for several years before somehow finding her way home. The traders had treated her much better than the Blackfeet had done, so when Clark arrived she told the warriors, "These are the people who helped me. Do them no hurt."[12]

First Sacagawea, now Watkuweis. The expedition owed more to Indian women than either captain ever acknowledged. And the United States owed more to the Nez Percé for their restraint than it ever acknowledged. When, in 1877, the army, carrying out government policy, drove Chief Joseph and the Nez Percé from their Idaho home, there were in the band old men and women who had as children been in Twisted Hair's village.

During the week Lewis was on his back, Clark moved camp to the junction of the North Fork of the Clearwater with the main stream, where there were Ponderosa pines of sufficient size to make canoes. On October 6 the canoes were finished. Clark made a cache for the saddles and a canister of powder. "I am verry Sick all night," he recorded, "pane in Stomach & the bowels." The next day, he opened his journal entry, "I continu verry unwell but obliged to attend every thing." Evidently Lewis was still so sick he couldn't even supervise the men's work. Lewis later wrote, "for my own part I suffered a severe Indisposition for 10 or 12 days, sick feeble & emiciated."[13]

Clark had the canoes put into the water and loaded. At 3:00 p.m., the party set out. The river was swift, with many bad rapids. Nevertheless, they made twenty miles. The expedition was once again waterborne, going downstream for the first time since Lewis had turned the keelboat from the Ohio into the Mississippi River, two years earlier. Ahead lay the Pacific.

---

[12] Moulton, *Journals of the Lewis and Clark Expedition,* 5:225; Ronda, *Lewis and Clark among the Indians,* 159.
[13] Jackson, *Letters of the Lewis and Clark Expedition,* 339.

11

"Marats, Dantons, and Robespierres"

Brother C. Edward

When Thomas Jefferson and the Republican Party came to power in 1801, the political fortunes of the Federalist Party in national affairs seemed to wane. New England Federalists were frequently frustrated by the policies of a government that, they believed, ignored the welfare of their region. The outbreak of the War of 1812 and the events which attended the war seemed to verify many New Englanders' suspicions that the likelihood of their influencing national events in the future was indeed bleak. In the latter part of 1814, at what appeared to be the nadir of the War of 1812, a group of concerned and basically responsible New Englanders met in Hartford, Connecticut, to discuss their concerns and to seek a course of action. The Hartford Convention proved to be a widely misunderstood movement and ultimately yielded nothing to the beleaguered New Englanders. It did, however, clearly delineate the divisions and tensions which complicated the relationships among the various sections of the United States in the early nineteenth century.

On Monday, February 13, 1815, Washington City savored the sweet, unfamiliar taste of victory. Andrew Jackson had routed the British at New Orleans, the Peace Treaty had been signed at Ghent, and the War of 1812 was over. Nothing more worth celebrating had happened in America since independence.

Harrison Gray Otis, Thomas H. Perkins, and William Sullivan tried hard to rejoice too. The end of hostilities removed a source of tragic national division, and they were pleased with that. But the hard fact was that the return of peace made fools of them sincere, honest fools, but fools all the same. How did three distinguished Massachusetts leaders get so out of harmony with their country's spirit? What quirk of history made them laughingstocks to a cheering nation? The answer is a painful story of intersectional stresses and strains, of misunderstandings and tensions that for decades threatened the survival of the Union.

The troubles began early. New England Federalists and Southern Democrats clashed even before their parties had names. Men of wealth, especially merchants dealing with England, usually believed their interests were best served by the Federalists. Those commercially involved with France and Asia, as well as farmers and artisans, were most often Democrats intensely concerned with national growth and eager to remove British influence from North American soil. Party distinctions were never that clear-cut, of course, but the generalization helps one to understand why the preponderance of Federalist strength centered in New England, a region whose prosperity was inextricably linked to trade with Great Britain.

There was some hope that these conflicting interests had been reconciled at the Constitutional Convention of 1787. There New England had succeeded in balancing its interests nicely against those of the other states. But this equilibrium was soon upset, and New England congressmen found themselves a dwindling fraction of the national legislature. Part of the decline was due to emigration. The opening of fertile lands north of the Ohio River, and later throughout the entire Louisiana Territory, was a powerful lure to the farmers of crowded New England. Their departure, swelling the population of the West, helped bring new states into existence. The once-powerful Northeast, suffering from a steady population drain, began losing political leverage.

There were other sources of friction too. The three-fifths clause of the Constitution, counting five slaves as the census equivalent of three freemen, gave Southern states additional seats in the House of Representatives. Nearly slaveless New England resented that. And there was the matter of immigration. Few of the arrivals from Europe settled in New England, but as they moved on, their numbers augmented the population and influence of other states.

Beginning in 1801, the presidencies of Jefferson and Madison increased the tension by presenting New England with sixteen years of administrations insensitive to the area's mercantile interests. These eclipsed states, prime movers in the founding of an independent America, failed repeatedly to obtain concessions from the national leadership. It had not always been like that, and New England's pride was stung to the quick.

The continual friction produced a sharp crisis in 1808. The Embargo Act of the previous year, an attempt to keep the United States out of the war between France and England, forbade American ships to engage in international trade. This unpopular law dealt a staggering blow to New England's economy. Their merchants were unhappy enough about losses from impressments and seizures, although they believed that they could survive those setbacks for a time. There was no way, however, to ride out a prolonged suppression of all European trade. Consequently, they demanded a prompt reopening of the ports.

The presidential election of 1808 gave the Federalists a chance to turn to the voters. Under the leadership of Harrison Gray Otis of Massachusetts, party officials met at New York in August and nominated Charles Cotesworth Pinckney of South Carolina for President and Rufus King of New York (formerly of Massachusetts) for Vice President. But the voters were no help; Madison won the election, and New England still chafed under the obnoxious embargo.

In January 1809, Congress rubbed salt in the wounds by authorizing use of the Army and Navy to hold American ships in port. The continuing idleness of New England seamen and shipyard workers brought hardship to rich and poor alike. But where could the people turn for relief? Federalist strength in Congress was insufficient to hold out much hope for help from that quarter. The sole alternative was the state government. Thus, indignant residents of cities like Newburyport, Massachusetts, pleaded with their legislatures "to interpose in our behalf for the removal of the recent distressing evils." Far more ominous, calls for secession broke out in the Federalist press. Hearing them, a worried Otis tried to head off trouble by proposing a convention to discuss the explosive situation.

Fortunately, the congressional Democrats took alarm, and the crisis passed. On March 1, 1809, a few days before he left office, Jefferson signed the repeal of the Embargo Act and the storm appeared to have blown over.

But not for long. With the declaration of war on June 18, 1812, the embargo was reinstated. New England Federalists protested military action against England by a government that had tolerated the same maritime depredations by France. The South and West, on the other hand, were eager to fight for freedom of navigation on the Mississippi and protection against Indians armed at Britain's western outposts. America had embarked on its first divisive war.

Federalist Governor Caleb Strong of Massachusetts gave vent to his party's indignation by proclaiming a statewide fast for peace. Calls for a New England convention rang out once more. It was 1808 all over again.

But again the trouble passed. The Democratic-controlled Massachusetts Senate stood immovably in the way of any effective action by that state. What did result was another New York meeting, this time to announce Federalist support of DeWitt Clinton for President. Young Clinton, a New York Democrat outside the Jefferson-Madison circle, was avidly seeking a route to the White House. The Federalists were glad to help him along in the hope that he might be able to retire Madison to his Virginia estate. Unhappily, Clinton lost, and the situation grew worse when Madison called the state militias into Federal service. Both Governors Strong of Massachusetts and Griswold of Connecticut defied the order, denouncing the requisition as unconstitutional.

The clamor for a convention grew louder as one military defeat followed another and the war stumbled aimlessly along. By 1814 pressure was mounting for nullification of the embargo, and for either the establishment of state customs agencies or state appropriation of Federal revenues. Governor Strong's resounding re-election in Massachusetts was a measure of the anti-nationalistic feeling in his state.

Yet the tension might again have eased had it not been for the success of British arms in Europe. Able to devote full time to America after defeating Napoleon, England stepped up her military efforts on all fronts. In August Washington was burned and Castine, Maine fell into British hands. Later the island of Nantucket was obliged to submit to British control. These events put Strong in a difficult position, with once friendly England now an obvious aggressor. Calling his legislature into special session on September 6, he faced a public demand for troops to defend the coastline, troops absent mainly because of his earlier failure to call them up. There was a real possibility of a Massachusetts ordinance of nullification, perhaps linked with a peace bid to England. Indeed, in mid-November Strong sent an emissary to Nova Scotia to explore the conditions for such an agreement. The cornered governor was keeping all his exits open.

Moderate Federalists could see the makings of rebellion all around them. Their leader, Harrison Otis, helped hold the line by gaining control of the Massachusetts special session and preventing any overt rupture with Washington. He achieved this as chairman of a select committee that listed grievances and called for a convention to discuss reforms in the Union to the States.

The Massachusetts General Court (Legislature) approved the recommendations, as well as the convention call. Strong responded promptly, dispatching letters of invitation to the governors of Connecticut, Rhode Island, New Hampshire, and Vermont. Connecticut replied favorably, offering the State House in Hartford as the site of the gathering. Rhode Island also agreed to send delegates. Governor John Taylor Gilman of New Hampshire, however, disliked the scent of secession he caught and declined to call his legislature into special session to consider the Massachusetts letter. And Governor Martin Chittenden of Vermont, himself nearly branded a traitor for his anti-war actions of the previous year, felt that with the invasion of New England the conflict had become exclusively defensive and was no longer torn by internal division. Hence, only three states appointed official delegates to Hartford. The two delegates from New Hampshire and the one from Vermont were chosen by county meetings, not by their state governments.

What sort of men were these twenty-six delegates? Were they the flaming firebrands one might expect at the onset of rebellion? Hardly. Massachusetts sent the largest delegation, twelve, but only one was any sort of radical. The chief voice for Massachusetts, and indeed for the whole convention, was cultured, wary Harrison Gray Otis. No one was a more dedicated Federalist, yet no one was less willing to take any unplanned plunges. His best-known Bay State colleague, George Cabot, was a reticent aristocrat who sought no office and hated public life. Nathan Dane, legal scholar and author of the Northwest Ordinance, was the very antithesis of a revolutionary. So were Stephen Longfellow, father of the poet, and William Prescott, father of historian George Prescott. The Massachusetts contingent was a notably solid conservative group, even by the estimate of political opponents.

The Connecticut delegation was equally conservative. The best-known of its seven members were ex-Governor John Treadwell, Lieutenant Governor Chauncey Goodrich, and Roger Minott Sherman, nephew of Declaration of Independence signer Roger Sherman. Rhode Island sent four exemplary citizens led by Samuel Ward, son of a Continental congressman and grandfather of Julia Ward Howe. Even the semi-official emissaries from New Hampshire and Vermont were moderates.

But the time had come to do something. How long could the Federalists sit on the pressure valve of New England opinion? As Otis saw it, the convention would at least provide a chance to let off steam before the whole boiler blew.

Despite their honorable intentions, however, these dignified statesmen took their share of lampooning. The hostile press delighted in associating their names with that of John Henry, a despised traitor of the day. The.Hartford town crier led a parade of convivial cronies around the State House, serenading the delegates with the lugubrious "Rogues March." Thomas Jefferson referred to the participants as "Marats, Dantons, and Robespierres." Probably John Adams, of all people, formed the fairest estimate. Not overly given to favorable opinions of his fellow men, Adams in this case spoke simply of "intelligent and honest men who had lost touch with reality."

On December 15, 1814, the convention assembled in the council chamber of the State House. Apparently the feeble winter sun shed very little light in the high-ceilinged second-floor chamber, for after electing George Cabot president, the convention voted so ill-advised a rule as secrecy. This blunder added fuel to the widespread suspicion that a conspiracy was under way, a suspicion Mrs. Longfellow recorded when she chided her husband for this lack of good judgment.

Yet there was no devious plotting, and the delegates hardly qualified as conspirators. On its first day the convention organized an agenda committee that recommended petitioning Congress for authority to unite against the British already encamped on the doorstep. To support this action, the committee proposed to appropriate Federal taxes collected in New England. In addition, the committee asked for the repeal of laws drafting state troops into Federal service. Another committee suggested several Constitutional amendments. On January 3, 1815, the full convention adopted these recommendations.

Only three committees functioned during the entire session, and their membership totaled but ten different individuals. Otis firmly controlled all three, and insisted to the end of his days that secession and a separate peace never came up for discussion. The assemblage adjourned *sine die* on January 5, with a committee of three empowered to call it back into session if events warranted.

The "Report" of the convention repeated the familiar New England grievances; inadequate representation in the national government, the harmful effects of embargoes, the unconstitutionality of drafting state militias into Federal service, and the injustice of denying Federal taxes to state governments for local defense. To help remedy these abuses, Otis and his colleagues proposed seven amendments to the Federal Constitution:

1. Abolishment of the three-fifths clause.
2. Approval by a two-thirds vote of Congress for the admission of new states to the Union.
3. Limitation of embargoes to sixty days.
4. Approval of embargo laws by a two-thirds vote of Congress.
5. Approval by a two-thirds vote of Congress for a declaration of war.
6. Disqualification of the foreign-born from national office.
7. Limitation of Presidents to one term, with no two successive Presidents to come from the same state.

Amendments 1, 6, and 7 were aimed at limiting the extent of non-New England influence in the national government. Numbers 2 through 5 attempted to protect the commerce which was the region's lifeblood.

The convention transmitted its report to the legislature of Massachusetts, Connecticut, and Rhode Island. The first responded by complimenting the delegates on their attachments to the Constitution and authorizing Governor Strong to send emissaries to present the resolutions to President Madison and Secretary of War Monroe. Strong named Otis, Boston merchant Thomas H. Perkins, and lawyer-historian William Sullivan.

The trio had little zest for their assignment, fearing that the moment for such a petition had passed. In this pessimistic mood they left Boston on Friday, February 3. Before reaching Baltimore on the 12th they knew of Jackson's victory at New Orleans. And the next day, when they reached Washington, they learned that another rumor was also true. The peace treaty had been signed at Ghent, and their mission had collapsed.

They did meet Madison and Monroe but, as they foresaw, no attention was paid to their now pointless protests. History had moved too fast, depriving New England of its chance for a dramatic confrontation with the Madison Administration. The anticlimactic ending was all the more unsatisfactory since there had never been a climax. Had it all been worthwhile? Probably not. The Hartford Convention was a responsible reaction to accumulated grievances. But the delegates forgot that they were no longer simply New Englanders; America had become a nation, not merely a loose association of sectional governments. This miscalculation might have proved tragic if Jackson had lost at New Orleans. In that event the war very likely would have resumed, peace treaty or not, and secession might have come almost a half-century before it did. Would it then have been the South that fought to preserve the Union? The road of history has taken stranger turns.

12

Eli Whitney:
Nemesis of the South

Arnold Whitridge

"Cotton is King," boasted Senator James Henry Hammond of South Carolina in 1858. "No power on earth dares to make war on it." Events from 1860 to 1865, however, would prove his words only partly correct. Cotton produced by slave labor did indeed rule the economy of the South, but when eleven southern states attempted to leave the Union in response to the election of a president who opposed the spread of slavery, the United States dared to make war on the cotton kingdom and did so successfully. Ironically, both the rule of King Cotton and the ability of the United States to defeat the South in the Civil War depended heavily on the inventive genius of a Massachusetts-born inventor named Eli Whitney. Whitney invented the cotton gin in 1793, and he later promoted the use of interchangeable parts in manufacturing. How, according to this article by Arnold Whitridge, did Whitney's inventive genius make him a nemesis (a cause of harm and failure) of the South?

Any American who ruminates about the origins of the Civil War—and that should mean not only professional historians but everyone in the United States, north and south, who has ever been spellbound by the story of their country—will find himself confronted sooner or later by an ingenious contraption for removing seeds from the cotton boll, known as the cotton gin.

This device, invented by Eli Whitney, a totally unknown young man just out of Yale College, changed the whole pattern of cotton production. No invention ever answered a more pressing need.

Immediately after graduating from Yale, in 1792, Whitney had been engaged as a private tutor for a family in Georgia. On his way to take up his post he made the acquaintance of Mrs. Nathanael Greene, widow of the Revolutionary general, who was returning to Savannah after spending the summer in the North. An invitation to stay at Mrs. Greene's plantation, all the more welcome when he discovered that his prospective employer had hired another man in his place, brought him into contact with the cotton aristocracy of the neighborhood. Whitney soon endeared himself to his hostess by his extraordinary "handiness." There was nothing that this big, rambling man with the extraordinary deft fingers could not make or mend.

As a boy on the farm, the oldest of five children, he had always preferred puttering around his father's workshop to doing the farm chores. He was born in Westboro, Massachusetts in 1765, the year of the Stamp Act. By the time he was grown the exciting days of the Revolution were over, and the farmers of Massachusetts were learning to their amazement that independence and prosperity did not necessarily go hand in hand. Some of them, discouraged by debts they could not pay, joined Shays' Rebellion against the state government, but Eli Whitney stuck to the farm and eked out the family income by manufacturing nails, even hiring a helper to fill his orders. When the demand for nails slacked off, he turned to making hat pins and walking canes. Neighbors got into the habit of looking up Eli Whitney, whenever they needed anything repaired. He even made a violin for one of them which was said to have produced "tolerable good music."

At the age of eighteen it came home to him that he needed a college degree if he was ever to be anything more than a clever mechanic. The family was not sympathetic: by the time he had prepared himself for college he would be too old, and besides the family could not afford it. Eli listened to all their complaints and then disregarded them. He taught school for three winters, finally won his father's consent, and was admitted to Yale in 1789, when he was 23 years old. He was not a brilliant student, but when the Reverend Ezra Stiles, the president of Yale, was asked to recommend a suitable person for a private tutor out of the graduating class of 1792, Eli Whitney was the man he chose. Though he was not planning to become either a minister or a lawyer, like most of his classmates, there was something about him that inspired confidence.

Evidently Mrs. Greene in Savannah had faith in him too, and when a party of her friends, officers who had served under the general in the Revolutionary War, were discussing the deplorable state of agriculture in their neighborhood, she referred them to the young Yale graduate who was staying with her. They were bemoaning the fact that there was no quick, practical way of separating short staple cotton from its seed. It took a slave ten hours to separate one pound of lint from three pounds of the small tough seeds. Under those conditions no one in the South could afford to grow cotton, and yet in other parts of the world cotton was becoming a semiprecious commodity. "Gentlemen," said Mrs. Greene, "tell your troubles to Mr. Whitney, he can make anything."

Mr. Whitney could and did. Within two weeks he had produced a model of the cotton gin, an ingenious device which was destined to have an ultimately disastrous effect upon the people it enriched. By the process he devised, the cotton was dragged through a wire screen by means of toothed cylinders revolving towards each other. A revolving brush cleaned the cylinders, and the seed fell into another compartment. A later model, run by water power, could produce 300 to 1,000 pounds a day.

Whitney wrote to his father that he hoped to keep his invention a "profound secret," but rumor spread so quickly that long before he could get to Washington and take out a patent his workshop had been broken open and his machine examined. The marauders discovered that the gin was easy enough to copy, and on the strength of what they saw they planted cotton on a scale never dreamed of before. In 1792 the United States was exporting only 138,000 pounds of cotton. Two years later that figure had risen to 1,601,000 pounds. Never had any invention made such an immediate impression upon society, abroad as well as at home.

In Great Britain the invention of spinning frames and power looms had created a demand which could be filled only from the southern states. The supplies from the Levant, from Guyana and from the West Indies, which had met nearly all needs down to 1794, fell into the back-ground as the export of American slave-grown and mechanically ginned cotton suddenly began to climb. By the end of the first quarter of the nineteenth century, America was shipping to Liverpool more than three-quarters of all the cotton consumed in the United Kingdom. Eli Whitney had conjured up an army of 450,000 cotton workers in England. Ten thousand power looms and 240,000 hand looms secured the cotton planters against the danger of a glutted market.

The existence of this market and the possibility of supplying it with ease and profit made cotton planting the one absorbing industry of the South. The Louisiana Purchase had opened to slave-holding settlement and culture a vast domain of the richest soil on earth in a region peculiarly adapted to the expanding production of cotton. As the production grew, so did the value of black slaves. By 1825, when cotton was selling at fifteen cents a pound, a good black field hand who had been worth only $500 twenty years earlier would often bring $1,500 on a New Orleans auction block.

The phenomenal success of the cotton industry, for which Eli Whitney was directly responsible, gave birth in the South to an entirely new conception of slavery. In the early days of the Republic the most thoughtful southerners, including Washington and Jefferson, had deprecated slavery as an evil, which must eventually be swept away. No one denied that slavery was a moral evil and a menace to the country. Almost every Virginian hoped to make real the opening words of Jefferson's Bill of Rights, "that all men are by nature free and independent." As the French traveler Chastellux wrote, "they are constantly talking of abolishing slavery, and of contriving some other means of cultivating their estates."

Such ideas gradually came to be regarded as old-fashioned. What, asked Daniel Webster in 1850, had created the new feeling in favor of slavery in the South, so that it became an institution to be cherished—

> no evil, no scourge, but a great religious, social and moral blessing? I suppose this is owing to the rapid growth and sudden extension of the cotton plantations of the South. It was the cotton interest that gave a new desire to promote slavery, to spread it, and to use its labor.

The doctrine that Cotton was King, and that all other interests in the nation would bow before it, had permeated the whole South by the middle of the century. Few of the northerners who scoffed at this doctrine remembered that it was a northern inventor who gave slavery its new lease on life. It was hard to protest against a system upon which the whole prosperity of one section of the country seemed to hinge. Unwittingly, Eli Whitney had set in motion an undercurrent against the notions of equality and freedom. He himself made nothing out of his cotton gin, but he was none the less the founder of the cotton empire, an empire which everybody believed would inevitably collapse if the under-pinning of slavery were removed. The cotton gin, like many other inventions, turned out to be so valuable to the world as to be worthless to its inventor. The government could offer him no protection against the infringement of patent rights. The suits he brought were tried before juries composed of the very men who were breaking the patents. Whitney discussed his predicament dispassionately in a letter to Robert Fulton, another disappointed inventor:

> The difficulties with which I have had to contend have originated principally in the want of a disposition in Mankind to do justice . . . My invention was new and distinct . . . I have always maintained that I should

have had no difficulty in causing my rights to be respected if it had been less valuable and used only by a small portion of the community.

Unable to make a living out of the cotton gin, he turned his back on the South. He settled in New Haven and determined to devote himself to the production of something profitable, something which could not easily be copied and appropriated by others. Alexander Hamilton's "Report on Manufactures," presented to Congress in 1791, had emphasized the importance of making the United States independent of foreign nations for military purposes. Alone of Hamilton's state papers, this report fell flat. It was only later that its wisdom came to be generally recognized, but Eli Whitney was one of those who did not have to be converted. In 1798, disturbed by the danger of war with France, he wrote to Oliver Wolcott, the secretary of the treasury, offering to manufacture "ten or fifteen thousand Stand of Arms." By "stand of arms" was meant the complete arms necessary to equip a soldier—the musket, bayonet, ramrod, wiper and screwdriver.

After some haggling the offer was accepted. Whitney journeyed down to Washington and returned to New Haven with a contract in his pocket for 10,000 muskets, costing $13.40 each, to be delivered within two years. He proposed to manufacture these muskets on a new principle, the principle of interchangeable parts.

Here was a man who as early as 1798 could visualize the government's need of a constant supply of firearms, who could devise methods of production that would guarantee such a supply, and who, handicapped by the lack of a machine that would enable workmen to cut metal according to pattern, proceeded to invent one which has remained unchanged in principle for a century and a half.

This milling machine, as it was called, was in itself a major innovation. It was the cornerstone of his new system of interchangeable parts, by means of which he was able to make the same parts of different guns as much like each other as "the successive impressions of a copper-plate engraving." Life in America had produced plenty of mechanics, particularly in New England, but few craftsmen. What Whitney did was to substitute for the skill of the craftsman the uniformity of the machine.

Foreigners have often observed as one of the characteristics of American industry that we build from the top down rather than from the ground up. Eli Whitney did not start with a few workmen and then gradually expand. He "tooled up" first. Before a single workman walked into his factory he designed and built all the machinery he would need for his method of production. At the same time he proved himself a practical businessman as well as an inventor. He understood how to obtain contracts, finance their execution and provide funds for future expansion.

The importance of what Eli Whitney was doing did not readily penetrate the official mind. His friend Oliver Wolcott had been replaced in the Treasury by Samuel Dexter, a Massachusetts lawyer, who instinctively distrusted theories not sanctioned by experience. Whitney's methods seemed to him unorthodox. As if to justify his suspicions, Whitney was soon running behind on his schedule of deliveries. In the first year only 500 guns were produced instead of the stipulated 4,000. Dexter was not surprised by his request for an advance of $10,000, but he took his time answering the letter and only agreed very grudgingly after insisting on further guarantees.

Fortunately the new President, Thomas Jefferson, was blessed with the receptive, ranging mind of his generation. The idea of inter-changeable parts was already familiar to him. In 1785, while minister to France, he had visited the workshop of a certain Monsieur LeBlanc who was engaged in manufacturing muskets on exactly that principle. He had himself put together the parts of fifty locks, "taking pieces at hazard as they came to hand." So impressed was he by this new method of manufacture that he suggested bringing Monsieur LeBlanc over to America, but the government was not interested in newfangled techniques. Nor indeed was the French government, which probably distrusted any invention that might possibly lead to unemployment.

Nothing more is heard of Monsieur LeBlanc. "I do not know what became of him," said Jefferson. He had flashed across the screen of history and disappeared. In England, too, other men had anticipated Whitney in the application of mass production to an article with inter-changeable parts. Joseph Bramah, the great machine designer, and Marc Brunel, a young French Royalist officer who had been driven out of his country during the Revolution, had manufactured pulley blocks on this system for the British Navy, but it was left to an American to develop the process and put it to the service of mankind.

Whitney himself probably never realized how far his system would reach. The new technique which had been adopted as a defense measure for the manufacture of firearms was soon found to be no less applicable to other industries. The Connecticut clockmakers began making brass clocks instead of wooden clocks, as soon as the advantages of inter-changeable manufacture were recognized. Elias Howe and Isaac Singer followed with the sewing machine, and before the outbreak of the Civil War Cyrus McCormick and his rivals were producing the harvesters and reapers that rolled back the frontier and revolutionized farming the world over.

For these inventions and a hundred others Eli Whitney paved the way. The successful application of his theory of interchangeable parts proved a landmark in the over-all growth of American mass production. In Europe, where there was no shortage of skilled labor, the idea of mass production made slow progress. It caught on only in the gun-making industry where the advantages were too obvious to be ignored. By the middle of the century nearly every government in Europe was supplied with American gun-making machinery, all planned to operate on what was known everywhere as the "American System."

In the southern states the rich planters who had profited so enormously from the cotton gin paid no attention to the increasing tempo of industrial activity in the North. One southern state, South Carolina, paid $50,000 to the inventor of the cotton gin as a belated acknowledgment of what society owed him, but no one in the South seemed to be aware of the new techniques in manufacture evolved by this same inventor, techniques of which the seceding states were soon to find themselves desperately in need. The fact was that conditions of labor, soil, and climate had produced a static society in the South which refused to accept the implications of the nineteenth century.

It is one of the ironies of history that the man who inadvertently contributed to the downfall of the South by his invention of the cotton gin should also have blazed the trail leading to the technological supremacy of the North. The loss of the will to fight in the closing days of the Confederacy can be traced in large part to the feeling that the South had reached the limit of its resources, whereas in the North every deficiency in equipment could always be made good.

As to inherent fighting ability no distinction can be made between the Union and Confederate soldier, but in the quantity as well as the quality of their equipment the advantage was all with the northerner. While it is true that the extraordinarily resourceful General Gorgas, the Confederate chief of ordinance, managed to keep the gray armies supplied with the necessary weapons and munitions up to the very end of the war, even General Gorgas could not keep pace with the inventiveness and the productivity of northern arsenals and northern factories. On more than one occasion a single northern regiment, armed with breech-loading rifles, held in check a whole brigade armed with the ordinary musket. As one Confederate soldier put it, "it is no use for us to fight you'uns with that kind of gun."

The disparity in clothing and equipment was even more marked than the disparity in weapons. The southern soldier had to find most of his own equipment, whereas the northerner was supplied by the government. If the northern soldier faced privation, as he often did, it was the fault of shady contractors and incompetent quartermasters.

The New England factories were turning out all the uniforms, the boots, and the varied accoutrements he could possibly need.

The Civil War, at bottom, was the first of the truly modern wars, in which the industrial potential of a nation forms the foundation on which all military plans and achievements must ultimately be built. Given that situation, the advantage was all with the North.

Before the war even began, William Tecumseh Sherman warned a southern friend that a purely agricultural nation, like the South, could not hope to fight against a nation of mechanics. "You are bound to fail," he said, sharply, and events bore out his contention. As the war progressed, the entire southern economy came under intolerable strain. In the end, it simply became impossible for the Confederacy to carry the burden any longer.

But the North could produce, in almost any required volume, the infinite variety and number of goods needed to support a nation at war. For this technique it was, to a large extent, indebted to Whitney.

Eli Whitney died in 1825, long before the "irrepressible conflict" had cast its shadow over American history. He himself was unaware of the part he had played in the expansion of slavery, just as he was unaware of the mighty industrial forces he had set in motion. He had invented the cotton gin and he had manufactured muskets on a new system for a war against France that never materialized, but by those two achievements he had affected the whole course of American history. By the first he riveted slavery on the South and thus created a tension between the two sections of the country which could only be resolved by war. And by the second he gave an impetus to the mass production of inexpensive goods which has created what the world knows as the American standard of living, and which has reunited us, in spite of all the differences in our backgrounds, into an amazingly homogeneous nation.

13

Engineering the Erie Canal

John Tarkov

The movement of people and goods along canals on boats pulled by draft animals may seem quaint in an age of railroads and superhighways; not to mention skies filled with jet airliners. In the early nineteenth century, however, canals played a key role in a Transportation Revolution that swept the United States, allowing a market-based economy to replace the older subsistence way of living and contributing greatly to the rise of industrialization and urbanization. This article tells the story of the first great canal, the Erie, which ran across New York State from Lake Erie to the Hudson River at Albany. Built between 1817 and 1825, the Erie Canal allowed New York City to become the center of commerce between the Atlantic coast and the old Northwest, one of the keys in making it the largest city in the United States. Moreover, the challenge of building a 363-mile canal, much of it through rugged terrain, produced the first generation of American engineers. Although railroads proved more effective and largely replaced canals as a means of transportation by the mid-nineteenth century, man-made waterways such as the Erie Canal were technological and commercial marvels in their day.

Thomas Jefferson had a good eye for real estate on a grand scale. But when the notion of a canal linking the Great Lakes with the Hudson River near Albany, New York, was put before him in 1809 by two New York State legislators, he dismissed it out of hand, "Why, sir," he said, " . . . you talk of making a canal three hundred and fifty miles long through a wilderness! It is a little short of madness to think of it at this day!"

The idea of the Erie Canal tended to arouse that kind of skepticism wherever it is broached, and it has been difficult for later historians writing about the canal not to disparage its many early critics. The Erie Canal turned out, after all, to be a resounding success, perhaps the single most important public work ever built in the United States. But at the time, its opponents were merely being prudent. There were many more reasons to believe the Erie would fail than that it would succeed.

Canal building was hardly an advanced craft, much less a science, in early nineteenth-century America. The two most ambitious artificial waterways attempted prior to the Erie were the twenty-two-mile-long Santee Canal near Charleston, South Carolina, and the twenty-seven-mile-long Middlesex Canal linking the Merrimack River with the Charles River and Boston Harbor. Neither had much to commend it. Completed in 1800, the Santee took eight years to build and was a fiscal nightmare. It wasn't much of a canal either. Political cronyism had pushed its path away from natural water sources, so that eventually two-thirds of its channel lay bone dry. The Middlesex, finished in 1803 after nine years of work, didn't pay a dividend to its stockholders until 1819.

The Santee and the Santee and the Middlesex were built at the approximate rate of two miles per year. If they were any yardsticks, the Erie, with its 363-mile length and its significantly larger channel (forty feet wide and four feet deep) might well be open by the millennium.

The most serious impediment to progress on both the Santee and Middlesex works was the lack of trained engineers. In the early nineteenth century there was not a single native-born engineer in America. The Santee Canal had been engineered by a peevish and none-too-honest Swede named Christian Senf. The Middlesex began in American hands, but the local magistrate chosen to lay out the canal line quickly proved incompetent, and an Englishman named William Weston was called in as consulting engineer.

Of the handful of European engineers working in this country around 1800, Weston was the most active, but he was not a man of prodigious talent; many of the structures he designed for the Middlesex Canal simply fell apart. The historian Elting E. Morison writes of Weston: "Knowing not much, he knew a great deal more than anyone else and was in frequent demand." He was in demand once again in 1816, when—after years of discussion, debate, and political maneuvering—New York State seemed poised to proceed with its canal undertaking. The state's board of canal commissioners offered him seven thousand dollars to come from England and oversee construction of the Erie, but Weston declined on the grounds of his advancing age and his desire to stay with his family.

At that point the canal commissioners discontinued their search for foreign expertise and instead appointed four residents of upstate New York—Benjamin Wright, James Geddes, Charles Broadhead, and Nathan S. Roberts—to be principal engineers on the canal. None of these men had ever even seen a canal before. Wright, Geddes, and Broadhead were judges. They knew surveying because such knowledge was useful to magistrates when they heard property cases. Roberts was a schoolteacher who taught himself surveying at Wright's urging.

But simple surveying, the kind that goes into making boundaries is of limited use when it comes to building a canal. Canal engineers must be able to measure elevations with a precision that allows for vertical errors measured in inches over horizontal stretches measured in dozens of miles. None of the four principal engineers appointed to building the Erie had ever taken a level before. But within a year they had taught themselves well enough so that when Geddes and Wright ran levels by different routes from Rome to Syracuse in the spring of 1818, enclosing a loop of one hundred miles, their final readings differed by less than two inches.

In all the many other details of canal building, they learned as they went, becoming engineers long after the title had been conferred on them. This was as true for the younger engineers on the canal as it was for men like Geddes and Wright. Virtually every American engineer of consequence during the first half of the nineteenth century learned his profession either on the Erie Canal or from an engineer who had been there. The Erie was truly, as a number of historians have said, America's first school of engineering. Men learned things there because they had to, and they learned them in whatever way they could: by mistakes, by watching and asking questions, and by accepting expert authority without regard to rank.

In 1818, for example, a minister and amateur mathematician named David Bates was serving as the resident engineer along a stretch of the canal east of Syracuse, and a young farmer named John Jervis was working as a target man in Bates's surveying party. Jervis had gained a rudimentary knowledge of leveling the previous year while felling trees for the canal and had buttressed this knowledge by studying two books on the subject. He ended up teaching Bates how to measure elevations.

Bates learned well from his subordinate. Later in life he was the principal engineer of the Ohio canal system. Jervis went on to become one of the greatest American engineers of the nineteenth century. Years later he wrote that on the Erie "the mechanical department of engineering was practically in its infancy. . . The plan for a timber trunk for the aqueducts was prepared and submitted by a carpenter,

Mr. Cady of Chittenango. This plan was adopted in nearly all the wood trunk aqueducts on the canal. At this day it stands as a well designed plan."

By 1819 local contractors and mechanics like Cady working on the first section of canal under construction—the ninety-four miles between the Seneca River and Utica—had invented three immensely valuable laborsaving devises. The land they were clearing was thick forest, and without their new machinery, the entire enterprise might have ground to a halt early on.

The first of the three inventions made it possible for one man to fell a tree of any size without using a saw or an ax. The worker would secure one end of a cable to the trunk of a tree some sixty feet above the ground and the other end to a roller turned by a gear with a crank. After anchoring the apparatus to the ground one hundred feet from the base of the tree, the workers would turn the crank. The tremendous leverage obtained by fastening the cable so high up made it only a matter of time and exertion before the tree crashed to the ground.

The stumps left behind could be extracted by another local invention. It rested on two huge wheels sixteen feet in diameter joined by an axle almost two feet thick and thirty feet long—in other words, a fair-sized tree. Midway along this axle-tree was a smaller wheel, fourteen feet in diameter, with its spokes firmly united to the axle barrel. A rope was fastened to the rim of this middle wheel, wound around it several times, and its loose end attached to a yoke of draft animals.

The middle wheel would be positioned almost directly over a stump, the two larger wheels braced, and a chain made fast to both the thick axle and the stump. When the team of horses or oxen pulled on the rope, the rotation of the wheel made the entire axle turn, winding the chain around it and gradually uprooting even fresh, green stumps. With this huge machine seven men and a pair of horses could pull thirty or forty stumps in a day.

The third invention was a plow with a heavy piece of sharpened iron attached to it; when draft animals pulled the plow, the plate traveled below the ground, cutting through roots as thick as two inches so that they could be easily scraped away.

From almost the beginning, plowing and scraping were the preferred method of excavation on the Erie, since the continual traffic of men and animals packed and strengthened the banks in a way that shoveling and carting could not. Spades and wheelbarrows did have to be used when the ground was wet, but on the Erie new spades were designed to cut through roots more easily, and new wheelbarrows provided greater ease in carting dirt away.

All these means for clearing and shaping the land were in use by 1819. So was a well-organized system—based on the accountability of contractors—for letting many small excavation and construction contracts to private citizens along the canal's route (the state put up major structures, such as aqueducts and dams). There was an ample supply of local labor, supplemented with Irish immigrants shipped north by New York City's Tammany Hall. There was a core of engineers whose diligence more than compensated for their inexperience.

And yet despite all that, the Erie Canal might have been a failure—even at the early state—for lack of one vital commodity: material for building durable locks. If the locks were built of wood, they would rot in a few years. Good stone locks needed hydraulic cement for waterproof mortaring, but the only known sources of hydraulic cement were in Europe, so the cost of that would be prohibitive. The only solution was to build the locks by uniting stone to stone with ordinary mortar and applying a thin coating of imported hydraulic cement at the joints between them. It was a concession to the apparently inevitable: The Erie's locks were destined to fall apart fast. The only question was how fast.

That question became academic almost as quickly as it became critical. In 1818, quite by accident, contractors along the canal line discovered natural cement rock. It was also discovered by a Herkimer County physician named Andrew Bartow, who demonstrated its potential for the benefit of Benjamin Wright and Wright's chief assistant engineer, Canvass White. In a tavern in the village of Chittenango, Bartow mixed the pulverized rock powder with sand and placed a ball of it into a bucket of water. By morning the mixture had hardened to the point where it could be rolled across the floor like a stone.

Canvass White, easily the most gifted engineer on the canal, had spent the previous winter in England—at his own expense—studying existing canals and learning about hydraulic cement. By the start of the 1819 construction season, he had perfected the process for refining this local rock into true cement powder. By the time the canal was completed, more than four hundred thousand bushels of it had been used. It firmly held together every bit of masonry on the canal, from mundane little culverts to gigantic aqueducts—and, of course, good stone locks. (The gates were of wood.)

White's discovery exploded on the scene so quickly that his patent on the process was conveniently ignored by all the manufacturers. Eventually the state legislature considered awarding him ten thousand dollars in compensation. He was entitled to at least six times that in royalties, but even the attempt at partial reparation fell through. It was a typical outcome for White. Perhaps an engineering genius, he was luckless in his financial affairs. He died young, in 1834, leaving his widow little more than the furniture she was compelled to sell.

The discovery of native hydraulic cement came as the building of the Erie Canal was about to enter a more technically difficult phase. The middle section had been chosen as the starting point for construction in 1817 because it offered advantages to both the engineers and the pro-canal politicians. Politically the advantage of starting in the middle was twofold. Results, measured in navigable canal miles, could be effected quickly there and then used as leverage to obtain more state fund for further work. At the same time as the middle section was completed, popular support for the rest of the canal would grow in the areas to the east and west.

Engineering a canal forty feet wide and four feet deep through the ninety-four miles of wilderness between Utica and the Seneca River was no mean technical feat, but the problems it presented were minor compared with the ones that lay in the later segments. If the canal was a school of engineering, the middle section offered the appropriate introductory course.

That course was completed in the fall of 1819, and the middle section was opened for navigation the following spring. Along the 270-odd miles of unfinished channel remaining, the most striking engineering problems (and solutions) were to be found in the 158-mile western portion, between the Seneca River and Buffalo, but the more difficult, if less spectacular, engineering had to be done in the east. There the canal dropped 419 feet in the 109 miles between Utica and the Hudson River; between Lake Erie and Utica the drop was only 146 feet over 252 miles.

The magnitude of the descent in the eastern section would have offered enough of a challenge by itself, but the difficulty was compounded by the inhospitable topography of the Mohawk River valley, through which eighty-six miles of the canal's line had to be laid out. The banks of the Mohawk were cramped by steep hillsides, which in places ended at the water's edge. This required construction of the canal channel in the river itself, supported on a masonry base and protected by high embankments. The canal's eastern section was a potential nightmare, and it fell to White, by now a principal engineer of the canal in everything but title, to make the best of it.

The key to his solution lay in his placement of locks, which automatically determined the location of pound levels—the stretches of channel between the locks. In order to take advantage of the better line available on the north bank, he ran the canal across the Mohawk four miles below Schenectady on a 748-foot-long aqueduct. Twelve miles farther east, at the Cohoes Falls, he recrossed to the south bank via a 1,188-foot-long aqueduct. White saw the work through in three years. By the end of 1823, the Erie was open from Brockport, some twenty miles west of Rochester, all the way to the Hudson River at Albany.

At that point, about eighty miles of channel, between Brockport and Buffalo, awaited completion. Already standing were two of the western Erie's engineering triumphs: the Irondequoit Embankment and the Genesee River Aqueduct.

Not far east of Rochester, an unexceptional stream called Irondequoit Creek had carved out a valley and an engineering challenge. Taking the canal across it without adding about one hundred and fifty feet of up-and-down lockage was imperative. The only thing that made the task even remotely possible was the presence of several natural ridges that could carry the canal at least partway over the valley it would have to span. James Geddes had long advocated linking these ridges together with great earthwork embankments and running the canal across the top; the canal commissioners were hesitant to approve so bold a plan, but finally realizing that they had few real options, they authorized the work to proceed as Geddes had proposed.

The Irondequoit Embankment, built entirely during the season of 1822, consisted of three natural ridges jointed together by two man-made ridges, one 1,320 feet long and the other 231 feet. The canal ran along the narrow summit for 4,950 feet, passing 76 feet above Irondequoit Creek, which flowed through a 245-foot-long culvert. Since the valley's soil was unsuitable for such enormous earthworks, small mountains of earth had to be hauled from elsewhere. Even so, there was no great confidence that the embankment would hold up; from its completion in October until the close of the 1822 season, the work was drained nightly.

A few miles farther west, in Rochester, a stone aqueduct carrying the canal over the Genesee River was completed in 1823; its combined span of 802 feet made it the second longest aqueduct on the canal. But impressive as the aqueduct and the embankment were, the engineering work that captured the most attention lay about sixty-five miles to the west, in Lockport, where the canal had to be lifted up into the Niagara Escarpment and where, for two miles, its channel would be blasted out of solid rock.

The work there began in 1822 and took three years. What stood at Lockport upon completion of the job were five double locks, one set of five for going up, a parallel set of five for going down. West of the locks, which quickly won popular renown as the Lockport Fives, the channel ran for seven miles through the Niagara ridge. To get through the most difficult portion—the two miles known as the Deep Cut—

workers had to blast free and haul away nearly 1.5 million cubic yards of rock.

While progress was being measured in feet and inches at Lockport, the final section of the canal, between Lockport and Buffalo, was being built more quickly—but nevertheless to an extraordinary standard of care. To propel water down from Lake Erie, the fifty miles of channel from Buffalo to Lockport were sloped at exactly one inch per mile. By the summer of 1825, the job was done. A few final details remained; then, on October 26, 1825, the Erie Canal formally opened amid statewide ceremony and celebration that lasted for weeks.

The ceremony and celebration ended with the year, but the effect of the canal on America had just begun. The Erie had cost the state about $ 7.9 million to build, but it attracted such a huge volume of commercial traffic that it paid for itself through toll revenues in less than ten years. Its awesome vitality as an avenue of commerce catapulted New York City into the position of preeminence that Philadelphia had always assumed would be its own. It turned western New York State from wilderness into a prosperous country of farms, towns, and busy manufacturing cities.

And as emigrants passed over the canal heading west, it had the same civilizing and nurturing influence on Ohio, Indiana, and the other states of the Old Northwest. The Erie appreciably advanced the timetable of American development.

But what if the canal had not been built? What if the task had proved too great and the work had been abandoned?

In his definitive History of the Canal System of the State of New York, written in 1905, Noble E. Whitford indulged in some fascinating speculative history. Without the Erie, he wrote, Canada would have been "enriched . . . commercially and strategically almost in proportion as it would have tended to impoverish us." With the completion of the Welland Canal across the isthmus between Lake Erie and Lake Ontario in 1831, the already established tendency of Northwestern trade to gravitate up the St. Lawrence would have been greatly accelerated. Moreover, Canada would have gained strategic control of the outlet to the Great Lakes, making it possible for the British government to translate that advantage into naval control of the lakes. All this at a time when their vital importance in the War of 1812 was still fresh in the memory.

Within the United States, the natural outlets for the northwestern trade were the Ohio and Mississippi rivers, and prior to the building of the Erie Canal, trade was drifting south along those routes just as it was drifting north to Montreal. Without the Erie Canal the impetus it gave for the building of other canals and, later, east-west railroads, geographic expediency would have routed that trade north and south. "Chicago could hardly have become so great an emporium," wrote Whitford, " . . .and not a little of the commercial prestige of Boston, New York and Baltimore . . . would then, perchance, have descended upon New Orleans and Mobile and Galveston. More portentous still than this commercial alliance between the Northwest and the South is the consequent probability that out of it there would have grown racial sympathy and political kinship, with what effect upon the great issues which culminated in the Civil War or upon present constituency of the American land and people, we can only conjecture."

But the canal had been built, and there was no conjecture as to its benefits. The men who built it found themselves in high demand as "canal fever" swept the country in the wake of the Erie's success. Benjamin Wright would still be referred to as the father of American engineering had he retired after the Erie, but he served as either the chief engineer or the consulting engineer for practically every major canal built in the United States for the next sixteen years, and for the Harlem and Erie railroads as well.

James Geddes was sixty-two when the Erie was done, but he continued canal work in Ohio and Maine before retiring. Canvass White served as the chief engineer of several canals, including the Delaware and Raritan. Nathan Roberts, who designed the famous Lockport Fives, was chief engineer on the Pennsylvania State Canal and at Muscle Shoals on the Tennessee River. After serving as chief engineer of the Ohio Canal System, David Bates moved on to success in railroad engineering. Before he too moved on to railroads, John Jervis's triumphs included the Delaware and Hudson Canal and New York City's Croton Aqueduct.

They did not build a perfect canal—no one does. The old Erie required a great deal of maintenance and repair, and it was alternately bedeviled by floods along streams that fed it or crossed its path and by low water due to leakage through its bed and banks. In 1836 the state began a twenty-six-year program of enlarging and improving the canal, guided by an authoritative, canal-long survey led by such men as John Jervis and Nathan Roberts. The survey found problems along every section of the canal, and some required substantial changes.

None of this detracts from the original accomplishment. That there was a profitable and maintainable canal in operation at all in 1837 speaks volumes about the kind of men who put it there. The few of them who had any technical knowledge at all had been nothing more than plain old-fashioned country surveyors before the Erie began. The rest had been farmers, craftsmen, merchants: the ordinary settlers of a wilderness. To do what they were asked to do, they had to reinvent themselves, and in reinventing themselves, they accomplished something unimagined and extraordinary. They invented the American engineer.

14

The Trail of Tears

Dee Brown

The displacement of the Amerindian commenced with the first English settlements along the Atlantic seaboard early in the seventeenth century and continued until after the American Civil War. Removals of Amerindians from their tribal lands occurred frequently in the colonial and national periods of American history, and each of the episodes was a tragically unhappy event. The Cherokees were an accomplished people who were widely renowned for their successes in modifying their culture to cope with the dramatic changes they faced as they were surrounded by white settlements. Finally, however, the lure of their fertile lands proved to be the downfall of the Cherokees. Even though the Cherokees had an impressive record of cooperation with the government of the United States, it all was to no avail. Like many other Amerindian nations who were forcibly moved westward so their lands could be appropriated by the expanding American frontier, the time for the relocation of the Cherokees finally arrived, and it is a chapter in American history replete with hardship and injustice.

In the spring of 1838, Brigadier General Winfield Scott with a regiment of artillery, a regiment of infantry, and six companies of dragoons marched unopposed into the Cherokee country of northern Georgia. On May 10 at New Echota, the capital of what had been one of the greatest Indian nations in eastern America, Scott issued a proclamation:

> The President of the United States sent me with a powerful army to cause you, in obedience to the treaty of 1835, to join that part of your people who are already established in prosperity on the other side of the Mississippi. . .
>
> The emigration must be commenced in haste. . . . The full moon of May is

already on the wane, and before another shall have passed away every
Cherokee man, woman and child . . . must be in motion to join their
brethren in the west . . . My troops already occupy many positions . . . and
thousands and thousands are approaching from every quarter to render
resistance and escape alike hopeless. . . . Will you then by resistance compel
us to resort to arms? Or will you by flight seek to hide yourselves in
mountains and thus oblige us to hunt you down? Remember that in
pursuit it may be impossible to avoid conflicts. The blood of the white
man or the blood of the red man may be spilt, and if spilt, however
accidentally, it may be impossible for the discreet and humane among you
or among us, to prevent a general war and carnage.

For more than a century the Cherokees had been ceding their land,
thousands of acres by thousands of acres. They had lost all of
Kentucky and much of Tennessee, but after the last treaty of 1819
they still had remaining about 35,000 square miles of forested
mountains, clean, swift-running rivers, and fine meadows. In this
country which lay across parts of Georgia, North Carolina, and
Tennessee they cultivated fields, planted orchards, fenced pastures
and built roads, houses, and towns. Sequoya had invented a syllabary
for the Cherokee language so that thousands of his tribesman quickly
learned to read and write. The Cherokees had adopted the white
man's way— his clothing, his constitutional form of government,
even his religion. But it had all been for nothing. Now these men who
had come across the great ocean many years ago wanted all of the
Cherokees' land. In exchange for their 35,000 square miles the tribe
was to receive five million dollars and another tract of land
somewhere in the wilderness beyond the Mississippi River.

This was a crushing blow to a proud people. "They are extremely
proud, despising the lower class of Europeans," said Henry
Timberlake, who visited them before the Revolutionary War. William
Barram, the botanist, said the Cherokees were not only a handsome
people, tall, graceful, and olive-skinned, but "their countenance and
actions exhibit an air of magnanimity, superiority and independence."

Ever since the signing of the treaties of 1819, Major General
Andrew Jackson, a man they once believed to be their friend, had
been urging Cherokees to move beyond the Mississippi. Indians and
white settlers, Jackson told them, could never get along together.
Even if the government wanted to protect the Cherokees from
harassment, he added, it would be unable to do so. "If you cannot
protect us in Georgia," a chief retorted, "how can you protect us from
similar evils in the West?"

During the period of polite urging, a few hundred Cherokee
families did move west, but the tribe remained united and refused to

give up any more territory. In fact, the council leaders passed a law forbidding any chief to sell or trade a single acre of Cherokee land on the penalty of death. In 1828, when Andrew Jackson was running for President, he knew that in order to win he must sweep the frontier states. Free land for the land-hungry settlers became Jackson's major policy. He hammered away this theme especially hard in Georgia where waves of settlers from the coastal lowlands were pushing into the highly desirable Cherokee country. He promised the Georgians that if they would help elect him President, he would lend his support to opening up the Cherokee lands for settlement. The Cherokees, of course, were not citizens and could not vote in opposition. To the Cherokees and their friends who protested this promise, Jackson justified his position by saying that the Cherokees had fought on the side of the British during the Revolutionary War. He conveniently forgot that the Cherokees had been his allies during the desperate War of 1812, and had saved the day for him in his decisive victory over the British-backed Creeks at Horseshoe Bend. (One of the Cherokee chiefs who aided Jackson was Junaluska. Said he afterward: "If I had known that Jackson would drive us from our homes I would have killed him that day at the Horseshoe.")

Three weeks after Jackson was elected President, the Georgia legislature passed a law annexing all the Cherokee country within the state's borders. As most of the Cherokee land was in Georgia and three-fourths of the tribe lived there, this meant an end to their independence as a nation. The Georgia legislature also abolished all Cherokee laws and customs and sent surveyors to map out lands in lot of 160 acres each. The 160-acre lots were to be distributed to white citizens of Georgia through public lotteries.

To add to the pressures on the Cherokees, gold was discovered near Dahlonega in the heart of their country. For many years the Cherokees had concealed the gold deposits, but now the secret was out and a rabble of gold-hungry prospectors descended upon them.

John Ross, the Cherokees' leader, hurried to Washington to protest the Georgia legislature's actions and to plead for justice. In that year Ross was 38 years old: he was well-educated and had been active in Cherokee government matters since he was 19. He was adjutant of the Cherokee regiment that served with Jackson at Horseshoe Bend. His father had been one of a group of Scottish emigrants who settled near the Cherokees and married into the tribe.

In Washington, Ross found sympathizers in Congress, but most of them were anti Jackson men and the Cherokee case was thus drawn into the whirlpool of politics. When Ross called upon Andrew Jackson to request his aid, the President bluntly told him that "no protection could be afforded the Cherokees" unless they were willing to move west of the Mississippi.

While Ross was vainly seeking help in Washington, alarming messages reached him from Georgia. White citizens of that state were claiming the homes of Cherokees through the land lottery, seizing some of them by force. Joseph Vann, a hard-working half-breed, had carved out an 800-acre plantation at Spring Place and built a fine brick house for his residence. Two men arrived to claim it, dueled for it, and the winner drove Vann and his family into the hills. When John Ross rushed home he found that the same thing had happened to his family. A lottery claimant was living in his beautiful home on the Coosa River, and Ross had to turn north toward Tennessee to find his fleeing wife and children.

During all this turmoil, President Jackson and the governor of Georgia pressed the Cherokee leaders hard in an attempt to persuade them to cede all their territory and move to the West. But the chiefs stood firm. Somehow they managed to hold the tribe together, and helped dispossessed families find new homes back in the wilderness areas. John Ross and his family lived in a one- room log cabin across the Tennessee line.

In 1831, the chiefs appealed to Congress with a memorial in which they stated that they would never voluntarily abandon their homeland, but proposed a compromise in which they agreed to cede the state of Georgia a part of their territory provided that they would be protected from invasion in the remainder. Furthermore, at the end of a definite period of years to be fixed by the United States they would be willing to become citizens of the various states in which they resided.

"Cupidity has fastened its eye upon our lands and our homes," they said, "and is seeking by force and by every variety of oppression and wrong to expel us from our lands and our homes and to tear from us all that has become endeared to us. In our distress we have appealed to the judiciary of the United States, where our rights have been solemnly established. We have appealed to the Executive of the United States to protect those rights according to the obligation of treaties and the injunctions of the laws. But this appeal to the Executive has been made in vain."

This new petition to Congress was no more effectual than their appeals to President Jackson. Again they were told that their difficulties could be remedied only by their removal to the west of the Mississippi.

For the first time now, a serious split occurred among the Cherokees. A small group of subchiefs decided that further resistance to the demands of the Georgia and United States governments was futile.

It would be better, they believed, to exchange their land and go west rather than risk bloodshed and the possible loss of everything. Leaders of this group were Major Ridge and Elias Boudinot. Ridge had adopted his first name after Andrew Jackson gave him that rank during the War of 1812. Boudinot was Ridge's nephew. Originally known as Buck Watie, he had taken the name of a New England philanthropist who sent him through a mission school in Connecticut. Stand Watie, who later became a Confederate general, was his brother. Upon Boudinot's return from school to Georgia he founded the first tribal newspaper, the *Cherokee Phoenix,* in 1827, but during the turbulence following the Georgia land lotteries he was forced to suspend publication.

And so in February 1835 when John Ross journeyed to Washington to resume his campaign to save the Cherokee nation, a rival delegation headed by Ridge and Boudinot arrived there to seek terms for removal to West. The pro-removal forces in the government leaped at this opportunity to bypass Ross's authority, and within a few days drafted a preliminary treaty for the Ridge delegation. It was then announced that a council would be held later in the year at New Echota, Georgia, for the purpose of negotiating and agreeing upon final terms.

During the months that followed, bitterness increased between the two Cherokee factions. Ridge's group was a very small minority, but they had the full weight of the United States Government behind them, and threats and inducements were used to force a full attendance at the council which was set for December 22, 1835. Handbills were printed in Cherokee and distributed throughout the nation, informing the Indians that those who did not attend would be counted as assenting to any treaty that might be made.

During the seven days which followed the opening of the treaty council, fewer than five hundred Cherokees, or about 2 percent of the tribe, came to New Echota to participate in the discussions. Most of the other Cherokees were busy endorsing a petition to be sent to Congress stating their opposition to the treaty. But on December 29, Ridge, Boudinot and their followers signed away all the lands of the great Cherokee nation. Ironically, thirty years earlier Major Ridge had personally executed a Cherokee chief named Doublehead for committing one of the few capital crimes of the tribe. That crime was the signing of a treaty which gave away Cherokee lands.

Charges of bribery by the Ross forces were denied by government officials, but some years afterward it was discovered that the Secretary of War had sent secret agents into the Cherokee country with the authority to expend money or bribe chiefs to support the treaty of cession and removal. And certainly the treaty signers were handsomely rewarded. In an era when a dollar would buy many times its worth today, Major Ridge was paid $30,000 and each of his followers received several thousand dollars each. Ostensibly they were being paid for their improved farm-lands, but the amounts were far in excess of contemporary land values.

John Ross meanwhile completed gathering signatures of Cherokees who were opposed to the treaty. Early in the following spring, 1836, he took the petition to Washington. More than three-fourths of the tribe, 15,964, had signed in protest against the treaty.

When the governor of Georgia was informed of the overwhelming vote against the treaty, he replied: "Nineteen-twentieths of the Cherokees are too ignorant and depraved to entitle their opinions to any weight or consideration in such matters."

The Cherokees, however, did have friends in Congress. Representative Davy Crockett of Tennessee denounced the treatment of the Cherokees as unjust, dishonest, and cruel. He admitted that he represented a body of frontier constituents who would like to have the Cherokee lands opened for settlement, and he doubted if a single one of them would second what he was saying. Even though his support of the Cherokees might remove him from public life, he added, he could not do otherwise except at the expense of his honor and conscience. Daniel Webster, Henry Clay, Edward Everett, and other great orators of the Congress also spoke for the Cherokees.

When the treaty came to a final decision in the Senate, it passed by only one vote. On May 23, 1836, President Jackson signed the document. According to its terms, the Cherokees were allowed two years from that day in which to leave their homeland forever.

The few Cherokees who had favored the treaty now began making their final preparations for departure. About three hundred left during that year and then early in 1837 Major Ridge and 465 followers departed by boats for the new land in the West. About 17,000 others, ignoring the treaty, remained steadfast in their homeland with John Ross.

For a while it seemed that Ross might win his long fight, that perhaps the treaty might be declared void. After the Secretary of War, acting under instructions from President Jackson, sent Major William M. Davis to the Cherokee country to expedite removal to the West, Davis submitted a frank report: "That paper called a treaty is no treaty at all," he wrote, "because it is not sanctioned by the great body of the Cherokees and was made without their participation or assent. . . . The Cherokees are a peaceable, harmless people, but you may drive them to desperation, and this treaty cannot be carried into effect by the strong arm of force."

In September 1836, Brigadier General Dunlap, who had been sent with a brigade of Tennessee volunteers to force the removal, indignantly disbanded his troops after making a strong speech in favor of the Indians: "I would never dishonor the Tennessee arms in a servile service by aiding to carry into execution at the point of the bayonet a treaty made by a lean minority against the will and authority of the Cherokee people."

Even Inspector General John E. Wool, commanding United States troops in the area, was impressed by the united Cherokee resistance, and warned the Secretary of War not to send any civilians who had any part in the making of the treaty back into Cherokee country. During the summer of 1837, the Secretary of War sent a confidential agent, John Mason, Jr., to observe and report. "Opposition to the treaty is unanimous and irreconcilable," Mason wrote. "They say it cannot bind them because they did not make it; that it was made by a few unauthorized individuals; that the nation is not party to it."

The inexorable machinery of government was already in motion, however, and when the expiration date of the waiting period, May 23, 1838, came near, Winfield Scott was ordered in with his army to force compliance. As already stated, Scott issued his proclamation on May 10: His soldiers were already building thirteen stockaded forts— six in North Carolina, five in Georgia, one in Tennessee, and one in Alabama. At these points the Cherokees would be concentrated to await transportation to the West. Scott then ordered the roundup started, instructing his officers not to fire on the Cherokees except in case of resistance. "If we get possession of the women and children first," he said, "or first capture the men, the other members of the same family will readily come in."

James Mooney, an ethnologist who afterwards talked with the Cherokees who endured this ordeal, said that squads of troops moved into the forested mountains to search out every small cabin and make prisoners of all the occupants however or wherever they might be found. "Families at dinner were startled by the sudden gleam of bayonets in the doorway and rose up to be driven with blows and oaths along the weary miles of trail that led to the stockades. Men were seized in their fields or going along the road, women were taken from their spinning wheels and children from their play. In many cases, on turning for one last look as they crossed a ridge, they saw their homes in flames, fired by the lawless rabble that followed on the heels of the soldiers to loot and pillage. So keen were these outlaws on the scent that in some instances they were driving off the cattle and other stock of the Indians almost before the soldiers had fairly started their owners in the other direction."

Long afterward one of the Georgia militiamen who participated in the roundup said: "I fought through the Civil War and have seen men shot to pieces and slaughtered by thousands, but the Cherokee removal was the cruelest work I ever knew."

Knowing that resistance was futile, most of the Cherokees surrendered quietly. Within a month, thousands were enclosed in the stockades. On June 6 at Ross's Landing near the site of the present-day Chattanooga, the first of many departures began. Eight hundred Cherokees were forcibly crowded onto a flotilla of six flatboats lashed to the side of a steamboat. After surviving a passage over rough rapids which smashed the sides of the flatboats, they landed at Decatur, Alabama, boarded a railroad train (which was a new and terrifying experience for most of them), and after reaching Tuscumbia were crowded upon a Tennessee River steamboat again.

Throughout June and July similar shipments of several hundred Cherokees were transported by this long water route—north on the Tennessee River to the Ohio and then down the Mississippi and up the Arkansas to their new homeland. A few managed to escape and make their way back to the Cherokee country, but most of them were eventually recaptured. Along the route of travel of this forced migration, the summer was hot and dry. Drinking water and food were often contaminated. First the young children would die, then the older people, and sometimes as many as half the adults were stricken with dysentery and other ailments.

On each boat deaths ran as high as five per day. On one of the first boats to reach Little Rock, Arkansas, at least a hundred had died. A compassionate lieutenant who was with the military escort recorded in his diary for August 1: "My blood chills as I write at the remembrance of the scenes I have gone through."

When John Ross and other Cherokee leaders back in concentration camps learned of the high mortality among those who had gone ahead, they petitioned General Scott to postpone further departures until autumn. Although only three thousand Cherokees had been removed, Scott agreed to wait until the summer drought was broken, or no later than October. The Cherokees in turn agreed to organize and manage the migration themselves. After a lengthy council, they asked and received permission to travel overland in wagons, hoping that by camping along the way they would not suffer as many deaths as occurred among those who had gone on the river boats.

During the waiting period, Scott's soldiers continued their searches for more than a thousand Cherokees known to be still hiding out in the deep wilderness of the Great Smoky Mountains. These Cherokees had organized themselves under the leadership of a chief named Utsala, and had developed warning systems to prevent captures by the bands of soldiers. Occasionally, however, some of the fugitives were caught and herded back to the nearest stockade.

One of the fugitive families was that of Tsali, an aging Cherokee. With his wife, his brother, three sons and their families, Tsali had built a hideout somewhere on the border between North Carolina and Tennessee. Soldiers surrounded their shelters one day, and the Cherokees surrendered without resistance. As they were being taken back toward Fort Cass (Calhoun, Tennessee) a soldier prodded Tsali's wife sharply with a bayonet, ordering her to walk faster. Angered by the brutality, Tsali grappled with the soldier, tore away his rifle, and bayoneted him to the ground. At the same time, Tsali's brother leaped upon another soldier and bayoneted him. Before the remainder of the military detachment could act, the Cherokees fled, vanishing back into the Smokies where they sought refuge with Chief Utsala. Both bayoneted soldiers died.

Upon learning of the incident, Scott immediately ordered that Tsali must be brought in and punished. Because some of his regiments were being transferred elsewhere for other duties, however, the general realized that his reduced force might be occupied for months in hunting down and capturing the escaped Cherokee. He would have to use guile to accomplish the capture of Tsali.

Scott therefore dispatched a messenger—a white man who had been adopted as a child by the Cherokees—to find Chief Utsala. The messenger was instructed to inform Chief Utsala that if he would surrender Tsali to General Scott, the Army would withdraw from the Smokies and leave the remaining fugitives alone.

When Chief Utsala received the message, he was suspicious of Scott's sincerity, but he considered the general's offer as an opportunity to gain time. Perhaps with the passage of time, the few Cherokees remaining in the Smokies might be forgotten and left alone forever. Utsala put the proposition to Tsali: If he went in and surrendered, he would probably be put to death, but his death might insure the freedom of a thousand fugitive Cherokees.

Tsali did not hesitate. He announced that he would go and surrender to General Scott. To make certain that he was treated well, several members of Tsali's band went with him.

When the Cherokees reached Scott's headquarters, the general ordered Tsali, his brother, and three sons arrested, and then condemned them all to be shot to death. To impress upon the tribe their utter helplessness before the might of the government, Scott selected the firing squad from Cherokee prisoners in one of the stockades. At the last moment, the general spared Tsali's youngest son because he was only a child.

(By this sacrifice, however, Tsali and his family gave the Smoky Mountain Cherokees a chance at survival in their homeland. Time was on their side, as Chief Utsala had hoped, and that is why today there is a small Cherokee reservation on the North Carolina slope of the Great Smoky Mountains.)

With the ending of the drought of 1838, John Ross and the 13,000 stockaded Cherokees began preparing for their long overland journey to the West. They assembled several hundred wagons, filled them with blankets, cooking pots, their old people and small children, and moved out in separate contingents along a trail that followed the Hiwassee River. The first party of 1,103 started October 1.

"At noon all was in readiness for moving," said an observer of the departure. "The teams were stretched out in a line along the road through a heavy forest, groups of persons formed about each wagon. The day was bright and beautiful, but a gloomy thoughtfulness was depicted in the lineaments of every face. In all the bustle of preparation there was a silence and stillness of the voice that betrayed the sadness of the heart. At length the word was given to move on. Going Snake, an aged and respected chief whose head eighty summers had whitened, mounted on his favorite pony and led the way in silence, followed by a number of younger men on horseback. At this very moment a low sound of distant thunder fell upon my ear. . . . a voice of divine indignation for the wrong of my poor and unhappy countrymen, driven by brutal power from all they loved and cherished in the land of their fathers to gratify the cravings of avarice. The sun was unclouded—no rain fell—the thunder rolled away and seemed hushed in the distance."

Throughout October, eleven wagon trains departed and then on November 4, the last Cherokee exiles moved out for the West. The overland route for these endless lines of wagons, horsemen, and people on foot ran from the mouth of the Hiwassee in Tennessee across the Cumberland plateau to McMinnville and then north to Nashville where they crossed the Cumberland River. From there they followed an old trail to Hopkinsville, Kentucky, and continued northwestward to the Ohio River, crossing into southern Illinois near the mouth of the Cumberland. Moving straight westward they passed through Jonesboro and crossed the Mississippi at Cape Girardeau, Missouri. Some of the first parties turned southward through Arkansas; the later ones continued westward through Springfield, Missouri, and on to Indian Territory.

A New Englander traveling eastward across Kentucky in November and December met several contingents, each a day apart from the others. "Many of the aged Indians were suffering extremely from the fatigue of the journey," he said, "and several were quite ill. Even aged females, apparently nearly ready to drop into the grave, were traveling with heavy burdens attached to their backs—on the sometimes frozen ground, and sometimes muddy streets, with no covering for the feet except what nature had given them.... We learned from the inhabitants on the road where the Indians passed, that they buried fourteen or fifteen at every stopping place, and they make a journey of ten miles per day only on an average. They will not travel on the Sabbath . . . they must stop, and not merely stop—they must worship the Great Spirit, too; for they had divine service on the Sabbath—a camp meeting in truth."

Autumn rains softened the roads, and the hundreds of wagons and horses cut them into morasses, slowing movement to a crawl. To add to their difficulties, tollgate operators overcharged them for passage. Their horses were stolen or seized on pretext of unpaid debts, and they had no recourse to the law. With the coming of cold damp weather, measles and whooping cough became epidemic. Supplies had to be dumped to make room for the sick in the jolting wagons.

By the time the last detachments reached the Mississippi at Cape Girardeau it was January, with the river running full of ice so that several thousand had to wait on the east bank almost a month before the channel cleared. James Mooney, who later heard the story from survivors, said that "The lapse of over half a century had not sufficed to wipe out the memory of the miseries of that halt beside the frozen river, with hundreds of sick and dying penned up in wagons or stretched upon the ground, with only a blanket overhead to keep out the January blast."

Meanwhile the parties that left early in October were beginning to reach Indian Territory. (The first arrived on January 4, 1839.) Each group had lost from thirty to forty members by death. The later detachment suffered much heavier losses, especially toward the end of their journey. Among the victims was the wife of John Ross.

Not until March 1839 did the last of the Cherokees reach their new home in the West. Counts were made of the survivors and balanced against the counts made at the beginning of the removal. As well as could be estimated, the Cherokees had lost about four thousand by deaths—or one out of every four members of the tribe—most of the deaths brought about as the direct result of the enforced removal. From that day to this the Cherokees remember it as "the trail where they cried," or the Trail of Tears.

15

All Men and Women are Created Equal

Constance Rynder

During the early nineteenth century, women in the United States generally lived within the boundaries of what one historian has called the "cult of true womanhood." That is, they were expected to honor the virtues of piety, purity, domesticity, and submissiveness. Men had the freedom to pursue careers and make a difference in the world; women did not. The best that a woman could hope for, in the words of Ralph Waldo Emerson, was to arrive "at the intellectual and moral elevations of her husband." By the 1840s, however, intelligent and educated women such as Elizabeth Cady Stanton, a housewife in Seneca Falls, New York, rejected these limitations on their lives. Stanton, with the encouragement of Lucretia Mott, a liberal Quaker preacher, called a convention in her hometown in 1848 to discuss the issues of women's rights. Seeking to dramatize their cause, they decided to re-write the Declaration of Independence, changing Jefferson's "All Men are Created Equal" to "All Men and Women are Created Equal" and making "man" rather than George III the tyrant. Constance Rynder's article describes the obstacles faced by the women who met at Seneca Falls and the long road to success for one of their key demands—woman suffrage.

One hundred and fifty years ago the people attending the first Women's Rights Convention adopted the radical proposition that All men & women are created equal"

The announcement of an upcoming "Woman's Rights Convention" in the Seneca County Courier was small, but it attracted Charlotte Woodward's attention. On the morning of July

219

19, 1848, the 19-year-old glove maker drove in a horse-drawn wagon to the Wesleyan Methodist Chapel in the upstate New York town of Seneca Falls. To her surprise, Woodward found dozens of other women and a group of men waiting to enter the chapel, all of them as eager as she to learn what a discussion of the social, civil, and religious rights of women" might produce.

The convention was the brainchild of 32-year-old Elizabeth Cady Stanton, daughter of Margaret and Judge Daniel Cady and wife of Henry Stanton, a noted abolitionist politician. Born in Johnstown, New York, Cady Stanton demonstrated both an intellectual bent and a rebellious spirit from an early age. Exposed to her father's law books as well as his conservative views on women, she objected openly to the legal and educational disadvantages under which women of her day labored. In 1840 she provoked her father by marrying Stanton, a handsome, liberal reformer and further defied convention by deliberately omitting the word "obey" from her wedding vows.

Marriage to Henry Stanton brought Elizabeth Cady Stanton - she insisted on retaining her maiden name - into contact with other independent-minded women. The newlyweds spent their honeymoon at the World Anti-Slavery Convention in London where, much to their chagrin, women delegates were denied their seats and deprived of a voice in the proceedings. Banished to a curtained visitors' gallery, the seven women listened in stunned silence as the London credentials committee charged that they were "constitutionally unfit for public and business meetings." It was an insult Cady Stanton never forgot.

Among the delegates was Lucretia Coffin Mott, a liberal Hicksite Quaker preacher and an accomplished public speaker in the American abolitionist movement, who was also disillusioned by the lack of rights granted women. A mother of six, Mott had grown up on Nantucket Island, "so thoroughly imbued with women's rights," she later admitted, "that it was the most important question of my life from a very early age." In Mott, Cady Stanton found both an ally and a role model. When I first heard from her lips that I had the same right to think for myself that Luther, Calvin and John Knox had," she recalled, and the same right to be guided by my own convictions . . . I felt a new born sense of dignity and freedom." The two women became fast friends and talked about the need for a convention to discuss women's emancipation. Eight years passed, however, before they fulfilled their mutual goal.

For the first years of her marriage, Cady Stanton settled happily into middle-class domestic life, first in Johnstown and subsequently in Boston, then the hub of reformist activity. She delighted in being part of her husband's stimulating circle of reformers and intellectuals and gloried in motherhood; over a 17-year period she bore seven children. In 1847, however, the Stantons moved to Seneca Falls, a small, remote farming and manufacturing community in New York's Finger Lakes district. After Boston, life in Seneca Falls with its routine household duties seemed dull to Cady Stanton, and she renewed her protest against the conditions that limited women's lives. "My experience at the World Anti-Slavery Convention, all I had read of the legal status of women, and the oppression I saw everywhere, together swept across my soul, intensified now by many personal experiences." A meeting with Lucretia Mott in July of 1848 provided the opportunity to take action.

On July 13, Cady Stanton received an invitation to a tea party at the home of Jane and Richard Hunt, wealthy Quakers living in Waterloo, New York, just three miles west of Seneca Falls. There she again met Lucretia Mott, Mott's younger sister, Martha Coffin Wright, and Mary Ann McClintock, wife of the Waterloo Hicksite Quaker minister. At tea, Cady Stanton poured out to the group the torrent of my long-accumulating discontent." Then and there they decided to schedule a women's "convention" for the following week. Hoping to attract a large audience, they placed an unsigned notice in the Courier advertising Lucretia Mott as the featured speaker.

Near panic gripped the five women as they gathered around the McClintocks' parlor table the following Sunday morning. They had only three days to set an agenda and prepare a document "for the inauguration of a rebellion." Supervised by Cady Stanton, they drafted a "Declaration of Sentiments and Resolutions," paraphrasing the Declaration of Independence. The document declared that "all men and women are created equal" and "are endowed by their Creator with certain unalienable rights. . . ." These natural rights belong equally to women and men, it continued, but man "has usurped the prerogative of Jehovah himself, claiming it as his right to assign for her a sphere of action, when that belongs to her conscience and to her God." The result has been "the establishment of an absolute tyranny over her."

There followed a specific catalog of injustices. Women were denied access to higher education, the professions, and the pulpit, as well as equal pay for equal work. If married they had no property rights; even the wages they earned legally belonged to their husbands. Women were subject to a high moral code, yet legally bound to tolerate moral delinquencies in their husbands. Wives could be punished, and if divorced a mother had no child custody rights. In every way, man "has endeavored to destroy [woman's] confidence in her own powers, to lessen her self-esteem, and to make her willing to lead a dependent and abject life." Above all, every woman had been deprived of "her inalienable right to the elective franchise."

Eleven resolutions demanding redress of these and other grievances accompanied the nearly 1,000-word Declaration. When Cady Stanton insisted upon including a resolution favoring voting rights for women, her otherwise supportive husband threatened to boycott the event. Even Lucretia Mott warned her, "Why Lizzie, thee will make us ridiculous!" "Lizzie," however, refused to yield.

Although the gathering was a convention for and of women, it was regarded as "unseemly" for a lady to conduct a public meeting, so Lucretia's husband, James Mott, agreed to chair the two-day event. Mary Ann McClintock's husband, Thomas, also participated. Henry Stanton left town.

When the organizers arrived at the Wesleyan Chapel on the morning of Wednesday, July 19, they found the door locked. No one had a key, so Cady Stanton's young nephew scrambled in through an open window and unbarred the front door. As the church filled with spectators, another dilemma presented itself. The first day's sessions had been planned for women exclusively, but almost 40 men showed up. After a hasty council at the altar the leadership decided to let the men stay, since they were already seated and seemed genuinely interested.

Tall and dignified in his Quaker garb, James Mott called the first session to order at 11:00 A.M. and appointed the McClintocks' older daughter (also named Mary Ann) secretary. Cady Stanton, in her first public speech, rose to state the purpose of the convention. "We have met here today to discuss our rights and wrongs, civil and political." She then read the Declaration aloud, paragraph by paragraph, and urged all present to participate freely in the discussions. The Declaration was re-read several times, amended, and adopted unanimously Both Lucretia Mott and Cady Stanton addressed the afternoon session, as did the McClintocks' younger daughter, Elizabeth. To lighten up the proceedings, Mott read a satirical article on "woman's sphere" that her sister Martha had published in local newspapers. Later that evening, Mott spoke to the audience on "The Progress of Reforms."

The second day's sessions were given over to the 11 resolutions. As Mott feared, the most contentious proved to be the ninth - the suffrage resolution. The other 10 passed unanimously. According to Cady Stanton's account, most of those who opposed this resolution did so because they believed it would compromise the others. She, however, remained adamant. "To have drunkards, idiots, horse racing rum-selling rowdies, ignorant foreigners, and silly boys fully recognized, while we ourselves are thrust out from all the rights that belong to citizens, is too grossly insulting to be longer quietly submitted to. The right is ours. We must have it." Even Cady Stanton's eloquence would not have carried the day but for the support she received from ex-slave and abolitionist Frederick Douglass, editor of the antislavery newspaper, North Star. "Right is of no sex," he argued; a woman is "justly entitled to all we claim for man." After much heated debate the ninth resolution passed, but by only a small majority.

Thomas McClintock presided over the final session on Thursday evening and read extracts from Sir William Blackstone's Commentaries on the Laws of England that described the status of women in English common law. Cady Stanton took questions before short speeches were given by young Mary Ann McClinlock and Frederick Douglass. Lucretia Mott closed the meeting with an appeal to action and one additional resolution of her own: The speedy success of our cause depends upon the zealous and untiring efforts of both men and women, for the over-throw of the monopoly of the pulpit, and for securing to women of equal participation with men in the various trades, professions, and commerce." It, too, passed unanimously.

In all, some 300 people attended the Seneca Falls Convention. The majority were ordinary folk like Charlotte Woodward. Most sat through the 18 hours of speeches, debates, and readings. One hundred of them - 68 women (including Woodward) and 32 men - signed the final draft of the Declaration of Sentiments and Resolutions. Women's rights as a separate reform movement had been born.

Press coverage was surprisingly broad and generally venomous, particularly on the subject of female suffrage. Philadelphia's Public Ledger and Daily Transcript declared that no lady would want to vote. "A woman is nobody A wife is everything. The ladies of Philadelphia . . . are resolved to maintain their rights as Wives, Belles, Virgins and Mothers." According to the Albany Mechanic's Advocate, equal rights would "demoralize and degrade [women] from their high sphere and noble destiny ... and prove a monstrous injury to all mankind." The New York Herald published the entire text of the Seneca Falls Declaration, calling it "amusing" but conceding that Lucretia Mott would "make a better President than some of those who have lately tenanted the White House." The only major paper to treat the event seriously was the liberal New York Tribune, edited by Horace Greeley, who found the demand for equal political rights improper, yet "however unwise and mistaken the demand, it is but the assertion of a natural right and as such must be conceded."

Stung by the public outcry, many original signers begged to have their names removed from the Declaration. "Our friends gave us the cold shoulder, and felt themselves disgraced by the whole proceeding," complained Cady Stanton. Many women sympathized with the convention's goals but feared the stigma attached to attending any future meetings. "I am with you thoroughly," said the wife of Senator William Seward, "but I am a born coward. There is nothing I dread more than Mr. Seward's ridicule." Even the McClintocks and the Hunts refrained from active involvement in women's rights after the Seneca Falls Convention.

But Cady Stanton saw opportunity in public criticism. "Imagine the publicity given our ideas by thus appearing in a widely circulated sheet like the Herald!" she wrote to Mott. "It will start women thinking, and men, too." She drafted lengthy responses to every negative newspaper article and editorial, presenting the reformers' side of the issue to the readers. Mott sensed her younger colleague's future role. "Thou art so wedded to this cause," she told Cady Stanton, "that thou must expect to act as pioneer in the work."

News of the Seneca Falls Convention spread rapidly and inspired a spate of regional women's rights meetings. Beginning with a follow-up meeting two weeks later in Rochester, New York, all subsequent women's rights forums featured female chairs. New England abolitionist Lucy Stone organized the first national convention, held in Worcester, Massachusetts, in 1850. Like Cady Stanton, Stone saw the connection between black emancipation and female emancipation. When criticized for including women's rights in her anti-slavery speeches, Stone countered: "I was a woman before I was an abolitionist - I must speak for the women."

Quaker reformer Susan B. Anthony joined the women's rights movement in 1852. She had heard about the Seneca Falls Convention, of course, and her parents and sister had attended the 1848 Rochester meeting. Initially, however, she deemed its goals of secondary importance to temperance and abolition. All that changed in 1851 when she met Cady Stanton, with whom she formed a life-long political partnership. Bound to the domestic sphere by her growing family, Cady Stanton wrote articles, speeches, and letters; Anthony, who never traveled the country lecturing and organizing women's rights associations. As Cady Stanton later put it, "I forged the thunderbolts and she fired them." In time, Susan B. Anthony's name became synonymous with women's rights.

Women's rights conventions were held annually until the Civil War, drawing most of their support from the abolitionist and temperance movements. After the war, feminist leaders split over the exclusion of women from legislation enfranchising black men. Abolitionists argued that it was "the Negro's Hour," and that the inclusion of female suffrage would jeopardize passage of the Fifteenth Amendment to the Constitution, which enfranchised all male citizens regardless of race. Feeling betrayed by their old allies, Cady Stanton and Anthony opposed the Fifteenth Amendment. Their protest alienated the more cautious wing of the movement and produced two competing suffrage organizations.

In 1869, Lucy Stone, Julia Ward Howe - well known author of "Battle Hymn of the Republic" - and others formed the moderate American Woman Suffrage Association, while Cady Stanton, Anthony, Martha Wright, and the radical faction founded the National Woman Suffrage Association (NWSA). Lucretia Mott, now an elderly widow, sought in vain to reconcile the two camps.

Both organizations sought political equality for women, but the more radical NWSA actively promoted issues beyond suffrage. Guided by the original Seneca Falls Resolutions, the NWSA demanded an end to all laws and practices that discriminated against women, and called for divorce law reform, equal pay, access to higher education and the professions, reform of organized religion, and a total rethinking of what constituted a "woman's sphere." Cady Stanton spoke about women's sexuality in public and condemned the Victorian double standard that forced wives to endure drunken, brutal, and licentious husbands. Anthony countenanced - and occasionally practiced - civil disobedience; in 1872 she provoked her own arrest by illegally casting a ballot in the presidential election.

By the time the two rival organizations merged in 1890 to form the National American Woman Suffrage Association (NAWSA), much had been accomplished. Many states had enacted laws granting married women property rights, equal guardianship over children, and the legal standing to make contracts and bring suit. Nearly one-third of college students were female, and 19 states allowed women to vote in local school board elections. In two western territories - Wyoming and Utah - women voted on an equal basis with men. But full suffrage nationwide remained stubbornly out of reach. NAWSA commenced a long state-by-state battle for the right to vote.

NAWSA's first two presidents were Cady Stanton and Anthony, by then in their seventies. Old age did not mellow either one of them, especially Cady Stanton. Ever the rebel, she criticized NAWSA's narrow-mindedness and viewed with increasing suspicion its newly acquired pious, prohibitionist allies. NAWSA's membership should include all "types of classes, races and creeds," she stated, and resist the evangelical infiltrators who sought to mute the larger agenda of women's emancipation.

Cady Stanton had long advocated reform of organized religion. "The chief obstacle in the way of woman's elevation today," she wrote, "is the degrading position assigned her in the religion of all countries." Whenever women tried to enlarge their "divinely ordained sphere," the all-male clerical establishment condemned them for violating "God's law." Using the Scriptures to justify women's inferior status positively galled her. In 1895, she published The Woman's Bible, a critical commentary on the negative image of women in the Old and New Testaments. Even Anthony thought she had gone too far this time and could do little to prevent conservative suffragists from venting their wrath. During the annual convention of NAWSA, both the book and its author were publicly censured. Henceforth, mainstream suffragists downplayed Cady Stanton's historic role, preferring to crown Susan B. Anthony as the stateswoman of the movement.

Elizabeth Cady Stanton died in 1902 at the age of 86, and Susan B. Anthony died four years later, also at 86. By then a new generation of suffrage leaders had emerged - younger, better educated, and less restricted to the domestic sphere. The now-respectable, middle-class leadership of NAWSA adopted a "social feminist" stance, arguing that women were, in fact, different from men and therefore needed the vote in order to apply their special qualities to the political problems of the nation.

However, more militant suffragists, among them Quaker agitator Alice Paul and Cady Stanton's daughter, Harriot Stanton Blatch, continued to insist upon women's absolute equality. They demanded a federal suffrage amendment as a necessary first step toward achieving equal rights. Paul's National Woman's Party gained the movement valuable publicity by engaging in confrontational tactics, including picketing the White House, being arrested, and going on hunger strikes while in prison.

Voting rights came in the wake of World War I. Impressed by the suffragists' participation in the war effort, Congress passed what came to be known as the "Susan B. Anthony Amendment" in 1919. Following state ratification a year later, it enfranchised American women nationwide in the form of the Nineteenth Amendment to the Constitution.

It had been 72 years since that daring call for female voting rights was issued at the Seneca Falls Convention. On November 2, 1920, 91-year-old Charlotte Woodward Pierce went to the polls in Philadelphia, the only signer of the Seneca Falls Declaration who had lived long enough to legally cast her ballot in a presidential election.

16

Children of Darkness

Stephen B. Oates

The first census of the United States in 1790 reported 697,624 slaves, by 1830 the number had reached two million, and on the eve of the Civil war it stood at nearly four million. In spite of these huge numbers, however, there were relatively few slave revolts in the Old South. The greatest uprising by slaves came in Southampton County, Virginia, on August 22, 1831. Planned and led by a man called Nat Turner, the revolt lasted several days and resulted in the deaths of nearly sixty whites before it was put down, and an even larger number of blacks, including Nat Turner, were put to death. Nat Turner's Rebellion frightened whites throughout the slave states and led to a general tightening of controls within the system and a rising fear of antislavery and abolitionism in the North.

Stephen B. Oates's account of Nat Turner's early life and events in Southampton County during August 1831 raises several basic questions. What led Nat Turner, among the millions of slaves in the South, to become the leader of this great rebellion? Why did it fail? Exactly how did the slave states during the 1830s and 1840s show an even greater determination to maintain the South's "Peculiar Institution"?

Until August, 1831, most Americans had never heard of Virginia's Southampton County, an isolated, impoverished neighborhood located along the border in the southeastern part of the state. It was mostly a small farming area, with cotton fields and apple orchards dotting the flat, wooded landscape. The farmers were singularly fond of their apple crops: from them they made a potent apple brandy, one of the major sources of pleasure in this hardscrabble region. The county seat, or "county town," was Jerusalem, a lethargic little community where pigs rooted in the streets and old-timers spat tobacco juice in the shade of the courthouse. Jerusalem lay on the bank of the Nottoway River some seventy miles south of Richmond. There had never been any large plantations in Southampton County, for the soil had always been too poor for extensive tobacco or cotton cultivation. Although one gentleman did own eighty slaves in 1830, the average was around three or four per family. A number of whites had moved on to new cotton lands in Georgia and Alabama, so that Southampton now had a population that was nearly 60 percent black. While most of the blacks were still enslaved, an unusual number—some seventeen hundred, in fact—were "free persons of color."

By southern white standards, enlightened benevolence did exist in Southampton County—and it existed in the rest of the state, too. Virginia whites allowed a few slave schools to operate—then a crime by state law—and almost without complaint permitted slaves to hold illegal religious meetings. Indeed, Virginians liked to boast that slavery was not so harsh in their "enlightened" state as it was in the brutal cotton plantations in the Deep South. Still, this was a dark time for southern whites—a time of sporadic insurrection panics, especially in South Carolina, and of rising abolitionist militancy in the North— and Virginians were taking no chances. Even though their slaves, they contended, were too happy and too submissive to strike back, Virginia was nevertheless almost a military garrison, with a militia force of some hundred thousand men to guard against insurrection.

Southampton whites, of course, were caught in the same paradox: most of the white males over twenty-one voluntarily belonged to the militia and turned out for the annual drills, yet none of them thought a slave revolt would happen here. *Their* blacks, they told themselves, had never been more content, more docile. True, they did get a bit carried away in their religious meetings these days, with much too much singing and clapping. And true, there were white preachers who punctuated their sermons with what a local observer called "ranting cant about equality" and who might inspire black exhorters to retail that doctrine to their congregations. But generally things were quiet and unchanged in this remote tidewater county, where time seemed to stand as still as a windless summer day.

It happened with shattering suddenness, an explosion of black rage that rocked Southampton County to its foundations. On August 22, 1831, a band of insurgent slaves, led by a black mystic called Nat Turner, rose up with axes and plunged southeastern Virginia—and much of the rest of the South—into convulsions of fear and racial violence. It turned out to be the bloodiest slave insurrection in southern history, one that was to have a profound and irrevocable impact on the destinies of southern whites and blacks alike.

Afterward, white authorities described him as a small man with "distinct African features." Though his shoulders were broad from work in the fields, he was short, slender, and a little knock-kneed, with thin hair, a complexion like black pearl, and large, deep-set eyes. He wore a mustache and cultivated a tuft of whiskers under his lower lip. Before that fateful August day, whites who knew Nat Turner thought him harmless, even though he was intelligent and did gabble on about strange religious powers. Among the slaves, though, he enjoyed a powerful influence as an exhorter and self-proclaimed prophet.

He was born in 1800, the property of Benjamin Turner of Southampton County and the son of two strong-minded parents. Tradition has it that his African-born mother threatened to kill him rather than see him grow up in bondage. His father eventually escaped to the North, but not before he had helped inculcate an enormous sense of self-importance in his son. Both parents praised Nat for his brilliance and extraordinary imagination; his mother even claimed that he could recall episodes that happened before his birth—a power that others insisted only the Almighty could have given him. His mother and father both told him that he was intended for some great purpose, that he would surely become a prophet. Nat was also influenced by his grandmother, who along with his white masters taught him to pray and to take pride in his superior intelligence. He learned to read and write with great ease, prompting those who knew him to remark that he had too much sense to be raised in bondage—he "would never be of any service to any one as a slave," one of them said.

In 1810 Benjamin Turner died, and Nat became the property of Turner's oldest son Samuel. Under Samuel Turner's permissive supervision Nat exploited every opportunity to improve his knowledge: he studied white children's school books and experimented in making paper and gunpowder. But it was religion that interested him the most. He attended black religious meetings, where the slaves cried out in ecstasy and sang hymns that expressed their longing for a better life. He listened transfixed as black exhorters preached from the Bible with stabbing gestures, singing out in a rhythmic language that was charged with emotion and vivid imagery. He studied the Bible, too, practically memorizing the books of the Old Testament, and grew to manhood with the words of the prophets roaring in his ears.

Evidently Nat came of age a bit confused if not resentful. Both whites and blacks had said he was too intelligent to be raised a slave; yet here he was, fully grown and still in bondage. Obviously he felt betrayed by false hopes. Obviously he thought he should be liberated like the large number of free blacks who lived in Southampton

County and who were not nearly so gifted as he. Still enslaved as a man, he zealously cultivated his image as a prophet, aloof, austere, and mystical. As he said later in an oral autobiographical sketch, "Having soon discovered to be great, I must appear so, and therefore studiously avoided mixing in society, and wrapped myself in mystery, devoting myself to fasting and prayer."

Remote, introspective, Turner had religious fantasies in which the Holy Spirit seemed to speak to him as it had to the prophets of old. "Seek ye the kingdom of Heaven," the Spirit told him, "and all things shall be added unto you." Convinced that he "was ordained for some great purpose in the hands of the Almighty," Turner told his fellow slaves about his communion with the Spirit. "And they believed," Turner recalled, "and said my wisdom came from God." Pleased with their response, he began to prepare them for some unnamed mission. He also started preaching at black religious gatherings and soon rose to prominence as a leading exhorter in the slave church. Although never ordained and never officially a member of any church, he was accepted as a Baptist preacher in the slave community, and once he even baptized a white man in a swampy pond. There can be little doubt that the slave church nourished Turner's self-esteem and his desire for independence, for it was not only a center for underground slave plottings against the master class, but a focal point for an entire alternate culture—a subterranean culture that the slaves sought to construct beyond the white man's control. Moreover, Turner's status as a slave preacher gave him considerable freedom of movement, so that he came to know most of Southampton County intimately.

Sometime around 1821 Turner disappeared. His master had put him under an overseer, who may have whipped him, and he fled for his freedom as his father had done. But thirty days later he voluntarily returned. The other slaves were astonished. No fugitive ever came back on his own. "And the negroes found fault, and murmured against me," Turner recounted later, "saying that if they had my sense they would not serve any master in the world." But in his mind Turner did not serve any earthly master. His master was Jehovah—the angry and vengeful God of ancient Israel—and it was Jehovah, he insisted, who had chastened him and brought him back to bondage.

At about this time Nat married. Evidently his wife was a young slave named Cherry who lived on Samuel Turner's place. But in 1822 Samuel Turner died, and they were sold to different masters—Cherry to Giles Reese and Nat to Thomas Moore. Although they were not far apart and still saw each other from time to time, their separation was nevertheless a painful example of the wretched privations that slavery placed on black people, even here in mellowed Southampton County.

As a perceptive man with a prodigious knowledge of the Bible, Turner was more than aware of the hypocrisies and contradictions loose in this Christian area, where whites gloried in the teachings of Jesus and yet discriminated against the "free coloreds" and kept the other blacks in chains. Here slave owners bragged about their benevolence (in Virginia they took care of their "niggers") and yet broke up families, sold blacks off to whip-happy slave traders when money was scarce, and denied intelligent and skilled blacks something even the most debauched and useless poor whites enjoyed: freedom. Increasingly embittered about his condition and that of his people, his imagination fired to incandescence by prolonged fasting and Old Testament prayers, Turner began to have apocalyptic visions and bloody fantasies in the fields and woods southwest of Jerusalem. "I saw white spirits and black spirits engaged in battle," he declared later, "and the sun was darkened—the thunder rolled in the heavens, and blood flowed in streams—and I heard a voice saying, 'Such is your luck, such you are called to see, and let it come rough or smooth, you must surely bare it.'" He was awestruck, he recalled, but what did the voice mean? What must he bare? He withdrew from his fellow slaves and prayed for a revelation; and one day when he was plowing in the field, he thought the Spirit called out, "Behold me as I stand in the Heavens," and Turner looked up and saw forms of men there in a variety of attitudes, "and there were lights in the sky to which the children of darkness gave other names than what they really were—for they were the lights of the Saviour's hands, stretched forth from east to west, even as they extended on the cross on Calvary for the redemption of sinners."

Certain that Judgment Day was fast approaching, Turner strove to attain "true holiness" and "the true knowledge of faith." And once he had them, once he was "made perfect," then the Spirit showed him other miracles. While working in the field, he said, he discovered drops of blood on the corn. In the woods he found leaves with hieroglyphic characters and numbers etched on them; other leaves contained forms of men—some drawn in blood—like the figures in the sky. He told his fellow slaves about these signs—they were simply astounded—and claimed that the Spirit had endowed him with a special knowledge of the seasons, the rotation of the planets, and the operation of the tides. He acquired an even greater reputation among the county's slaves, many of whom thought he could control the weather and heal disease. He told his followers that clearly, something large was about to happen, that he was soon to fulfill "the great promise that had been made to me."

But he still did not know what his mission was. Then on May 12, 1828, "I heard a loud noise in the heavens," Turner remembered, "and the Spirit instantly appeared to me and said the Serpent was loosened, and Christ had laid down the yoke he had borne for the sins of men, and that I should take it on and fight against the Serpent." Now at last it was clear. By signs in the heavens Jehovah would show him when to commence the great work, whereupon "I should arise and prepare myself, and slay my enemies with their own weapons." Until then he should keep his lips sealed.

But his work was too momentous for him to remain entirely silent. He announced to Thomas Moore that the slaves ought to be free and would be "one day or other." Moore, of course, regarded this as dangerous talk from a slave and gave Turner a thrashing.

In 1829 a convention met in Virginia to draft a new state constitution, and there was talk among the slaves—who communicated along a slave grapevine—that they might be liberated. Their hopes were crushed, though, when the convention emphatically rejected emancipation and restricted suffrage to whites only. There was also a strong backlash against antislavery publications thought to be infiltrating from the North, one of which—David Walker's Appeal—actually called on the slaves to revolt. In reaction the Virginia legislature enacted a law against teaching slaves to read and write. True, it was not yet rigorously enforced, but from the blacks' viewpoint slavery seemed more entrenched in "enlightened" Virginia than ever.

There is no evidence that Turner ever read antislavery publications, but he was certainly sensitive to the despair of his people. Still, Jehovah gave him no further signs, and he was carried along in the ebb and flow of ordinary life. Moore had died in 1828, and Turner had become the legal property of Moore's nine-year-old son—something that must have humiliated him. In 1829 a local wheelwright, Joseph Travis, married Moore's widow and soon moved into her house near the Cross Keys, a village located southwest of Jerusalem. Still known as Nat Turner even though he had changed owners several times, Nat considered Travis "a kind master" and later said that Travis "placed the greatest confidence in me."

In February, 1831, there was an eclipse of the sun. The sign Turner had been waiting for—could there be any doubt? Removing the seal from his lips, he gathered around him four slaves in whom he had complete trust—Hark, Henry, Nelson, and Sam—and confided what he was called to do. They would commence "the work of death" on July 4, whose connotation Turner clearly understood. But they formed and rejected so many plans that his mind was affected. He was seized with dread. He fell sick, and Independence Day came and passed.

On August 13 there was another sign. Because of some atmospheric disturbance the sun grew so dim that it could be looked at directly. Then it seemed to change colors—now pale green, now blue, now white—and there was much excitement and consternation in many parts of the eastern United States. By afternoon the sun was like an immense ball of polished silver, and the air was moist and hazy. Then a black spot could be seen, apparently on the sun's surface—a phenomenon that greatly aroused the slaves in southeastern Virginia. For Turner, the black spot was unmistakable proof that God wanted him to move. With awakened resolution he told his men that "as the black spot passed over the sun, so shall the blacks pass over the earth."

It was Sunday, August 21, deep in the woods near the Travis house at a place called Cabin Pond. Around a crackling fire Turner's confederates feasted on roast pig and apple brandy. With them were two new recruits Jack, one of Hark's cronies, and Will, a powerful man who intended to gain his freedom or die in the attempt. Around mid afternoon Turner himself made a dramatic appearance, and in the glare of pine-knot torches they finally made their plans. They would rise that night and "kill all the white people." It was a propitious time to begin, because many whites of the militia were away at a camp meeting. The revolt would be so swift and so terrible that the whites would be too panic-stricken to fight back. Until they had sufficient recruits and equipment, the insurgents would annihilate everybody in their path—women and children included. When one of the slaves complained about their small number (there were only seven of them, after all), Turner was quick to reassure him. He had deliberately avoided an extensive plot involving a lot of slaves. He knew that blacks had "frequently attempted similar things," but their plans had "leaked out." Turner intended for his revolt to happen completely without warning. The "march of destruction," he explained, "should be the first news of the insurrection," whereupon slaves and free blacks alike would rise up and join him. He did not say what their ultimate objective was, but possibly he wanted to fight his way into the Great Dismal Swamp some twenty miles to the east. This immense, snake-filled quagmire had long been a haven for fugitives, and Turner may have planned to establish a slave stronghold there from which to launch punitive raids against Virginia and North Carolina. On the other hand, he may well have had nothing in mind beyond the extermination of every white on the ten-mile route to Jerusalem. There are indications that he thought God would guide him after the revolt began, just as He had directed Gideon against the Midianites. Certainly Turner's command of unremitting carnage was that of the Almighty, who had said through his prophet Ezekiel:

"Slay utterly old and young, both maids and little children, and women . . . ."

The slaves talked and schemed through the evening. Night came on. Around two in the morning of August 22 they left the woods, by-passed Giles Reese's farm, where Cherry lived, and headed for the Travis home-stead, the first target in their crusade.

All was still at the Travis house. In the darkness the insurgents gathered about the cider press, and all drank except Turner, who never touched liquor. Then they moved across the yard with their axes. Hark placed a ladder against the house, and Turner, armed with a hatchet, climbed up and disappeared through a second-story window. In a moment he unbarred the door, and the slaves spread through the house without a sound. The others wanted Turner the prophet, Turner the black messiah, to strike the first blow and kill Joseph Travis. With Will close behind, Turner entered Travis' bedroom and made his way to the white man's bed. Turner swung his hatchet—a wild blow that glanced off Travis' head and brought him out of bed yelling for his wife. But with a sure killer's instinct Will moved in and hacked Travis to death with his axe. In minutes Will and the others had slaughtered the four whites they found in the house, including Mrs. Travis and young Putnam Moore, Turner's legal owner. With Putnam's death Turner felt that at last, after thirty years in bondage, he was free.

The rebels gathered up a handful of old muskets and followed "General Nat" out to the barn. There Turner paraded his men about, leading them through every military maneuver he knew. Not all of them, however, were proud of their work. Jack sank to his knees with his head in his hands and said he was sick. But Hark made him get up and forced him along as they set out across the field to the next farm. Along the way somebody remembered the Travis baby. Will and Henry returned and killed it in its cradle.

And so it went throughout that malignant night, as the rebels took farm after farm by surprise. They used no firearms, in order not to arouse the countryside, instead stabbing and decapitating their victims. Although they confiscated horses, weapons, and brandy, they took only what was necessary to continue the struggle, and they committed no rapes. They even spared a few homesteads, one because Turner believed the poor white inhabitants "thought no better of themselves than they did of negroes." By dawn on Monday there were fifteen insurgents—nine on horses—and they were armed with a motley assortment of guns, clubs, swords, and axes. Turner himself now carried a light dress sword, but for some mysterious reason (a fatal irresolution? the dread again?) he had killed nobody yet.

At Elizabeth Turner's place, which the slaves stormed at sunrise, the prophet tried once again to kill. They broke into the house, and there, in the middle of the room, too frightened to move or cry out, stood Mrs. Turner and a neighbor named Mrs. Newsome. Nat knew Elizabeth Turner very well, for she was the widow of his second master, Samuel Turner. While Will attacked her with his axe the prophet took Mrs. Newsome's hand and hit her over the head with his sword. But evidently he could not bring himself to kill her. Finally Will moved him aside and chopped her to death as methodically as though he were cutting wood.

With the sun low in the east, Turner sent a group on foot to another farm while he and Will led the horsemen at a gallop to Caty Whitehead's place. They surrounded the house in a rush, but not before several people fled into the garden. Turner chased after somebody, but it turned out to be a slave girl, as terrified as the whites, and he let her go. All around him, all over the Whitehead farm, there were scenes of unspeakable violence. He saw Will drag Mrs. Whitehead kicking and screaming out of the house and almost sever her head from her body. Running around the house, Turner came upon young Margaret Whitehead hiding under a cellar cap between two chimneys. She ran crying for her life, and Turner set out after her—a wild chase against the hot August sun. He overtook the girl in a field and hit her again and again with his sword, but she would not die. In desperation he picked up a fence rail and beat her to death. Finally he had killed someone. He was to kill no one else.

After the Whitehead massacre the insurgents united briefly and then divided again, those on foot moving in one direction and Turner and the mounted slaves in another. The riders moved across the fields, kicking their horses and mules faster and faster, until at last they raced down the lane to Richard Porter's house, scattering dogs and chickens as they went. But the Porters had fled—forewarned by their own slaves that a revolt was under way. Turner knew that the alarm was spreading now, knew that the militia would soon be mobilizing, so he set out alone to retrieve the other column. While he was gone Will took the cavalry and raided Nathaniel Francis' homestead. Young Francis was Will's owner, but he could not have been a harsh master: several free blacks voluntarily lived on his farm. Francis was not home, and his pregnant young wife survived Will's onslaught only because a slave concealed her in the attic. After killing the overseer and Francis' two nephews Will and his men raced on to another farm, and another, and then overran John Barrow's place on the Barrow Road. Old man Barrow fought back manfully while his wife escaped in the woods, but the insurgents overwhelmed him and slit his throat.

As a tribute to his courage they wrapped his body in a quilt and left a plug of tobacco on his chest.

Meanwhile Turner rode chaotically around the countryside, chasing after one column and then the other, almost always reaching the farms after his scattered troops had done the killing and gone. Eventually he found both columns waiting for him at another pillaged homestead, took charge again, and sent them down the Barrow Road, which intersected the main highway to Jerusalem. They were forty strong now and all mounted. Many of the new recruits had joined up eager "to kill all the white people." But others had been forced to come along as though they were hostages. A black later testified that several slaves—among them three teen-age boys "were constantly guarded by negroes with guns who were ordered to shoot them if they attempted to escape."

On the Barrow Road, Turner's strategy was to put his twenty most dependable men in front and send them galloping down on the home-steads before anybody could escape. But the cry of insurrection had preceded them, and many families had already escaped to nearby Jerusalem, throwing the village into pandemonium. By midmorning church bells were tolling the terrible *news—insurrection, insurrection—and* shouting men were riding through the countryside in a desperate effort to get the militia together before the slaves overran Jerusalem itself.

As Turner's column moved relentlessly toward Jerusalem one Levi Waller, having heard that the blacks had risen, summoned his children from a nearby schoolhouse (some of the other children came running too) and tried to load his guns. But before he could do so, Turner's advance horsemen swept into his yard, a whirlwind of axes and swords, and chased Waller into some tall weeds. Waller managed to escape, but not before he saw the blacks cut down his wife and children. One small girl also escaped by crawling up a dirt chimney, scarcely daring to breathe as the insurgents decapitated the other children—ten in all—and threw their bodies in a pile.

Turner had stationed himself at the rear of his little army and did not participate in these or any other killings along the Barrow Road. He never explained why. He had been fasting for several days and may well have been too weak to try any more killing himself. Or maybe as God's prophet he preferred to let Will and the eight or nine other lieutenants do the slaughtering. All he said about it afterward was that he "some-times got in sight in time to see the work of death completed" and that he paused to view the bodies "in silent satisfaction" before riding on.

Around noon on Monday the insurgents reached the Jerusalem highway, and Turner soon joined them. Behind them lay a zigzag path of unredeemable destruction: some fifteen homesteads sacked and approximately sixty whites slain. By now the rebels amounted to fifty or sixty—including three or four free blacks. But even at its zenith Turner's army showed signs of disintegration. A few reluctant slaves had already escaped or deserted. And many others were roaring drunk, so drunk they could scarcely ride their horses, let alone do any fighting. To make matters worse, many of the confiscated muskets were broken or too rusty to fire.

Turner resolved to march on Jerusalem at once and seize all the guns and powder he could find there. But a half mile up the road he stopped at the Parker farm, because some of his men had relatives and friends there. When the insurgents did not return, Turner went after them—and found his men not in the slave quarters but down in Parker's brandy cellar. He ordered them back to the highway at once.

On the way back they met a party of armed men—whites. There were about eighteen of them, as far as Turner could make out. They had already routed his small guard at the gate and were now advancing toward the Parker house. With renewed zeal Turner rallied his remaining troops and ordered an attack. Yelling at the top of their lungs, wielding axes, clubs, and gun butts, the blacks drove the whites back into Parker's cornfield. But their advantage was short-lived. White reinforcements arrived, and more were on the way from nearby Jerusalem. Regrouping in the cornfield, the whites counterattacked, throwing the rebels back in confusion. In the fighting some of Turner's best men fell wounded, though none of them died. Several insurgents, too drunk to fight any more, fled pell-mell into the woods.

If Turner had often seemed irresolute earlier in the revolt, he was now undaunted. Even though his force was considerably reduced, he still wanted to storm Jerusalem. He led his men away from the main highway, which was blocked with militia, and took them along a back road, planning to cross the Cypress Bridge and strike the village from the rear. But the bridge was crawling with armed whites. In desperation the blacks set out to find reinforcements: they fell back to the south and then veered north again, picking up new recruits as they moved. They raided a few more farms, too, only to find them deserted, and finally encamped for the night near the slave quarters on Ridley's plantation.

All Monday night news of the revolt spread beyond Southampton County as express riders carried the alarm up to Petersburg and from there to the capitol in Richmond. Governor John Floyd, fearing a statewide uprising, alerted the militia and sent cavalry, infantry, and artillery units to the stricken county. Federal troops from Fortress Monroe were on the way, too, and other volunteers and militia outfits were marching from contiguous counties in Virginia and North Carolina.

Soon over three thousand armed whites were in Southampton County, and hundreds more were mobilizing.

With whites swarming the countryside, Turner and his lieutenants did not know what to do. During the night an alarm had stampeded their new recruits, so that by Tuesday morning they had only twenty men left. Frantically they set out for Dr. Simon Blunt's farm to get volunteers—and rode straight into an ambush. Whites barricaded in the house opened fire on them at pointblank range, killing one or more insurgents and capturing several others—among them Hark Travis. Blunt's own slaves, armed with farm tools, helped in the defense and captured a few rebels themselves.

Repulsed at Blunt's farm, Turner led a handful of the faithful back toward the Cross Keys, still hoping to gather reinforcements. But the signs were truly ominous, for armed whites were everywhere. At last the militia overtook Turner's little band and in a final, desperate skirmish killed Will and scattered the rest. Turner himself, alone and in deep anguish, escaped to the vicinity of the Travis farm and hid in a hole under some fence rails.

By Tuesday evening a full-scale manhunt was under way in south-eastern Virginia and North Carolina as armed whites prowled the woods and swamps in search of fugitive rebels and alleged collaborators. They chased the blacks down with howling dogs, killing those who resisted—and many of them resisted zealously—and dragging others back to Jerusalem to stand trial in the county court. One free black insurgent committed suicide rather than be taken by white men. Within a week nearly all the bona fide rebels except Turner had either been executed or imprisoned, but not before white vigilantes—and some militiamen—had perpetrated barbarities on more than a score of innocent blacks. Outraged by the atrocities committed on whites, vigilantes rounded up blacks in the Cross Keys and decapitated them. Another vigilante gang in North Carolina not only beheaded several blacks but placed their skulls on poles, where they remained for days. In all directions whites took blacks from their shacks and tortured, shot, and burned them to death and then mutilated their corpses in ways that witnesses refused to describe. No one knows how many innocent blacks died in this reign of terror—at least a hundred twenty, probably more. Finally the militia commander of Southampton County issued a proclamation that any further outrages would be dealt with according to the articles of war. Many whites publicly regretted these atrocities but argued that they were the inevitable results of slave insurrection. Another revolt, they said, would end with the extermination of every black in the region.

Although Turner's uprising ended on Tuesday, August 24, reports of additional insurrections swept over the South long afterward, and dozens of communities from Virginia to Alabama were seized with hysteria. In North Carolina rumors flew that slave armies had been seen on the highways, that one—maybe led by Turner himself—had burned Wilmington, butchered all the inhabitants, and was now marching on the state capital. The hysteria was even worse in Virginia, where reports of concerted slave rebellions and demands for men and guns swamped the governor's office. For a time it seemed that thousands of slaves had risen, that Virginia and perhaps the entire South would soon be ablaze. But Governor Floyd kept his head, examined the reports carefully, and concluded that no such widespread insurrection had taken place. Actually no additional uprisings had happened anywhere. Out of blind panic whites in many parts of the South had mobilized the militia, chased after imaginary insurgents, and jailed or executed still more innocent blacks. Working in cooperation with other political and military authorities in Virginia and North Carolina, Floyd did all he could to quell the excitement, to reassure the public that the slaves were quiet now. Still, the governor did not think the Turner revolt was the work of a solitary fanatic. Behind it, he believed, was a conspiracy of Yankee agitators and black preachers—especially black preachers. "The whole of that massacre in Southampton is the work of these Preachers," he declared, and demanded that they be suppressed.

Meanwhile the "great bandit chieftain," as the newspapers called him, was still at large. For more than two months Turner managed to elude white patrols, hiding out most of the time near Cabin Pond where the revolt had begun. Hunted by a host of aroused whites (there were various rewards totalling eleven hundred dollars on his head), Turner considered giving himself up and once got within two miles of Jerusalem before turning back. Finally on Sunday, October 30, a white named Benjamin Phelps accidentally discovered him in another hideout near Cabin Pond. Since the man had a loaded shotgun, Turner had no choice but to throw down his sword.

The next day, with lynch mobs crying for his head, a white guard hurried Turner up to Jerusalem to stand trial. By now he was resigned to his fate as the will of Almighty God and was entirely fearless and unrepentant. When a couple of court justices examined him that day, he stated emphatically that *he* had conceived and directed the slaughter of all those white people (even though he had killed only Margaret Whitehead) and announced that God had endowed him with extraordinary powers. The justices ordered this "fanatic" locked up in the same small wooden jail where the other captured rebels had been incarcerated.

On November 1 one Thomas Gray, an elderly Jerusalem lawyer and slaveholder, came to interrogate Turner as he lay in his cell "clothed with rags and covered with chains." In Gray's opinion the public was anxious to learn the facts about the insurrection—for whites in Southampton could not fathom why their slaves would revolt. What Gray wanted was to take down and publish a confession from Turner that would tell the public the truth about why the rebellion had happened. It appears that Gray had already gathered a wealth of information about the outbreak from other prisoners, some of whom he had defended as a court-appointed counsel. Evidently he had also written unsigned newspaper accounts of the affair, reporting in one that whites had located Turner's wife and lashed her until she surrendered his papers (remarkable papers, papers with hieroglyphics on them and sketches of the Crucifixion and the sun). According to Gray and to other sources as well, Turner over a period of three days gave him a voluntary and authentic confession about the genesis and execution of the revolt, recounting his religious visions in graphic detail and contending again that he was a prophet of Almighty God. "Do you not find yourself mistaken now?" Gray asked. Turner replied testily, "Was not Christ crucified?" Turner insisted that the uprising was local in origin but warned that other slaves might see signs and act as he had done. By the end of the confession Turner was in high spirits, perfectly "willing to suffer the fate that awaits me." Although Gray considered him "a gloomy fanatic," he thought Turner was one of the most articulate men he had ever met. And Turner could be frightening. When, in a burst of enthusiasm, he spoke of the killings and raised his manacled hands toward heaven, "I looked on him," Gray said, "and my blood curdled in my veins."

On November 5, with William C. Parker acting as his counsel, Turner came to trial in Jerusalem. The court, of course, found him guilty of committing insurrection and sentenced him to hang. Turner, though, insisted that he was not guilty because he did not feel so. On November 11 he went to his death in resolute silence. In addition to Turner, the county court tried some forty-eight other blacks on various charges of conspiracy, insurrection, and treason. In all, eighteen blacks—including one woman—were convicted and hanged. Ten others were convicted and "transported"—presumably out of the United States.

But the consequences of the Turner revolt did not end with public hangings in Jerusalem. For southern whites the uprising seemed a monstrous climax to a whole decade of ominous events, a decade of abominable tariffs and economic panics, of obstreperous antislavery activities, and of growing slave unrest and insurrection plots, beginning with the Denmark Vesey conspiracy in Charleston in 1822 and culminating now in the worst insurrection Southerners had ever known. Desperately needing to blame somebody besides themselves for Nat Turner, Southerners linked the revolt to some sinister Yankee-abolitionist plot to destroy their cherished way of life. Southern zealots declared that the antislavery movement, gathering momentum in the North throughout the 1820s, had now burst into a full-blown crusade against the South. In January, 1831, William Lloyd Garrison had started publishing *The Liberator* in Boston, demanding in bold, strident language that the slaves be immediately and unconditionally emancipated. If Garrison's rhetoric shocked Southerners, even more disturbing was the fact that about eight months after the appearance of *The Liberator* Nat Turner embarked on his bloody crusade—something southern politicians and newspapers refused to accept as mere coincidence. They charged that Garrison was behind the insurrection, that it was his "bloodthirsty" invective that had incited Turner to violence. Never mind that there was no evidence that Turner had ever heard of *The Liberator;* never mind that Garrison categorically denied any connection with the revolt, saying that he and his abolitionist followers were Christian pacifists who wanted to free the slaves through moral suasion. From 1831 on, northern abolitionism and slave rebellion were inextricably associated in the southern mind.

But if Virginians blamed the insurrection on northern abolitionism, many of them defended emancipation itself as the only way to prevent further violence. In fact, for several months in late 1831 and early 1832 Virginians engaged in a momentous public debate over the feasibility of manumission. Out of the western part of the state, where antislavery and anti-black sentiment had long been smoldering, came petitions demanding that Virginia eradicate the "accursed," "evil" slave system and colonize all blacks at state expense. Only by removing the entire black population, the petitions argued, could future revolts be avoided. Newspapers also discussed the idea of emancipation and colonization, prompting one to announce that "Nat Turner and the blood of his innocent victims have conquered the silence of fifty years." The debate moved into the Virginia legislature, too, and early in 1832 proslavery and antislavery orators harangued one another in an unprecedented legislative struggle over emancipation. In the end most delegates concluded that colonization was too costly and too complicated to carry out. And since they were not about to manumit the blacks and leave them as free men in a white man's country, they rejected emancipation. Indeed, they went on to revise and implement the slave codes in order to restrict blacks so stringently that they could never mount another revolt. The modified codes not only strengthened the patrol and militia systems, but sharply curtailed the rights of free blacks and all but eliminated slave schools, slave religious meetings, and slave preachers. For

Turner had taught white Virginians a hard lesson about what might happen if they gave slaves enough education and religion to think for themselves.

In the wake of the Turner revolt, the rise of the abolitionists, and the Virginia debates over slavery, the other southern states also expanded their patrol and militia systems and increased the severity of their slave codes. What followed was the Great Reaction of the 1830s and 1840s, during which the South, threatened it seemed by internal and external enemies, became a closed, martial society determined to preserve its slave-based civilization at whatever cost. If Southerners had once apologized for slavery as a necessary evil, they now trumpeted that institution as a positive good—"the greatest of all the great blessings," as James H. Hammond phrased it, "which a kind providence has bestowed." Southern postmasters set about confiscating abolitionist literature, lest these "incendiary" tracts invite the slaves to violence. Some states actually passed sedition laws and other restrictive measures that prohibited blacks and whites alike from criticizing slavery. And slave owners all across the South tightened up slave discipline, refusing to let blacks visit other plantations and threatening to hang any slave who even looked rebellious. By the 1840s the Old South had devised such an oppressive slave system that organized insurrection was all but impossible.

Even so, southern whites in the antebellum period never escaped the haunting fear that somewhere, maybe even in their own slave quarters, another Nat Turner was plotting to rise up and slit their throats. They never forgot him. His name became for them a symbol of terror and violent retribution.

But for antebellum blacks—and for their descendants—the name of Nat Turner took on a profoundly different connotation. He became a legendary black hero who broke his chains and murdered white people because slavery had murdered blacks. Turner, said an elderly black man in Southampton County only a few years ago, was "God's man. He was a man for war, and for legal rights, and for freedom."

17

Gold!

Ralph K. Andrist

Gold! The lure of easy wealth often drives gold-hungry prospecters to alter both local environments and national histories. Such was the case with the great gold discovery in California in 1848. California barely had been annexed to the United States at the conclusion of the Mexican War when the stampede to search for gold began. John Sutter, a wealthy landowner whose property was located in the vicinity of modern-day Sacramento, decided to build a sawmill along the South Branch of the American River where his construction crew accidentally found gold in the stream in early 1848. News of the strike soon spread to nearby settlements, and by the end of the year, the Atlantic coast states' newspapers announced the gold discovery. Almost immediately a horde of adventurers set out for California. In 1849 alone, at least 56,000 men came to California in search of a fortune. Many were disappointed, but others prospered. Between 1848 and 1852 gold worth approximately $250,000,000 was extracted from the California gold-fields. The great California gold-rush subsided late in the 1850s. Not only did it change the economy of the nation, it also caused California's population to grow rapidly and promoted statehood for the region long before anyone originally expected. It was a colorful, exciting, and productive episode in our nation's history.

The California Gold Rush was the biggest and the richest of them all, but it was no different from any of those that followed in providing the majority of its participants with much rushing and little gold.

When forty-niners reminisced through beards grown longer and whiter, the strikes of the past became richer and the nuggets bigger, but the mournful truth is that most gold hunters would have done better financially staying at home—and been considerably more comfortable.

Let there be no misunderstanding, though; the gold across the Sierra Nevada was rich beyond belief, and many miners made strikes that deserve the adjective "fabulous." It was just that there was not enough gold in the streams to make everyone rich. Hubert Howe Bancroft, historian of the West, estimated that during the peak years of 1849 and 1850 the gold taken out averaged about $600 per miner. Averages are usually misleading: this one, on examination, can mean only that for every miner who struck it rich, there must have been a platoon who hardly got to see what gold looked like.

It all began, as every schoolchild is taught, at the sawmill of John Sutter one January day in 1848. A Swiss immigrant, Sutter at the time ruled, benevolently and graciously, over an estate of 49,000 acres which he had received from the Mexican government and had built into what amounted to a self-sustaining kingdom. It lay in the valley of the Sacramento, still almost empty of settlers, and his settlement, called Sutter's Fort, was situated where Sacramento now stands.

In the summer of 1847 he sent a carpenter named James Marshall, in charge of a crew of men, up the South Branch of the American River to build a sawmill. Work proceeded through the next several months until January, when Marshall turned water into the millrace for the first time. He let it run all night to wash the race clean of debris; the next morning, January 24, 1848, he saw yellow specks glinting through the running water, and the famous discovery was made.

Sutter was deeply disturbed by the finding of the metal; gold and the pastoral serenity of his pleasant empire were incompatible, and he had a foreboding of things to come—although the results were to be more devastating than he could possibly have imagined: his cattle butchered, his fields trampled and untended, his land taken by squatters, until he had not a thing left. At the moment all he could do was ask the men at the mill to keep the secret for another six weeks, so that his ranch workers would not desert him to dig gold before spring planting was done. The men at the mill did not leave but continued to work as before, panning for gold only on Sunday, until the sawmill was finished in March.

So far, the discovery had produced no gold fever at the scene, nor did it do so farther afield. The news began trickling into San Francisco within two or three weeks (Sutter's request for six weeks of secrecy had been ignored), carried by letter and by word of mouth. Both of the town's two newspapers duly reported the discovery, but no one became excited. The people of San Francisco—there were 850 or 900 of them—were still not convinced that this amounted to anything.

But the reports kept coming in, and with them samples of gold. Several Mormons were discovered quietly digging about twenty-five miles from the sawmill; their site, which inevitably became known as Mormon Diggings, turned out to be richer than the first. San Francisco was impressed; the gold was more plentiful and widespread than anyone had thought. By the end of April, men who had gone up the American River to see for themselves were returning with fat pouches of gold, replenishing their supplies, and then hurrying back. Now, at last, the town was filled with excitement, though restraint still prevailed. Men talked about gold, but went about their business as usual. It needed a little more to turn the excitement into roaring gold fever, however, and a man named Sam Brannan supplied the extra bit of frenzy.

Brannan was a ubiquitous figure in early California, always on hand when there was a dollar to be made, and shrewd enough to make it. He was in turn a storekeeper, a hotel owner in Sacramento when miners were willing to pay anything for a bed and meal, a merchant in San Francisco so respected that he was elected to head the first Vigilante organization, a newspaper publisher, and a wealthy landowner. A man of formidable talents, Sam Brannan.

In 1848, he was operating a store in Sutterville, a small settlement near Sutter's Fort. He was an elder in the Mormon Church and had gone up to Mormon Diggings to look the situation over and talk to his brethren there. Some of the excitement had begun to stir in his own veins, and he felt moved to get his share of the wealth—but not by digging, an activity which had no charm for him. His approach, at first glance, appears completely irrelevant. During the second week of May, he traveled by boat to San Francisco with a bottle of gold dust. It has become folklore that he spent the day walking the streets, waving the vial of gold and shouting, "Gold! Gold! Gold from the American River!" It is more likely that he collected groups on corners and in stores and saloons, passing the gold around and telling how he had seen plenty like it being panned out up at Mormon Diggings. Whatever he did, he left them burning with gold fever.

Brannan came to town about May 12; fleets of boats left on the fourteenth and fifteenth for Sutter's Fort, where all passengers had to disembark and set out on foot for the diggings. Sam Brannan's store was right at hand as they left the boats, and Brannan had thoughtfully laid in a large stock of provisions and mining supplies. He was one of the first to demonstrate something that would be proved again and again during the gold rush: the surest way to prosper was to leave the mining to others, and concern oneself with selling the miners what they needed.

San Francisco became almost hysterical. More gold arrived, this time from the Fort, about a week after the first exodus, and another large group of citizens dropped everything and left. It is usually estimated that less than one hundred people remained by the end of June. Doctors, lawyers, bakers, blacksmiths, laborers, schoolteachers—all went. There was no government left; the first and second alcaldes were gone (the Americans had adopted from the recently dispossessed Mexicans the alcalde system, a kind of hybrid mayor-magistrate), and so was the sheriff. Women and children also departed; this first gold-rush year was different in many ways from those that followed.

Now the fever spread to other California settlements: Monterey, San Diego, Sonoma, Benicia, San Jose, Santa Cruz, Santa Barbara, Los Angeles. Walter Colton, alcalde at Monterey, wrote of the way the people of his village disappeared when the first proof of the gold strike reached them in June, leaving little more than women and soldiers at the army post. A crew of carpenters who were at work on a schoolhouse "threw down their saws and planes, shouldered their picks, and are off for the Yuba. Three seamen ran off from the *Warren,* forfeiting their four years' pay; and a whole platoon of soldiers left only their colors behind."

Ranches were deserted or left with only women to tend them, grain went unharvested, cattle and horses roamed wild. Sailors deserted from the U.S. Pacific Squadron in San Francisco Bay and at Monterey, and the Army lost 716 enlisted men in the eighteen months beginning July 1, 1848. Said one soldier: "The struggle between *right* and six dollars a month and *wrong* and seventy-five dollars a day is rather a severe one."

By early June ships had carried the news to the Sandwich Islands (Hawaii); by July it reached Oregon; and in August, the neighboring Mexican state of Sonora. In each case there was skepticism at first, then wild-eyed gold mania. In less than four months, nineteen ships left Honolulu with 300 foreigners, most of the Islands' white colony, and an unknown number of Kanakas, or natives. An estimated 5,000 to 6,000 Mexicans headed north. In Oregon many settlers had very recently refused to do military duty against the Native Americans because they did not want to leave their families without protection; now, as the gold fever seized them, they said a hasty good-by to families, possibly added a few brief words of caution about locking the doors at night, and were off.

Young Mormons returning home carried news of the discovery east across the mountains to Salt Lake City. Once again the first reaction was tepid, but when a second group of young men came, carrying considerable gold, "the cry was raised, 'To California—To the Gold of

Ophir our brethren have discovered! To California!" (Men gave voice to more rousing cries in those days than now.) Brigham Young tried to hold them, without success; gold had more appeal for many of the young Saints than did building the Mormon garden in the desert.

Sometime between August and September the news got back to the Atlantic states and the Mississippi Valley—and once again was ignored. But as later ships brought increasingly sensational accounts, interest mounted. There were tales of men who had dug out thousands of dollars' worth of gold in a matter of days. Walter Colton, the alcalde of Monterey, and Thomas Larkin, Navy agent in the same town, laid it on with a heavy trowel in their letters and reports, talking of streams "paved with gold," and claiming that the mines exceeded "all the dreams of romance and all the golden marvels of the wand of Midas." That sort of thing made pretty heady reading for a New England farm boy after a day of building rock walls. Once again excitement gradually built up to a point where it needed only a spark to touch it off, and that came on December 5 when President James K. Polk, in his annual message, gave official recognition to the stories. They were, he said, of such an extraordinary character as "would scarcely command belief" were they not corroborated by the authentic reports of officers in the public services.

Almost literally overnight, tens of thousands of men were on their way. The overland route, of course, was closed until spring. The Argonauts, as the gold seekers inevitably came to be called, had a choice of two sea routes. One was the all-water route around Cape Horn. The other took the traveler by ship to the Isthmus of Panama, which he crossed; then he boarded another ship on the Pacific side (a small proportion crossed at Nicaragua). In 1849, the Cape Horn passage was by far the most popular; the ratio swung the other way in subsequent years.

The trip around South America was long and expensive, but it was passably comfortable for a man on a good ship with an able skipper and a fair break in the weather. One Franklin Buck who left New York on January 18, 1849, did not reach San Francisco until August 6; but he passed the time without undue tedium: he had included in his baggage a backgammon board, a library of 250 volumes, and a good supply of wine. As the demand for ships grew, all possible vessels were diverted to carrying California-bound passengers. The New England whaling fleet was taken over almost in its entirety. Merchant vessels were, for the most part, only minimally converted for passenger comfort (but this was not vital if these ships were sound and well-handled). What was criminal was the way in which get-rich-quick operators dragged rotten-bottomed ships out of retirement, patched the worst of their leaks, and, as often as not, gave command of them to incompetents or drunks who could no longer hold a berth under normal conditions.

But it made no difference to the clamoring crowds of Argonauts: they would board anything headed for California. Many ships went down, especially in the stormy passage around Cape Horn—how many no one knows—and gold-rush diaries frequently record sighting the wreckage of some unfortunate craft, and speak of the chilling effect it had on those who saw it.

The Panama route was much shorter and, in terms of actual traveling time, faster: six to eight months via Cape Horn, six weeks by way of Panama. The only trouble was that there were often months of waiting mixed in with the six weeks of traveling. The Argonaut landed at Chagres on the Isthmus, crossed the seventy-five-mile stretch of jungle, partly by native boat on the swirling, treacherous Chagres River and partly by mule train along narrow, dripping, insect-infested trails fetid from the rotting carcasses of mules, and finally reached the moribund city of Panama on the Pacific, whence another ship could be had to take him on to California. But there were few ships on the Pacific, especially in 1849, and as fast as they arrived in San Francisco, their crews deserted them to go mining. Argonauts found themselves stranded in Panama for weeks and months while the floating population of the town continued to swell—for passenger agents back East went on selling tickets with bland assurances of connections at Panama. Hundreds died of malaria, cholera, and other diseases as a result of the inevitably unsanitary conditions. Some men, as foolhardy as they were impatient, started up the coast in various small craft. Most were never heard of again.

When a ship did come, four or five times as many men crowded aboard as the vessel was meant to carry. As a result, the passage was usually miserable. Hiram Pierce, a dour, middle-aged blacksmith from Troy, New York, who left a wife and seven children to go after gold, described mealtime as an alfresco affair on deck with sailors carrying food between a double row of passengers while everyone grabbed: "Many behave so swineish that I prefer to stay a way unless driven to it by hunger." The ship's doctor was a drunk; one night he got himself entangled in his hammock and was suspended with his head dangling. Another time, "The same worthy took a dose of medicine to a patient & haveing a bone in his hand knawing, he took the medicine & gave the bone to the patient."

Most of those who came by sea arrived at San Francisco. The town had gained back all the population it had lost to the mines, and thousands more. It was an ephemeral place of tents and wooden walls with canvas roofs, changing so fast that the diary-keeping Argonaut, passing through and then returning three or four months later, invariably noted that nothing was as it had been. San Francisco was the great warehouse of the gold fields, the port of debarkation for gold seekers, the place when a miner down from the hills could purchase various pleasures more titillating than anything he had dreamed of back home.

The strange hysteria that gripped men, many of them sober, level-headed citizens until that moment, was variously known as gold fever, yellow fever, California fever, California mania, and gold mania. The term "fever" seems to fit it best because, like a real fever, its peak or crisis could almost be pinpointed and the period of recovery charted. In the Atlantic coast states it raged at its height from December of 1848 into the following March and then began a slow decline through the rest of 1849. In the Mississippi Valley it was a little later getting started, reaching its peak from February through May of 1849.

To those living in the Mississippi Valley, the natural route was overland (although many gold seekers from seaboard states also joined the wagon companies). A number took various southern routes, such as the Sonora Trail, which swings down into Mexico, and the Santa Fe Trail and its westward extensions. But by far the overwhelming majority followed the Oregon and Mormon trails, which parallel each other on opposite sides of the Platte River over the Great Plains; once through the Rockies they swung down toward the California passes along various routes and cutoffs, none of them easy.

Travelers began gathering in March at the three Missouri River towns that became the outfitting places for the overland trip: Independence and St. Joseph, Missouri, and Kanesville (now Council Bluffs), Iowa. Accommodations in the towns were quickly filled and tent cities grew up on the outskirts. Steamboats arrived almost daily with men, mules, and supplies to add to the growing chaos; the river front was a continual jam of wagons, herds of oxen and mules, and cursing teamsters. Almost every man wore a gun and a bowie knife, but more as a sort of California Ho! uniform than because he had any thought of using them. This was not a gun-fighting crowd, and there was remarkably little shooting or stabbing.

The trip had a rigid timetable. The wagons could not start before late April, when the grass on the prairie was green and high enough to provide food for teams, and they had to be over the Sierra Nevada in California before snow began to fall in the high passes, which meant the last wagon had to be on its way before June was over.

A great many men on the trail never should have been there. There were carts pulled by a single mule or ox, wagons with a mule and oxen hitched together, and various other makeshift evidences of shoestring ventures. A man with a rifle and bulldog was in Independence in 1849, planning to walk all the way to California; he very well might have, because he had already walked from Maine. Another man was planning to push a wheelbarrow to the gold fields.

The first part of the trip presented no undue difficulties or dangers. The grass was new and plentiful, the ground solid, animals and men fresh, and equipment still new. But the picnic atmosphere soon began to evaporate. The wagons formed an almost continuous line at times, and all but those in the lead drove in a cloud of choking dust. In the western part of present-day Nebraska, sandier ground and the upward-trending trail made pulling difficult, and animals began to show the effects; break-downs occurred more often as equipment became worn, and more and more of the faint-hearted turned back.

Now the Argonauts began divesting themselves of excess baggage until the trail looked like the line of retreat of a routed army. Alonzo Delano, a forty-niner, wrote on June 3:

> We were compelled to throw away a quantity of iron, steel, trunks, valises, old clothes, and boots, of little value and I may observe here that we sub-sequently found the road lined with cast-off articles, piles of bacon, flour, wagons, groceries, clothing, and various other articles which had been left, and the waste and destruction of property was enormous. In this the selfish nature of man was plainly exhibited. In many instances the property thus left was rendered useless. We afterwards found sugar on which turpentine had been poured, flour in which salt and dirt had been thrown, and wagons broken in pieces or partially burned, clothing torn to pieces, so that they could not be worn, and a wanton waste made of valuable property, simply because the owners could not use it themselves and were determined that nobody else should.

Besides being marked with debris, wrecked wagons, and animal carcasses, the trail was soon lined with graves, mainly those of cholera victims. The disease had come to New Orleans from Europe late in 1848, had been spread by steamboat up the Mississippi Valley, and was carried onto the plains by the wagon trains. It is a disease spread by human filth, and with the travelers' lack of concern for sanitation, it rampaged among the gold seekers. Their comrades buried the victims and hurried on—though there were dark stories of stricken men carried out of sight of the trail and left to die.

Travel through the mountains was hard going; there were places where wagons had to be eased down some of the steeper slopes with ropes, and spots on one or two of the cutoffs where they were actually lowered down cliffs. But beyond the Rockies the way really got difficult. In Utah and Nevada water and grass, scarce enough anyhow, were very often bitter, and even poisonous, from the alkali, salt, and sulphur they contained. The worst part of this dry stretch was the final drive over a searing, lifeless desert that had to be crossed in one single stage, requiring usually about twenty-four hours. Here, a traveler had the option of two routes. One took him to the life-giving water of the Truckee River with Boiling Springs at the midpoint, where unappetizing but drinkable water for the animals could be had by pouring it from the hot springs into troughs and allowing it to cool. The other way led to the Carson River across the Forty-Mile Desert, where there was no water of any kind.

Animals already in poor condition collapsed and were left to die. In many cases, companies tried to save weakening animals by leaving their wagons with a guard and driving their mules or oxen without loads on to the river, hoping that two or three days of rest, water, and good grass would revive them so that they could go back into the desert and haul the wagons the rest of the way. Forty-niner Joshua Breyfogle spent more than three days on the Forty-Mile Desert guarding his company's wagons while waiting for the mule teams to be brought back. "From twelve o'clock till sunrise the emigrants are passing in crowds, nearly perishing for water," he wrote in his diary while he waited, "and are leaving mules, horses and oxen to starve on the plains for they can't drive them on. I don't know what will become of the back trains." At the end of his last night on the desert he noted: "This is the most horrid night I ever passed. The road was strewd with the carcasses of dead mules, horses and cattle, and most of them with pieces of flesh cut out by the Indians. . . . " And two days later, after safely crossing the desert: "There is about four thousand wagons behind that will have to pass about three hundred miles without any grass and very little water. There must hundreds perish on the plains. The forty-five mile stretch is now almost impassable because of the stench of the dead animals along the road which is literally lined with them and there is scarcely a single train or wagon but leaves one or more dead animal, so that it must be getting worse every day."

That, too, was part of rushing for gold. And having got through the desert, they had the Sierra Nevada to cross, once again a land of ups and downs, where wagons had to be worked through boulder-strewn canyons and eased down steep slopes with ropes. Some of the gold seekers no longer had any wagons. After the crossing of the desert, there were groups that salvaged so few animals that they had to give up their wagons and use their remaining beasts as pack animals. Some lost all, and slung packs on their backs, and went on foot with what few miserable possessions they could carry.

And so, finally, they crossed the last mountain barrier and came down the American River to Sutter's Fort and the new boom town of

Sacramento, where potatoes and onions were selling for a dollar each. But what did it matter?—prices meant nothing to a man who would soon be up in the hills where there was gold waiting to be picked up from the ground.

How many miners came to California in 1849 is not known, and estimates differ widely. By the overland trails, at least 35,000 is a plausible guess. The ships around Cape Horn brought 15,000 more; another 6,000 arrived by way of Panama. How many died on the plains or in the jungles or left their bones at the bottom of the sea cannot even be guessed, but it reached tens of thousands before the gold rush ended, late in the 1850s. The tide of gold seekers continued as high during the next three or four years, but there never was another year quite like 1849, when the gold fever still raged, when hills and streams still lay untouched and waiting, and no disillusion had yet thrown the slightest shadow over the most fantastic visions of great and sudden wealth.

What happened to these gold-fevered men when they finally reached California? Most of them worked harder than they had ever worked before, and suffered a large variety of ailments and injuries which youth and clean living usually helped them to survive. A few found enough gold to make themselves wealthy, but most probably just managed to break even.

For mining involved more than swishing a little gravel and water around in a basin; it was hard, back-straining work. Placer gold, the only kind really known during the gold rush, consists of gold dust and occasional nuggets scattered thinly through sand and gravel (a miner never called it anything but "dirt"). To obtain the gold, it was necessary to wash a great deal of dirt, taking advantage of the fact that gold is about eight times as heavy as sand and will settle to the bottom while the sand is being carried off by the water. The gold pan, traditional symbol of the miner, was used only in very rich claims or for testing samples of dirt to see whether they were worth working further. In ordinary circumstances, a hopperlike device of wood and perforated sheet iron called a cradle, or rocker, was employed in a two-man operation: while one shoveled in the dirt, the other rocked the device and poured water with a dipper. The dirt was washed through, and the gold was caught in settling pockets.

After 1849, an invention called the long tom was used wherever there was a good supply of running water. It was simply a wooden flume with water running through it; dirt was shoveled in and sluiced through while the gold caught on a slatted bottom. A long tom was worked by several men and could handle four or five times as much dirt per man per day as could a cradle. That meant, of course, that a miner had to shovel four or five times as much dirt into it as he would into a cradle to keep it operating at full efficiency. A man usually had to pay for what he got, even in the gold fields.

The terrain on which the prospectors worked did little to make things easier for them; it was usually difficult. The diggings were chiefly along the tributaries of the Sacramento and San Joaquin rivers, which flowed out of the Sierra Nevada; each river, fork, branch, and creek was eventually followed by prospectors to its source. In the lower foothills the land might be only moderately rocky and hilly at best; near the head-waters rushing streams flowed in the clefts of deep, precipitous gorges whose bottoms were often cluttered with boulders and fallen rocks and choked with jackstraw tangles of dead trees. Even under these conditions, miners persevered at the ever-absorbing task of separating a small amount of gold from a mountain of gravel, and with amazing energy and ingenuity constructed hydraulic works to enable them to move the stream here or there or otherwise exploit it in their search for wealth.

Sometimes these constructions reached the proportions of major engineering works—and were often complete wastes of time and talent. Louise Clappe—"Dame Shirley" she called herself in her letters—who lived with her doctor husband in the mining camps of Indian Bar and Rich Bar on a high fork of the Feather River for a year, wrote of a company of thirteen men who worked from February almost through September on a project to divert a section of the stream so they could mine the bed. It involved building a dam six feet high and three hundred feet long, as well as a flume and other supporting works. Lumber had cost $1,000 and thirty laborers had been hired for nine and a half days; in all, the dam cost $2,000. When the company totaled its take in gold dust at the end of the venture, it amounted to $41.70.

While such experiences were frequent, they were very far from universal, or else a crowd of amateurs would not have been able to take out, between 1848 and 1852, a quarter of a billion dollars' worth of gold, more or less—no one knows exactly how much—before the rich placer deposits began to give out. For a great many men, the gold fields yielded up a very good day's wage for a day's work. But a day's wage was not what started the gold rush and kept it going; the Argonauts came expecting nothing less than a strike that would make them rich over-night. And there were places where the new Eldorado was almost as rich as the wildest stories ever told about it—locations like those at Auburn, where four cart loads of dirt yielded $16,000, and where, during the first delirious days, it was not at all unusual for a man to dig $1,000 to $1,500 worth of gold between dawn and dusk. Even the stories about gold being found at the roots of bushes turned out to be true: a man hunting rabbits near Angel's Camp jammed his ramrod into the roots of a manzanita bush and turned up a piece of gold-bearing quartz; he scratched out $ 700 worth of gold the rest of the day using the rod, but with better implements gathered $2,000 the next day and $7,000 the third.

There were stories of men digging gold flakes out of cracks in the rock in stream beds with spoons. Three German prospectors taking a short cut home through unexplored country found just such a situation on a high tributary of the Feather River and were reported to have taken out $36,000 in four days without even having to wash any gravel. The story of the find leaked out—miners seemed able to smell a gold strike—and the location, named Rich Bar, was quickly swarming with men. It was so rich that it was agreed that claims should be limited to ten square feet. Single panfuls of dirt here contained $1,500 to $2,000 in gold often enough to be considered almost commonplace; the record for one panful was said to have been $2,900. One company of four men took out $50,000 in a single day.

Such strikes were largely phenomena of the early part of the gold rush, however, when men were prospecting virgin ground. Even as early as 1850 such surprises had become quite rare, and by the end of 1852 the gold rush was just about over. By that time all the rivers had been prospected, almost all the big strikes made. The gold fields no longer had much place for a man operating on only a dream and a shoestring. Hard-rock mining, beginning to become common, involved tunneling into rock and crushing and treating gold-bearing quartz, and so necessitated tremendous capital outlays. Hydraulic mining, a new development, was making it possible to recover gold from very low-grade placer deposits, but it required tremendous amounts of water under very high pressures, which were obtained from the high Sierra by complex canal and flume systems far too costly for an independent prospector.

But the gold seekers kept coming, though in rapidly diminishing numbers, until 1859. That was the year the great Comstock Lode was discovered in what is now Nevada. Virtually every miner in California dropped what he was doing and headed through the passes of the Sierra Nevada to the new Eldorado. It was a great rush, but it was anticlimax after the one in California. But then, so has been every other gold rush since.

18

The Unexpected Mrs. Stowe

David McCullough

"So this is the little woman," Abraham Lincoln supposedly said to Harriet Beecher Stowe when they met in 1862, "who made this big war." The president was referring, of course, to Stowe's novel, Uncle Tom's Cabin, the single most important piece of antislavery literature ever published and indeed one of the most famous books in the history of the United States. When the novel appeared in 1851-1852, it caused an immediate international sensation. Stowe succeeded not because she presented carefully reasoned arguments to convince her readers that slavery was wrong but because readers of her story were moved emotionally to recognize the humanity of enslaved African-Americans. The slaves in Uncle Tom's Cabin had the same feelings, thoughts, and desires as did all men and women. They were not sub-humans fit only for servitude. Stowe's novel did not convert a majority of northerners to abolitionism, but it aided mightily in convincing them that slavery was an evil that should not be allowed to spread.

This article explains how Stowe came to write the book that made her famous, and it also gives an account of the very full life that she led. Only a woman of great strength could have dealt with the many problems that she faced in her personal life and still write more than twenty books and numerous essays, poems, articles, and children's stories. Doubtless Lincoln exaggerated when he gave her "credit" for the Civil war, but Harriet Beecher Stowe was indeed a special person.

She had been brought up to make herself useful. And always it suited her. As a child she had been known as Hattie. She had been cheerful but shy, prone to fantasies, playful, and quite pretty. After she became famous, she would describe herself this way: "To begin, then, I am a little bit of a woman,—somewhat more than forty, about as thin and dry as a pinch of snuff; never very much to look at in my best days, and looking like a used-up article now." She wasn't altogether serious when she wrote that, but the description was the one people would remember.

She was born in Litchfield, Connecticut—in a plain frame house that still stands—in 1811, when Lincoln was two years old and when Dolley Madison was in the White House. She was the seventh of the nine children Roxana Foote bore Lyman Beecher before being gathered to her reward, and she was such a worker, even when very small, that her preacher father liked to say he would gladly have given a hundred dollars if she could have been born a boy.

As a child she had found most of his sermons about as intelligible as Choctaw, she wrote later, and never would she be at peace with his religion. But she loved him, and for all his gloomy talk of sin and damnation it is not hard to understand why. He was a powerful, assertive figure who had an almost fiendish zest for life for hunting and fishing with his sons, for listening to all music, and for playing the violin, which he did badly. But could he only play what he heard inside him, he told them all, he could be another Paganini. Best of all he loved to go out and "snare souls," as he said. In a corner of the cellar he kept a pile of sand, and if his day was not enough to use him up, and stormy weather kept him from outdoor exercise, down he would go; shovel in hand, to sling sand about.

Sunday mornings he would come bounding along through the sunshine, late again for that appointed hour when weekly he brought down Calvinist thunder upon the heads of upright Litchfield people. He had a special wrath for drunkards and Unitarians, and he believed passionately in the Second Coming. But something in him made him shy away from the strictest tenet of his creed—total predestination—and its logic. Once when he had agreed to exchange pulpits with another pastor, he was told that the arrangement had been preordained. "Is that so?" he said. "Then I won't do it!" And he didn't.

The happiest times in her childhood, Hattie would write later, were the days spent away from him, visiting an Aunt Harriet in Nutplains, Connecticut, in a house filled with books and pictures gathered by a seafaring uncle and a wonderful old Tory grandmother, who in private still said Episcopal prayers for the king and queen.

At twelve Hattie often wandered off from the noisy parsonage to lie on a green hillside and gaze straight into a solid blue sky and dream of Byron. One month she read *Ivanhoe* seven times.

In 1832, when Hattie had turned twenty-one, Lyman Beecher answered the call to become the first president of the Lane Theological Seminary in Cincinnati. He packed up his children and a new wife and set off for what he called "the majestic West." A New Jerusalem was to be established on the banks of the Ohio. The family spirits were lifted; and crossing the Alleghenies, they all sang "Jubilee." A Philadelphia journal likened the exodus of the Reverend Mr. Beecher and his family to the migration of Jacob and his sons.

The following summer the Lane Theological Seminary's first (and at that time, only) professor, Calvin Ellis Stowe, a Biblical scholar and Bowdoin graduate, travelled west in the Beechers' wake. For all his learning and devotion to the Almighty, Stowe was a very homely and peculiar worker in the vineyard.

He was accompanied by a beautiful young bride, Eliza, who soon became Hattie Beecher's best friend in Cincinnati but died not very long afterward. Apparently it was a shared grief over Eliza that brought Hattie and Calvin Stowe together. Years later, with some of the proceeds from *Uncle Tom's Cabin,* they would commission an artist to do a portrait of Eliza, and every year thereafter, on Eliza's birthday, the two of them would sit before the portrait and reminisce about Eliza's virtues.

The wedding took place in early January, 1836. What exactly she saw in him is a little hard to say. The night before the ceremony, trying to describe her emotions in a letter to a school friend, she confessed she felt "nothing at all." But Lord Byron had not appeared in Cincinnati. At twenty-four she may have felt she was getting on.

Calvin was thirty-three, but he seemed as old as her father. He was fluent in Greek, Latin, Hebrew, French, Italian, German; he was an authority on education; he knew the Bible better than her father. Also, it is recorded, he had a grand sense of humor. But he was as fat and forgetful and fussy as an old woman. In the midst of a crisis, as she would soon discover, he had a bad habit of taking to his bed, and he had absolutely no "faculty," that Yankee virtue she defined simply as being the opposite of shiftlessness.

He also had an eye for pretty women, as he admitted to Hattie, and a taste for spirits, but these proclivities, it seems, never got him into any particular trouble.

But there was more. Calvin, from his boyhood until his dying day, was haunted by phantoms. They visited him most any time, but favored dusk. They appeared quite effortlessly out of the woodwork, the floor, or the furniture. There was a regular cast of characters, Calvin said, as real and familiar to him as anyone else he knew. Among his favorites were a giant Native American woman and a dark dwarf who between them carried a huge bull fiddle. There was a troupe of old Puritans from his native Natick, all shadowy and dark blue in color, and one "very pleasant-looking human face" he called Harvey. They performed music for Calvin Stowe, and somehow or other they talked to him without making any sound at all, or so he said. He had no reluctance about discussing the subject, and there is no indication that any of his circle thought the less of him for it.

Still, the marriage proved difficult soon enough. Hattie became pregnant almost immediately, and just about then Calvin was asked by the state of Ohio to go to Prussia to study educational systems there. Professing a profound fear of the salt sea, he told her he would never see her again in this life. She insisted that he go, and had twin daughters while he was away. There was a third child two years later, then another, and another and two more later on. A professor's wages were never enough, even when old Lyman could pay Calvin in full, which was seldom. Hattie's health began to fail. "She lived overmuch in her emotions," one son would explain years later.

"It is a dark, sloppy, rainy, muddy disagreeable day," she wrote once to Calvin when he was in Detroit attending a church convention. ". . . I am sick of the smell of sour milk, and sour meat, and sour everything, and then the clothes *will* not dry, and no wet thing does, and everything smells mouldy; and altogether I feel as if I never wanted to eat again."

She began going off on visits to relatives, leaving Calvin and the children behind. The visits grew longer. She went to the White Mountains, then to Brattleboro, Vermont, to try the water cure. The expenses were met by gifts from distant admirers of the family: the Stowes felt that the Lord had a hand in it. Hattie stayed on for nearly a year at Brattleboro, living on brown bread and milk, enduring the interminable sitz baths of one Dr. Wesselhoeft, and writing home exuberant letters about moonlight snowball fights. And no sooner did she return to the cluttered house in Cincinnati than the professor hauled himself off to Brattleboro, there to stay even longer than she had. When a cholera epidemic broke out in Cincinnati and more than a hundred people a day were dying, she wrote to tell him to stay right where he was. She would manage.

In all they were separated a total of three years and more, and their letters back and forth speak of strong, troubled feelings. The hulking, clumsy Stowe, bearded, nearsighted, complained that she never folded his newspaper properly and that her letters of late were too uninteresting for him to read aloud to his friends. She in turn would run on about her own miseries. The house depressed her, she worried about money, she hated the climate in Cincinnati. She thought too much about death.

But she also told him, "There are a thousand favorite subjects on which I could talk with you better than anyone else. If you were not already my dearly loved husband I should certainly fall in love with you."

And Calvin would write to her when she was visiting her sister in Hartford, "And now my dear wife, I want you to come home as quick as you can. The fact is I cannot live without you and if we were not so prodigious poor I would come for you at once. There is no woman like you in this wide world."

In this same letter Calvin proclaimed to her—and apparently he was the first to do so—"My dear, you must be a literary woman. It is so written in the book of fate." He advised her to make all her plans accordingly, as though she had little else to do. "Get a good stock of health and brush up your mind," he declared. And he told her to drop her middle initial, E (for Elizabeth), from her name. "It only incumbers it and interferes with the flow and euphony." Instead: "Write yourself fully and always Harriet Beecher Stowe, which is a name euphonious, flowing, and full of meaning."

She had already written quite a little—temperance tracts, articles on keeping the Sabbath, New England "sketches," for which she drew heavily on Calvin's seemingly inexhaustible fund of childhood reminiscences. Once she had done an article about a slave. She had been selling these pieces to *Godey's Lady's Book* and one or two other magazines. She got two dollars a page on the average, which was more profitable than taking in boarders, she decided. But no one in the family, other than Calvin, had taken her writing very seriously.

She worked at the kitchen table, confusion all around, a baby in a clothes basket at her feet. She couldn't spell very well, and her punctuation would always be a puzzle for her publishers. She dreamed, she said in a letter to Calvin, of a place to work without "the constant falling of soot and coal dust on everything in the room."

Then in July of 1849 she was writing to tell him that their infant son Charley was dead of cholera. The summer before she had nearly died of it herself, with her father praying over her all through one terrible, sweltering night, the room alive with mosquitoes. She had been unable to do a thing for the child, she told Calvin. For almost a week she watched him die, with no way to help, she said, no way even to ease his suffering.

Calvin returned to her very soon after that, determined to leave Cincinnati for good. He had accepted a professorship at Bowdoin College, in Brunswick, Maine, and before he could settle up his affairs in Cincinnati, he characteristically sent Harriet and three of the children off to Maine ahead of him.

She left Cincinnati in the early spring of 1850, a shabby little figure, perfectly erect, perhaps no more than five feet tall, nearly forty, and pregnant once again. She boarded a riverboat at the foot of town, saying farewell with no misgivings. She was going home, she felt.

She was also heading for a sudden and colossal notoriety of a kind never known by any American woman before, and very few since; but of that she had no notion whatever. Nor did she or anyone else alive have any idea how important those seventeen years in Cincinnati had been to her and, as things turned out, to the whole course of American history.

She sailed up the Ohio to Pittsburgh, where she changed to a canalboat. Already she was feeling so good she got out and walked the towpath between locks. At Johnstown the boat and all its passengers were hoisted up and over the Allegheny Mountains by that thrilling mechanical contrivance of the nineteenth century, the Portage Railroad. East of the mountains she went by rail to New York and there crossed by ferry to Brooklyn to see her younger brother, Henry Ward, pastor of Plymouth Church. As children they had sometimes been taken for twins, only Henry Ward had been thick of speech and considered the slow one. Now she took note of his obvious success, and they went out for a drive in a spotless six-hundred-dollar carriage, a recent gift from his parishioners.

In a few days she went on to Hartford, still looking after the children and all their baggage. Her spirits were soaring. At Hartford she stayed with her sisters Mary and Isabella; in Boston with her brother Edward, who was growing ever more militant over the slavery issue. All the Beechers were growing more militant over one thing or another. For Isabella it was women's rights; for the brilliant Catherine, education; for Charles, freedom from theological authority. From Boston, Harriet took the Bath Steamer to Maine, sailing headlong into a northeaster.

On the day they were scheduled to arrive at Brunswick, one story goes, the president of Bowdoin sent a professor named Smith down to greet the new faculty wife, but Smith returned disappointed, saying she must have been delayed. Nobody got off the boat, he said, except an old Irish woman and her brats.

Brunswick offered precious few of the eastern civilities Mrs. Stowe had longed for, and the house Calvin had taken in advance turned out to be deserted, dreary, and damp, to use her words. She went straight to work, refinishing floors, putting up wallpaper—the pioneer again. When Calvin wrote from Cincinnati to say he was sick and plainly dying and that she and theirs would soon be plunged into everlasting debt, she read the letter with humor and stuffed it into the stove.

Calvin showed up before summer, her baby was born, she rested two weeks. When winter came, there were holes in her shoes, and the house was so cold during one long storm that the children had trouble sitting still long enough to eat their meals. They were living on $1,700 a year. It was during the following spring that she began *Uncle Tom's Cabin*.

People are still trying to interpret the book and to explain just how and why she came to write it. At first she said she really didn't write it at all. She said the book came to her in visions and all she did was write down what she saw. When someone reproached her for letting Little Eva die, she answered, "Why, I could not help it. I felt as badly as anyone could! It was like a death in my own family and it affected me so deeply that I could not write a word for two weeks after her death." Years later she stated categorically, "God wrote it." And a great many of her readers were quite willing to let it go at that.

The truth is, the subject of the book had been all around her for a very long time. Old Lyman had been able to make Litchfield farmers weep when he preached on slavery. In Cincinnati she had opened her own Sunday school to black children, and the Lane Seminary had been a hotbed of abolitionist fervor. The Underground Railroad, she later claimed, went directly through her Cincinnati house, which was a bit of an exaggeration; but on one occasion Calvin and her brother Charles did indeed help a black woman and her child elude a slave hunter. The only time she was in an actual slave state, during a visit across the Ohio River in Kentucky, she made no show of emotion about it. But stories she heard from the black women she knew in Cincinnati moved her enormously, particularly those told by a gentle person named Eliza Buck, who helped her with housework and whose children, Harriet Stowe discovered with incredulity, had all been fathered by the woman's former master in Kentucky. "You know, Mrs. Stowe," she had said, "slave women cannot help themselves."

Eliza Buck told her of lashings and of black families split up and "sold down the river." Once on an Ohio River wharf Mrs. Stowe had seen with her own eyes a husband and wife torn apart by a slave trader.

By the time she came east to Maine, Henry Ward was using his Brooklyn pulpit to raise money to buy children out of slavery. In Boston she and Edward had talked long and emotionally about the Fugitive Slave Bill, then being debated in Congress, which made it a federal crime to harbor or assist the escaped "property" of a slave master. Her duty was plain. There was, she said, a standard higher than an act of Congress.

She did some research in Boston and corresponded with Frederick Douglass on certain details. But for all that, the book would be written more out of something within her, something she knew herself about bondage and the craving for liberation, than from any documentary sources or personal investigation of Negro slavery in the South. Indeed she really knew very little about Negro slavery in the South. Her critics would be vicious with her for this, of course, and she would go so far as to write a whole second book in defense of her sources. But *Uncle Tom's Cabin* could never be accounted for that way.

There is probably something to the story that she began the book as a result of a letter from Edward's wife. "Hattie," wrote her sister-in-law from Boston, "if I could use the pen as you can, I would write some-thing that will make this whole nation feel what an accursed thing slavery is." To which Hattie answered, "As long as the baby sleeps with me nights, I can't do much at anything, but I will do it at last. I will write that thing if I live."

The story appeared first as a serial in the *National Era,* an antislavery paper, beginning in June, 1851. It took her a year to write it all, and apparently she did Uncle Tom's death scene first and at a single sitting, writing on brown wrapping paper when her writing paper ran out. The finished story was brought out in book form by the publisher, John P. Jewett, in two volumes on March 20, 1852, a month before the serialized version ended.

Calvin thought the book had little importance. He wept over it, but he wept over most of the things she wrote. Her publisher warned that her subject was unpopular and said she took too long to tell her story. On the advice of a friend who had not read the manuscript, she decided to take a 10 percent royalty on every copy sold instead of a fifty-fifty division of profit or losses, as had also been offered to her.

She herself expected to make no money from it; she thought it inadequate and was sure her friends would be disappointed with her. Within a week after publication ten thousand copies had been sold. The publisher had three power presses running twenty-four hours a day. In a year sales in the United States came to more than three hundred thousand. The book made publishing history right from the start. In England, where Mrs. Stowe had no copyright and therefore received no royalties, sales were even more stupendous. A million and a half copies were sold in about a year's time. The book appeared in thirty-seven different languages. "It is no longer permissible to those who can read not to have read it," wrote George Sand from France, who said Mrs. Stowe had no talent, only genius, and called her a saint.

The book had a strange power over almost everyone who read it then, and for all its Victorian mannerisms and frequent patches of sentimentality much of still does. Its characters have a vitality of a kind comparable to the most memorable figures in literature. There is sweep and power to the narrative, and there are scenes that once read are not forgotten. The book is also rather different from what most people imagine, largely because it was eventually eclipsed by the stage version, which Mrs. Stowe had nothing to do with (and from which she never received a cent) and which was probably performed more often than any play in the language, evolving after a few years into something between circus and minstrel show. (One successful road company advertised ". . . a pack of genuine bloodhounds; two Toppsies; Two Marks, Eva and her Pony 'Prince'; African Mandolin Players; 'Tinker' the famous Trick Donkey.") In the book, for example, no bloodhounds chase, Eliza and her baby across the ice.

What the book did at the time was to bring slavery out into the open and show it for what it was, in human terms. No writer had done that before. Slavery had been argued over in the abstract, preached against as a moral issue, its evils whispered about in polite company. But the book made people at that time *feel* what slavery was about. ("The soul of eloquence is feeling," old Lyman had written.)

Moreover, Harriet Stowe had made a black man her hero, and she took his race seriously, and no American writer had done that before.

The fundamental fault, she fervently held, was with the system. Every white American was guilty, the Northerner no less than the slaveholder, especially the church-going kind, *her* kind. Simon Legree, it should perhaps always be remembered, was a Vermonter.

That Uncle Tom would one day be used as a term of derision ("A Negro who is held to be humiliatingly subservient or deferential to whites," according to *American Heritage Dictionary)* she would have found impossible to fathom, and heartbreaking. For her he was something very close to a black Christ. He is the one character in all her book who lives, quite literally, by the Christian ideal. And if one has doubts that she could see black as beautiful or that she saw emancipation for the black man as a chance for full manhood and dignity, there is her description of Eliza's husband, George Harris, as straight-backed, confident, "his face settled and resolute." When George and his family, having escaped into Ohio, are cornered by slave hunters, Mrs. Stowe writes a scene in which George is fully prepared to kill his tormentors and to die himself rather than permit his wife and son to be taken back into slavery. " . . . I am a free man, standing on God's free soil," George yells from the rock ledge to which he has retreated, "and my wife and my child I claim as mine.... We have arms to defend ourselves and we mean to do it. You can come up if you like; but the first one of you that comes within the range of our bullets is a dead man, and the next, and the next, and so on till the last."

She seems to have been everywhere at once after the book was published—Hartford, New Haven, Brooklyn, Boston. Almost immediately the South began boiling with indignation. She was a radical, it was said. All the Beechers were radicals. She began receiving threatening letters from the South, and once Calvin unwrapped a small parcel addressed to her to find a human ear that had been severed from the head of a black slave. Calvin grew more and more distraught. They decided it was time to move again, now to Andover, Massachusetts, to take up a previously offered teaching job at the seminary there.

Then they were sailing to England, where huge crowds waited for her at railroad stations, hymns were composed in her honor, children came up to her carriage with flowers. She went about in a gray cloak carrying a paint box. She was a tireless tourist. And she worried. "The power of fictitious writing, for good as well as evil is a thing which ought most seriously to be reflected on. No one can fail to see that in our day it is becoming a very great agency."

When war came, everyone told her it was her war, and she thought so too. In South Carolina, as the war commenced, the wife of a plantation owner wrote in her diary that naturally slavery had to go, but added, "Yes, how I envy those saintly Yankee women, in their clean cool New England homes, writing to make their fortunes and to shame us."

Harriet Stowe never saw the Civil War as anything but a war to end slavery, and all her old Beecher pacifist principles went right out the window. "Better, a thousand times better, open, manly, energetic war, than cowardly and treacherous peace," she proclaimed. Her oldest son, Frederick, put on a uniform and went off to fight. Impatient with Lincoln for not announcing emancipation right away, she went down to Washington when he finally proclaimed that the slaves would be free, and was received privately in the White House. The scene is part of our folklore.

"So this is the little woman who made this big war," Lincoln is supposed to have said as he shook her hand.

She was sitting in the gallery at the Boston Music Hall, attending a concert, on January 1, 1863, the day the Emancipation Proclamation became effective. When an announcement of the historic event was made from the stage, somebody called out that she was in the gallery. In an instant the audience was on its feet cheering while she stood and bowed, her bonnet awry.

After the war she kept on writing. In fact, as is sometimes overlooked, that is what Harriet Beecher Stowe was, a writer, and one of the most industrious we have ever had. Unwittingly she had written the abolitionist manifesto, although she did not consider herself an abolitionist. She agreed with her father that abolitionists "were like men who would burn down their houses to get rid of the rats." She was not a crusader pure and simple. She never considered herself an extremist, and she seldom took an extreme position on any issue. She was a reformer, and there was an evangelical undercurrent to just about everything she wrote. But writing was her work, her way to make herself useful.

Her life was about half over when she wrote *Uncle Tom's Cabin*, but for thirty years more she wrote almost a book a year on the average, plus innumerable essays, poems, children's stories, and magazine articles, many of which she did under the pseudonym Christopher Crowfield. Perhaps her most artful novel, *The Minister's Wooing*, ran to fifty printings, and a magazine article, "The True Story of Lady Byron's Life," which appeared in the *Atlantic Monthly* in 1869, caused more furor than anything published in America since *Uncle Tom's Cabin*.

During a second visit to England she had become fast friends with the widow of Lord Byron, who confided the terrible secret that the great Byron had committed incest with his half sister and that a child had been born as a result. Mrs. Stowe kept the secret for thirteen years, but when Byron's former mistress, Countess Guiccioli, published her memoirs and portrayed Lady Byron as a self-righteous tyrant who would drive any mortal male to excesses, Harriet Stowe decided it was time to strike a blow in her friend's behalf, Lady Byron by this time having been dead for nearly a decade. So she told the whole story.

All kinds of accusations were hurled at her, some quite unpleasant. She rode out the storm, however, and again, as with *Uncle Tom*, she wrote a book to justify what she had written. But her standing with the American public would never be the same.

She could write in all kinds of places, under every kind of condition. She was always bothered by deadlines, and it seems she was always in need of money. The royalties poured in, but the more she had the more she spent—on a huge Gothic villa in Hartford that was all gables and turrets and was never finished completely; on a cotton plantation in Florida where she intended to provide blacks with a program of work and education; and later, when that failed, on an orange and lemon grove at Mandarin, Florida, "where the world is not," she said, and where she hoped her unfortunate son Frederick might find himself.

Frederick had trouble staying sober. His problem had started before the war, but at Gettysburg he had been hit in the head by a shell fragment, and, his mother would always believe, he had never been himself again. "After that," one of her grandsons would write, "he not only was made drunk by the slightest amount of alcohol but he could not resist taking it."

Calvin grew enormously fat, ever more distant, and of even less use than before when it came to the everyday details of life. Moreover, Harriet found fame increasingly difficult. She had become a national institution. Her correspondence alone would have drained a less vigorous spirit.

Tragedy struck repeatedly. In 1857, upon returning from Europe, she learned that her son Henry, a student at Dartmouth, had drowned while swimming in the Connecticut River. In 1870 Frederick, unable to endure his mother's Florida experiment any longer, wrote her a touching apology and went to sea, shipping around the Horn. It is known that he got as far as San Francisco, but after that he disappeared and was never heard from again. She would go to her grave with every confidence that he would return one day.

But it was the Brooklyn scandal that hurt her worst of all, she said. In November of 1872 a New York paper reported that her beloved brother Henry Ward, by then the most popular preacher in America, had been carrying on an adulterous affair with one of his parishioners. His enemies swept in for the kill. For all the Beechers the gossip was agonizing. A sensational trial resulted, the husband bringing suit against Beecher for alienation of his wife's affections. It dragged on for six months and was the talk of the country. Whether Beecher was guilty or innocent was never proved one way or the other. He denied everything, the jury was unable to agree on a verdict, and as far as his sister was concerned his character was never even in question.

The whole story was a slanderous fabrication, she said, and she stood by him through the entire grisly, drawn-out business, as did all the Beechers except Isabella Beecher Hooker, who was only a half sister, it was noted, and was regarded by many as just a little unbalanced. (Isabella, who called herself *"the* inspired one," wanted to take charge of a service at Plymouth Church herself and "as one commissioned from on high" declare her brother's guilt from his own pulpit. Years later, when he was dying, she even tried to force her way into his house to get a deathbed confession.)

But it would be mistaken to suggest that Harriet's life became increasingly burdensome. Quite the contrary. As time passed she seems to have grown even more liberated from her past. She drew further and further from the shadow of her harsh Calvinist heritage, eventually rejecting it altogether. She had long since discarded the doctrine of original sin. Neither man nor nature was necessarily corrupt, she now held. Hers was a faith of love and Christian charity. She had a seemingly limitless love for the whole human family. Years before, Catherine, her spinster sister, had been the first of the Beechers to rebel against the traditional faith when a young man she was engaged to marry, a gifted Yale professor of philosophy, was lost at sea and Catherine had had to face the terrible Calvinist conclusion that the young man was consigned to eternal damnation because he had never repented. In time all of Lyman Beecher's offspring would desert the faith. Henry Ward would even go so far as to preach that there is no hell.

For Harriet, Calvinism was repugnant, a "glacial" doctrine, although she admired enormously the fervor it had given the Puritan colonists of her native New England and the solid purpose and coherence of the communities they established. Like many of her time she sorely lamented the decline of Christian faith in the land. It was the root of the breakdown of the old order, she believed. Mostly, it seems, she admired the backbone the old religion gave people. "They who had faced eternal ruin with an unflinching gaze," she wrote, "were not likely to shrink before the comparatively trivial losses and gains of any mere earthly conflict." If she herself could not accept the articles of the Puritan faith, she seemed to wish everybody else would. And once from Florida she wrote: " . . . never did we have a more delicious spring. I never knew such altogether perfect weather. It is enough to make a saint out of the toughest old Calvinist that ever set his face as a flint. How do you think New England theology would have fared, if our fathers had landed here instead of on Plymouth Rock?"

Like numerous other literary figures of the day she tried spiritualism and claimed that her son Henry had returned from somewhere beyond to pluck a guitar string for her. She became an Episcopalian, and she developed an open fondness for such things as Europe (Paris and Italy especially), Rubens, elegant society, and Florida, in particular Florida (" . . . this wild, wonderful, bright, and vivid growth, that is all new, strange and unknown by name to me ... "). The theatre and dancing were no longer viewed as sinful. She rejected the idea that "there was something radically corrupt and wicked in the body and in the physical system." She took a little claret now on occasion. An account of a visit to Portsmouth, New Hampshire, suggests that once at least she may have taken a little too much claret.

She was asked to give readings, to go on the lyceum, as the contemporary lecture circuit was called, like Robert Ingersoll, P. T. Barnum, and the feminists. She needed the money, so at age sixty-one, having never made a public speech before, she embarked on a new career with its endless train rides, bad food, and dreary hotels. She was very shy at first and not much good at it. But she got over that and in time became quite accomplished. "Her performance could hardly be called a reading," reported the *Pittsburgh Gazette*, "it was recitative and she seldom glanced at the book. Her voice betrayed the veritable Yankee twang.... Her voice is low, just tinged in the slightest with huskiness, but is quite musical. In manner she was vivacious and gave life to many of the pages, more by suggestive action than by utterances. . . . She seemed perfectly possessed on the stage, and read with easy grace. . . . "

She found she could move her audiences to great emotional heights, but to laughter especially. And she loved the life. Her health picked up. "I never sleep better than after a long day's ride," she wrote.

Her appearance never changed much. She put on no new airs. Nothing, in fact, good or bad, seemed capable of changing that plain, earnest, often whimsical manner. She acquired a number of new friend-ships that meant a great deal to her, with Oliver Wendell Holmes and Mark Twain particularly. Henry Drummond, the noted Scottish religious writer, wrote, after a visit to Hartford: "Next door to Twain I found Mrs. Harriet Beecher Stowe, a wonderfully agile old lady, as fresh as a squirrel still, but with the face and air of a lion." And he concluded: "I have not been so taken with any one on this side of the Atlantic."

Her affections for Calvin seem to have grown stronger, if anything. He had become absorbed in Semitic studies, let his beard grow, and took to wearing a skullcap. She began calling him "My Old Rabbi." His apparitions took up more and more of his time, and for a while he was having nightly encounters with the Devil, who came on horseback, Calvin said. But otherwise his mind stayed quick and clear until the end, and she found him exceedingly good company.

In their last years they seem also to have had few financial worries. Among other things a book of his, *The Origin and History of the Books of the Bible,* had a surprisingly large sale. And their affairs in general were being capably managed by their twin daughters, Eliza and Harriet, maiden ladies who apparently had considerable "faculty."

Calvin died peacefully enough, with Harriet at his bedside, on August 6, 1886. She lived on for another ten years, slipping off ever so gradually into a gentle senility.

In a letter to Oliver Wendell Holmes she wrote: "I make no mental effort of any sort; my brain is tired out. It was a woman's brain and not a man's, and finally from sheer fatigue and exhaustion in the march and strife of life it gave out before the end was reached. And now I rest me, like a moored boat, rising and falling on the water, with loosened cordage and flapping sail."

She was eighty-two. She spent hours looking at picture books, bothering no one, or went out gathering flowers, "a tiny withered figure in a garden hat," as one writer described her. On occasion she took long walks beside the river, an Irish nurse generally keeping her company.

Sometimes, Mark Twain would recall, she "would slip up behind a person who was deep in dreams and musings and fetch a war whoop that would jump that person out of his clothes."

And every now and then, during moments of astonishing clarity, she would talk again about *Uncle Tom's Cabin,* the book that had just "come" to her in visions. Once, years earlier, when she was having trouble writing, she had said: "If there had been a grand preparatory blast of trumpets or had it been announced that Mrs. Stowe would do this or that, I think it likely I could not have written; but nobody expected anything ... and so I wrote freely."

She died near midnight on July 1, 1896.

19

The Father of American Terrorism

Ken Chowder

John Brown's raid on Harper's Ferry, Virginia (now West Virginia), in October 1859 earned him a place among the most controversial figures in American history. Already known for murderous attacks on settlers in Kansas whom he regarded as proslavery, Brown achieved lasting fame with his attempt to take the federal arsenal at Harper's Ferry, arm slaves in the area, and create a republic of free blacks to encourage slave insurrections across the South. The attack, which failed, infuriated southerners and met with disapproval from most northerners, who condemned the use of violence and regarded Brown as misguided at best. A minority of highly articulate Abolitionists, however, hailed John Brown as an agent of the Lord sent to strike down slavery. He "will make the gallows glorious like the cross," said Ralph Waldo Emerson.

Strongly differing views of John Brown continue nearly 150 years after his raid on Harper's Ferry and subsequent execution for treason against the State of Virginia. Was he a fanatical terrorist or a martyred hero of the fight against slavery? Was slavery so immoral, so wrong, that any action against it, including insurrection and murder, was moral and just? The answer, like the reply to all questions involving moral issues, is an individual matter, and in the wake of the attacks of September 11, 2001 on the World Trade Towers and the Pentagon, every American might re-think his or her reaction to the man called "The Father of American Terrorism."

On December 2, 1859, a tall old man in a black coat, black pants, black vest, and black slouch hat climbed into a wagon and sat down on a black walnut box. The pants and coat were stained with blood; the box was his coffin; the old man was going to his execution. He had just handed a last note to his jailer: "I John Brown am now quite certain that the crimes of this guilty, land: will never be purged away; but with Blood. I had ... vainly flattered myself that without very much bloodshed; it might be done."

As he rode on his coffin, John Brown gazed out over the cornfields of Virginia. This is a beautiful and animal husbandry, but his most conspicuous talent seemed to be one for profuse and painful failure.

In the 1830s, with a growing network of canals making barren land worth thousands, Brown borrowed deeply to speculate in real estate - just in time for the disastrous Panic of 1837. The historian James Brewer Stewart, author of Holy Warriors, says that "Brown was a typical story of someone who invested, as thousands did, and lost thousands, as thou-sands did as well. Brown was swept along in a current of default and collapse."

He tried breeding sheep, started another tannery, bought and sold cattle—each time a failure. When one venture lost money, Brown quietly appropriated funds from a partner in a new business and used it to pay the earlier loss. But in the end his farm tools, furniture, and sheep went on the auction block.

When his farm was sold, he seemed to snap. He refused to leave. With two sons and some old muskets, he barricaded himself in a cabin on the property. "I was makeing preparation for the commencement and vigorous prosecution of a tedious, distressing, wasteing, and long protracted war," Brown wrote. The sheriff got up a posse and briefly put him in the Akron jail. No shots were fired, but it was an incident people would remember, years later, when the old man barricaded himself at Harpers Ferry.

Brown's misadventures in business have drawn widely varying interpretations. His defenders say he had a large family to support; small wonder he wanted badly to make money. But others have seen his financial dreams as an obsession, a kind of fever that gave him delusions of wealth and made him act dishonestly.

Perhaps it was this long string of failures that created the revolutionary who burst upon the American scene in 1856. By that time Brown had long nurtured a vague and protean plan: He imagined a great event in which he—the small-time farmer who had failed in everything he touched—would be God's messenger, a latter-day Moses who would lead his people from the accursed house of slavery. He had already, for years, been active in the Underground Railroad, hiding runaways and guiding them north toward Canada. In 1837 he stood up in the back of a church in Ohio and made his first public statement on human bondage, a single pungent sentence: "Here before God, in the presence of these witnesses, I consecrate my life to the destruction of slavery." For years, however, this vow seemed to mean relatively little; in the early 1850s, as anger over slavery began to boil up all over the North, the frustrated and humiliated Brown was going from courtroom to courtroom embroiled in his own private miseries.

Finally it happened. The John Brown we know was born in the place called Bloody Kansas. Slavery had long been barred from the territories of Kansas and Nebraska, but in 1854 the Kansas-Nebraska Act decreed that the settlers of these territories would decide by vote whether to be free or slave. The act set up a competition between the two systems that would become indistinguishable from war.

Settlers from both sides flooded into Kansas. Five of John Brown's sons made the long journey there from Ohio. But Brown himself did not go. He was in his mid-fifties, old by the actuarial tables of his day; he seemed broken.

Then, in March of 1855, five thousand proslavery Missourians— the hard-drinking, heavily armed "Border Ruffians"—rode into Kansas. We came to vote, and we are going to vote or kill every God-damned abolitionist in the Territory," their leader declared. The Ruffians seized the polling places, voted in their own legislature, and passed their own laws. Prison now awaited anyone who spoke against slavery.

In May, John Junior wrote to his father begging for his help. The freesoilers needed arms, more than we need bread," he said. Now we want you to get for us these arms." The very next day, Brown began raising money and gathering weapons and in August the old man left for Kansas, continuing to collect arms as he went.

In may 1856 a proslavery army sacked the free-soil town of Lawrence; not a single abolitionist dared fire a gun. This infuriated Brown. He called for volunteers to go on "a secret mission." The old man, in his soiled straw hat, stuck a revolver in his belt and led a company of eight men down toward Pottawatomie Creek. Proslavery people lived in the cabins there.

Late on the night of May 23, 1856, one of the group, probably Brown, banged on the door of James Doyle's cabin. He ordered the men of the family outside at gun-point, and Brown's followers set upon three Doyles with broadswords. They split open heads and cut off arms. John Brown watched his men work. When it was over, he put a single bullet into the head of James Doyle.

His party went to two more cabins, dragged out and killed two more men. At the end bodies lay in the bushes and floated in the creek; the murderers had made off with horses, saddles, and a bowie knife.

What came to be called the Pottawatomie Massacre ignited all-out war in Kansas. John Brown, the aged outsider, became an abolitionist leader. In August some 250 Border Ruffians attacked the free-soil town of

Osawatomie. Brown led thirty men in defending the town. He fought hard, but Osawatomie burned to the ground.

A few days later, when Brown rode into Lawrence on a gray horse, a crowd gathered to cheer "as if the President had come to town," one man said. The spinning of John Brown had already begun. A Scottish reporter named James Redpath had found Brown's men in their secret campsite, and "I left this sacred spot with a far higher respect for the Great Struggle than ever I had felt before." And what of Pottawatomie? Brown had nothing to do with it, Redpath wrote. John Brown himself even prepared an admiring account of the Battle of Osawatomie for Eastern newspapers. Less than two weeks after the fight, a drama called Ossawattomie Brown was celebrating him on Broadway.

That autumn, peace finally came to Kansas, but not to John Brown. For the next three years he traveled the East, occasionally returning to Kansas, beseeching abolitionists for guns and money, money and guns. His plan evolved into this: One night he and a small company of men would capture the federal armory and arsenal at Harpers Ferry, Virginia. The invaders would take the guns there and leave. Local slaves would rise up to join them, making an army; together they all would drive south, and the revolution would snowball through the kingdom of slavery.

On the rainy night of October 16, 1859, Brown led a determined little procession down the road to Harpers Ferry. Some twenty men were making a direct attack on the U.S. government; they would liberate four million souls from bondage. At first the raid went like clockwork. The armory was protected by just one man, and he quickly surrendered. The invaders cut telegraph lines and rounded up hostages on the street.

Then Brown's difficulties began. A local doctor rode out screaming, "Insurrection!," and by midmorning men in the heights behind town were taking potshots down at Brown's followers. Meanwhile, John Brown quietly ordered breakfast from a hotel for his hostages. As Dennis Frye, the former chief historian at Harpers Ferry National Historical Park, asks, The question is, why didn't John Brown attempt to leave? Why did he stay in Harpers Ferry?" Russell Banks, the author of the recent John Brown novel Cloudsplitter, has an answer: "He stayed and he stayed, and it seems to me a deliberate, resigned act of martyrdom."

At noon a company of Virginia militia entered town, took the bridge, and closed the only true escape route. By the end of the day, John Brown's revolution was failing. Eight invaders were dead or dying. Five others were cut off from the main group. Two had escaped across the river; two had been captured. Only five raiders were still fit to fight. Brown gathered his men in a small brick building, the enginehouse, for the long, cold night.

The first light of October 18 showed brown and his tiny band an armory yard lined with U.S. Marines, under the command of Col. Robert E. Lee. A young lieutenant, J. E. B. Stuart, approached beneath a white flag and handed over a note asking the raiders to surrender. Brown refused. At that Stuart jumped aside, waved his cap, and the Marines stormed forward with a heavy ladder. The door gave way. Lt. Israel Green tried to run Brown through, but his blade struck the old man's belt buckle; God, for the moment, had saved John Brown.

A few hours later, as he lay in a small room at the armory, bound and bleeding, Brown's real revolution began. Gov. Henry A. Wise of Virginia arrived with a retinue of reporters. Did Brown want the reporters removed? asked Robert E. Lee. Definitely not. "Brown said he was by no means annoyed," one reporter wrote. For the old man was now beginning a campaign that would win half of America. He told the reporters: "I wish to say ... that you had better—all you people of the South—prepare yourselves for a settlement of this question.... You may dispose of me very easily—I am nearly disposed of now; but this question is still to be settled—this negro question I mean; the end of that is not yet.

His crusade for acceptance would not be easy. At first he was no hero. Leaders of the Republican party organized anti-Brown protests; "John Brown was no Republican," Abraham Lincoln said. Even the Liberator, published by the staunch abolitionist William Lloyd Garrison, called the raid "misguided, wild, and apparently insane."

In the South the initial reaction was derision—the Richmond Dispatch called the foray "miserably weak and contemptible"—but that soon changed to fear. Stuart's soldiers found a carpetbag crammed with letters from Brown's supporters; a number of prominent Northerners had financed the raid. It had been a conspiracy, a wide-ranging one. But how wide?

A reign of terror began in the South. A minister who spoke out against the treatment of slaves was publicly whipped; a man who spoke sympathetically about the raid found himself thrown in jail. Four state legislatures appropriated military funds. Georgia set aside seventy-five thousand dollars; Alabama, almost three times as much.

Brown's trial took just one week. As Virginia hurried toward a verdict, the Reverend Henry Ward Beecher preached, "Let no man pray that Brown be spared! Let Virginia make him a martyr!" John Brown read Beecher's words in his cell. He wrote "Good" beside them.

On November 2 the jury, after deliberating for forty-five minutes, reached its verdict. Guilty. Before he was sentenced, Brown rose to address the court: "I see a book kissed here, . . . the Bible. . . . [That] teaches me to 'remember them that are in bonds, as bound with them.' I endeavored to act up to that instruction. . . . I believe that to have interfered . . . in behalf of His despised poor was not wrong, but right. Now, if it is deemed necessary that I should forfeit my life . . ., and mingle my blood further with the blood of my children and with the blood of millions in this slave country whose rights are disregarded . . . I say let it be done!"

For the next month the Charlestown jail cell was John Brown's pulpit. All over the North, Brown knew, people were reading his words. He wrote, "You know that Christ once armed Peter. So also in my case I think he put a sword into my hand, and there continued it so long as he saw best, and then kindly took it from me."

The author of the Pottawatomie Massacre was now comparing himself to Jesus Christ. And he was not alone. Even the temperate Ralph Waldo Emerson called him "the new Saint whose fate yet hangs in suspense but whose martyrdom if it shall be perfected, will make the gallows as glorious as the cross." There were rescue plans, but John Brown did not want to escape. "I am worth inconceivably more to hang than for any other purpose," he wrote.

He got that wish on December 2, and the mythologizing of the man began in earnest. Thoreau, Emerson, Victor Hugo, Herman Melville, and Walt Whitman all wrote essays or poems immortalizing him. James Redpath eagerly waited for the moment when "Old B was in heaven"; just a month after the execution, he published the first biography. Forty thousand copies of the book sold in a single month.

Less than a year and a half later, the guns began firing on Fort Sumter. If the country had been a tinder box, it seemed to many that John Brown had been the spark. "Did John Brown fail?" Frederick Douglass wrote. ". . . John Brown began the war that ended American slavery and made this a free Republic."

His reputation seemed secure, impermeable. The first biographies of the man James Redpath called the "warrior saint" all glorified him. But then, in 1910, Oswald Garrison Villard, grandson of the abolitionist William Lloyd Garrison, wrote a massive and carefully researched book that pictured Brown as a muddled, pugnacious, bumbling, and homicidal madman. Nineteen years later Robert Penn Warren issued a similar (and derivative) study. Perhaps the most influential image of John Brown came, not surprisingly, from Hollywood: In Santa Fe Trail Raymond Massey portrayed him as a lunatic, pure and simple.

It wasn't until the 1970s that John Brown the hero re-emerged. Two excellent studies by Stephen B. Oates and Richard Owen Boyer captured the core of the conundrum: Brown was stubborn, monomaniacal, egotistical, self-righteous, and sometimes deceitful; yet he was, at certain times, a great man. Boyer, in particular, clearly admired him: At bottom Brown "was an American who gave his life that millions of other Americans might be free."

Among African-Americans, Brown's heroism has never been in doubt. Frederick Douglass praised him in print; W. E. B. Du Bois published a four-hundred-page celebration of him in 1909; Malcolm X said he wouldn't mind being with white people if they were like John Brown; and Alice Walker, in a poem, even wondered if in an earlier incarnation she herself hadn't once been John Brown.

But, as Russell Banks points out, Brown's "acts mean completely different things to Americans depending upon their skin color." And the image that most white people today have of John Brown is still of the wild-eyed, blood-thirsty madman. After all, he believed that God spoke to him; he killed people at Pottawatomie in cold blood; he launched an attack on the U.S. government at Harpers Ferry with not even two dozen men. How sane could he have been?

Let's look at those charges one by one. First: He conversed with God. Brown's religious principles, everyone agrees, were absolutely central to the man. As a child he learned virtually the entire Bible by heart. At sixteen he traveled to New England to study for the ministry. He gave up after a few months but remained deeply serious about his Calvinist beliefs. Brown had a great yearning for justice for all men, yet a rage for bloody revenge. These qualities may seem paradoxical to us, but they were ones that John Brown had in common with his deity. The angry God of the Old Testament punished evil: An eye cost exactly an eye.

If God spoke directly to John Brown, He also spoke to William Lloyd Garrison and to the slave revolutionary Nat Turner. To converse with God, in Brown's day, did not mean that you were eccentric. In fact, God was on everyone's side. John Brown saw the story of Moses setting the Israelites free as a mandate for emancipation, but at the same time, others used the Bible to justify slavery (Noah did, after all, set an ever-lasting curse on all the dark descendants of Ham). It was all in the Bible, and Americans on both sides went to war certain that they were doing God's bidding. So it is that John Brown believed that God had appointed him "a special agent of death," "an instrument raised up by Providence to break the jaws of the wicked."

Second: He killed in cold blood. Brown was a violent man, but he lived in increasingly violent times. Slavery itself was of course a violent practice. In 1831 Nat Turner led seventy slaves to revolt; they killed fifty-seven white men, women, and children. A few years later a clergyman named Elijah Lovejoy was gunned down for speaking out against slavery. By the 1850s another distinguished clergyman, Thomas Wentworth Higginson, could lead a mob to the federal courthouse in Boston and attack the place with axes and guns. "I can only make my life worth living," Higginson vowed, "by becoming a revolutionist." During the struggle in Kansas Henry Ward Beecher's Plymouth Church in Brooklyn was blithely shipping Sharps rifles west; "there are times," the famous preacher said, "when self-defense is a religious duty." By the late fifties, writes the historian James Stewart, even Congress was "a place where fist fights became common . . . a place where people came armed . . . a place where people flashed Bowie knives." On February 5, 1858, a brawl broke out between North and South in the House of Representatives; congressmen rolled on the floor, scratching and gouging each other.

Brown's Pottawatomie Massacre was directly connected to this national chaos. On the very day Brown heard about the sacking of Lawrence, another disturbing report reached him from Washington: A Southern congressman had attacked Sen. Charles Sumner, a fierce abolitionist, on the floor of Congress, caning him almost to death for insulting the South. When the news got to Brown's campsite, according to his son Salmon, the men went crazy—crazy. It seemed to be the finishing, decisive touch." Brown ordered his men to sharpen their broadswords and set off toward Pottawatomie, the creek whose name still stains his reputation.

So it is that "Brown is simply part of a very violent world," according to the historian Paul Finkelman. At Pottawatomie, Finkelman says, "Brown was going after particular men who were dangerous to the very survival of the free-state settlers in the area." But Dennis Frye has a less analytical (and less sympathetic) reaction: "Pottawatomie was cold-blooded murder. [It was] killing people up close based on anger and vengeance."

To Bruce Olds, the author of Raising Holy Hell, a 1995 novel about Brown, Pottawatomie was an example of conscious political terrorism: "Those killings took place in the middle of the night, in the dark—that was on purpose. In his writings, [Brown] uses the word terror' and the word 'shock.' He intended to produce both of those, and he did."

Maybe Pottawatomie was insane, and maybe it was not. But what about that Harpers Ferry plan—a tiny band attacking the U.S. government, hoping to concoct a revolution that would carry across the South? Clearly that was crazy.

Yes and no. If it was crazy, it was not unique. Dozens of people, often bearing arms, had gone South to rescue slaves. Secret military societies flourished on both sides, plotting to expand or destroy the system of slavery by force. Far from being the product of a singular cracked mind, the plan was similar to a number of others, including one by a Boston attorney named Lysander Spooner. James Horton, a leading African-American history scholar, offers an interesting scenario. "Was Brown crazy to assume he could encourage slave rebellion? . . . Think about the possibility of Nat Turner well-armed; well-equipped. . . . Nat Turner might have done some pretty amazing things," Horton says. It was perfectly rational and reasonable for John Brown to believe he could encourage slaves to rebel."

But the question of Brown's sanity still provokes dissension among experts. Was he crazy? He was obsessed," Bruce Olds says, he was fanatical, he was monomaniacal, he was a zealot, and . . . psychologically unbalanced." Paul Finkelman disagrees: Brown "is a bad tactician, he's a bad strategist, he's a bad planner, he's not a very good general—but he's not crazy."

Some believe that there is a very particular reason why Brown's reputation as a madman has clung to him. Russell Banks and James Horton make the same argument. The reason white people think he was mad," Banks says, is because he was a white man and he was willing to sacrifice his life in order to liberate black Americans." We should be very careful," Horton says, "about assuming that a white man who is willing to put his life on the line for black people is, of necessity, crazy."

Perhaps it is reasonable to say this: A society where slavery exists is by nature one where human values are skewed. America before the Civil War was a violent society, twisted by slavery. Even sober and eminent people became firebrands. John Brown had many peculiarities of his own, but he was not outside his society; to a great degree, he represented it, in its many excesses.

The past, as always, continues to change, and the spinning of John Brown's story goes on today. The same events—the raid on Harpers Ferry or the Pottawatomie Massacre—are still seen in totally different ways. What is perhaps most remarkable is that elements at both the left and right ends of American society are at this moment vitally interested in the story of John Brown.

On the left is a group of historical writers and teachers called Allies for Freedom. This group believes that the truth about the Harpers Ferry raid has been buried by the conventions of history. Its informal leader, Jean Libby, author of John Brown Mysteries, says, "What we think is that John Brown was a black nationalist. His ultimate goal was the creation of an independent black nation." The Allies for Freedom believes, too, that far from being the folly of a lunatic, Brown's plan was not totally unworkable, that it came much closer to succeeding than historians have pictured. Libby thinks that many slaves and free blacks did join the uprising—perhaps as many as fifty. Why would history conceal the fact of active black participation in Harpers Ferry? The South was anxious to cover up any indication that the raid might have been successful," Libby says, "so slaves would never again be tempted to revolt."

Go a good deal farther to the left, and there has long been admiration for John Brown. In 1975 the Weather Underground put out a journal called Osawatomie. In the late 1970s a group calling itself the John Brown Brigade engaged in pitched battles with the Ku Klux Klan; in one confrontation in Greensboro, North Carolina, in 1979, five members of the John Brown Brigade were shot and killed. Writers also continue to draw parallels between John Brown and virtually any leftist who uses political violence, including the Symbionese Liberation Army (the kidnappers of Patty Hearst in the 1970s), the Islamic terrorists who allegedly set off a bomb in the World Trade Center in Manhattan, and Ted Kaczynski, the Unabomber.

At the same time, John Brown is frequently compared to those at the far opposite end of the political spectrum. Right-to-life extremists have bombed abortion clinics and murdered doctors; they have, in short, killed for a cause they believed in, just as John Brown did. Paul Hill was convicted of murdering a doctor who performed abortions; it was, Hill said, the Lord's bidding: "There's no question in my mind that it was what the Lord wanted me to do, to shoot John Britton to prevent him from killing unborn children." If that sounds quite like John Brown, it was no accident. From death row Hill wrote to the historian Dan Stowell that Brown's "example has and continues to serve as a source of encouragement to me. . . . Both of us looked to the scriptures for direction, [and] the providential similarities between the oppressive circumstances we faced and our general understandings of the appropriate means to deliver the oppressed have resulted in my being encouraged to pursue a path which is in many ways similar to his." Shortly before his execution Hill wrote that "the political impact of Brown's actions continues to serve as a powerful paradigm in my understanding of the potential effects the use of defensive force may have for the unborn."

Nor was the murder Hill committed the only right-wing violence that has been compared to Brown's. The Oklahoma City bombing in 1995 was a frontal attack on a U.S. government building, just like the Harpers Ferry raid. Anti-abortion murders, government bombings, anarchist bombs in the mail—nearly every time political violence surfaces, it gets described in the press as a part of a long American tradition of terrorism, with John Brown as a precursor and hero, a founding father of principled violence.

He gets compared to anarchists, leftist revolutionaries, and right-wing extremists. The spinning of John Brown, in short, is still going strong. But what does that make him? This much, at least, is certain: John Brown is a vital presence for all sorts of people today. In February PBS's The American Experience is broadcasting a ninety-minute documentary about him. Russell Banks's novel Cloudsplitter was a critical success and a bestseller as well. On the verge of his two hundredth birthday (this May 9), John Brown is oddly present. Perhaps there is one compelling reason for his revival in this new millennium: Perhaps the violent, excessive, morally torn society John Brown represents so aptly was not just his own antebellum America but this land, now. Ken Chowder wrote "John Brown's Holy War," the documentary that will appear on PBS's The American Experience on February 28.

20

Combat Trauma in the American Civil War

John E. Talbott

The American Civil War cost the lives of approximately 618,000 Union and Confederate soldiers, far more than the United States has lost in any of its other military conflicts. Historians have told and re-told the story of how so many men died from wounds received in battle and from the diseases that often raged through entire armies. However, much less attention has been given to the men who survived and to the possibility that the war inflicted wounds on them that were unseen as well as seen. The danger, fear, noise, smoke, and confusion of military combat is horrifying, and those who live through it often experience extreme psychological and emotional reactions. Following World War I the term "shell shocked" was applied to soldiers who suffered from combat-induced mental disorders, and in the post-Vietnam War era there are frequent references to "post-traumatic stress syndrome." Does it not seem reasonable that the Civil War inflicted similar unseen wounds on its veterans? John Talbott's article, which is notably different from most historical investigations of the conflict, argues that it did.

When Civil War soldiers 'saw the elephant,' as they called going into action, some of them sustained injuries they could not name. Wounds to the mind left them open to imputations of malingering, allegations of cowardice or charges of desertion. For the Union army had no label like shell shock, battle fatigue or post-traumatic stress disorder to help explain and legitimise a mysterious condition, no category short of lunacy to account for peculiar behaviour. In late

November 1864, for instance, Captain J. McEntire, a provost marshal, wrote of Private William Leeds, a prisoner in his charge:

> He has been strolling about in the woods, and has procured his food from soldiers . . . He has a severe cut on his nose and his eyes are in mourning for the loss of his character.

Since enlisting the previous January, Leeds had been trying to escape the Army of the Potomac: 'We have not been able to keep him a moment except in confinement,' his colonel wrote. On Christmas Eve 1864 Leeds was committed, under escort, to the Government Insane Asylum—St Elizabeth's Hospital—in Washington, D.C.

Perhaps Leeds was lucky. For men whom medical officers might have diagnosed for combat trauma in 1916, 1944 or 1968 were hauled before courts martial in 1864, and some of them probably wound up at the end of a noose or in front of a firing squad. The human response to stress did not change between the Civil War and the Vietnam War, but under-standing and interpreting the response were transformed.

The evidence bearing on combat trauma in the Civil War is anecdotal, ambiguous and fragmentary. Traces usually appear in such narratives as soldiers' diaries, journals, and letters home. Sometimes evidence appears in stories written long after the war. James Thurber, for instance, often mentioned his grandfather's awakening from nightmares of the Federal retreat from Fredericksburg. An Ohio volunteer who spent a lifetime recrossing the Rappahannock in his dreams probably suffered from combat trauma. Such mind wounds afflicted many fewer people and drew far less attention from either physicians or the public than 'nervous breakdown,' the Victorians' term for incapacitating depression. Combat trauma led an underground, phantom-like existence until bursting into full view, and grudging recognition, in the war of 1914–18. For all its elusiveness, it leaves tracks.

Consider the case of the James boys—William, Henry, Garth, or 'Wilky,' as he was called, and Robertson or 'Bob.' The two older boys, the philosopher and the novelist, did not serve in the Civil War; the two younger ones did. Wilky, an officer in the 54th Regiment of Massachusetts Volunteer Infantry, was twice wounded in the assault on Fort Wagner; Bob was an officer in the 55th Massachusetts, a less famous regiment that also saw some hard fighting.

A mysterious back injury sustained fighting a fire in Newport, Rhode Island, kept Henry out of the army that so many of his friends and contemporaries rushed to join. William James shared Henry's ambivalent feelings about military service but not the back problem that went with it. Later on, however, he became deeply interested in the relationship between psychological trauma and psychopathology. Henry James' 'obscure hurt' and William's debilitating bouts of depression are far better documented than the fate of the foot soldiers Wilky and Bob. While the older brothers emerged as two of the most influential men in American intellectual life, the two combat veterans dwelled in obscurity. Wilky moved from town to town, concocting grandiose financial schemes in which he repeatedly lost his shirt. Bob became an alcoholic. To ascribe the postwar fortunes of the junior members of the Jamesian quartet solely to their war experiences is too simple. Still, Wilky's chronic restlessness and Bob's alcoholism are tell-tale signs of combat trauma.

Other evidence bearing on mind wounds is more indirect. Combat is replete with episodes of anomalous, peculiar or unusual behaviour. Such behaviour falls within the pattern the psychologist Pierre Janet called 'dissociation.' As a response to traumatic events—indeed, as a defence *against* trauma—dissociation is an adaptive strategy. It allows a person under stress to continue functioning, although often in an autonomic and sometimes inappropriate way. Three such cases among many that might be adduced involve high-ranking officers, not the infantrymen or 'grunts' who were at greater risk of combat trauma.

On June 30th, 1862, toward the close of the ill-fated Peninsula campaign and the sixth day of the ferocious Seven Days' Battle, General George B. McClellan, Commander of the Army of the Potomac, boarded the gunboat *Galena* and steamed up the James River, putting a great number of miles between himself and the responsibilities of his command. What could account for such behaviour? The judgement of McClellan's biographer, Stephen Sears, is harsh: the general 'had lost the courage to command'. This moral judgement might be softened by guessing that McClellan, never eager to commit his army to battle and chagrined by the consequences, was suffering from dissociation, a response to trauma rather than a loss of nerve. Indeed, Sears goes on to qualify his own remark: '[McClellan] was drained,' he says, 'in both mind and body.' This is a Janet-like acknowledgement of the psychosomatic consequences of stress. In any event, McClellan recovered his equilibrium, if not his fitness for high command.

The other two examples derive from eye-witness accounts. In late November 1862 Lieutenant Henry L. Abbott, 20th Massachusetts Volunteers, wrote to his father about the alarming behaviour of Raymond Lee, the colonel commanding his regiment:

> Col. Lee. . . is undoubtedly very much shaken in his intellects, at any rate at times. . . It seems the horrors of Antietam his previous fatigues and his

drinking, completely upset him. After the battle he was completely distraught. He didn't give any orders. He Wouldn't do any thing. The next morning he mounted his horse, without any leave of absence, without letting any body [know] where he was going, he set out alone. Macy, who was bringing up some recruits, met him about ten miles away from the regt. without a cent in his pocket, without any thing to eat or drink, without having changed his clothes for four weeks, during all which time he had this horrible diarrhea-just getting ready to turn into a stable for the night. Macy gave him a drink and some money and got him into a house, put him to bed stark naked, and got his wits more settled, and then came on. When the poor old man came back to the regt. they thought he had been on an awful spree, he was so livid and shaky. Macy says he was just like a little child, wandering away from home.

The third episode of dissociation is more ambiguous. Around mid-morning on May 6th, 1864, the second day of the Battle of the Wilderness, the 20th Massachusetts was dug in behind log and earthen breastworks hastily thrown up along the Orange Plank Road. During a lull in the firing, Brigadier General James S. Wadsworth came galloping up and ordered the regiment to advance toward a wall of saplings and scrubby pines believed to conceal rebel troops.

At fifty-nine Wadsworth was the oldest senior officer in the Army of the Potomac, a wealthy and well-connected New Yorker admired for serving competently and without pay in a position of great danger. Yet on the morning of May 5th, a 20th Massachusetts officer recalled, Wadsworth rode up 'in a very wild and excited manner' demanding to know who was in command. Told by Colonel George Macy that his own brigade commander had ordered him to hold his position at any cost, 'Wadsworth then said very excitedly,' according to the Massachusetts captain, "'I command these troops and order you forward."' In fact, Wadsworth commanded a division of the 5th Corps, under Gouverneur Warren. The 20th Massachusetts belonged to the 2nd Corps, under Winfield Hancock. In the confusion of battle Wadsworth had either lost or deliberately left, for a purpose known only to him (perhaps an attempt to impose order where he saw none?), his own division. In any event, when the jurisdictional issue was raised Wadsworth 'became still more excited,' according to our informant, 'throwing his arms in the air, and said something which I did not catch, but to which [Macy] answered "very well sir, we will go.' "

Accounts of what happened next are markedly at odds. Either Wadsworth led the charge of the 20th Massachusetts or, as a survivor of the assault remembers it, the general 'immediately galloped off and disappeared' before regimental officers managed to pry their men loose from the breastworks and walk them into the muskets of the 8th Alabama, lying in wait on the ground. 'Great God!,' Macy told his captains, 'That man is out of his mind.' Shot through the head that afternoon, Wadsworth died a few days later. In the space of fifteen minutes, the 533 men who charged into the woods were reduced to the three of four officers and 110 men who eventually reformed on the Brock Road.

General Alexander S. Webb, who had anchored his brigade's line on the strong position occupied by the 20th Massachusetts, later called Wadsworth's command to put his twelve regiments at Wadsworth's disposition 'the most astonishing and bewildering order.' Indeed his actions on the morning of May 6th make little sense. Seeking to arrest the disintegration of the Federal line, Wadsworth accelerated it. Why was he so far from where he belonged? Why did he countermand the instructions of the experienced and able commander on the scene? Why did he so frantically urge a reliable, veteran regiment to assault an invisible enemy? This episode illustrates both the fog of war and the disorientation of Wadsworth. In the hours before the incident in question, the general admitted to an aide that 'he was exhausted and worn out' and wondered about his own fitness for command. Dissociation may help account for his 'most astonishing and bewildering' behaviour.

The best-known case of dissociation in the Army of the Potomac lived only in Stephen Crane's imagination. Despite his preternatural sense of the realities of warfare, when he wrote *The Red Badge of Courage* (1895), a tale of a Union soldier's coming of age, young Crane had never been in combat. From what he had read and heard from friends and relatives, however, he created one of the truly great American novels. For verisimilitude, his 'Tattered Man' is unsurpassed. He embodies the straggler, a whole category of armed and uniformed refugees, soldiers in search of (or in flight from) an army. In a vast penumbra around every battlefield, I suspect, wandered many acute cases of combat trauma.

Crane's story of wounds physical and mental unfolds at Chancellorsville, virtually the same ground as the Wilderness and its equal as a scene of savage fighting. In the year separating the first battle from the second, the character of the Civil War changed drastically. From First Bull Run in July 1861 to Gettysburg in July 1863, weeks, often months, passed between battles. From the crossing of the Rapidan on May 4th, 1864, until the end came nearly a year later, however, the Army of the Potomac and the Army of Northern Virginia were seldom out of rifle shot, and scarcely a day passed when shots were not exchanged. Two different wars were fought: one (1861-63) looked back to European wars of the seventeenth and eighteenth centuries; the other (1864-65) looked forward to the twentieth—to the Russo-Japanese War, the First World War and beyond.

Different wars have created different hells. At one end of the spectrum lies the Greek hoplite way of war, a deadly and terrifying rugby scrum over in minutes and definitive in outcome. 'It was *a brief* nightmare, ' its historian, Victor Hanson, emphasises. At the other end of the spectrum lies Clausewitz's 'absolute war,' a theoretical realm of unrestrained violence. Over the last two centuries, especially, warfare has lurched toward the Clausewitzian end. In studies of twentieth-century wars, psychiatrists and social scientists have emphasised duration and intensity as key variables in the incidence of combat trauma. 'There is no such thing as 'getting used to combat,' an official study of infantrymen in the European theatre in the Second World War found. 'Each moment. . . imposes a strain so great that men will break in direct relation to the intensity and duration of their exposure.'

Combat veterans who forded the Rapidan in the spring of 1864 quickly recognised the war had changed. The conditions struck them with overwhelming force. 'These last few days have been very bad,' Oliver Wendell Holmes Jr wrote his parents on June 24th, seven weeks after the Army of the Potomac had crossed the river. 'Many a man has gone crazy since this campaign begun (sic) from the terrible pressures on mind and body... I hope to pull through but don't know.' Holmes left the army later in the summer, against the urgings of his father, when his three-year enlistment ran out. 'Doubt demoralises me as it does any nervous man,' he had written earlier by way of explanation, 'I cannot now endure the labors and hardships of the line.' Holmes, in fact, served as a headquarters staff officer during his last campaign, but as a member of the 20th Massachusetts he had been in the thick of many of the Army of the Potomac's battles since the autumn of 1861.

Indeed, scarcely any Union regiment was in the heart of the storm longer than the 20th Massachusetts. At the end of June 1864, Captain H. L. Patten reckoned the toll exacted on his outfit:

> [The men] have been so horribly worked and badgered that they are utterly unnerved and demoralised. They are easily scared as a timid child at night. Half our brigade were taken prisoners the other day, in the middle of the day, by a line no stronger than themselves, without firing a shot. You had a campaign of one day, we of fifty-three days; *every day* under fire, every night either digging or marching. We, our brigade, have made fourteen charges upon the enemy's breastworks, although at last no amount of urging, no heroic example, no threats, or anything else, could get the line to *stir one peg*. For my own part, I am utterly tired and disheartened and if I stay at all, it will be like a whipt dog—because I think I must.

The diary of Private Austin Carr, 82nd New York Volunteers, of the same brigade and division as the 20th Massachusetts, catalogues the pressures to which Holmes alluded in his letters home. Carr joined up in August 1862, right before Antietam, so his perspective is that of a seasoned grunt—just how seasoned is apparent from his entry of May 1st, 1863, the eve of Chancellorsville:

> Eight days rations in our knapsacks and haversack, one change of clothes, an overcoat, an oil cloth blanket, a woolen blanket and a shelter tent will make an awful load to carry. . . Ten rounds more of ammunition served out to us, making fifty in all, that's the way they load us down, so that when we come to march, we can't go but a short distance before we are tired out. Forty rounds is all I want to carry, so when we start, I will throw the extra ten rounds away.

Like all veteran infantrymen, Carr keenly sensed the relative usefulness of, to use the title of Tim O'Brien's book on Vietnam, *The Things They Carried.*

New recruits, he discovered in the Wilderness, posed a greater danger to their own side than to the enemy. Wildly firing his rifle, a man named Clark hit one comrade in the head and nicked Carr in the finger. 'That riled me somewhat,' Carr wrote, 'So I put my rifle to his head and threatened to blow his brains out if he fired again.' Now the risk of being killed came not only from the front but from all sides. Following the refusal of Webb's brigade to obey his order to charge (by no means an uncommon occurrence in the Army of the Potomac that spring), two intermingled lines of infantry fired into each other, dissolving momentarily into a fleeing mob. 'The boys don't fight as they used to,' Carr lamented. Still more fearful than misdirected small-arms fire was an artillery bombardment, friendly or hostile. In most accounts from the incoming end, including the following from Carr, terror vies with helplessness:

> We lay upon a knoll close to the enemies' works and under their artillery, which they didn't hesitate to use, they having perfect range of the knoll. A deadly fire of shells was poured into us, killing and wounding a great many, without our having the means to retaliate. It was a fearful spot, and the sights I was compelled to witness was horrible. . . Our feeling can better be imagined than described while we were laying out under that destructive shelling. I trust that I will never get in another such position as I have been in today.

Eighty years later, an American Marine found himself in another such position. 'As Peleliu dragged on,' Eugene Sledge wrote:

> I feared that if I ever lost control of myself under shell fire my mind would
> be shattered. . . To be under heavy shell fire was to me by far the most
> terrifying of combat experiences. . . Fear is many-faceted and has many
> subtle nuances, but the terror and desperation endured under heavy
> shelling are by far the most unbearable.. .

W. H. R. Rivers, who treated countless British soldiers for shell shock
during the Great War, was convinced that his patients' sense of
helplessness contributed far more to their condition that the routine
horrors of combat. Perched beneath balloons tethered high over the
trenches, artillery observers were sitting ducks to the riflemen and
machine-gunners below. These utterly helpless observers, Rivers
pointed out, suffered the highest incidence of breakdown of any
branch of the service.

Digging in offered Austin Carr and his comrades one means of
escape from the intensity of small arms and artillery fire. 'We entrench
ourselves as soon as we halt for the night,' he wrote on May 27th.
'That much despised weapon of McClellan, the spade, is constantly
brought in use'—despised, perhaps, but long since become the foot
soldier's friend. Satellite mapping of the Chancellorsville battlefield is
beginning to reveal that pickets on duty in front of their regiments'
positions in May 1863 had dug in, fully a year before the idea of
entrenching battle lines had become generally accepted. Henry
Abbott, Major of the 20th Massachusetts, had noted after Gettysburg in
July of the same year that the failure of Pickett's charge 'demonstrates
. . . that . . . a front attack over an open field against even the
slightest pit cannot be successful.'

But if a trench gives shelter, it also imprisons, immobilising its
occupants and inducing a powerful urge to escape. 'We have to lay all
day in the [rifle] pits,' Carr complained:

> . . . amongst the dirt and sand. We have dug places in the ground for
> water, and places to go to attend the wants of nature. We are packed in
> here rather close, making it rather difficult to walk; if we do walk it is in a
> stooping posture. We are covered with sand, eat sand, drink sand, and
> breathe sand, until we have almost become pillars of sand.. .

Straggling kept pace with entrenching. The provost guard, or
military police, Carr noted, 'is getting very strict and ugly. It is
rumored that two of them was shot this evening.' Although gloomily
aware of his own fraying nerves, he never wrote of deserting. In any
event, he was spared the temptation. On June 22nd, 1864, Carr fell
into the hands of the rebels, who happened upon a regiment
stuporous from drink. Whisky was to the Army of the Potomac what

dope became for the American army in Vietnam: the favoured means of self-medication against the stresses of war.

The war of movement, or at least the war of two large armies stumbling and crashing into each other in the woods of northern Virginia, had become a stationary war even before Austin Carr was captured. Rifle pits hastily scratched in the dirt each day gave way to elaborate fortifications stretching around Petersburg as far as the eye could see. One infantryman wrote to his hometown newspaper:

> We are close up to the enemy's guns besieging his works. The breastwork against which I am leaning is not more than 200 yards from the enemy's lines . . . The field is open between us, but it is a strip of land across which no man dares to pass . . . An attacking party from either side would be mown down like grass. We have abattis in front of our works, and so have they . . . [T]hese saairly prongs extending outward are no very pleasant things to get over in the face of a murderous fire at close range. I believe if the enemy should attack us, we could kill every man of them before any could get into our works . . . a man's head isn't safe a moment above the protection of the breastworks. Our work here is built zigzag, . . . which gives us a chance to protect ourselves from a cross fire. We can only get from place to place . . . by walking in trenches that we have dug for that purpose. Relieving is accomplished in the night, and as slyly as possible.

In virtually every particular, the war being described here could be the war of 1914–1918: the war of shell shock. The evidence for combat trauma in the Civil War seems far more diffuse and ambiguous than the disorder this term suggests. Yet 'shell shock' is misleadingly precise. It expresses an inference drawn in the early months of the Great War, when the novel and alarming symptoms front-line British soldiers displayed were attributed to the concussive effect of exploding projectiles on their brains and spinal columns. As combat trauma revealed its protean character, medical officers challenged this organic hypothesis. Nevertheless, the label stuck. In our day, journalists describe Democrats who lose control of the U.S. Congress as 'shellshocked.'

In terms of the terrible pressures they endured, combat soldiers of the last year of the Civil War had more in common with those of the first year of the Great War than either had with civilians of their own times. In terms of mental disorder, the so-called 'Front Experience' reached not only between belligerents but across generations. What changed in the half century between the Civil War and the First World War was not the response of the human species to stress, but the cultural expression of the response. In 1914 far more was known and admitted about what went on in mind, brain and body than had been the case in 1861. Mental disorder had been re-constructed. And so it has been re-constructed since 1918. Yet a little cultural construction goes a long way. In the realm of the historical understanding of combat trauma, it can easily go too far.

It would be well to remember a premise drawn from evolutionary psychology, a discipline historians have not been especially eager to borrow from. 'The evolved structure of the human mind,'—the one we all carry around in our heads today—'is adapted to the way of life of Pleistocene hunter-gatherers, and not necessarily to our modern circumstances.' Modern war is a concatenation of hells, none of them good for hunter-gatherers.

FOR FURTHER READING:

Eric Dean, 'We Will All Be Lost and Destroyed: Post-traumatic Stress Disorder and the Civil war,' *Civil War History*, 37 (June 199 1); Mark de Wolfe Howe, ed. *Touched with Fire: Civil War Letters of Oliver Wendell Holmes, Jr., 1861-1864* (Harvard University Press, 1946); Abram Kardiner, *The Traumatic Neuroses of War* (New York 1941); James M. McPherson, *Battle Cry of Freedom: The Civil War Era* (Oxford University Press, 1988), Tim O'Brien, *The Things They Carried* (Houghton-Mifflin, 1990); Daniel Pick, *War Machine: The Rationalization of Slaughter in the Modern Age* (Yale University Press, 1993).

John E. Talbott is Professor of History at the University of California, Santa Barbara.